THE GOLDEN LABYRINTH
A STUDY OF BRITISH DRAMA

THE
GOLDEN
LABYRINTH

A Study of
British Drama

by

G. WILSON KNIGHT

*Formerly Professor of English Literature in the University of
Leeds and President of the Leeds University
Union Theatre Goup*

NEW YORK

W · W · NORTON & COMPANY · INC ·

Same title Program as in hardbound Same pagination

To

Francis Berry,

maker of poetic narratives,

is dedicated

this study of poets in the sister art of

DRAMA

There is some soul of goodness in things evil
  Would men observingly distil it out.

WILLIAM SHAKESPEARE, *Henry V*, IV. i.

In Death I see not Overthrow.

HENRIK IBSEN, *Brand*, V.

*This Greek vision dimly reflects existence in that world
beyond death which I have called 'Eidos'. It conveys,
shadowily, the spirit of that splendid world, where the
subtle body, in glowing perfection, expresses form in
its greatest and in its highest intensity, where the mere
act of living may be accompanied by an exultation
that transcends the lofty ecstasy of the greatest earthly
artist.*

As from F. W. H. MYERS, through
GERALDINE CUMMINS, *Beyond
Human Personality*, I.

PREFACE

THOUGH I was at first reluctant to bind myself to a task for which my reading seemed inadequate, it is a pleasure now that it is done to express my gratitude to Mr John Baker of Phoenix House for having pressed me to undertake it. I am also grateful to Professor Bonamy Dobrée, whose invitation to me to come to Leeds after the war to inaugurate and run a World Drama course and take an active interest in the ever-vigorous work of the Leeds University Union Theatre Group has given me an extended period of dramatic saturation, enriched now for many years by happy association with Mr Frederick May as the Group's Chairman, without which the work would have been the harder. It may be worth recording that my views on the dramatic power of the fifth act in Tennyson's *Becket* and of the Madman in Masefield's *Good Friday*, together with my comments on the inward strength and upward lift of Shakespeare's protagonists, are based on acting experience.

My pages on Webster, Marlowe, Tennyson, Ibsen, Shaw, Sherriff and O'Casey are in part revisions of typescripts I have had by me for a number of years. An earlier appreciation of Lyly's plays appeared in *The Review of English Studies*, XV, lviii, April 1939; essays on *The Tragedy of Nan* and *Hassan* have also been published (pp. 332, 337 below); and so has my present account of the dramas of Nathaniel Lee, in a recent issue of *Venture*, Karachi. A fair amount of new reading has been involved. Among the main guides who have both furthered my understanding and directed me to works that I should otherwise have missed are: J. R. Allardyce Nicoll's *British Drama* and other indispensable works; F. S. Boas's valuable handbooks on Tudor, Stuart and eighteenth-century drama; Una Ellis-Fermor for both the Jacobeans and the Irish dramatists; M. C. Bradbrook for Jacobean comedy; Bonamy Dobrée for the Restoration; R. Bertrand Evans for the Gothic movement; M. Willson Disher and George Rowell for the popular theatre of the nineteenth century; and Priscilla Thoulless and J. C. Trewin for the moderns. I have used with profit *The Oxford Companion to the Theatre*, edited by Phyllis Hartnoll, finding some of its articles, including those of Professor G. D. F. Kitto on the Greeks, very helpful. Other authorities are recorded in my text.

I am grateful to both Professor J. A. Davison and my brother W. F. Jackson Knight for bringing expert knowledge to discussion of my first chapter, though it contains elements for which they must not be supposed to have assumed responsibility; to Mr Martial Rose for reading, and in general approving, my second chapter; and to Mr Arthur Creedy for a peculiarly fertile piece of advice. I am deeply indebted to Dr Patricia Ball, who has read the whole book in proof, checked many of my plot-details, references and dates, commented on my judgements, and in particular brought a critical eye to bear on, and helped me to clarify, my reactions to Dryden and Congreve.

Many influences, I am sure, remain unrecorded. A general obligation must be expressed to the staff, post-graduate students and students of the University of Leeds for all that I have gained through conversation, class discussions and the reading of theses and essays. To record those instances that linger in my mind might be unfair to the many that have been forgotten. One exception may be made: whilst I was planning out my new Shakespeare essay, Mr Wole Soyinka wrote an examination answer that touched and clarified my plans, both in that essay and elsewhere.

I offer my thanks to Mr Douglas Jefferson, Mr Arthur Creedy, Mr Arnold Taylor, Mr E. G. Hauger and Miss Theo Brown for suggestions and the loan of books; to Miss Helen White and Mr Norman Talbot for looking up some research details; to Dr G. S. Bedagkar for help with dates; to Dr Sylvia England for the checking of references and facts; to Dr Saros Cowasjee for interrupting his researches on Sean O'Casey to help me with the preparation of my text; to Mrs Nancy Berry for compiling the index; and to Miss Lona M. Mont-Clar of Phoenix House, whose sense of detail, patience and care have removed a number of imperfections.

Books have not always been easy to find, but my labours have been eased by the courtesy of the staff at the following libraries: the Brotherton Library at Leeds and the Roborough Library at Exeter; the City libraries at Leeds, Birmingham and Exeter; the Leeds Library; and the British Museum.

I express my gratitude to Mrs E. M. Hands, who has for thirty-five years been turning my untidy scripts into neat type; to Mrs O. F. B. Hewetson for daily sympathy and happy surroundings; and to Professor A. N. Jeffares for generous, departmental, consideration.

I confess to having invaded the territories of specialists without specialist equipment. I have tried to restrict my discussion of dramatic

origins to the most general terms; in addition to the authorities
quoted I have clearly been influenced by Sir James Frazer's *The
Golden Bough*; and also by Gilbert Murray and F. M. Cornford,
though I am aware that their theories have been questioned. Apart
from such controversial fields, I shall be glad to hear of any factual
errors elsewhere, with a view to rectification. My hope is that the
book will be used for its interpretative quality, and not as a work of
reference. Dates especially should be checked against the established
authorities. A play's first appearance may come through either production or publication; production may be first in London, Dublin,
Europe or America; there may be an entry in the Stationers' Register;
or we may have some evidence of composition earlier than any
recorded appearance. I have picked my way as best I could among the
authorities,[1] who do not always tally with each other, and tried,
following the practice of Professor Allardyce Nicoll in *British Drama*,
to settle on a single date for each play, not too far out, only introducing such qualifications as 'prod.' or 'pub.', 'c.' or '?', where there
seemed a strong reason for doing so. Exact dating is a study in itself,
and for it we must go to the experts who are skilled in the relevant
researches, and have space for their discussion.

Most of my textual references are self-explanatory. For the older
dramatists I am myself responsible for details of typography and
punctuation. Act and Scene numerals follow those used by the
following editors: Lyly, R. W. Bond (1902); Kyd, F. S. Boas (1901);
Marlowe, R. H. Case as general editor (1930–3); Greene, J. Churton
Collins (1905); Peele, A. H. Bullen (1888); Jonson, Percy Simpson
and C. H. Herford (1925–52); Chapman, T. M. Parrott (1910–14);
Marston, H. Harvey Wood (1934–9); Middleton, A. H. Bullen
(1885–6); Tourneur, Allardyce Nicoll (1930); Webster, F. L. Lucas
(1927); Ford, Havelock Ellis (1888); Beaumont and Fletcher, Arnold
Glover and A. R. Waller (1905–12); Massinger, Arthur Symons
(1889; *The Bondman*, F. Cunningham, 1871); Davenant, J. Maidment
and W. H. Logan (1872–4); Brome, Anonymous (1873); Crowne,
Anonymous (1873–4); Dryden, Walter Scott, re-edited by G. Saintsbury (1882); Boyle, Earl of Orrery, W. S. Clark II (1937); Lee,
Thomas B. Stroup and Arthur L. Cooke (1954–5); Etherege, H. F. B.
Brett-Smith (1927); Wycherley, Montague Summers (1924); Congreve, Montague Summers (1923); Farquhar, Charles Stonehill

---

[1] Among these I would draw attention to Professor Kenneth Muir's 'The
Chronology of Marlowe's Plays', *Proceedings of the Leeds Philosophical Society:*
V. vi, 345–56.

(1930); Southerne, Anonymous (1774).[1] For Shakespeare, Milton and the Romantic poets I have followed the Oxford editions. With my references to other dramatists, confusions are unlikely.

In referring to works of commentary I have noted the place of origin for foreign publications only; where no place is noted the publication is British. My system of references is: XII; 12, for volume and page; XII. 12, for chapter and page (for the Bible, xii. 12); XII, xii, for volume and issue. For poetry, XII. 12 signifies canto and stanza, and for plays I use 2; II. ii. 2, to signify, respectively, part, act, scene and line or page. Shakespearian sonnets and Nietzschean sections are given ordinary numerals.

A friend has urged that my book should have an end-piece, summing up its findings. It has not, partly because the story is not yet concluded and partly because such a discussion would make another book. If I were asked to define briefly what the material here collected suggests to be the nature of drama, I might say that we discover its essence, whether tragic or comoedic, in a tension between normal experience and another order of being. These are often found shaping themselves into an opposition of some dark hero against some person of seraphic grace; and my views on what in the following pages I have called the 'seraphic' have been developed further in the essay 'The Seraphic Intuition' appended to the 1962 reissue of *The Christian Renaissance*. Whatever the particular forms, both terms must be present, and must be co-present in tension and release. When you find the one without the other, or variations in sequence rather than interaction in simultaneity, we are unlikely to have drama of quality.

In conclusion, I should add that some of the material in this book formed part of the Clark Lectures for 1962. I would record my gratitude to the Master and Fellows of Trinity College, Cambridge, for the honour of their invitation.

G. W. K.

Leeds, 1962.

---

[1] The plays were published in three volumes. In writing of *Sir Antony Love* I have followed the editor's spelling 'Antony' in place of the 'Anthony' of older editions.

CONTENTS

ACKNOWLEDGMENTS

THE author and publishers are grateful to the following for permission to quote copyright passages from the books named:

George Allen & Unwin Ltd for *The Shadow of the Glen* and *The Playboy of the Western World* by John M. Synge; The Bodley Head Ltd and Professor C. Colleer Abbott, editor, for 'Cruach' in *Poems and Plays* by Gordon Bottomley; Jonathan Cape Ltd for *The Emperor Jones* by Eugene O'Neill; Constable & Co. Ltd for 'A Sleeping Clergyman' and 'Dr Angelus' in *John Knox and Other Plays* by James Bridie; Gerald Duckworth & Co. Ltd for *Maeve* by Edward Martyn; Faber and Faber Ltd for *Sweeney Agonistes* and *The Family Reunion* by T. S. Eliot, *The Dog Beneath the Skin* and *The Ascent of F6* by W. H. Auden, and *Trial of a Judge* by Stephen Spender; Victor Gollancz Ltd for *Journey's End* by R. C. Sherriff; Rupert Hart-Davis Ltd for 'The Saloon' in *The Complete Plays of Henry James*; William Heinemann Ltd for *The White Carnation* by R. C. Sherriff; Mr J. B. Priestley and William Heinemann Ltd for *Time and the Conways* and *Music at Night*; Mr W. Somerset Maugham and William Heinemann Ltd for *The Circle* and *The Sacred Flame*; Mrs Flecker and William Heinemann Ltd for *Don Juan* and *Hassan* by James Elroy Flecker; Professor O. L. Zangwill and William Heinemann Ltd for *The Melting Pot*, *The War God* and *The Next Religion* by Israel Zangwill; Miss Clemence Dane and William Heinemann Ltd for *Adam's Opera* and *Will Shakespeare*; Mr Sean O'Casey and Macmillan & Co. Ltd for 'Juno and the Paycock', 'The Silver Tassie', 'Within the Gates' and 'The Shadow of a Gunman' in Sean O'Casey's *Collected Plays*; The Trustees of the Hardy Estate and Macmillan & Co. Ltd for *The Dynasts* by Thomas Hardy; Miss H. H. R. Sturge Moore and Macmillan & Co. Ltd for *Medea* by Thomas Sturge Moore; Mrs W. B. Yeats and Macmillan & Co. Ltd for *The King's Threshold* and *The Unicorn from the Stars* by W. B. Yeats; The Richards Press Ltd for *The Triumph of Mammon* by John Davidson; Dr John Masefield, O.M., and The Society of Authors for *The Tragedy of Nan*, *A Play of St George* and *Good Friday*; The Public Trustee and The Society of Authors for *Major Barbara*, *Caesar and Cleopatra*, *On the Rocks* and *Too True to be Good* by G. Bernard Shaw.

PART 1

CHAPTER I

Greek

This say I, of no mortal father born,
Dionysus, son of Zeus. Had ye but known
To have been pious when ye might, Zeus' son
Had been your friend; ye had been happy still.
EURIPIDES, *The Bacchae*, trans. Dean H. H. Milman.

I

DRAMA aims to make profitable terms with the alien powers surrounding man. Tragedy engages evil and death, the numinous and the eternal; though solemn it is not sad; and rhythms of dance, music or metre, deep analogues to the rhythms of sexual activity, assist in establishing the harmony. In comedy the sexual element is stronger. Here the civilized ego is related to natural forces: to food, to drink, and to sexual instinct. A disparity is admitted, mental dignities are dethroned, and resolution comes not by reason or harmony but through the other and more directly sexual rhythms, or ripples, of laughter. Both tragedy and comedy work for an expansion of conscious being; they are more than conductors of thought: they are active powers.

The word 'drama' denotes 'action'. Drama exists when we have (i) a coherent action deliberately performed by people representing persons other than themselves and (ii) an audience drawing advantage from this performance. The actor's art flowers from the exhibitionist instinct, like the sex display of birds, but he is being urged to exhibit more than his ordinary social self. This he deliberately casts off, touching a deeper spring from which he re-creates himself as another, experiencing a kind of possession. In assuming his part he has broken the limits of his individuality and released his anti-self, exulting in the thrill of the new person's suffering, shame or glory. The audience too identify themselves with what is strange and opposite; they are sadist lovers, enjoying the persons shown, their troubles, their folly, their grandeur and their beauty. The actor experiences an enlargement, the audience a recognition.

In ancient Greece the presiding deity of the civic dramatic festivals was Dionysus. Dionysus is best known as the god of fertility and reproduction, and of the release of suppressed instincts through drink; as an uninhibited god. Sir William Ridgeway in *The Origin of Tragedy* (1910) and *The Dramas and Dramatic Dances of Non-European Races* (1915) argued that Greek tragedy, with its heavy emphasis on ghosts, tombs and burial rites, could not have derived from such a deity and must be related rather to hero and ancestor worship and the cult of the dead. His general argument would be overpowering if Dionysus were no more than a vine god; but Erwin Rohdë in *Psyche: The Cult of Souls and Belief in Immortality among the Greeks* (trans. W. B. Hillis, London, 1925) had seen more in Dionysus, regarding him as a god of the occult. Dionysus certainly became the patron deity of drama, and we may provisionally regard him as inclusive, but if he was the god of both nature and that which was behind nature, of both life and death, we may reasonably ask, 'What was he not?' Fortunately the answer is simple. He was, and is, not the god of man's inhibited, ethical, civilized self-consciousness; instead he is always threatening it, both with lusts, indecencies and indignities and with crimes, ghosts and death. There is nothing respectable or civilized about him: he is the enemy of such qualities.

Man had risen through mastery of want and danger; the agriculturist, the herdsman and the hunter had provided food and the warrior had won territory. Drama may have grown from sympathetic magic, from rituals imitating what was wanted, making rain for fertility or fire for warmth; tragedy may be related to sacrifices meant either to release powers or placate spirits and deities, and to the many age-old cults centred on a dying and resurrected hero or god. Conflicts, dyings and resurrections were envisaged in close relation to the conquest of winter by spring. Deeds of great heroes may have been enacted to bring more victories either magically or by inspiring the onlookers to heroism. Ritual and drama are agents; as civilization advances the agency becomes more psychological but its action persists. Even more is involved than the facing and surmounting, which Aristotle observed, of the pity and terrors of existence. The aim is to make terms with and draw fertility and power from the dread non-human deities conditioning earthly life, striving through conflict for new kinds of mastery and self-mastery; at the limit, for death-conquest and the superman.

But the drive for and through civilization must have had its own god, standing for what Dionysus alone was not; a human god, a god of those ideals and visions which first prompted man's ascent. This god we may call Apollo, the god whose male yet delicate beauty symbolizes the dream-ideal of Hellenic culture.

Among the rituals forming the hinterland of Greek drama was that of the 'young and beautiful' Adonis as 'the victim of a tragic and untimely death'; he is resurrected, and 'only after his tragic death does he appear to assume divine attributes', in his 'death and resurrection' alike becoming the 'personification of natural energies' (Jessie Weston, *From Ritual to Romance*, X, XII, U.S.A., 1957; originally 1920). In Adonis is the quintessence of (i) human idealism and (ii) the tragic; and in drama and elegiac he has had a long line of descendants, such as Milton's Lycidas and Byron's Thyrza. These tragic definitions lend undying power to the central intuition of youth as a cosmic perfection and ultimate hope. If it dies it must live: this is the Apollonian trust.

To the Greeks, quite apart from metaphysics, male youth was, in their daily life, a star. Its aesthetic appeal at warrior exercise, athletic contests, dance, song and music—for all these were felt as parts of one harmony—was highly honoured; and boys, as Kenneth J. Freeman in his *Schools of Hellas* (1907; [1] IV. 142–9) tells us, were carefully selected to make their peculiar contributions at public displays of choral and semi-dramatic dance, so forecasting much that was to follow in Medieval and Renaissance drama. To the Greeks the beautiful was the good, and physical proportion and perfection a visual symbol of highest virtue. Apollo is a god of light, of ideals, of ethic.

The balance is precarious. Human beauty is as fragile as that of Adonis, slain by a boar, by an inhuman universe; more, it may open the flood-gates to lust, and in self-defence idealism hardens into moral convention, which is too often, in every age, the enemy of the best. So, though Apollo remains our ideal, he is perpetually challenged by Dionysus. This is the archetypal conflict from which all our dramatic conflicts derive; and the desired end is union. Drama labours to create from the marriage of Dionysus with Apollo a new and higher humanity, a new greatness on earth, or beyond. It is accordingly rich with figures of heroes, kings and supermen asserting their powers within mortality and sometimes breaking free from mortal limitation.

[1] Published with an introduction by A. W. Verrall, and often reprinted. Freeman's account was followed by P. A. Coggin in *Drama and Education*, 1956; and see Ruby Ginner, *Gateway to the Dance*, 1960. Young boys were presumably wanted in part for their voices, as in the Medieval Church dramas. Freeman notes that one died from a dose intended to improve his voice (IV. 148–9).

We are thinking now in terms of Friedrich Nietzsche's *The Birth of Tragedy from the Spirit of Music* (1872, trans. W. A. Haussmann, 1909), a thesis inspired by the music dramas of Richard Wagner. Though ante-dating our other authorities, it covers their findings. Much of it applies to comedy too, but our best authority for that is John Cowper Powys (p. 14 below).

Greek drama is made of chorus and actors. The chorus Nietzsche, following Aristotle, relates to the ecstatic lyric, the dithyramb, and Dionysus; the actors, to sculpture, epic poetry, and Apollo. Drama is seen as made from these two art deities of ancient Greece. Dionysus is the god of sound, of music, of the darkness behind threatening and interpenetrating creation, and to be associated with the 'titanic powers of nature' (3), the orgiastic (2) and all that is unindividual, unhuman and mysterious; he is the 'Primordial Unity' (1) and creative origin. Dionysus comes from the East (1). But against him stands the more Western assertion of Apollo, a god of precise visual forms, of intellect and individuality, of ethics (4) and politics (21), a dream of formal and individualized perfection. The Dionysian [1] principle corresponds to the deepest 'I' or selfhood, a oneness with all life far deeper than the individual ego as normally known (5); to a subjectivity tapping depths below moral categories, ranging from sexual orgy to religious insight. Both principles, Dionysian and Apollonian, are active, but the activity of the one we may call vertical, corresponding to the moment-by-moment immediacy, the 'now' of dramatic composition, and that of the other narrative and horizontal. Nietzsche compares them to the two sexes (1); the Dionysian is as clearly female in tone as the Apollonian is male; they are sexual archetypes or universals corresponding to the sex split of human creation. Both have their nobler and less worthy aspects, the one tending to vice and the other to convention: we may refer to the 'higher' or 'lower' 'Dionysian' or 'Apollonian'.

In Greek tragedy the Dionysian chorus moves and chants in ritual deliberation from its place in the 'orchestra' interpreting and dominating the epic action. As music throws off the 'picture sparks' of lyric poetry (5, 6), so the chorus from which drama has been born (7) may be regarded as the 'mother-womb' (8) of the stage persons and their tragic story. The process is felt by Nietzsche throughout in

---

[1] I follow the standard translation by W. A. Haussmann under the general editorship of Oscar Levy in using the terms 'Dionysian' and 'Apollonian' instead of 'Dionysiac' and 'Apollinian' or 'Apolline', the terms in professional use by classical scholars. The distinction is worth preserving in order to limit the understanding of these principles to the Nietzschean sense.

close relation to the cosmic scheme; we are invited to see Greek
drama as a microcosm or condensation of that scheme conceived on
the pattern of Indian philosophy wherein the god Brahma projects
the shapes of Maya—a term Nietzsche uses (1, 2)—on to the stage of
life and withdraws them to himself. In watching our highest human
excellence striving and withdrawn, we enjoy recognition of the
Primordial Unity at 'the heart of things' (16), which is also our own
deepest selfhood, the 'I' which is 'from the abyss of being' (5), an
otherness whither appearance flees as 'into the bosom of the true
and only reality' (22; also 16, 17, 24). Within destruction itself is a
great mystery hinting 'another existence and a higher joy' (21).
Tragedy is the fruit not of pessimism but of rapture.

The emphasis of *The Birth of Tragedy* falls inevitably on the
Dionysian principle, both because it is in danger of neglect as the
Apollonian is not, and because it is the peculiar purpose of drama as
such to force us to face and use it. But the final aim of *each* is a
'fraternal union' (21, 24; also 1, 2, 4, 25) corresponding to the form
of Greek drama. In his other great imaginative work, *Thus Spake
Zarathustra* (1883–91), Nietzsche develops a statement beyond
drama celebrating this integration (pp. 293–7 below).

Nietzsche's dramatic scheme exists in its own right independently
of any particular criticisms that might be levelled on archaeological
grounds. For the study of all acting and all drama it is invaluable.
Acting is itself a plunging from Apollonian individuality into the
Dionysian otherness from which alone a new impersonation may be
successfully re-created. Though the chorus has gone we still have our
'orchestra' to distend and prepare our minds, and whenever we
recognize the *uncanny* power of off-stage sounds, the Dionysian
principle is at work, giving depth to the Apollonian story. It covers
all that is mysterious, all that is atmospheric, in stage projection; and
we have only to think of the ghost scene in *Hamlet* to realize that
what we regard as the specifically 'dramatic' is close to the specifically
'Dionysian'. Or again, whenever a dramatic art-form, speech, scene,
or whole play, is found to exist less as a horizontal sequence than as
a growth from within surprising with a sudden access of power,
unfurling and explosive, then Dionysus, god of mystery and of
fertility, is active. Since our two principles are sexual archetypes,
they may be felt within all dramas of sexual antagonism or approach.
Often we shall find dramatic women levelling the irrational powers
against male valuation. We shall also find an important and recurring
opposition of (i) some power-impregnated man or woman as against

(ii) some figure of youthful and seraphic, bisexual grace. Power is balanced against love. The final aim of the Dionysian-Apollonian harmony is shadowed alike by the catharsis of tragedy, the marriage conclusions of romance, and the recurring conception of bisexual persons. The normal symbol of an achieved integration is gold; where such impressions occur attainment is not far off. When the harmony is mastered, as by Plato's Socrates and Nietzsche's Zarathustra, drama as such has ceased to exist, having surmounted itself.

II

Nietzsche's two principles, which correspond on the human plane to the sexes, female and male, can be found at work within the content as well as the form of Greek tragedy. We shall next discuss the tragedies of Aeschylus (525–456 B.C.), Sophocles (c. 496–406 B.C.) and Euripides (480–406 B.C.) in sexual terms.

Greek tragedy grew, like Elizabethan drama, from a soil of national victory and self-realization. Behind, as a Bible, was Homer; and more recently the Grecian city-states had combined to defend themselves against the Persian Empire, defeating King Darius and his son Xerxes. Aeschylus' drama *The Persae* dramatizes the victory of Salamis, from the Persian view; it is a short, but gripping, play, with great power in the raising of the ghost of Darius, to pronounce judgement on his defeated son.

Aeschylus' most comprehensive surviving work is the *Oresteia* trilogy, which wrestles with the problem of self-propagating evil, revenge, justice, and the will of Zeus, or God. In the *Agamemnon* Clytemnestra murders her husband King Agamemnon on his victorious return from the Trojan war. She is prompted in part by the ancestral curse, the demon haunting the family generation by generation, and in part by revenge for the death of her daughter Iphigenia, sacrificed by Agamemnon in pursuance of his military aims. A general sense of disquietude is expressed by the chorus regarding the nature of war and the suffering it brings to women. The female emphasis is maintained by the Apollo-tormented Cassandra's clairvoyant reading of the curse saturating the House of Atreus, to which she has been brought; a scene that can stand beside the ghost scenes in *Hamlet* to point the identity of the specifically 'dramatic' and the specifically 'occult'.

The emphasis of the *Choephoroe* is male. Much of it is devoted to long chorus passages labouring to arouse the spirit of the murdered Agamemnon against his queen, though the ghost does not actually appear, such effects being more proper on the female and Dionysian side of our opposition. His son, Orestes, has been commanded by Apollo, god of male reason, to avenge his father. He obeys, but is soon aware of the Erinues, or Furies, dark, female, and snake-haired, atavistic earth-spirits corresponding to irrational layers of guilt and crime below the threshold of consciousness, at once avengers of evil and themselves evil. Though Orestes was impelled by duty and ethic, he endures the torment of a mother's murder.

When in the *Eumenides*, the third play of the trilogy, Clytemnestra's ghost appears to urge on the Furies in the temple of Apollo to which Orestes has fled for sanctuary, we have a clear sexual opposition,[1] which also corresponds to Nietzsche's two principles, with the chorus of Furies as Dionysian equivalents. Next Orestes is brought for trial before the court of Areopagus in Athens, with Apollo as counsel for the defence and the Furies demanding punishment. As president of the court we have Athena, the warrior-goddess, a Valkyrie figure, pre-eminently bisexual. During the arguments, Apollo tells the Furies that their proper home is the execution ground, where impalings and other torments are done; like Nietzsche, like Bernard Shaw in *Caesar and Cleopatra*, Aeschylus sees more evil in such executions than in an honourable revenge, and in deliberately relating his Furies to this horror he sets the tone for many a future dramatization of judicial torment. Another argument concerns the relative demands of father and mother on a child's duty, Athena favouring the father; and that she, though a woman, should do this, underlines her bisexual function. The votes of the Areopagus are equally divided and the casting vote is given by Athena for mercy. It is arranged that the Furies, who are henceforward to be known as the 'Eumenides' or 'kindly ones', should go underground and be duly reverenced as guardian deities provided always that they remain hidden.

The *Oresteia* is a universal study of evil descending, as in Ibsen's *Ghosts*, from generation to generation. A darkly feminine, Dionysian force from the past disrupts civilization and clogs advance. But it has its rights. In bringing his mythical action to contemporary Athens, Aeschylus suggests that freedom from inherited compulsions may be

---

[1] Aeschylus' Apollo and Furies have been compared to C. G. Jung's concepts of 'animus' and 'anima' (W. F. Jackson Knight, 'The Aeschylean Universe', *The Journal of Hellenic Studies*, LXIII, 1943).

won provided that we do not reject but rather honour the dark entities, who then become guardians and kindly powers. There is a breaking through from mechanical law into a justice which is mercy, as in the New Testament; and it is personified by the bisexual Athena, who functions like Shakespeare's Portia speaking her 'mercy' speech through male disguise in *The Merchant of Venice*.

The *Prometheus Bound*, which may have either followed or preceded the *Oresteia*, is the central and only surviving part of its trilogy. The Titan Prometheus has incurred the wrath of the newly instated god-king Zeus by bringing fire, and so civilization, to man; and for punishment he is enchained and tormented on a mountainside. Zeus represents the universal cruelty, the hostile Dionysian, but the superhuman support of man's aspiration, Prometheus, contains, as Nietzsche himself observes (*The Birth of Tragedy*, 9), both principles. Much space is given to a woman, Io, who, pursued by the desires of Zeus and the consequent anger of his wife Hera, visits Prometheus in the form of a cow tormented by a gadfly. If Prometheus corresponds to contemporary man, Io is contemporary woman, personifying the torment consequent on woman's sexual contact with the cosmic or Dionysian powers. As Prometheus is the archetype of male aspiration, so Io is the archetype of Clytemnestra, Medea, Lady Macbeth, Phèdre and Hedda Gabler. Eventually Io's descendant and her torment's justification, Herakles-as-superman, will release Prometheus, and Io find Zeus' love more gentle. Some relevant thoughts occur in Dryden's *Amphitryon* (p. 132). Other dramatists, such as Shakespeare, Chapman, Byron, Wagner, Ibsen, and Shaw are to follow Aeschylus in looking for a superman.

Aeschylus' survey is bisexually balanced, Sophocles' tilted towards the Apollonian, and Euripides' towards the Dionysian. Sophocles' emphasis is humanistic and ethical. In both the *Ajax* and the *Philoctetes* the stress falls on nobility of action. In his handling of the Orestes myth in the *Electra* he favours the male side, showing brother and sister rightly and successfully avenging Agamemnon's death and so removing the curse on the House of Atreus. Electra is strong and good. So is Antigone in the *Antigone*, who injects a religious and feminine sensibility into male statecraft, and in so doing sets the type of all future dramatic striving, such as Ibsen's in *Emperor and Galilean*, for a synthesis of Church and State. Resolution comes through the death of Creon's son, forecasting *The Winter's Tale* and the many youth sacrifices in Ibsen (p. 290 below), which may be called dramatic descendants from Adonis.

Sophocles' two greatest surviving works are the *Oedipus Tyrannus* and its sequel the *Oedipus Coloneus*. In the first he faces a grim destiny; the supernatural powers remain distant and enigmatic and do not interpenetrate the human story as in Aeschylus; and his deity, though functioning as an awe-inspiring agent, is not Zeus or Dionysus, but Apollo.

Oedipus tries to escape the oracular prophecy that he is destined to slay his father and marry his mother, but in the attempt rushes unwittingly and blamelessly on his fate. After killing his unrecognized father Laius, King of Thebes, in a just quarrel, he comes to Thebes itself, which is being tormented by the Sphinx, an anomalous monster who has been slaughtering everyone who could not answer the riddle: 'What is he who walks first on four legs, next on two, and finally on three?' Oedipus solves it, the answer being Man, who uses a stick in old age. Sophocles does no more than refer to the riddle, assuming knowledge of it; but it demands our attention. The Sphinx is an abnormal creature, half woman and half lion, symbolizing a higher state of being, as in Shaw's *Caesar and Cleopatra* (pp. 284-5, 346 below). Oedipus is regarded as a man of deep penetration and the riddle should surely shadow a profundity. If it does so, the 'stick' must correspond to man matured in the wisdom of old age, like Shaw's Captain Shotover in *Heartbreak House* and the Ancients of *Back to Methuselah*. When attaining superman status in his second play the blinded Oedipus will probably carry a stick. So three stages of the human story, animal, man, and superman, are being indicated, and the society that could not read this riddle suffers until Oedipus' answer makes him its saviour. He becomes king and marries his mother, Jocasta. His descent into sexual abnormality, which has given its name to a well-known 'complex', tones naturally with the superlative part he is playing, since sexual abnormalities regularly characterize genius; they are its signature, psychologically at least, for the superstate will be as abnormal as the Sphinx itself.

The horror is revealed and he is cast out of the city. In the second play, the *Oedipus Coloneus*, he has grown to full stature. Proudly he recalls and reiterates his innocence; there has been no tragic fault; as in all true tragedy, we have an upward progress. Like many such super-types, like Shakespeare's Timon, rejection is followed by recognition: Thebes wants him back, for his presence will be a magical power to protect the city. But, like Timon, he now spurns the community that had rejected him. Instead he has come to Colonus, near Athens, where a pastoral sweetness replaces the dread Mount

Cithaeron which overwatched his tragedy; and now he offers libations in the grove of the Eumenides, the earth-spirits of the *Oresteia*, here associated with natural sweetness, with milk and honey. To Athens he offers the blessing of his tomb after death, and the good and enlightened Theseus, with the courtesy recaptured by Shakespeare in *A Midsummer Night's Dream*, protects him; as in every age the genius, the embryo-superman, needs secular protection. So Sophocles, like Aeschylus, brings his myth to Athenian ground for its solution: both are patriots.

Thunder sounds. Oedipus' hour is come, and in as marvellous a messenger speech as Greek drama offers us, his lifting to a state beyond what we call 'man' is reported. This is how Sophocles approaches what lies beyond. He does not deal in ghosts. His darkest destiny is the work of Apollo, and points directly to a sublime, yet human, transcendence. His one other strikingly supernatural occurrence is the appearance of the god-man or superman Herakles to solve human problems in the *Philoctetes*.

Sophocles is Apollonian, Euripides Dionysian; the one's emphasis is male, the other's female. In Euripides' *Ion* Apollo is the subject of violent criticism from a woman's viewpoint. In his *Electra* and *Orestes* the revenge commanded by Apollo is as grimly and bitterly presented as in Sophocles it is honoured. *The Trojan Women* is a noble study of women suffering from man's warfare. Euripides has one ghost, but it is less interesting than is his Dionysian psychology. The *Hippolytus* is a study in repression. Aphrodite, goddess of sexual love, executes a horrible revenge on the young hero who, in scorn of a goddess whose rites are suited only to nocturnal indulgence, has dared to reject sexual activity for a life of athletic prowess and hunting; that is, for male pursuits without any taint of female alloy or allure. The *Medea* is even more directly feminist. Wronged by her unfaithful and self-seeking husband Jason, Medea uses her witchcraft to murder his new wife and his and her own children. Here occult and feminist energies are levelled against man's callous disregard of a woman's rights, the feminist argument being as clearly pointed as in Ibsen's *Doll's House*. Medea goes free, escaping to Athens by help of the sun god.

What we have called the 'Dionysian' principle we have hitherto been finding expressed in other terms: in the Furies, in Zeus, in ghosts. Euripides' last play *The Bacchae* introduces us to Dionysus himself. The god has come in disguise to Pentheus, King of Thebes, who with his mother Agave has refused the new Dionysian cult from the East, which he regards as effeminate and immoral. Dionysus' worshippers are mainly women, and they engage in nocturnal, Walpurgis Night orgies on the slopes of Mount Cithaeron, becoming wild and bestial creatures of nature, unhumanized, tearing animals, lustful and sadistic. Dionysus sets to work on Pentheus; gradually he gains the ascendancy; mesmerizes him; persuades him to *dress as a woman* and join the women Bacchantes in the mountain woods. Out there, by night, his own mother Agave is deluded by the god into slaughtering her son, thinking him an animal. When all is known Dionysus is coldly triumphant. Asked, like Iago, *why* he has done all this, his answer is simple: because Pentheus and Agave refused to worship his deity.

So Euripides drives home the dangers of ethic unrelated to the deeper sources. The sexual and Dionysian powers must be accepted; more, they must be honoured, as the Erinues are honoured in the *Oresteia*, for only so can they become sweet and Sophoclean, as in the pastoral idealism of their worship at Colonus. Sophocles' emphasis is male and Euripides' female, but each dramatically strives for an inclusiveness corresponding to the Aeschylean balance. All three alike labour for that synthesis of Dionysian and Apollonian which Nietzsche saw as the purpose and meaning of tragic drama.

III

Greek tragedy may have a natural background. Mountains and ocean are elemental powers in the *Prometheus Bound*; Mount Cithaeron is a dominating presence for Sophocles and still more, with a fine realization of its woods and beasts, for Euripides; and Sophocles' Colonus is a pastoral haven. But the main emphases are inward and spiritual. Comedy is more directly concerned with natural forces. Greek comedy, made like the tragedies from chorus and actors, appears to have derived jointly from the phallic sex festivals of the *Komos*, or 'revel', and from various fertility or other mummeries of impersonated conflict, death and resurrection, the two composing elements corresponding to the dithyramb and epic fictions within tragedy. Fertility revels and rituals were known throughout the ancient world, varying from saturnalia in which participants disguised themselves in animal skins with long ears and tails or rioted in sex disguise, to the more solemn ceremonials of the mystery cults. Spring folk dramas dramatized the rebirth of nature;

they may have been intended to act magically and assure successful harvests, and simultaneously the cosmic scheme was being used as an interpretation of human destiny: man's drama was being integrated into the drama of the seasons, where spring follows winter. In what remains of these folk dramas we often find a slain champion resurrected, sometimes humorously, by a doctor.[1] Within the area of comic origins we can detect a flowering from sex to resurrection.

Comedy in later ages has a natural stock-in-trade of sexual audacity and miraculous happy endings such as would scarcely meet the moral and rational demands of civilized thinking were it not for the humour. For at some point in our story the primitive and positive response to the mysteries of nature became clouded by taboo and unbelief, and it was at this point that laughter, in itself a simple product of child-like joy, came in to assist with its peculiar wisdom man's reintroduction to a lost simplicity and challenge his more sophisticated assurances. 'Humour' was born. Though in part intellectual, its purpose is to support and not deny the natural powers. Laughter is on the side of instinct, of life, of joy, and miracle; from these it sprang as surely as tragedy sprang from death; and because comedy grew from cults honouring these bright powers, its proper critical targets ever since have been man's moral and mental valuations and insincerities. In so far as it attacks natural instincts, it is the less comic, and if it invites us to *laugh* at them from a moral or rational view, it becomes suicidal. A moralistic comedy is a contradiction in terms. The best defence of the iconoclastic obscenities of great comedy is probably that offered in the concluding chapters of John Cowper Powys's *Rabelais* (1948). Powys sees great humour as marking an advance beyond constricting taboos and the poisons of ingrown spiritualities towards common sense and cosmic health. Humour is on every level the key to re-creation and resurrection: it is no chance that Euripides' drama of resurrection, the *Alcestis*, touches comedy. That comedy associates readily with miracle and immortality is witnessed by Eugene O'Neill's *Lazarus Laughed* and the plays of Shakespeare and Bernard Shaw.

In Greece the great master of comedy was Aristophanes (*c.* 448–380 B.C.). His dramas cover both social criticism and poetic fantasy, but a general relation to the old rituals is reflected by his titles: *The Clouds*, *The Wasps*, *The Frogs*, *The Birds*. There is a running emphasis on drink, food, cooking, and sex. Plays often end with

[1] E. K. Chambers, *The Medieval Stage* (p. 27 below), I; 207, 210, 213.

feasting and sometimes a marriage. In all of them he makes fun of accepted values, social or religious.

The Acharnians and *The Knights*, written and performed during the war between Athens and Sparta, are attacks on war-psychology, the war party and its leader, Cleon. *The Acharnians* amusingly contrasts the absurdities of war with culinary and sexual enjoyment. Food, cooking and drink are regularly relied on, for contrast or as symbols. In the *Lysistrata* the women go on strike, refusing sexual intercourse until the war is stopped. In the *Thesmophoriazusae* Euripides is in trouble from the women for his delineations of the feminine temperament and is defended by a relative who disguises himself as a woman. Both Euripides and Socrates are satirized in *The Clouds*, which contains attacks on the rising generation and modern sophistication, with an amusing hit at a science that replaces Zeus as the cause of thunder by a scientific term which is scarcely calculated to sustain divine honours. The *Plutus* makes philosophic comedy from the rationalization of wealth, its conclusion celebrating a new alignment of wealth and justice. Aristophanes denounces accepted values and mental aims in the name of basic life principles. He is optimistic. Old men are miraculously rejuvenated, new and more splendid systems replace injustice and folly; and he likes to end with festivity.

His two most imaginative works are *The Frogs* and *The Birds*. In *The Frogs* Dionysus as god of drama is a comically nervous and effeminate person venturing into Hades to bring back a dramatic poet from the dead: the choice lies between Aeschylus and Euripides and there is an amusing contest. But is it not strange, even in a comedy, that such a presentation of Dionysus should be performed in his honour? And that such a god should be also the god of high tragedy?

As we have seen, Ridgeway argued that Dionysus as god of fertility and the vine could not have been the original god of tragedy, though it was later put under his care; when, we may suggest, it had become less ritual than entertainment. Ridgeway's argument appears to be supported by *The Frogs*. Much of the fun derives from Dionysus disguising himself as the great Herakles in order to make his dread journey; he is a nature deity aiming to master the heroic, adventure into death, and find a tragic dramatist. The most memorable scene is probably that of his conflict with the Frogs, whose insistent and sub-human chorus of 'Brek-kek-kek-kex, co-ax, co-ax' he has to quell whilst trying to cross the Styx. These frogs are creatures of cold, reptilian life, recalling Aeschylus' snaky-haired Furies and their similarly repetitive and sub-human noises. So Dionysus is really being shown as having to surmount the lower elements of the 'Dionysian' in order to enter the realms of Death; and when he gets there, he at once finds another *contrasted* chorus of the initiates in Elysium hymning 'Iacchus', a deity sometimes associated with Dionysus as mystery god. The journey accordingly appears to represent Dionysus' self-surmounting from nature deity to god of tragedy and Elysian intimations. The choice of Dionysus as tragic patron may have derived from the desire to place human death within the harmonies of nature, where spring follows winter; he was a deity who could reclaim tragedy from death, and that is precisely what we see him doing for a tragic poet in *The Frogs*. Whatever be the exact truth, there appears to be a second level of meaning below the surface plot and surface humour. Both the veiling and the humour may be supposed ways of approach to a problem too baffling and perhaps too theologically dangerous for a more direct exposition.

Theology is again central to *The Birds*. *The Frogs* takes us to the depths, *The Birds* to the heights. The hero Peisthetairos is an astute old man sick of the vices of civilization who solicits help from the Birds to found a new city in air, which they call 'Cloud-Cuckoo-Town'. It is to be an ideal community, and the rejection of unsuitable applicants gives opportunity for some amusing political and social satire.

But here too there are deeper meanings. Atmospheric phenomena had already been given a spiritualized and almost Shelleyan poetry in *The Clouds*, and bird life is in every age an imaginative analogue to spirit life. In Plato's *Phaedrus* (p. 18 below) feathers and flight are reiterated images of spiritual ascent. Though their present king was once a mortal (75, 97–8, 114), the Birds as a group claim to be 'immortal' beings descended from the winged Eros or Love conceived as a mighty bird, and to antedate the official gods as well as the rest of earthly creation (685–722). They are 'winged deities' (903) who must be reinstated in their ancient sovereignty (1600–1) with men praying only to them (1058–60). Such thoughts are entangled with a firm sense of them as real birds, the relation being knotted by reference to the contemporary belief in birds as omens. Such an entanglement is more dramatically useful than would be any direct exploitation of esoteric truth; Ibsen does much the same with the sea (pp. 290, 292). Without departing too far from actuality we are shown the building of an ethereal city interpenetrating our higher atmosphere. Aristophanes presents a poetic analogue to the 'etheric' plane, or dimension.

The comedy is rich. The new community acts as a besieging force, cutting off sacrificial nourishment from the gods and so forcing their surrender. Prometheus is one of our visitors, with a kind of umbrella to guard himself from Zeus' thunderbolts; and so is Aeschylus' superman, Herakles. We are within the context of man's Promethean and spiritual self-assertion towards a higher, more magical, being, using but surpassing man's religious consciousness. The hero Peisthetairos is finally honoured as, pretty nearly, Zeus; he becomes divine, and is given the sceptre of rule and a noble *gamos*, or marriage, with Basileia (=sovereignty), daughter of Zeus, as bride and Eros as his strength; just as Dante during his upward progress is invested with 'Crown and Mitre' as 'sovereign' of himself (*Purgatorio*, XXVII). Like Bernard Shaw's, Aristophanes' humour serves to make approaches too bold for direct argument.

IV

Tragedy captures dark powers and at high moments transfigures them; comedy takes a short cut and assumes joy in terms of humour. Both work for the integration and the sublimation personified by Socrates (469–399 B.C.).

Socrates' teaching as reported by Plato (427–348 B.C.) was itself dramatic both in conception and in form, searching for truth through opposites and dialogue. His teaching ranged over politics, ethics, love, and immortality. He is shown as in full mastery of that for which Western drama darkly strives. Dramatic thought labours continually for a synthesis of religion and politics, church and state; and the *Republic* has its philosophic ruler or rulers.

The Socratic wisdom, though rationally presented, has its foundations in mystery. In Plato's most impassioned dialogue, the *Phaedrus*, emphasis is laid on poetic and prophetic ecstasy, and in the *Symposium* Socrates' understanding of love is derived from the prophetess, or medium, Diotima. The aspersions on certain kinds of poetry in the *Phaedo* and the *Republic* mark no rejection of the essence but rather an assimilation and a transcending of poetic fictions, like that represented by Nietzsche's Zarathustra (p. 294 below), into a life-wisdom of poetic substance. Reason becomes part of an Apollonian mysticism transmuting the Dionysian powers to a golden flame.

There is an ascent from passion to purpose. The central doctrine is a doctrine of love in tune with the prevailing cult of *paederastia*, or educational love for a boy or youth. Love is described in the *Phaedrus*. Though the extreme of vice is rejected, the doctrine is planted firmly in the physical and the love advocated has fire and passion; it is a seething madness wherein the soul feels itself recovering the wing feathers of its divine origin; it is an awakening beyond reason into supernal recognition and remembrance. That Eros, the love god, should be called 'the patron of beautiful boys' (265) is not strange, for we are being pointed to the beauty of the unfolding bud more perfect than any earthly maturity and so reflecting the creative and divine essence, at once the heart of life and the earnest of immortality. So in the *Symposium*, after the various speakers have offered their different accounts of love, the crowning truth is that reported by Socrates from Diotima: what the true lover primarily desires is to 'beget upon the thing of beauty' (206) immortal flowerings in the realms of wisdom and virtue. Earthly beauty mirrors a divine reality and Eros is defined as the spirit-link, the angel messenger, between the gods and man. In Greek art he is depicted as a winged youth, so forming the archetype of what we shall often, in the following pages, call the 'seraphic intuition'.

Socrates lived his own gospel. Himself physically far from beautiful, his own soul harmony delighted in the visible excellence of the young lives he gathered round him. 'His relation to his young disciples', wrote G. Lowes Dickinson, 'was that of a lover and a friend' (*The Greek View of Life*, 1896, 1907; III. 150). Though *paederastia* was an accepted custom, Socrates' imposing development of it aroused opposition, and he was accused of atheism and the corruption of youth. In *The Clouds* Aristophanes' attack on Socrates is at one point, the contest of personified vice and virtue, couched in terms of homosexual aspersion. If this dialogue was added because the original text had been regarded as too favourable to Socrates,[1] we have one cause of his unpopularity. In the *Apology* Socrates appears to have thought that Aristophanes' play helped to weight the scales against him.

Beyond love and ethic Socrates, through Plato, asserts immortality. In the *Apology* he refers to his spirit guardian, telling how he listens, like Shaw's Joan, to its voice. In *The Birds* (1553–5) Aristophanes refers to him as engaging in spiritualistic cults. His thoughts on

---

[1] Stated in *The Oxford Companion to Classical Literature* (Sir Paul Harvey, 1937, 1946; 112).

death may be called 'spiritualistic'. In the *Republic* the future life is described by one who has died and returned; [1] and in the *Phaedo*, just before his own death, Socrates describes the beyond, to which at death each is guided by his spirit guardian, as our same nature transfigured, of richer colouring and more etheric texture; not so much another, transcendent, world, as a new dimension of this that we know, such as that experienced by a butterfly emerged from its chrysalis.

As we read the *Apology*, Socrates' defence before his judges, and the account of his last hours before death in the *Phaedo*, we are reminded of Christ. There is the same poise, the same repudiation of retaliation or escape and the same assurance regarding death. The true superman must always be one to whom death is no ogre, but rather the 'death', if so we can call it, of Sophocles' hero at Colonus.

Greek tragedies were translated or adapted by the Romans, and many works of quality and stature may have been created, though nothing survives except the dramas of Seneca (*c.* 4 B.C.–A.D. 65), composed during the reign of Nero. These redevelop the old themes, but were probably meant for reading rather than performance. In Seneca the two dramatic principles, Dionysian and Apollonian, are driven to the extremes of an exaggerated sensationalism countered by passages of stoic moralizing. Rome has left us no great tragedy. For links with the central dramatic tradition we must look to Virgil's *Aeneid*: to his tragic Dido; his Adonis equivalent, the slaughtered Pallas; the bisexually conceived Camilla; and the Dionysian and subversive fury Allecto. However, Seneca exerted a main influence on Renaissance drama.

Much the same happened in comedy. The 'old comedy' of Aristophanes was succeeded by the 'new comedy' of Menander (342–292 B.C.) along lines heralded by Euripides' *Ion* and characterized by realism, domestic wrangling, intricacy of plot, lost and found children and other errors, complications and discoveries, with heterosexual romance and happy endings. Menander's plays were adapted and imitated by Plautus (*c.* 254–184 B.C.) and Terence (*c.* 190–159 B.C.), whose works set the type for Renaissance comedy. Though the type became a convention, it only did so because it had a perennial appeal corresponding to certain truths of human destiny; and whenever a great dramatist uses it, we must be prepared to recognize a profundity.

[1] See W. F. Jackson Knight, 'The After-Life in Greek and Roman Antiquity', *Folklore*, LXIX, December 1958.

CHAPTER II

Medieval

ANGELI: Quem quaeritis in sepulchro, Christicolae?
MULIERES: Jesum Nazarenum crucifixum, O caelicolae.

I

WHILE the Greeks were cramming the history of culture into a few centuries an Eastern people were forging one no less exciting though of a longer span. The correspondences are interesting.

In Genesis man's intellectual ascent incurs God's wrath, just as in the myth of Prometheus: both can be read as evolution myths. Israel's epic story of wandering, warfare and heroism corresponds to the *Odyssey* and the *Iliad*, with David's dirge over Saul and Jonathan (2 Samuel i. 19–26) to match Achilles' grief for Patroclus; the great prophets, Isaiah and Jeremiah, correspond to the dramas of Aeschylus and Sophocles, penetrating the divine purpose, willing harmony and union; Job and the *Prometheus Bound* make similar pleas for cosmic justice. Israel has its law-giver and leader, Moses, like Greece's Solon, or the great Pericles. Both are small nations, fighting for life under threats from great empires, Assyria and Persia. St Paul's claim to have surmounted the Judaic Law through Christ corresponds to the raising in Aeschylus' *Oresteia* of the rule of blood and law to a solution under the child of Zeus, Athena; and the lost conclusion to the *Prometheus* would have provided another analogy, with Herakles uniting man and Zeus. Sophocles' peculiarly incarnate wisdom culminating in Oedipus' ascension forecasts the New Testament. Beyond prophecy and drama is the living Man, Socrates and Jesus, unrecognized and condemned but afterwards honoured and their life and teaching recorded by disciples and followers, Plato and Xenophon, the evangelists and St Paul. As the elixir cools, thought becomes more analytic, in Aristotle and the Church fathers. From St Paul and St John onwards the Greek blends with the Hebraic; St Augustine's thought is conditioned by the later Platonists; and Aristotle becomes the thought-companion of Thomas Aquinas.

In calling himself the 'Son of Man' Jesus claims to be the fulfilment of prophecy. The conception may well be more than evolutionary, but it is not less: St Paul regards him as 'the first-born of a great brotherhood' (Romans viii. 29). The traditional picturing of him as a new-born child with his Mother suggests the end of a biological progress, and he has no children himself. His divine birth resembles that of Euripides' hero in *Ion*, the close mother relationship and comparative slighting of human fatherhood corresponding, we may suggest, to the 'Oedipus complex' often supposed to be strongly functioning in men of genius. Jesus is unmarried. In tone with both the Platonic fervour and the love 'beyond a woman's love' of his ancestor David (2 Samuel i. 26),[1] his first affection is given to the Beloved Disciple, John (John xiii. 23–5; xix. 26; xxi. 20), and it is natural that John should be our main authority on Jesus' doctrine of love. Both John's Gospel and his First Epistle announce a love circuit from God through Jesus to his disciples and thence expanding (e.g. at John xiii. 34; xv. 12); or it may go, Platonically, through love of man to God (1 John iv. 20); the teaching's core being the statement 'God is love' (1 John iv. 8). For various reasons Jesus' teaching, like Socrates', aroused opposition. The pictures showing his Mother and John beside the Cross make a statement of undying significance.[2]

Though the main emphasis is male, women are beautifully presented in the Gospels, especially Luke's, and we have a number of parables on marriage festivity. The sexual problem is clarified, whatever our opinions on either its authorship or its orthodoxy, by the recently published Gospel of Thomas wherein Jesus tells Peter, who has objected that a woman is 'not worthy of life', meaning eternal life, that she can be made 'a living spirit' by becoming male (Thomas, 112).[3] The price of entry, for either sex, is bisexuality, the childlike and angelic state counselled by Jesus (Matthew xviii. 2–5, 10; xix. 14; Mark x. 14–15) being here re-emphasized and next interpreted as

[1] See also 1 Samuel xx. 41.

[2] In *The Arrow and the Sword* (1947, 1955) Hugh Ross Williamson observes that the traditional depicting of 'the Crucified between the Beloved and the Mother' has 'a significance which is not always understood' (V. 86). Christopher Marlowe was said to have insisted on a homosexual strain in the New Testament, quoting John, xiii. 23–5. See p. 57 below.
For some notes on the authorship of the Gospel, and First Epistle attributed to John, see my 'Epilogue' to the 1962 reissue of *The Christian Renaissance*.

[3] My references follow the text published in *The Secret Sayings of Jesus* by Robert M. Grant and David Noel Freedman, 1960. These do not tally with *The Gospel according to Thomas* by A. Guillaumont and others, 1959.
I discuss more fully the implications of this Gospel and of Gnosticism in general in the 1962 reissue of *The Christian Renaissance*.

an *internal* marriage making 'the man' and 'the woman' into 'a single one' (Thomas, 23) with a view to the perfected self-integration. The psychological teaching is summed up: 'When you make the two one, you will become sons of man' (Thomas, 103). This is as the state of 'the angels in Heaven', who know nothing of sexual mating (Matthew xviii. 10; xxii. 30; Mark xii. 25; Luke xx. 36). Jesus' high rating of celibacy (Matthew xix. 11–12) springs less from self-denial than from a self-fulfilment.

The *paederastia* of the Greeks and the love celebrated in Plato's *Phaedrus* and *Symposium* were in part educational relationships, in which romance blended with care and an almost parental tone; and this especial caring is far more strongly developed in Christianity. It is vivid in the art that clusters round the Nativity, but it originates from the Gospel of John, with its reiterations to Peter of 'Feed my sheep' (xxi. 15–17). In this gospel we have our strongest emphasis on the personal relationship of Jesus, as lover, to the disciples, and ever since Christianity has diverged from other religions in its reliance on this peculiarly personal love relationship, descending through John, Peter and the others to the whole Christian Church as Christ's Bride. It is all one process, from the personal centre, asking a personal response.

Yet Jesus was more than Socrates, more than prophet, lover-genius, or hero. He breathes too an uncompromising ethical fervour and a terrifying spirituality with a sense of urgency and impending judgement. Occult and magic powers, clairvoyance and clairaudience, were in him, powers such as great drama regularly implies and uses: miracles, control of the elements, healings, revival of the dead, and his own resurrection. That central quest from the old rituals downwards, the quest of victory over death, is here mastered. The ascension of Oedipus is lived; Aristophanes' fantasy in *The Birds* of man becoming the equal of Zeus is lived; Prometheus is released. The Son of Man, or Superman, has blasted the limits of earth-locked humanity.

Nature to Jesus is kindly, with God as love, creating the lily and caring for the birds, and all its horrors somehow by-passed. Yet if blood forms no part of the doctrine, it does of the drama. He who has surpassed the categories of blood and sacrifice becomes himself a royal victim; and for us, the only whole truth is in the drama. The New Testament is strongly dramatic, showing an interpenetration of the natural and the supernatural similar to Shakespeare's, and Jesus as an appallingly dominating protagonist. The quiet before the end, the last supper and prayer in the garden, resemble and must have influenced those scenes of fourth-act quiet in Shakespearian tragedy.

Christian theology is the science of an unprecedented happening, alien to common sense. The law of blood still holds, its grip unloosened: in nature 'red', as Tennyson puts it, 'in tooth and claw' (*In Memoriam*, LVI.); in man's warring and civil justice; above all in the sadistic instinct, which is the reflection in man's sexual self-consciousness of the blood rhythm present within the voracities of nature. We remember the hideous execution grounds in the *Oresteia* and the tearing of animals in *The Bacchae* (pp. 9 and 13 above). These are the horrors that tragic drama labours to catch and cleanse, and if Christ has surpassed them we have not. We are therefore invited to direct our instincts on the Cross, which marks the relationship of Christ to ourselves. The naked and tortured figure is a sadistic and masochistic symbol in cosmic display. Whatever our perversions we can place them here; especially does the Crucifix drain off the blood lust, replacing other sacrifices and other cruelties, and twisting them painfully into love. This love is not quite natural to us. St Paul realizes that the whole creation 'sighs and throbs with pain' (Romans viii. 22), and the release he looks for is so far beyond our comprehension that we are forced into dogma and metaphysics. So the mighty fabric of Christian theology arose.

Since Christ is both so human and so alien, he must be both Man and God. The paradox is given a universal significance in the Trinity, wherein the Father is the all-creator, containing good and evil; the Son, Christ preaching love; and the Holy Spirit, for us, the unifier. In the Greek-Nietzschean scheme our correspondences would be Dionysus-Brahma, the primordial origin, for the Father; Socrates or the bisexual Athena of the *Oresteia*, for the Son; and the Platonic Eros, for the Holy Spirit. Such systems make miniature yet all-embracing dramas. The Greek analogies are not out of place, since the continuity with Greek thought was never for long broken: St Paul, St John, St Augustine and St Aquinas, all show Greek influences. But in Christianity there is a new tug, a compulsion and drive, based on ethical conflict, of a kind unknown to the Greeks, descending from the New and Old Testaments and beyond that perhaps from ancient Mazdaism; and so we have a fourth person, the Devil, who must presumably be regarded as an aspect of the Father. Christianity is at heart a drama, a conflict becoming unity, a Three-in-One which is neither One nor Three, but both, an ever-present reciprocity and interaction. More paradoxes recur in the Mass, finding God in the inanimate (pp. 316-7 below) and asserting the contemporaneity of a past sacrifice, with all the immediacy of the dramatic 'now'. Christianity is saturated in the dramatic: its great theologians, Abélard and Aquinas, work, as did Plato, in terms of 'disputation', or dialogue, posing the contrapuntal. If the medieval synthesis attained an inclusive harmony unknown before or since, this was through no denial of paradox, but rather through the firm acceptance of dramatic paradox at its heart, with resultant harmony out-flowering. Later ages show confusion at the heart and multitudinous dramas on the circumference.

This system dominated throughout the Dark and Middle Ages. The abnormal sexology of the New Testament was accepted as the human ideal, and devoted men, officers of the Church, lived it; sometimes through a natural attunement but also through intellectual conviction, will-power, ritual exercise and help from higher spheres. So we have the growth of a celibate priesthood and monastic communities. Sexual intercourse was slighted. The central emphasis was still male, yet softened by love, matching the bisexuality of the integrated Christ. The aim was astringent. Nature and reason demanded a redressing of balance and the cult of the Virgin Mother grew, to assure the rights of the female as female and of procreation; for the superman ideal, in Plato, in the New Testament, in Nietzsche, in the thought of Tolstoy's last years, procreates spiritually rather than biologically. For most people life went on normally enough. It was even perhaps easier to be normal, since all the abnormal compulsions were safely enclosed in religious houses or set above the altar for worship, whence they radiated power throughout the community of Christendom. That is how the Middle Ages grasped the best of both worlds; it was an astounding accomplishment, dominating Europe for twelve centuries.

Meanwhile human turbulences persisted. The Roman Empire dissolved, Europe was a collection of scattered principalities or chiefdoms, without political coherence. Charlemagne re-established (800-814) the Western empire, aiming to align imperial control with official Christianity, and from his time onwards there was a running interplay of Pope and Emperor, and many rivalries of secular and ecclesiastical power, such as those of Pope Gregory VII with the Emperor Henry IV and Becket with King Henry II of England; both of which we shall find treated in British dramas (pp. 261-2, 265-9 below). The aim, which we today would call the fusion or at least harmonization of Church and State, was noble; but the emperors were little more than princes wielding a power of limited range; the last of consequence was Frederick II, who became emperor in 1215. National kings grew in importance; Europe was being divided into strong sovereign states; the Holy Roman Empire became a lost cause.

Even so the attempt was made, the note sounded. The overtones of the term 'chivalry' witness to a harmonization of warrior and Christian unknown since; and a lustre still surrounds chivalric romance, as in the music dramas of Wagner. But only a unique cause can justify a Christian warriorship. Such a cause was behind the great Crusades, in which the medieval ideal, though fitfully and with many failings, became action, leading to the formation of new orders of soldier monks, both religious and military, such as the Knights Templars.

Chivalry suggests 'courtesy' and touches 'courtly love'. Here again there is an antagonism between Church and man; and still more, between Church and woman. The New Testament gives us little help regarding politics and sexual relationships, and the Church's doctrine regarding sexual sin remained uncompromising. But instincts have their way. The romantic love cult, originating in Provence in the eleventh century, spread widely. The loved one might be either male or female, though open and social recognition was only accorded love for a woman.[1] Though aiming at sexual fulfilment in deliberate dissociation from marriage, the cult nevertheless marked a refinement of sexual impulse and was accompanied by a host of Christian virtues, such as humility and service. Subtle poetry was made of it; it became itself a second and rival religion with Love as deity and in some songs sexual romance shades imperceptibly into the cult of the Virgin.

In both politics and sexual relations a compromise was intermittently reached and union consistently sought; and yet harmony was not in practice achieved. Perhaps the most important political theorist was Dante, whose De Monarchia (c. 1312) makes a strong plea for a revitalized monarchy and empire in descent from Rome as a means to man's earthly fulfilment, through one world community, of the divine purpose. Dante's emperor is to derive his authority not from the Pope, to whom is due only the reverence due to St Peter, but directly from God. Emperor and Pope are to be as two separate guides to the earthly and heavenly paradises respectively, working in

[1] Terms of address such as 'lord' cannot always be read as metaphors for a lady: Michelangelo's Sonnets will not submit to such a reading.
The extent of homosexuality in the Middle Ages has been fruitfully discussed in Hugh Ross Williamson's The Arrow and the Sword (p. 21 note).

harmonious independence. 'Dante', writes John B. Morrall, 'seems to have been the first thinker to elevate the earthly destiny of Man . . . into an end in itself' (*Political Thought in Medieval Times*, 1958; 101). The *De Monarchia* is as a bridge from the Middle Ages to the Renaissance.

In the sexual sphere Dante's *Divina Commedia* (1300–20) harmonizes erotic instinct and Christianity. Beatrice personifies that youthful pre-sexual perfection which is elsewhere, as we shall see, more usually expressed through boys disguised as angels or girls.[1] She inspires a love as ideal as Plato's and as fervent as that of the troubadours, whilst also symbolizing the mystery of the Incarnation. She exists as a medium between the divine and man, as an 'angel' properly under-stood as a 'messenger', corresponding to the Platonic Eros and what we may generically call the 'seraphic intuition' running as a golden and unifying thread through medieval culture, both sacred and secular; and it is she who leads Dante through the paradisial spheres. The great poem is made throughout of circles and circling motion; in it the triangularities of scholastic thought are contained and harmonized; and the final insight of man fitted within the divine circling finds all human agonies and inconsequences as constituent to the one perfection. Again, Dante both sums and includes the medieval heritage and casts light ahead into the Renaissance.

II

A break between the Church and classical drama was inevitable. Revulsion from the horrors and indecencies associated with the stage in fourth-century Rome merely forced a natural divergence. Christianity claimed to include and place the dramatic substances. Literary gestures towards superhumanity were no longer in request, since the Superman had come; no tragedy could rival the Cross; and comic obscenities were to be repressed rather than indulged. As for the spirit world, there was no need for oracles and mediums, the Church being the one oracle and only true medium. Poetic reports regarding the Elysian life paled before Christ's staggering victory.

Drama did not wholly die. The comic tradition of the Mediter-ranean West was kept alive by wandering mimes and minstrels.[2]

[1] In John Cowper Powys's *Owen Glendower*, 1941, XIX. 722, the bisexually conceived Tegolin is compared directly with Dante's Beatrice.
[2] I am relying on Allardyce Nicoll's study *Masks, Mimes and Miracles*, 1931.

There is some evidence of a more literary drama. The Saxon nun Hrotsvitha modelled religious plays on Terence in the tenth century, and about this time plays were being done at Constantinople, perhaps along the lines, in the semi-Greek manner, of the mysterious *Christos Paschon*, or *Christ Suffering*, the text of which survives. Throughout Europe indigenous festivals and folk drama of pagan ancestry and tone were continuous, sometimes, as in the 'Mummers' Play', with a combat, death and resurrection, the persistent themes of all drama, setting the type for more sophisticated works.

However, Europe in the Dark Ages had no comprehensive drama. The all-dominating Church felt no need of it. But the one concentration was hard: Christ had indeed risen, but men still died. Though the Mass relived Christ's suffering and triumph, it remained distanced by devotion and beyond the senses, which it deliberately contradicted. Under Charlemagne, however, made emperor in 800, there was a renaissance of learning, which led to fresh extensions. Certain notes and vowel sounds in the office of the Mass were soon to be given additional phrases, embellishments called 'tropes', in adjustment to the music, sometimes in the vernacular. The creative impulse took wing, and drama was reborn.

The Church plays of the Middle Ages have been studied in E. K. Chambers's *The Medieval Stage* (1903) and more exhaustively in Karl Young's *The Drama of the Medieval Church* (1933). Two points must be emphasized. First, the new drama was born from music, coming from 'beyond the very borders of articulate speech' (Chambers, II; 7) and recalling Nietzsche's title *The Birth of Tragedy from the Spirit of Music*; second, it was, again in tune with Nietzsche, (p. 7 above; pp. 308–9 below), born not in grief but in joy, being inspired *not by Christ's suffering but by his resurrection*. The first known liturgical drama comes somewhere about the year 900 (Young, II; 397) in the Easter Mass, clerics chanting before the altar the dialogue between the two, or three, Marys and the Angel, or Angels, at Christ's sepulchre. Translated from the Latin it goes:

ANGELS: Whom do you seek in the sepulchre, worshippers of Christ?
MARYS: Jesus of Nazareth, the crucified, O heavenly ones.
ANGELS: He is not here: he has risen as he had foretold.
   Go, report that he has risen from the sepulchre.

Once started progress was rapid. The dialogue was detached from the Mass, impersonation and costuming developed, the drama was elaborated and the action used the whole church, with procession.

New persons, Peter and John, were brought in, and finally Christ himself. This resurrection drama met not merely a need but a craving, spreading widely with various elaborations across Europe. Resurrection had passed from the occult to the visible, from devotion to experience. The congregations shared in it and joined in with a paean of triumph. Christ's resurrection had for a moment become theirs too.

As impersonation grew the parts were carefully allotted. In the Gospel of Mark, who records only one, the angel at the tomb is like a 'youth' (xvi. 5); and for their angels the Church regularly used choir-boys whose youthful purity and silvery voices could make the heavenly seem real (Young, I; 240, 244, 275, 283, 288, 290, 294, 299). The Marys were young clerics or 'scholars' (Young, I; 262, 289, 294); John was a youth, Peter old (Young, I; 364–5). The boy angels were carefully 'ornati sicut Angeli', sometimes with wings and lilies; or they might be hidden aloft, their voices only heard (Young, I; 244, 294, 299). In the getting up of these angels, in a fourteenth-century text, Karl Young finds his first striking example of a visual impersonation (I; 244); this appears to have been the Church's first properly dramatic creation; and the implications for our study of Western drama are important. We shall find many later dramatists presenting, in one way or another, seraphic equivalents; often in what we may call bisexual disguise, with suggestions of a state beyond sex, like 'the angels in Heaven' (p. 22 above).

There followed dramatizations of events subsequent to the Resurrection, of Jesus' appearance on the road to Emmaus and of the Ascension. There were also the laments of Mary and John at the Crucifixion, and other passion pieces—the first recorded is from Italy in 1200 (Chambers, II; 75)—but the early emphasis was all on the Resurrection. Karl Young writes: 'In comparison with the multitude of medieval Church plays treating events relating to the Resurrection, the number of dramatic representations of the Crucifixion is astonishingly small' (I; 492). Even the Nativity plays come in only as 'imitations' of the Easter play, boys acting midwives and angels (Young, II; 3, 12–13, 19). The Christmas story lends itself better to plastic representations of Virgin and Child than to drama, whereas resurrection is close to drama's heart. For the massacre of the Holy Innocents the children's parts were played by choir-boys, who were duly resurrected with the help of angels; and there were dramatizations of the raising of Lazarus (c. 1200; A. W. Pollard, *English Miracle Plays*, 1927; xvii–xviii; Young, II; 114; 199–219). The emphasis was still on miracle and victorious life. The actions of saints were turned into dramas, of which there are four extant in Latin (*c.* 1100–1200; Young, II; 309–11) about St Nicholas, the patron of youth, who has been called 'the most popular saint in Christendom' (Young, II; 308). One of these, *Tres Filiae*, dramatizes his rescue of three girls from prostitution; another, *Tres Clerici*, his prayer for the raising of three murdered scholars and an angel's announcement of its success; and a third, *Filius Getronis*, is a full-length drama about a Christian boy, Deodatus, captured by heathens and restored to his parents by the saint's powers, the boy's characterization and spirited talk being peculiarly well developed (Young, II; 357–8). The main emphasis of these Latin plays falls on resurrection, angels, and youth.

Though doctrine was as always severe, the ritual life of the Church had its diversions. E. K. Chambers describes the two most important, the Feast of Fools and the cult of the Boy Bishop. The first, held during the new year, recalls the Greek *komos*. The minor clergy engaged in obscene and ludicrous behaviour and speech within the sanctuary and during the actual saying of the Mass, and also in the streets. Priests dressed as women, rousing laughter with a ludicrous burlesquing of the sacred and indulgence in licentious behaviour. Every kind of filth, including ordure, was involved; it was an orgy reversing all decency, practised from the twelfth to the fifteenth century.

In England the Feast of Fools was less popular than the cult of the Boy Bishop celebrated during the cluster of youth festivals around Christmas: St Nicholas' Day, 6 December; the Feast of St John and Holy Innocents Day, 27 and 28 December; the Feast of the Circumcision, 1 January; and Epiphany, 6 January. The choir-boys elected their own bishop some time about St Nicholas' Day. At Padua during the thirteenth century he is recorded as assuming authority at vespers on St John's Day (Young, I; 109). Other boys impersonated other church dignitaries. The Boy Bishop held his office for some days, officiating at services, preaching a sermon, questioning the real bishop as to his stewardship and giving a state banquet. Sometimes he went on a progress, visiting various church centres. Sometimes during these ceremonies boys dressed as girls and visited convents. At the Reformation objection was raised in England, in 1541, to having children 'decked and apparelled to counterfeit priests, bishops, and women' on 'Saint Nicholas, Saint Catherine, Saint Clement, the Holy Innocents, and such like'; but the custom

was reinstated under Mary, to die out again under Elizabeth I
(Chambers, I; 366–8).[1]

There must have been much fun involved, but the central idea was
serious. In what Karl Young calls 'The Christmas Play from Bene-
dictbeuern', an elaborated and heavy work on the opposition of
Judaism and Christianity, the Boy Bishop suddenly invades the
drama to speak without musical accompaniment *as the authoritative
voice of Christian theology* (see Young, II; 175, 190, 192). The cult
was in clear alignment with the dramatic use of boys to impersonate
angels. From Plato down male youth had been the normal sense
equivalent to the seraphic, and to this intuition England traditionally
owes her conversion through the offices of Pope Gregory the Great
in the sixth century. The Venerable Bede recounts how St Gregory
had seen 'some boys put up for sale, of a white body and fair countenance, and with hair of remarkable beauty', and on being told that
they were Angles, replied: 'Non Angli, sed angeli', for 'they have the
faces of angels and shall be made co-heirs with the angels in Heaven'
(*A History of Britain*, 1937, E. H. Carter and R. A. F. Mears;
II. 41). It was ruled that the Boy Bishop himself had to be sufficiently
good-looking, 'formosus', and there was a respond used at York and
at Salisbury: *Corpore enim formosus es, O fili*. He also had to have
a good voice (Chambers, I; 356). C. S. Lewis defines the peculiar
charm of medieval love poetry as 'that boy-like blending (or so it
seems) of innocence and sensuousness which could make us believe
for a moment that paradise had never been lost' (*The Allegory of
Love*, 1936; III. 135). It is what Dante saw in, or through, Beatrice;
and Chaucer in his boy squire, 'He was as fresh as is the month of
May' (*The Canterbury Tales*, Prologue, 92).

The remoteness of Christian transcendentalism was countered in
two ways: by the lower Dionysian of orgiastic release in the Feast of
Fools and by opposing to the inadequacies of human maturity the
seraphic excellence of youth. Within the soaring architecture, bright
colours and golden display and lights of the medieval churches, these
silver-voiced choristers were used to reinstate among fallen mankind
an evident and authoritative perfection.[2]

[1] On the Boy Bishop Karl Young gives (I; 552) the following references: J. M. J.
Fletcher, *The Boy-Bishop at Salisbury and Elsewhere*, Salisbury, 1921; also
(Note on I; 110) A. F. Leach in *Educational Charters and Documents, 598 to
1909*, Cambridge, 1911, xlvi. A. F. Leach emphasizes the ritual's effect on drama.
[2] This is the 'perfection' symbolized by the Phoenix in *Love's Martyr* (p. 67
below). The dramatic powers of youth were recognized in the Orient. See *The
Nō Plays of Japan* (Arthur Waley, 1921, 1954; 21, 30, 45). The 'flower of youth',
was considered to have 'a natural grace' subsequently lost but forecasting the
'true flower' of the great actor's maturity.

III

In fourteenth-century England religious and social disturbances were active. New impulses were rising, in love lyric, in Chaucer and Langland; in Wycliffe; in the Peasants' Revolt. Secular and sacred met on equal terms, interpenetrated, clashed. At the new festival of Corpus Christi the Host was taken in open procession through the streets; and this was the main occasion for the performance of the Mystery cycles.

There are three stages in the development of our religious drama. The first is the Mass, only indirectly dramatic; the second, the Church plays, only by slow stages freeing themselves from Latin and from chant; and the third, the Mystery cycles, done as civic performances in ordinary English. Earlier biblical plays were joined together into an epic drama, starting with God and the falls of Lucifer and Adam, using key incidents of the Old Testament, dealing elaborately with the New, and ending with Judgement Day. We have the following cycles: the York; the 'Towneley', probably from Wakefield; the Chester; and that formerly called the Coventry Cycle, now known as the 'N-Town' Cycle, from the East Midlands. Traditional elements from folk drama, minstrelsy and other spectacles must have contributed to these elaborate and successful open-air performances, which met a communal need and received a widespread response. Trade guilds were variously responsible for separate scenes. The occasion was one of festivity and display; effects of Heaven and Hell were spectacular; colours, with the flash of gold, vivid; and the whole enlivened by music and song. God, Christ, angels, and devils mingled with Jews, Romans, and simple shepherds, but the action was felt by its audience as contemporary and as part of a communal self-dramatization.

The complete York Cycle has been published in J. S. Purvis's semi-modernized version *The York Cycle of Mystery Plays* (complete version, 1957). This vast drama is impressive: from the fall of Lucifer on the tension is maintained.

Jesus is lovingly presented, with a naïve, physical delight. As a baby he is a 'sweet thing' and 'blessed flower' (xiv. 96–7); as a boy in the temple, a 'lovely lad' giving promise of a 'pretty swain' (xx. 140, 147). But sweetness is countered by strength. We are shown Symeon's anxious waiting crowned by recognition that the Christ-child, the 'royal rose', has at last come. Connotations both pastoral

and royal combine to honour him as the praise of this 'giant' and
'mightiest master' builds up (xli; originally xviii. 129–31), gathering
power:

> Therefore, babe, shield us that we here not spill,
> And farewell, who formedst all at thy will.
> Farewell, star stablest by loud and by still
>   In soothfastness.
> Farewell, the royalest rose that is reigning;
> Farewell, the babe best in thy bearing,
> Farewell, God's Son. Grant us thy blessing,
>   To end our distress.
>   (xli; xviii. 131.)

'Distress': medieval life was grim, but conviction and hope were sure,
sensing shafts of angelic light slanting from Heaven to Earth. At the
Transfiguration Jesus' visible excellence, already great, is heightened
(xxiii. 161). At his entry into Jerusalem accompanied by his apostles,
six rich and six poor men, and seven boys with palm branches,
singing, the people acclaim him in stanzas warm in human feeling
and secular honour as 'king' and 'sovereign', as 'prince of peace',
'comely', and 'courteous', as both prince and loved one:

> Hail, flourishing flower that ne'er shall fade!
> Hail, violet vernal with sweet odour!
> Hail, mark of mirth, our medecine made!
> Hail, blossom bright; hail our succour:
>   Hail, king comely!
>   (xxv. 184.)

Flowers, 'rose' and 'lily', mix with precious stones, 'beryl', 'diamond' and 'jasper'. He is a 'comely knight' 'David's son', come to
release man from his 'bitter' lot; he is the all-powerful 'conqueror'
and final judge, welcome to 'our city'; and 'our city' is not simply
Jerusalem, but also York. Drama was not merely entertaining
the community; it was being injected into its blood-stream, like an
elixir.

As tragedy closes in there is much else. The Church plays made
comparatively slight use of the Passion, concentrating rather on the
Resurrection and on seraphic intimations. Here we are among the
city crowds, and the communal festivity has its reverse side. Those
violent and brutal instincts of the lower Dionysian so bitterly impugned by Nietzsche in *The Birth of Tragedy* (2), and which the
Crucifix exists to grapple and transmute, are here appallingly awake.

Jesus' agonized prayers in Gethsemane (xxviii) are burdened by a physical fear; the physical feeling hitherto so romantically sweet meets now its balance in physical horror and physical agony. From then on the torment is horribly, it might seem unnecessarily, drawn out. Jesus comes before Cayphas and then before Pilate; is sent to Herod; is before Pilate again, is prepared for crucifixion; is crucified. Pilate is a proud figure of worldly place and power; Herod a well-realized character study in bluster; the Jewish priests, who bear the main guilt, are less vital. Minor persons are vigorous: there is confusion and clamour, a raucous crowd of bullying and mocking people, drunk with blood lust, like hounds. Every possible detail is played up, developed, revelled in: buffeting, binding, stripping, bloody whipping, crushing down of the thorns, the mock sceptre. Earlier dramatic ideals are hideously reversed: not only do the boy idealisms of Church drama and ritual give place to the reiterated use (from xxix. 210 onwards) of 'boy' and 'lad' as terms of scorn and despisal applied to Peter and Jesus, but a full part in the mockery is played by the 'sons' (xxx; xxxi.). And all this is merely a preparation for the supreme fun—for that above all it is—of the Crucifixion. The soldiers, called 'knights', take their time over it. There is a second stripping:

<pre>
1 KNIGHT: Ay me!
              Methinks our wits do doting speed;
              He must be naked now indeed.
              Although he call himself a king,
              In all his clothes he shall not hang,
              But naked as a stone be stead.
2 KNIGHT: That call I a full fitting thing.
              But to his sides I trow they cling,
              For blood that he has bled.
3 KNIGHT: Whether they cling or cleave
              Naked shall he be led . . .
                              (xxxiv. 280.)
</pre>

So the clothes are torn from the wounds. Then follows the nailing to the cross laid on the ground, discussed detail by detail, including the tugging of the limbs with ropes to draw them out to the required distance, followed by the thrill of raising it 'on height that men might see' (xxxv. 286), and lastly the pleasure of dropping it suddenly into the mortice prepared:

<pre>
3 KNIGHT: Heave up!
4 KNIGHT: Let down, so all his bones
              Asunder now on all sides tear.
</pre>

1 Knight: This falling was more fell
            Than all the harms he had.
            Now well may all men tell
            The least bone of this lad.
                                    (xxxv. 288.)

One of them in obvious pleasure points out, and proceeds to demonstrate, that the cross is too loose and can be made to sway,
as 'thou mayest well wit' (xxxv. 288). When Jesus thirsts, a sprightly
boy promises 'a draught that is daintily dight' and brings a mixture
of 'vinegar and gall', addressing Jesus as 'sweet sir' and saying
'Drink it ye shall' (xxxvi. 295–6). From the arrest of Jesus till his
death we have had one long sequence of extended and elaborated
torment.

The audiences unquestionably enjoyed the cruelties just as, despite
theology and fears of damnation, they are known to have enjoyed
the devils at Hell mouth. Psychologically speaking we can say that
Christ was, in present actuality, taking on himself the sins and
sadisms of the community. What had always been implicit in the
Crucifix was now being amplified: that is all. The New Testament is
followed closely and there is authority for every main turn of the
action. We can justify such drama by saying that these worst instincts,
though usually unconscious or controlled in the individual, are
ready to break out communally. The dramatic emphasis here is not,
as so often in later drama, on the cruelty of an individual as such:
neither Pilate nor Herod want Jesus crucified, and the Jewish priests
who do act on theological principles. What we find is rather the
unleashing of sadistic instinct in the mass mind or in individuals as
part of a group, like the soldiers; and we may suppose a corresponding response in the mass mind of the audience. An overruling reverence and sympathy would simultaneously have been accorded Jesus,
and the proper result would be a release of sinful stuff in direct
relation to a sense of wrong and an attunement to good. We can
only hope that that is what happened.

The Resurrection and Ascension are less vivid. The power has
been expended and the conditions must have precluded effects comparable with those attained in the atmospheric surrounds of the
Church plays. Memory of the physical horrors lingers on, in the talk
of Lukas and Cleophas (xl) and in the preaching of Thomas (xlvi),
as though their branding were indelible. Dominating interests centre
now on Mary and John, whom Jesus had told to replace him as her
son, and on Jesus himself, who is to have Mary as his heavenly

consort, 'to be crowned for his queen and he himself King' (xlv. 354). Poetic praise is lavished on her (xlvi. 365). As 'chief of chastity' she is to enjoy delights in Heaven said by an angel to be as sweet as any conceivable by 'man' or 'wife' (xlvii. 371). She and Jesus will dwell there 'together' in 'bliss' (xlvii. 368):

> Receive this crown, my dear darling;
> Where I am king thou shalt be queen.
> (xlvii. 372.)

The maternal relationship now carries the overtones of marriage. The romance felt earlier in Mary's motherhood is recaptured by the romance of her Son's reunion with her in Heaven, as King and Queen.

The tonings are strongly royalistic in thoughts of 'sovereign', 'prince' and 'empire' (xlvi. 362, 365). Intimations of grandeur, earthly or spiritual, pervade the cycle. There is throughout an interlocking of Earth and Heaven, and the linking is done by angels. Angels are the cycle's principle of unity. We open with God and the angelic host, and from then on angels appear in scene after scene; sometimes in grand chorus, sometimes in smaller groups, or singly. They, as messengers from God, control the action. An angel visits Jesus after the temptation; an angel supports him in Gethsemane. Angels announce the birth of Jesus and his resurrection, and visit Mary, before her motherhood and before her assumption. Often they sing. As surely as in the Church plays they dominate, and sometimes Jesus himself appears in comparison no more than—to use a phrase from our text—'true Man' (xxxviii. 319). Sometimes he appears to be no more than a passive dramatic centre or occasion for our main conflict of the sadistic and the angelic. The world is vividly human and intensely physical in both romance and horror, yet visited throughout by 'mine angels lovely to see, lighter than the leven' (xlv. 358); and framed, at start and conclusion, by the transcendent. At the Judgement (xlviii) the wounds of Christ are again remembered; it is this, the physical and sadistic horror, that is here the central evil; men are divided up, for Heaven or Hell; and the scene ends with angel music. This great Judgement overarches for us the judgement in the *Oresteia* and the judgement conclusions to Renaissance drama (pp. 53–4 below). The relation of drama to judgement is exact, and here we have our supreme exemplar.

The other extant cycles have their peculiar qualities. The Wakefield Cycle is characterized by two peculiarly strong dramatic movements in its Nativity and Passion sequences.[1] In the First Shepherds' Play of this cycle the wearied and care-worn shepherds are startled by the visiting angel's wondrous appearance, illuminating the whole meadow like lightning, and by the 'piercing sound' of his voice in song. In the second play—for there are two—the description is more homely, admiring in particular his vocal 'trills'. This second play is famous for the burly comedy which preludes the angelic announcement and the shepherds' visit to the Christ-child.[2]

The Chester Cycle [3] is more theological and less exciting than the York and Wakefield cycles. It has qualities of its own, including a touching pathos in the words of the boy Isaac when about to be sacrificed by his father, Abraham. There is also an interesting piece on Antichrist, the false Christ come to deceive man as foretold in the New Testament (Matthew xxiv. 5; Mark xiii. 22; Luke xxi. 8; 1 John (Epistle) ii. 22; iv. 3), here shown raising the dead and communicating with spirits.

IV

The full scope of dramatic activity during the later medieval period is not known. Among the religious plays extant there are many of the type known as 'Morality Plays'; these were numerous and influential. The Mystery cycles are warmly human, the Moralities more generalized and abstract. Based, as the Mystery cycles are not, on the supposition that the human problem can be defined in ethical terms, they tend to lack drama, which is more properly a labouring towards some final judgement than a derivative of it. They may be regarded as symptoms of a fear that the Church was losing its hold.

Our first and one of the best Morality plays is *The Castle of Perseverance* (*c.* 1405) in which *Humanum Genus*, or Mankind, is shown tempted by various worldly sins such as Pleasure, Folly, Scandal and Avarice with such virtues as Charity, Abstinence and Chastity on the other side. He falls; there is a heavenly judgement, Mercy pleading against Justice; and the Father is merciful. Important to the action are the hero's two companion angels, good and bad. The conception gives the drama a certain metaphysical, at once

---

[1] I owe this judgement to a conversation with Mr Martial Rose, whose modernized version of the whole Wakefield Cycle was published in 1961.

[2] I have quoted from the versions of the two plays by A. C. Cawley in the Journal of The Yorkshire Dialect Society, 1950 and 1951.

[3] Modernized selections by Maurice Hussey were published in 1957.

human and spiritual, reality, since it cannot safely be denied that such spirit entities, apart from all dogma, exist. Medieval drama is regularly empowered by its angels.

Of the more ambitious Moralities the most famous is *The Summoning of Everyman*, which may be a reworking of a Flemish play printed in 1495. To Everyman comes Death with his peremptory summons. Everyman solicits the companionship of his friend Fellowship on his dread journey, and is refused. Kindred and Cousin desert him too, and Goods, or Possessions, also. Good Deeds is willing, but weak. Knowledge counsels resort to religion and Everyman confesses and endures his penance. Now Beauty, Strength, Discretion, and Five Wits all come to his aid, but as he nears his grave they too leave him. Knowledge, who corresponds to Dante's Virgil, stays to the last to assure his safety; but only Good Deeds actually goes with him, like Dante's Beatrice, to paradise. Angel voices are heard singing and an angel speaks of the 'heavenly sphere' to which Everyman has gone. The people, especially Fellowship, have a vitality beyond abstraction. The play's lasting impact derives from the universality of the situation and the overpowering presence of that supreme abstraction, so deeply rooted in drama, Death. Death, as a stage person, is as convincing as the ghost in *Hamlet*. Church doctrine is used, but whatever our beliefs the reading of the relation of life to death rings true. This is our one drama on Death as Death, moving from threat to song, from terror to the angelic sphere.

The transition to the secular dramas of our next period is hard to trace. In his *Early English Stages 1300 to 1660* (I; 1959) Glynne Wickham argues that elaborated indoor entertainments were customary among the aristocracy from the reign of Richard II, and that their nature can be gleaned from Chaucer's *Frankleyn's Tale*, Froissart's *Chronicle* and John Lydgate's *The Troy Book* (*c*. 1430; Wickham, I; 191–5). From the turn of the fifteenth century the main developments appear to have been devised for aristocratic entertainment and there is simultaneously a shift of emphasis from Church doctrine to more general issues. In John Skelton's *Magnificence* (*c*. 1516 ?) the wealthy hero is misled by false advisers such as Counterfeit and Crafty Conveyance and comes under the control of Adversity, Poverty and Despair, to be eventually reinstated by Sad Circumspection and Perseverance. We are reminded of *Everyman*, yet the teaching is nearer to a worldly than to a heavenly wisdom, like Polonius' advice in *Hamlet*. Many short plays or 'interludes', more or less in descent from the Moralities, were acted before noblemen in the sixteenth century. In them the effects of the new learning are often apparent; anti-ecclesiastical or other satire may be contained; Renaissance influences are felt, and the way is open for new developments.

The Morality tradition lasted well into the sixteenth century. In Marlowe's *Doctor Faustus* it is felt clashing with the new drama; in Shakespeare, though less obtrusive, it remains active.

Christendom had split into sovereign nations, whose kings now received all the glorification which Dante would have accorded his ideal emperor. A transference of spiritual allegiance is discernible from Christ to monarch; sanctity is associated with the king; and the community dramatizes itself in royal celebrations.

Ceremonies were gorgeous and stately in gilt and gold. E. K. Chambers and, more recently, Glynne Wickham have described them. Stages were erected in the streets for personified *tableaux vivants*, and the delivery of speeches. On such occasions angels again dominated. In 1392 Richard II was greeted at St Paul's by 'a youth enthroned amongst a triple circle of singing angels'; and at Henry V's return after Agincourt in 1415 singing boys represented 'the heavenly host'; on a castle 'stood boys feathered like angels, who sang *Te Deum* and flung down gold coins and boughs of laurel'; and virgins on a tower—who were probably boys in disguise—'wafted golden leaves out of golden cups, while above were wrought angels in gold and colours, and an image of the sun enthroned' (Chambers, II; 167–9). The sanctities of religion, of the heavenly, were, in accord with the principles of Dante's *De Monarchia*, being injected into a royal adulation, and such civic adulations, after an interruption during the Wars of the Roses, were to continue. 'A figure prominent in all pageants', writes Glynne Wickham, 'was the angel', and when there were angels and virgins, 'boys usually played the parts of both'. Angels were strikingly presented. We hear of Raphael 'with his golden and glittering wings and feathers of many and sundry colours' (Wickham, I; 106). Such pageantry was still vivid under Elizabeth I, who was to see at Norwich 'an excellent boy, well and gallantly decked, in a long white robe of taffeta, a crimson scarf wrought with gold, folded on the Turkish fashion about his brows, and a gay garland of fine flowers on his head' (Wickham, I; 109, quoting Thomas Churchyard).

Angels are the key to medieval drama. Their function is to link men to higher spheres and announce victories over death. The seraphic intuition, persisting from Plato and Gregory the Great to the

Elizabethans, binds our story. Church, Holy Roman Emperor and national kings are in various rivalries, theological controversies are rife, the secular gains gradually on orthodox sanctities; but throughout all, above the iniquities and the horrors; standing aside from codes of courtly adultery; independent of dogma and more omnipresent than Christ himself; throughout Liturgical drama, Mysteries, Moralities, and royal pageantry, runs the one golden thread of the seraphic glimpsed within what Byron in *Don Juan* (IV. 11) called 'the precious porcelain of human clay'.

These, 'mine angels lovely to see' (p. 35 above), are, like Plato's winged Eros, etheric beings, from the etheric sphere, or beyond. The root dramatic conflict of the Middle Ages is the conflict of (i) the sadistic instinct, reflected in the Crucifix and the torments of the Mystery plays; and (ii) the seraphic. We may call it an opposition of power and love. Later drama is to show a recurring balance of power-impregnated protagonists and ideal, seraphic beings of a love beyond sex, 'like the angels in Heaven'.

PART 2

PART 2

CHAPTER III

Elizabethan

That we have as great care to govern in peace as conquer in war; that whilst arms cease arts may flourish, and, joining letters with lances, we endeavour to be as good philosophers as soldiers, knowing it no less praise to be wise than commendable to be valiant.

JOHN LYLY, *Alexander and Campaspe*, I. i.

I

AT THE Renaissance Christianity ceased to dominate the drama. The change began in Italy and spread to the west. Sexual and political necessities reasserted themselves; a new dynamism was felt; ancient pieties lost prestige.

When so thrown back on himself, man discovers a world of unruly instincts. The city-states of Renaissance Italy saw corruption in the Church, princes maintaining themselves and ambitious men rising by treachery and crime; sex instincts in natural and unnatural forms; jealousies, antagonisms, vengeances, and vendettas. The evils for which the Crucifix had for centuries acted as a conductor now flared in its despite with an unholy confidence. This confidence was not altogether inept, since, the whole man being now engaged, such self-realizations could at the best produce remarkable personalities combining the qualities of statesman, soldier, scholar and connoisseur. Patron princes, secular or ecclesiastic, aimed high. Life was not only glorified: it was magical. Shows were staged on land and water with machinery for aerial effects, and elaborated decoration and symbolism. Prodigious artistry showed man in relation to a splendid nature directly or mythologically dramatized; or, by use of heavenly bodies, to a splendid cosmos. Nature was no longer under a ban; Lucifer was again scaling the heavens.

Modern liberalism was embryonic. Women had new rights, and shared in education and learning. Consciousness was instinctively focused to the culture of the ancients, and Greco-Roman myth became the instinctive grammar of a new psychology. The ancients gave authority for belief in supernatural powers other than those approved by the Church, and it was believed that beneficent as well as evil spirits could be contacted.[1] Man's life was extended, his consciousness strained, by infinite possibilities. At choice moments he could feel himself being happily integrated into a wondrous universe.

A new drama was inevitably sought. The Greek dramatists were known and used, but the favourite was Seneca, from the age of Nero, a period of religious scepticism, speculative philosophy, abounding licence and grandiose display with which the Renaissance had more in common than with the pietistic culture of ancient Greece. Seneca's philosophic sensationalism well suited the speculations and extravagances to which medieval religion bore much the same relation as the age of Pericles to the age of Nero.

Since the Italian Renaissance was lacking in moral conflict no great tragic dramatist emerged. British drama was to take a different course. The influence of Italy on Tudor England was strong, but never exclusive. The medieval tradition was not broken; indigenous drama of one kind or another was continuous across England, though little has survived. What has survived relates mainly to performances in educational and aristocratic circles.

From the end of the fifteenth century secular 'interludes', or short plays, were frequently performed. Henry Medwall's *Fulgens and Lucrece* (c. 1497) is an early romantic comedy. Attributed to John Rastell (born c. 1475) we have the love play *Calisto and Meliboea* and *The Interlude of the Four Elements* (after 1517), a scientific piece influenced by the new learning. The English climate is the subject of John Heywood's amusing *The Play of the Weather* (pub. 1533). In Chaucerian vein satiric fun is made from church officials in Heywood's *The Four P's* (pub. c. 1544), and in *The Pardoner and the Frere* (pub. 1533), attributed to Heywood. John Bale's *King Johan* (c. 1537) is a blend of history and morality, with John as national hero against Rome.

Our most interesting transitional drama is from Scotland. Sir David Lindsay's *The Satire of the Three Estates*, first acted at Linlithgow Palace in 1540, uses a morality form for an expansive purpose. In the first part Divine Correction rescues King Humanity from Sensuality; in the second, moving on from royalism to democracy, the centre of interest shifts to John the Commonweal, whose complaints are redressed and who is finally given his share of

[1] See C. S. Lewis's *English Literature in the Sixteenth Century*, 1954, 8–14.

political power. Attacks are levelled against the wickedness and injustice of society; poverty gets a hearing rare in early drama; and the vices and oppressions of church dignitaries are scathingly denounced. We conclude with a trial and the hanging of Deceit and Falsehood. Stage action is vigorous, comedy effective, and the characters, both good and bad, alive. It has been well called 'propaganda for the Reformation'[1]; it could equally well be called propaganda for socialism. The 'three estates' of Church, aristocracy and merchants are brought to the bar of an enlightened human critique, which still registers after four centuries of social advance.

To return to England. Boys did Terence and Plautus at school to develop their manners and personalities. New comedies were written on classical models but with a native humour, the most famous extant example being Nicholas Udall's *Ralph Roister Doister* (1553) with its hero-braggart Ralph, the frolicsome Matthew Merrygreek, and word coinage of nonsense sort to give impetus to the bustling action. Schools took plays to court. Richard Edwardes's powerful piece on friendship, *Damon and Pythias*, was done before the Queen (*c.* 1564) by boys of the Royal Chapel. The song schools of the Royal Chapel and Paul's played a vital part in Elizabethan drama. Beside *Ralph Roister Doister* we can place the farcical *Gammer Gurton's Needle* of unknown authorship done at Cambridge in the 1560's. Both universities were developing a comprehensive dramatic tradition of classical plays heavy and light, in Latin or in translation, and others of original composition. The Queen's visits in 1564 and 1566 were greeted by dramatic performances.

Meanwhile the lawyers and students of the Inns of Court in London were concentrating on heavy works of Senecan tone. Translations of Seneca had been published in English; and soon after we have the first English blank-verse tragedy, *Gorboduc or Ferrex and Porrex*, by Thomas Norton and Thomas Sackville (1561). It is a grim story of political dissension and a dominating and ferocious queen. Despite its long speeches, the blank verse has a modulation and variation of pause and flow to which commentators have scarcely done justice. *Gismond of Salerne* by Robert Wilmot and others, acted before the queen in 1567, is interesting for the violence of its passions. The foundations of our later drama were being laid. The Inns of Court performances were given elaborate productions, often with dumb shows carefully directed and demanding a high degree of skilled miming.

[1] By Robert Kemp, in the preface to his adaptation of the play, 1951.

We find another important line of development in the Masque. The masque was a blend of symbolic disguising and dancing in honour of some great lord or a sovereign. Its ancestry goes far back, but it gained impetus in England under Henry VIII, who had Italian artists to assist in his festivities. With the masque we can group the many public ceremonies arranged for Queen Elizabeth on her progresses through the country, and all their pageantry and symbolism. In such activities drama was being lived; though dramatic, they are not limited to fiction, and are part, like the many performances by school, university, or lawyers' college, of a royal occasion. Medieval ritual, especially towards the close, and perhaps especially in France, saw a similar self-dramatization, but the Renaissance tapped new vitality in its recurring and emphatic use of Hellenic mythology. The old emblems and symbols were reinforced, in drama they were soon overpowered, by classical myths.

Under Elizabeth I the Renaissance ideal, the ideal of Castiglione's *Il Cortegiano*, of the 'magnanimous' or fully developed man, the 'courtier's, soldier's, scholar's, eye, tongue, sword' as Shakespeare puts it in *Hamlet* (III. i), was not only admired, but realized; an ideal of which Sir Philip Sidney was the recognized type. Yet the Renaissance in England, though it drew much from Italy, diverged too, and reacted in self-defence. There was as much of the Reformation in it as of the Renaissance, and the philosophy of Machiavelli was regarded as a threat. The medieval tradition was not lost; instead we have a composite of what was best in both the new and the old. In a compact island, enjoying the keen vitality attendant on a sharp acceleration of change, both social and economic, a moment of poise was felt, in which new and old, Church and State, existed in a reciprocity unknown before or since. The Queen was both emperor and pope, ruling and inspiring a culture which appeared to be enjoying for a brief span that integrity for which medieval Europe had striven in vain.[1] The little island realm was already a world power. Elizabethan England matched Italy in culture and Spain in sea adventure. The new world was open and gold was coming in from trade and buccaneering. It was an age of music and an age of royalism. Dominating it all was Elizabeth I.

What was this woman whose single personality dominated so remarkable a culture? She had male qualities, as surely as Edmund

---

[1] A similar comparison, though with emphasis falling on the Jacobean rather than the Elizabethan, has been developed by Patrick Cruttwell in *The Shakespearean Moment*, 1954.

Spenser's Britomart in *The Faerie Queene*. Renaissance women could vie with men in intellectual power and scholarly attainment, while the men could be simultaneously brave and effeminate. It was to this extent a bisexual culture, an age 'sexually ambiguous' (Havelock Ellis, *From Marlowe to Shaw*, 1950; 85), its quality being neatly reflected in the sexual delineations and disguises of Sidney's *Arcadia*; [1] and it was natural enough to apply the bisexual connotations of the term 'Phoenix' to its living personification in a queen of passionate nature, male intellect and royal prerogative. She was, or symbolically acted the part of, a fully integrated being; and she was also, or symbolically acted the part of, a virgin, Shakespeare's 'imperial votaress' (*A Midsummer Night's Dream*, II. i) replacing the Queen of medieval culture by a royal incarnation.

Within this pervading sense of the bisexual, marriage too comes, at long last, into its own. This is the period of Spenser's marriage paeans, when, as C. S. Lewis tells us, the romance of marriage succeeds the medieval romance of adultery (*The Allegory of Love* 1936, VII). That there were less attractive qualities in Elizabethan England is true, and to these we shall return. Meanwhile, we have said enough to introduce the plays of John Lyly.

II

Lyly's court plays are pastoral in atmosphere, delicate in texture, and written in a style which lends itself variously to wit, fun, philosophy, and passion. They were acted by boy companies, the children of the Royal Chapel or Paul's. These boy performers aroused a puritanical criticism. During the year 1569 we find a disapprover writing: 'Plays will never be supprest while Her Majesty's unfledged minions flaunt it in silks and satins'; and 'Even in Her Majesty's chapel do these pretty upstart youths profane the Lord's Day by the lascivious writhing of their tender limbs'. [2] Dramatically the advantages were considerable. The boy companies, together with the use of boys for female parts in the adult companies, encouraged dramatists to rely for certain effects of primary importance on a long succession of ideal, bisexually felt, persons throughout the dramas of the sixteenth and seventeenth centuries.

Lyly's drama is fond of witty pages and beautiful young men, and

---

[1] See John F. Danby's *Poets on Fortune's Hill*, 1952, II.
[2] E. K. Chambers, *The Elizabethan Stage*, 1923, II; 34.

his girls may disguise themselves back again to the boys which they
really are. These plays are rich in psychological subtlety; they honour
love in all its variations and contradictions, normal or abnormal;
they are moralities with Cupid as God.

Alexander and Campaspe (1580) has a simple pattern: Alexander,
the chivalrous, wise and kindly conqueror; Campaspe whom he
wants for himself; and his humble rival Apelles, the painter. The inter-
relations of kingship, love and art are pithily discussed. Compressed
dialogue can be brilliant:

> ALEXANDER: Is love a vice?
> HEPHAESTION: It is no virtue.
> (II. ii.)

But Alexander, the world conqueror, must learn to command himself (v. iv): he does so, and leaves the lovers in peace. Alexander's
court with its blending of valour, philosophy and art (I. i) mirrors
Elizabeth's; and so does his control of sexual desire. The reference is
more obvious in *Sapho and Phao* (1583), wherein the virgin pride of
Queen Sapho, who is praised in terms clearly intended for Elizabeth,
so offends Venus that she makes Cupid tempt her with the pheno-
menally beautiful young Phao, whom she is later forced to relinquish
through the goddess's own infatuation for him. But in Venus' despite
she adopts Cupid, Venus' son, as her own, so making herself 'the
Queen of Love' (v. ii). Love is to be treasured within virginity.

Endimion or The Man in the Moon (1585) is strong in contemporary
meaning:

> GYPTES: They are thrice fortunate that live in your palace, where truth
> is not in colours but life, virtues not in imagination, but execution.
> CYNTHIA: I have always studied to have rather living virtues than
> painted gods; the body of Truth than the tomb.   (IV. iii.)

Cynthia, the Moon, is 'always one, yet never the same—still incon-
stant yet never wavering' (III. iv): the tight paradoxes serve well to
characterize Elizabeth's reign. Tellus, the Earth, may be Mary Queen
of Scots, and Endimion, set between these, the ideal and the natural,
may or may not be the Earl of Leicester. The seemingly light dialogue
has profundity:

> TELLUS: She shall have an end.
> ENDIMION: So shall the world.
> TELLUS: Is not her beauty subject to time?
> ENDIMION: No more than time is to standing still.
> TELLUS: Wilt thou make her immortal?
> ENDIMION: No, but incomparable.   (II. i.)

A metaphysical essay could be written on each reply, but it remains stage talk. What better entrance could an actor ask than 'No rest, Endimion? Still uncertain how to settle thy steps by day, or thy thoughts by night?' (ii. iii). The delicate prose handles emotional conflict with a fine artistry.

The story has atmospheric weight, solidified into dramatic symbol. Endimion sleeps on a 'lunary bank' (ii. iii) and there is an oracular fountain wherein you may read divine secrets (iii. iv). Magic can be fearsome: Tellus pursues her possessive desires with the aid of witchcraft. In contrast are Cynthia's virginity, Endimion's aspiration, and male friendship regarded in Platonic wise as 'the image of eternity' surpassing sexual love (iii. iv). Values intershade: Tellus has her own nature-embedded divinity and Cynthia's changefulness is not denied. Yet Cynthia rules throughout and dominates the conclusion with royal authority. She is conceived like Alexander as a sovereign in whom mercy counters justice (v. iii), and all ends happily. Endimion realizes that she is above him; in his dream he has seen the dangers threatening her throne and is content to serve. Lyly shows us Elizabeth I dominating a drama of erotic idealism accompanied by natural and cosmic marvels.

The 'dangers' threatening Elizabeth are shown in *Midas* (1589), written just after the Armada. Midas is Philip of Spain, a tyrannic monster driven on by Bacchus, or Dionysus, god of unruly instincts, to lust for power and gold: 'That iron world is worn out, the golden is now come' (i. i). However, he is made to realize the futility of attacking a heaven-guarded nation. He is further defined by his preference of Pan, the earth deity, to Apollo. Lyly is far too honest a dramatist not to give Pan, as he gave Tellus, a good case (iv. i), though the victory is with Apollo.

Elizabethanism breathes love, and male beauty is as important as female. In *Gallathea* (1584) two girls, Gallathea and Phyllida, disguised by their fathers as boys to save them from being chosen as a sacrifice to Neptune, meet and fall in love: 'Yonder boy is in mine eye too beautiful' (ii. i). The dialogue continues:

> PHYLLIDA: It is pity that nature framed you not a woman, having a face so fair, so lovely a countenance, so modest a behaviour.
> GALLATHEA: There is a tree in Tylos whose nuts have shells like fire, and being cracked, the kernel is but water.
> PHYLLIDA: What a toy is it to tell me of that tree, being nothing to the purpose: I say it is pity you are not a woman.
> GALLATHEA: I would not wish to be a woman, unless it were because thou art a man.   (iii. ii.)

The dialogue concludes with: 'Come, let us into the grove and make much one of another . . .' (III. ii). Cupid also appears disguised as a woman; is captured by Diana with whom he is naturally at enmity, and comes in bedraggled, arrows broken, wings clipped. Even so, love's autonomy is urged; if slighted its wound will 'fester to the death within' (v. iii), and Cupid is finally released. As for the two girls, one is to be changed to a boy since love must not be thwarted (v. iii).

That changes of dress or other transformations may correspond to the psychological disparity sometimes found between physical sex and emotional temperament is suggested by the words 'my manly shape hath yet a woman's mind' (IV. ii) in *The Maid's Metamorphosis*, a verse-play posthumously attributed to Lyly wherein the heroine Eurymine's sex is changed by Apollo—who has already recounted his own love for the boy Hyacinth (III. i)—to the confusion of her love relationship with Ascanio: 'Doth kind allow a man to love a man?' (v. i).

Lyly is quite as interested in normal love and in woman as woman as he is in sovereign virginity or sylph-like disguise. *The Woman in the Moon* (c. 1591–3), on the creation of woman, is Lyly's Genesis. We open with Nature, Concord, and Discord. Discord grumbles that when working through 'contraries' to project 'some wondrous deed' (I. i) she is regularly hampered by Concord. Nature makes a neat commentary on tragic drama in insisting that this is precisely the conflict which she wants. Anyway, the source of discord is woman. Pandora is given all possible excellences by the various planets, but since each influences her too powerfully, she turns out to have all the vices: in turn passionate, ambitious, and deceitful, and then again virtuous, and sweet. Her changes are kaleidoscopic, varying from lust to Sibylline inspiration. Her chosen deity is the Moon since 'change is my felicity' (v. i). Pandora is raw material for Shakespeare's Cleopatra. The conception is one of which medieval drama knew, or at least said, little.

In *Love's Metamorphosis* (c. 1586–8) Cupid, here a ruling and dignified god, punishes three of Ceres' girls who in rejecting their suitors are respectively guilty of cruelty, pride and lightness, by turning them respectively at the men's request into a stone, a flower, and a bird. Though the girls prove strangely content, Cupid's answer is conclusive and the psychology of it true:

> If they yield not, I will turn them again, not to flowers, or stones, or birds, but to monsters no less filthy to be seen than to be named hateful.   (v. iv.)

The men now phrase their penitence in terms of the same three symbols and the girls relent with the reservations that any future complaints of hardness, thorny behaviour, or freedom must be related to the experiences they have undergone. The changes rung on the symbols are happily conceived and the thought deep. We hear of jealousy, 'without which love is dotage and with which love is madness; without the which love is lust, and with which love is folly' (IV. i). The embarrassing truth is honestly faced.

Mother Bombie (1590) is in the Plautine or Terentian vein. The tone is homely. Intricacy of plot and structure makes it an impressive technical achievement, but there is less exciting psychology, though we again meet an unorthodox love. A supposed brother and sister who are in love realize that 'that which nature warranteth laws forbid' (III. i); then the good and kindly Mother Bombie, fortune-teller and clairvoyant, assures them of success, and they turn out not to be related. Mother Bombie is the centre of action, consulted by the various people in turn: her mystical powers suggest a universal meaning, and we may suppose such a meaning not only in this but in all such comedies, in descent from Menander, of mistake, discovery, and recognition. Their age-long attraction comes from their hinting a solution of life's manifold and baffling confusions.

Lyly's psychology is always dramatic; indeed only drama can unravel such knots. The tone is throughout sympathetic; dark figures such as Tellus, Bacchus, Pan and Neptune are accorded their rights. The subtlety which so catches fleeting paradoxes on the wing precludes any too sharp a moralizing. Love is intricate and baffling, but the eye is on its essence whatever the daring, and safety is maintained. Setting and ritual lend support, with focal objects, fountain, sacred tree, or temple, or some central deity or sovereign, to harmonize the action, and various magicians or clairvoyants to give it depth. We must imagine performance by candlelight and the glamour of glinting costume and architectural surrounds. With Lyly we are at the heart of Elizabethan culture, and a just appreciation of his esoteric sexology will assist our understanding of the recurring emphasis on bisexual, boy-girl figures in subsequent comedy and romance.

III

Drama of more native stock and a wider social appeal appears to have been continuous, though it was not till it blended with the academic that it became firmly established. Plays were done at inn yards and the first popular theatre, open to the sky, was erected in 1576. Others followed. Professional drama, using adult actors for the men and boys for women, developed rapidly. Acting, led by men such as Edward Alleyn and Richard Burbage, became strong.

Thomas Kyd's *The Spanish Tragedy* (*c.* 1587) is Senecan in tone, though the form is episodic. The theme is revenge, a theme dating back to the Greeks, and newly alive in Renaissance Europe when new responsibilities were weighing on the individual. Revenge is personified, and a ghost impels the bloody story. The setting helps, since both Italy and Spain suggested horrors threatening from abroad and awaiting their chance at home. There is a strong villain, Lorenzo, prototype of Iago and others, but the main interest converges on old Hieronimo. Speech has dramatic immediacy:

> What outcries pluck me from my naked bed?
>
> * * * *
>
> Who calls Hieronimo? Speak, here I am.
> I did not slumber; therefore 'twas no dream.
>
> (II. v.)

The economic pressure on a popular playwright serves a purpose in forcing the dramatist to eschew the interminable sequences of literary Seneca and rivet his audience's attention through immediate and inward experience. Hieronimo's son has been murdered:

> O eyes! no eyes, but fountains fraught with tears;
> O life! no life, but lively form of death;
> O world! no world, but mass of public wrongs,
> Confus'd and fill'd with murder and misdeeds!
> O sacred Heavens! if this unhallow'd deed,
> If this inhuman and barbarous attempt,
> If this incomparable murder thus
> Of mine, but now no more, my son,
> Shall unreveal'd and unrevenged pass,
> How should we term your dealings to be just?
>
> (III. ii.)

Rhetorical antithesis becomes a surge and swell. The rhythms accumulate; vocal colour changes at 'but now no more'; syntax is wedded to emotion. In an age of disrupted faith the old Aeschylean cry is again heard; is the universe unjust? Nature should, it *must*, join with him in grief:

> The blustering winds, conspiring with my words,
> At my lament have mov'd the leafless trees . . .
>
> (III. vii.)

Though they have ruined meadows and reduced mountains to marshland, his complaint still rises, 'soliciting for justice and revenge'. Nature sympathizes, yet the 'empyreal heights' and 'walls of diamond' remain 'impregnable': God seems deaf (III. vii). The attempt is to integrate human suffering into its natural and divine context, to fuse warm humanity and gentle nature with the cold diamonds of Heaven. The revenge themes to be so popular from now on reflect an attempt to right a cosmic balance.

Evil may however have its own grim, part-Senecan and part-medieval, geography. Asked where Lorenzo lives, Hieronimo replies with a speech of suspended action which forces us as we listen ourselves to make the awful journey:

> There is a path upon your left-hand side,
> That leadeth from a guilty conscience
> Unto a forest of distrust and fear—
> A darksome place and dangerous to pass:
> There shall you meet . . .
>
> (III. xi.)

It piles up, growing in horror, passing through the murk to where the whole world's iniquities 'cast up filthy and detested fumes'; where murderers 'have built a habitation for their cursed souls'; there shall you find Lorenzo in everlasting torment. Seneca was a master at generating a fearsome atmosphere,[1] and it was perhaps this more than anything that made him a Renaissance favourite.

Hieronimo's distraction attains a peculiar strength of meaningful madness in the mysterious additions to the text by an unknown author. His antisocial role is throughout fantastic, leading to his arrangement of a stage play wherein his enemies are cast for parts in which they are actually murdered. Such ritual conclusions, in descent from the feast in Seneca's *Thyestes*, occur regularly in our revenge plays: feast, play, masque, or formal duel may be used. Renaissance

---

[1] Clarence W. Mendell has observed that Seneca's prologues set the peculiar *tone* of what is to follow (*Our Seneca*, New Haven, U.S.A., 1941).

man had to do for himself what the medieval scheme, with its
Judgement Day conclusions to the Mystery cycles, had claimed to do
for all men. Though in England revenge never assumed the proportions it reached in Italy, the basic problem was similar: compulsions
of honour existed, social evils abounded, and each revenger is an
embryo revolutionary. Revenge, said Lord Bacon, is a kind of 'wild
justice'; and it naturally likes to ritualize itself, following the judgement conclusions of Aeschylus' *Oresteia* and the Mystery cycles, in
a miniature doomsday.

IV

Elizabethan idealism does not tell the whole truth of the national
soul. Poetic refinement coexisted with barbaric cruelty; bear or bull
baitings, whippings and hideously prolonged executions, were sources
of public delight. Christopher Marlowe faces this all too human
co-presence of sweetness and sadism with almost too uncompromising an honesty.

The two parts of *Tamburlaine the Great* (*c.* 1587) show us the
Scythian conqueror rising from humble origin to world power. His
appearance is god-like (1; II. i) and throughout he feels himself as
backed by cosmic energies. The sequence of conquests is repetitive
and would be boring were it not for the splendid verse. The poetry
has fire and fervour but little of Kyd's modulation; it rings rather
than pulsates. There is imagery of sun, spheres and meteors and a
glitter of crowns and weapons. Of earth and its vegetation we hear
little. Colours are sharp.[1] Proper names can be grand and geography,
as so often in this expanding age, an intoxication. Kingship is avidly
apprehended:

> To wear a crown enchas'd with pearl and gold,
> Whose virtues carry with it life and death;
> To ask and have; command and be obeyed ...
>
> 　　　　　　　　　　　　　　　　(1; II. v.)

The lines on man's questing Renaissance intelligence, opening with

> Our souls whose faculties can comprehend
> The wondrous architecture of the world,
> And measure every wandering planet's course ...

---

[1] The imagery of *Tamburlaine* was beautifully handled by U. M. Ellis-Fermor
in *Christopher Marlowe*, 1927, IV.

see this straining aspiration coming to rest in

> That perfect bliss and sole felicity
> The sweet fruition of an earthly crown.
>
> (1; II. vii.)

The juxtaposition is a true reading of Renaissance ambition. Tamburlaine even aims to

> march against the powers of heaven
> And set black streamers in the firmament,
> To signify the slaughter of the gods.
>
> (2; v. iii.)

Such excess, near comedy, is saved by the strong rhetoric and also by a grim realism.

For there is no sentimentalizing. Though he can speak rhapsodies of aesthetic idealism such as the famous 'If all the pens that ever poets held . . .' (1; v. ii), Tamburlaine is quite ruthless; in him all chivalric values are reversed; his enemies he not only conquers but degrades. Bajazet, the Turkish king, is caged and mockingly treated as an animal, he and his queen providing indecent amusement for Tamburlaine and his followers (1; IV. ii, iv). A rebellious viceroy is to be bitted, 'harnessed', whipped, fed, and stabled like a horse (2; III. v). Tamburlaine enters in a chariot drawn by kings with bits in their mouths, whipping them (2; IV. iii). Others await their turn and their curses are stifled by the bits, Tamburlaine's boy engaging in the fun: 'How like you that, sir king? Why speak you not?' (2; IV. iii). Apart from these incidents, human beings are naturally here regarded as cattle: 'With naked negroes shall thy coach be drawn' (2; I. iii). More entertainment is provided by the hoisting up and shooting of the Governor of Babylon (2; v. i); sadism here is a matter less of causing pain than of reducing the victim's human dignity, or integrity. Whilst claiming god-like status for himself, Tamburlaine would render others ludicrous. Irrelevant extremes face each other in contrast to the spiritualized humanism of Lyly and Kyd. No doubt the first audiences roared with delight, but it is more than slapstick; it is a terrible revelation of an enduring human instinct. We are not invited, except by the sufferers, to criticize: there is no catharsis, the juxtaposition of idealism and sadism being left unresolved.

Tamburlaine lacks depth; it is narrative rather than dramatic. Only one of Tamburlaine's characterizing actions, as apart from his words, is conceived poetically: when, encamped before an enemy city, he shows tents first white and next, failing a surrender, red; and finally advances accoutred in black (1; IV. ii).

Marlowe was fascinated by the Italian Renaissance and the prologue to *The Jew of Malta* (*c*. 1589) is spoken by Machiavelli:

> I count religion but a childish toy,
> And hold there is no sin but ignorance.
> Birds of the air will tell of murders past?
> I am asham'd to hear such fooleries.
> Many will talk of title to a crown:
> What right had Caesar to the empery?
> Might first made kings, and laws were then most sure
> When, like the Draco's, they were writ in blood.

There is talk of Italian poisons, Caesar Borgia is remembered (III. iv) and treachery called a 'kingly' trade (v. v). Barabbas the Jew starts impressively, counting his wealth and meditating on his princely merchandise. Afterwards he degenerates into an exaggerated figure of burlesque villainies and meets a ludicrous end by falling into the cauldron he has prepared for another. Merchant trade was a living issue to Elizabethan London, but Marlowe's study scarcely serves a coherent purpose.

Perhaps what most interests him is the Renaissance itself and all that it stands for, and this is his subject in *Doctor Faustus* (*c*. 1590–2), written round a third form of the power quest: magic. In dramatizing a revolt from medieval theology this extraordinary work sets the type for a long mythology of future Faust plays. The conception is vast, involving the conflict of two cultures, but the working out is disturbing. Dissatisfied with the unnatural constrictions of theology, Faustus solicits the aid of the devil Mephistophilis, whose gifts include the imaginative treasures of ancient Greece:

> Have I not made blind Homer sing to me
> Of Alexander's love and Oenon's death,
> And hath not he that built the walls of Thebes,
> With ravishing sound of his melodious harp,
> Made music with my Mephistophilis?
>
> (II. ii.)

Helen appears: 'Was this the face that launch'd a thousand ships?' (v. i). Aligned with these superb poetic excursions are Mephistophilis' offer of whores, and chaste maids, too, for his lust, with a deliberate repudiation of marriage (II. i). Renaissance idealism appears to be one with vice and both are from the Devil: instinct is simultaneously inflamed and condemned, and man trapped. Faustus is given great powers, and performs marvels, including materializations of the dead, his magic at this early stage in Europe's history blending occult practices with a symbolization of scientific advance in the centuries to follow:

> And what wonders I have done, all Germany can witness, yea all the world; for which Faustus hath lost both Germany and the world, yea Heaven itself . . .   (v. ii.)

Once only, in this quiet prose, does Marlowe touch a Shakespearian tragic dignity. And retribution and self-abasement swiftly follow: 'See, see, where Christ's blood streams in the firmament' (v. ii). Devils take Faustus to Hell and a choric figure moralizes.

Even when the poetry of Faustus' agonized self-conflict is great, its virtues remain those of a dramatic monologue and in total structure the drama is fragmentary. The middle scenes, with the show of Deadly Sins and the cheap comedy of Faustus' practical jokes on the Pope, sag. The dramatized conflict is one of cultural externals without penetration to that centre from which alone a coherent action can mature. Renaissance and Christianity are not merely opposed; they are in desperate incompatibility; the drama itself endures the conflict it should harmonize. Poetry, vice, the occult and science stand on the one side and religion on the other, in mutual exclusion. Aiming at both 'tragedy' and 'morality' Marlowe achieves neither, whilst nevertheless bestriding the centuries like a Colossus. In *Doctor Faustus* two ages clash.

During his life Marlowe was accused of homosexual interests.[1] In his *Massacre at Paris* (1592) King Henry has his minions and *Dido, Queen of Carthage* (c. 1587; pub. 1594) opens to discover 'Jupiter dandling Ganymede upon his knee' (I. i.). Strong homosexual feeling is written into his poem *Hero and Leander* (c. 1592), and it may be significant that his only drama of satisfying artistry, *Edward II* (c. 1591), is concerned primarily with homosexuality. Here is Gaveston, the King's favourite, speaking of his seductive arts:

> I must have wanton poets, pleasant wits,
> Musicians that with touching of a string
> May draw the pliant king which way I please.
> Music and poetry is his delight,
> Therefore I'll have Italian masques by night,
> Sweet speeches, comedies, and pleasing shows;

[1] See C. F. Tucker Brooke, *The Life of Marlowe, etc*, 1930; Apps. IX and XII; 99, 107; also Paul H. Kocher, *Christopher Marlowe*, University of North Carolina Press, 1946; VIII. 209–11.

> And in the day when he shall walk abroad,
> Like sylvan nymphs my pages shall be clad;
> My men like satyrs grazing on the lawns
> Shall with their goat-feet dance the antic hay.
> Sometime a lovely boy in Dian's shape,
> With hair that gilds the water as it glides,
> Crownets of pearl about his naked arms,
> And in his sportful hands an olive tree
> To hide those parts which men delight to see,
> Shall bathe him in a spring, and there hard by
> One like Actaeon peeping through the grove,
> Shall by the angry goddess be transformed;
> And running in the likeness of an hart,
> By yelping hounds pulled down, shall seem to die.
> Such things as these best please his majesty.
>
> (I. i.)

The King's passion for Gaveston is central and defended by a comparison with similar passions in Alexander, Hercules, Achilles,
Cicero and Socrates (I. iv); it is also condemned. The people are
either weak or otherwise unlikable, and the verse comparatively
bare, but the structure is firm and the action coherent. Edward's end
in a dungeon is given a remorseless realism:

> O water, gentle friends, to cool my thirst,
> And clear my body from foul excrements.
>
> (v. iii.)

He describes his plight:

> And there in mire and puddle have I stood
> This ten days' space . . .   (v. v.)

At his murder he cries piteously for mercy. Shakespeare would never
allow a king to be so presented and the not dissimilar Richard II dies
royally. Marlowe, like Tamburlaine, is a king-degrader and iconoclast.

His people do not grow, as do Shakespeare's, through suffering.
Tamburlaine becomes more and more repellent, the Jew disintegrates, Edward II is embarrassingly pathetic; and even Faustus' final
declamation is no more than a sublime expression of terror. In
Marlowe the most exquisite apprehensions are associated with the
lascivious; he seems to be tormented by things at once hideously
suspect yet tormentingly desirable; and he leaves us simultaneously
aware of intoxication and degradation. His feminine interests are
slight, and where there is humour it is cruel. He forecasts both Jonson
and Milton and what he reveals is vastly important and deeply true.
Yet revelation and truth are only half the tragic dramatist's task; the

other half is transmutation, or catharsis, and this he does not master. His reach, admittedly titanic, exceeds his grasp.

Marlowe is the less 'Elizabethan' in that he shows the clash rather than the synthesis of Renaissance and Reformation, but no one was more truly Elizabethan than George Peele. He was a patriot and a deviser of public pageants. Patriotic passages in his plays *The Battle of Alcazar* (c. 1589; II. iv) and *Edward I* (pub. 1593; I. i) forecast John of Gaunt's lines on England in Shakespeare's *Richard II* (II. i). He wrote fervent poetry on the chivalry of Elizabethan knights: male excellence was for him touched with romance. Such a remark as this in *The Battle of Alcazar* appears naturally, with no particular comments or extensions:

> Christopher de Tavera, next unto myself,
> My good Hephaestion and my bedfellow ...
>
> (II. iv.)

Hephaestion was Alexander's loved companion, referred to in defence of the King's behaviour in Marlowe's *Edward II*. In Peele's romantic drama *Sir Clyomon and Sir Clamydes* (pub. 1599) the princess Neronis in male disguise will be 'the bravest shepherd's boy in our town', staggering the church-wardens with his beauty (xv). Elizabethan poets, living on the Arcadian knife-edge between friendship and homosexuality, turned naturally to pastoral, and in pastoral Peele was at his happiest.

The Arraignment of Paris (pub. 1584) is a court masque, based on Paris' presentation of the golden apple as the prize of beauty to the goddess Venus and the consequent hostility of Juno and Pallas. Since Venus symbolizes beauty and love, Juno majesty and wealth, and Pallas wisdom and chivalry, much is involved in Paris' judgement. Arraigned by the gods, Paris offers a defence of the erotic impulse, denying guilty thoughts and insisting that the judgement of his eyes and heart can be rationally defended (IV. i). He asserts the trustworthiness of love-sight as against the erotic dangers so evident in Marlowe; he is really claiming, like so much Elizabethan poetry, to have by-passed the Fall and to be living in a golden age. Since Elizabeth I is queen of this 'Elysium', this 'ancient seat of kings' and 'second Troy', whose people are called 'Angeli' (v. i), it is only right that the Apple should finally go to her; and so it does. The masque is happily devised with mime and song and a delightful intermixing of classical mythology and English flowers.

The Old Wives' Tale (c. 1590) is a strangely satisfying medley of country life, romance, a bad magician, and a kindly ghost who sets confusions in order. A homely rusticity cohabits harmoniously with more literary traditions. It is a precursor of both *A Midsummer Night's Dream* and Milton's *Comus*.

All Peele's main interests are active within his central work, *The Love of David and Fair Bethsabe* (c. 1590). He was naturally drawn to the Old Testament's greatest figure, David, by turns shepherd boy, poet, hero and king. The atmosphere is one of 'gentle zephyr', 'soft and sacred air', 'bushy' thickets and 'delicate perfumes' (i; or I. i). David's love of Bethsabe is given an idyllic expression: 'Now comes my lover tripping like the roe . . .' (i; or I. i). The poetry is full-throated and nature-rooted, with sap and softness, with less of vigour than Kyd's but less mentalized than Marlowe's. There follows David's sin in arranging for Bethsabe's husband to be placed in the forefront of battle, and consequent accusations, curses and remorse. The revolt of his son Absalom is seen as the punishment of that 'traitor to our souls' (viii; or III. i), lust. But David's sin interests Peele less than the revolt of his son Absalom. Absalom is beautiful and his beauty is our central concern, male idealism being balanced against heterosexual lust, as in Shakespeare's Sonnets. To the Elizabethan, female sweetness was often a delight, but even more tormentingly wonderful in blend of beauty and power was the splendour of man, especially in youth. This splendour burns in Absalom.

He is a miniature Tamburlaine, with a difference. Tamburlaine's physique was stupendous and Herculean; Absalom's, 'flowering in pleasant spring-time of his youth' (vii; or II. iii), is sweeter. 'In all his body is no blemish seen' (vii. or II. iii). His golden hair radiates a mysterious power, like music, being compared to the 'golden wires of David's ivory lute', or harp (vi, vii; or II. ii, iii). His beauty intoxicates everyone: David, the stern Joab, and even Absalom himself, who believes that the heavens themselves must 'burn in love' with it (ix; or III. ii). The narcissistic apprehension blends with service to God:

> Why should not Absalom, that in his face
> Carries the final purpose of his God,
> That is, to work him grace in Israel,
> Endeavour to achieve with all his strength
> The state that most may satisfy his joy,
> Keeping his statutes and his covenants pure?
> His thunder is entangled in my hair,
> And with my beauty is his lightning quenched:
> I am the man he made to glory in . . .
>
> (ix; or III. ii.)

Since through human excellence an ultimate is glimpsed of God's purpose in creating man, all the terrors of religion are gone, 'entangled' in Absalom's beauty: beauty and piety are one. Herein is the positive elixir of the Elizabethan Renaissance.

Passage after passage pays its tribute to 'Jove's fair ornaments' in 'lovely' Absalom (x; or III. iii). The thought flames even in Absalom's own revolutionary address (xii; or III. v). And yet, with an exquisite symbolic irony, he is caught by a branch and 'hangs by the hair', between 'heaven and earth'. He who is God's 'especial glory', the 'choicest fruit of Nature's workmanship', is snared by a tree, his 'beauty' finding itself unable to influence the 'senseless' vegetation (xiii; or III. v). Nature has trapped its choicest creation, and as he hangs there Joab draws the obvious moral; so do the soldiers, as, reviling the 'beauteous rebel', they kill him (xiii; or III. v). A chorus seals the condemnation. But we must not confuse the framework with the picture: Absalom's assertion stands, as surely as Paris' defence. He is an early example, like so much in Marlowe, of a long line to follow, in Chapman and others, of dramatic persons who assert their native sovereignty against the established order symbolized by the king. Here the signature of excellence is beauty. We are reminded of the narcissistic pride of Lucifer in medieval drama; and of the ritual laments over Adonis in the ancient cults. We are left asking, must the glory be evanescent? Can the ultimate authority be simultaneously the ultimate cheat? Is beauty a lie?

If the youthful hero of this blend of pastoral and power quest is Peele's Tamburlaine, David's other son Solomon, ever searching for the wisdom and science which Pallas offered Paris, is his Faustus. David urges him not to press 'too far', to rely on God and put no trust in secondary revelations. Solomon reasserts his impatient will to rise 'on the burning wings of zeal divine', treading 'the golden starry labyrinth', his eagle eye on Jehovah (xv; or IV. ii). The balances are held: human aspiration is in part divine and cannot easily be checked.

Robert Greene's *Orlando Furioso* (*c.* 1591) is little more than a medley of adventure and magic, but *Alphonsus, King of Arragon* (*c.* 1588), perhaps composed in rivalry to Marlowe's *Tamburlaine*, is more interesting. The deposed prince wins back his rights by a series of clever strokes culminating in an attack on the Turkish Empire. When the enchantress Medea raises Calchas to show King Amurack the dangers ahead, and the official priests get Mahomet to prophesy through 'a Brazen Head' an encouragement to resistance, we have a

neat contrast of spiritualism and priest-craft, the latter proving
fallacious. There is no underlining of brutality, and when the
victorious Alphonsus on being rejected by Amurack's daughter
becomes threatening, his old father turns up in pilgrim's dress to act
as peace-maker, and the marriage is arranged. Marlowe's ringing
magnificence may be beyond Greene; he offers instead human
warmth and chivalry.

In *Friar Bacon and Friar Bungay* (*c.* 1589) Greene blends his
interest in the occult with an English pastoralism. Prince Edward,
son of Henry III, gets Lacy, Earl of Lincoln, to act as go-between to
further his passion for a country girl, Margaret. Through a television
apparatus of Friar Bacon the prince learns from a distance that Lacy
and Margaret love each other, and after a temporary submission to
tyrannic jealousy he renounces his claim, recognizing that Lacy's
intentions are honourable whereas his own were not. This edifying
story is delicately handled with a delightful realization of the girl
Margaret through a typically Elizabethan blend of native rusticity
and classical myth:

> Into the milk house went I with the maid
> And there amongst the cream-bowls she did shine,
> As Pallas 'mongst her princely huswifry:
> She turned her smock over her lily arms
> And dived them into milk to run her cheese . . .
>
> (I. i.)

Greene is justly famous for a sense of warm-blooded womanhood in
advance of his contemporaries.

Interwoven with the romance we have Friar Bacon's magical
fabrication of a Brazen Head, like the Head in *Alphonsus*, destined
to speak oracles of national import. Merry comedy is provided by
the block-headed servant Miles. Bacon's contest in magical power
with the continental Vandermast is played out before the King of
England, followed by a vindication of England's honour and a final
prophecy (v. iii) of Elizabeth. The association of magic and patriotism makes a happy contrast to *Doctor Faustus*.

Whether he was part, or sole, author of *George-a-Greene* (*c.* 1592)
is uncertain, but the meeting of the sturdily independent George of
Wakefield and another King of England serves a not dissimilar
purpose to the harmonizing of royalty and rusticity in *Friar Bacon
and Friar Bungay*.

Greene's plays curiously parallel Marlowe's, though the dates are
too uncertain for statements of priority. In *James IV* (*c.* 1591) the

weak Scottish king is led astray, like Edward II, by a favourite, Ateukin, who is explicitly associated with Machiavelli (III. ii), poses as a magician, and tempts the King to connive at the murder of his wife Dorothea, to make way for his love for another lady, Ida. Like Marlowe, though without his nerve-jarring results, Greene can align an ideal poeticizing with a strong evil:

> Go to mine Ida: tell her that her hairs
> Shall be embellished with orient pearls,
> And crowns of sapphires compassing her brows
> Shall war with those sweet beauties of her eyes.
>
> (IV. v.)

A golden poetry, as never in Shakespeare, accompanies abysmal sin. Fortunately the murder fails and the King repents.

Subsidiary people, especially the Machiavellian Ateukin and the irate Bishop of St Andrews, are firmly drawn, and the two women are exquisite. Dorothea, disguised like Imogen as a boy to escape from her husband's plots, forecasts the sweetness and forgiveness of Shakespeare's heroines. The action is imagined as a performance before Oberon as King of the Fairies devised by the melancholy Bohan.

V

The Greek-toned humanism that so tormented and illuminated the Elizabethan consciousness is variously interpenetrated or countered by Christian feeling. We conclude with consideration of a remarkable work which serves to sum and clarify our discussions.

A Looking Glass for London and England (*c.* 1590), first published as by 'Thomas Lodge and Robert Greene', and included by J. Churton Collins in his edition of Greene's dramas, sets the golden apprehensions of the age beside its accompanying evils. In Rasni, King of Nineveh, are contained all the vices of Marlowe's Tamburlaine and Greene's James IV; and the underplot shows poverty cheated by a usurer, thwarted of justice, and finally driven to thieving. A clown and ragamuffins provide comedy and an exposure of alehouse drunkenness. The glamour of high life contrasts with the sufferings of the low, and a chorus commentary relates the action to contemporary London.

Rasni, conqueror of Jerusalem, has Absalom's god-like beauty and Tamburlaine's martial looks 'sparkling revenge and dire disparagement' (I. i), together with the wealth of Lyly's Midas-Philip, Peele's Juno, and Marlowe's Jew. He is formally presented as a composite of all this, and more, being guilty of an incestuous love for his sister. His poetry is of the usual world-ranging sort:

> Lordings, I'll have my wedding sumptuous,
> Made glorious with the treasures of the world.
> I'll fetch from Albia shelves of margarites,
> And strip the Indies of their diamonds,
> And Tyre shall yield me tribute of her gold . . .
>
> (I. i.)

But his pride is to be short-lived. The prophet Oseas is 'brought in by an Angel' (I. ii) to act as choric moralizer and drive home the condemnation.

The occult, so pressing in Greene's plays, comes under the ban: even Friar Bacon was shown as repenting of his devices. Here, just after Rasni and his sister Remilia, who has been glorying in her triumphant beauty, have been presented with a marvellous arbour by the enchantments of the Magi, Remilia is suddenly found 'strucken with thunder, black' (II. i): the effect is terrifying. When a lady poisons her husband in order to enjoy Rasni's love, her act is greeted by the King in a speech of typical exuberance, promising to have the very winds perfumed for her with myrrh and ambergris (II. iii); but his love interchanges with her are interrupted by a hand from the clouds, holding a burning sword (IV. iii). When Rasni is confronted by a poor woman's accusation of her son, Radagon, who after having risen to the King's favour at court now repudiates his parents, he supports his favourite's atrocious philosophy with 'I like thy pride, I praise thy policy' (III. ii); but when the boy's mother, like old Hieronimo, calls on God for justice

> Oh all you heavens and you eternal powers,
> That sway the sword of justice in your hands . . .
>
> (III. ii.)

a 'flame of fire' swallows up her son, leaving Rasni to deplore the loss of his 'lovely Radagon'. Ghosts cry 'Woe' upon the city (IV. iii).

The choric Oseas addresses the audience, scene by scene. The moral is contemporary:

> Repent, all you that hear, for fear of plagues.
> O London, this and more doth swarm in thee!
>
> (III. ii.)

In Act V Oseas is replaced by the prophet Jonas, or Jonah, who arrives to bring Rasni and his wicked city to repentance. God's judgement is softened:

> And should not I have great compassion
> On Nineveh the City of the world,
> Wherein there are a hundred thousand souls . . .
>   (v. iii.)

Jonas comforts the stricken king and the rest, and speaks a final and moving address to London.

The vast design draws on the Miracles and Moralities, Seneca's five-act structure and chorus, Italian Machiavellianism, Marlovian excess, and Elizabethan conscience. The scenes from low life are organic and the humour really amusing. The placing of aristocratic pleasures within a context of social injustice goes far to clarify Marlowe's magnificent confusions; the dangers of excess are rationally related to the religious tradition; and many dark themes of Jacobean drama are forecast and placed. It is more than a document of its age: it could, and should, be revived.

CHAPTER IV

Shakespeare

I have in this rough work shap'd out a man.
Timon of Athens, I. i.

I

THOUGH great writing outspaces its age we can say that it was the Elizabethan life-joy that lifted William Shakespeare into his orbit. He was young enough to be influenced by the harmonies of Lyly, the pastoralism of Peele and Greene, the revenge motif and tragic poetry of Kyd, and by Marlowe's men of power; all these he used, combined and improved. Yet the old elements are rendered subtly different within the Shakespearian organization. There is nothing like the disjointed art-forms of Marlowe, or the moral patterning of *A Looking Glass for London and England*; rather we have a harmony, like Lyly's, only more inclusive. Bright pleasures are not, as in Marlowe and Greene, associated with evil; whatever is to be so associated itself takes on the colourings of evil, and, so coloured, has its own peculiar dignity and appeal. The total result is a harmony which enables us to survey ethical conflicts from a god-like view, without ethical confusion. All coheres. Man and his society are in close interaffective relationship to nature, to flowers and the seasons, the sea, sun and moon, the cosmos; and also to abysmal evil and to the divine. Myth, folklore and magic assert their age-old powers; Medieval religion and Renaissance art are in balance; and a total dramatic truth matures. This truth cannot be defined in terms of any system, though systems are used. The dominating Shakespearian symbols of thunder-tempests and music address themselves respectively to atavistic terrors and aspiration beyond thought. They are simple, vast, and universal. So is the Shakespearian royalty, appealing to mind-layers and traditional associations more deep and distant than Tudor rights. Shakespeare is the great dramatist of kingship.

Shakespeare's Sonnets (pub. 1609; composition dates unknown) follow the balance of his *Rape of Lucrece* (1594) as against his *Venus and Adonis* (1593), recording a sexual fascination, sinking to lust, for a Dark Lady, and an adoration of Socratic tone for a Fair Youth. The one arouses revulsion; the other is an experience of the bisexual, like the 'Phoenix' poems in *Love's Martyr* (1601) to which Shakespeare contributed *The Phoenix and the Turtle*. The adolescent harmony of the poet's seraphic young 'master-mistress' (Sonnet 20) awakes in the dramatist a corresponding harmony of apprehension which sees *all human creation, including the worst, as stamped with the one sovereignty* (Sonnets 113 and 114). The Dark Lady stands for sexual duality, the lower Dionysian; the Fair Youth, called the poet's 'better angel' (Sonnet 144) and acting as his own spiritual reflection, for the higher Apollonian. Shakespeare's angels are regularly imagined as young men (*The Wheel of Fire*, enlarged edition, 1949, etc.; Appendix B). If we provisionally call Greene heterosexual and Marlowe homosexual, Shakespeare, though he can handle homosexuality in *The Merchant of Venice* and *Twelfth Night*, may be called bisexual. From this bisexuality his dramas are created.[1]

II

The romantic comedies range from political dissension and tragic loss to wit and gaiety, with love central and conclusion in marriage. Marriage is deeply honoured, and the rights and qualities of the sexes beautifully distinguished. It is the woman's part to surrender to man, as lord; and yet the women, not the men, are the controlling powers. They are of two kinds: the strong, intellectual woman, and the gentler girls who take to male disguise.

The first type appears in *Love's Labour's Lost* (*c.* 1594), wherein the King and other young lords reject feminine society only to be subdued by the Princess and her attendant ladies. The theme is re-developed in the sex antagonism and verbal duels of *Much Ado about Nothing* (*c.* 1598). Benedick and Beatrice are entrenched in their own sexes: Beatrice is keen-witted, Benedick is a normal male, blunt and un-at-home with poetic refinements (v. ii). They are strong types; and we watch their semi-reluctant but deeply desired coming together. They are on a plane of sexual realism above the more deliberately fictionalized Claudio-Hero story of love, distrust, sin,

---

[1] My comprehensive study of Shakespeare's Sonnets and the Phoenix poems of *Love's Martyr* appears in *The Mutual Flame*, 1955.

repentance and reunion. Beatrice's intuition blasts the absurd plot, and Benedick's manly strength is her implement. She tells him to 'kill Claudio'. 'O, that I were a man', she cries, 'or that I had any friend would be a man for my sake' (IV. i.) The dialogue takes fire:

> BENEDICK: Tarry, good Beatrice. By this hand, I love thee.
> BEATRICE: Use it for my love some other way than swearing by it.
> BENEDICK: Think you in your soul the Count Claudio hath wronged Hero?
> BEATRICE: Yea, as sure as I have a thought or a soul.
> BENEDICK: Enough! I am engaged, I will challenge him . . .
>
> (IV. i.)

This is the perfect marriage of feminine insight and male action. Their apartness has been a symptom of their built-in, sexual individualities: here their personalities, while remaining different, collaborate. Though separate, each touches the other's sex, Beatrice by her desire to be a man, Benedick, less closely, by his trust in woman's intuition. On the stage the male impact of Benedick's simple 'I am engaged' can be overpowering.

Not until *Antony and Cleopatra* (*c.* 1607) are the sexes again so well balanced. In other early romances we find less vigorous heroes and gentler heroines who make their approaches in male disguise. Sexual disguise is used by many dramatists to signify pictorially an ideal state, but Shakespeare uses it more purposefully, *for it is only when in male disguise that these heroines are given their best wisdom.* So Julia in *The Two Gentlemen of Verona* (*c.* 1593) and Viola in *Twelfth Night* (*c.* 1600) comment wistfully, as from a higher wisdom, on their men's love:

> VIOLA: My father had a daughter lov'd a man,
>   As it might be, perhaps, were I a woman,
>   I should your lordship.
> ORSINO: And what's her history?
> VIOLA: A blank, my lord. She never told her love . . .
>
> (*Twelfth Night*, II. iv.)

Viola continues with a criticism of male passion. Now Orsino is meanwhile growing to love his page and, the truth of her identity revealed, Viola finally wins from him a devotion deeper than his flashy infatuation for Olivia. In *As You Like It* (*c.* 1599) Rosalind, disguised as the youth Ganymede, pretends to be herself in order to give Orlando a training in love; in Rosalind, Shakespeare had a boy actor playing a girl disguised as a boy pretending to be a girl. Her

words are by turn satiric, fantastic, amusing and wistful, blending
wit with pathos:

> But these are all lies: men have died from time to time, and worms
> have eaten them, but not for love. (IV. i.)

She—or he—and Orlando act a mock-marriage:

> ORLANDO: For ever and a day.
> ROSALIND: Say 'a day' without the 'ever'. No, no, Orlando, men
> are April when they woo, December when they wed: maids are
> May when they are maids, but the sky changes when they are
> wives . . . (IV. i.)

The supposed boy's acting of woman's peevishness—'Ay, go your
ways, go your ways; I knew what you would prove' (IV. i)—is as
pretty a self-satire as we could wish. Rosalind-Ganymede rings all
the changes on love (III. ii; IV. i).

Since true love is more than sexual, the love-wisdom of Viola and
Rosalind is rightly spoken from this disguise. When Jessica in *The
Merchant of Venice* (*c.* 1596) appears 'in the lovely garnish of a boy'
(II. vi) we are aware of a natural charm or grace; but more than
nature is involved: a spark is struck, with seraphic illumination. In
Cymbeline (*c.* 1610) the disguised Imogen draws from Belarius the
words:

> By Jupiter, an angel! Or, if not,
> An earthly paragon! Behold divineness
> No older than a boy! (III. vi.)

The impressions continue (IV. ii). And yet in these Shakespearian
disguises we never feel, as we do in Lyly, that the boy actor's natural
pertness is in play; that is reserved for Puck in *A Midsummer Night's
Dream* and Ariel in *The Tempest*. Viola and Rosalind are always
feminine, and that their exquisite and authoritative realizations of
womanhood come through disguise suggests that within the bisexual
dimension whatever is best in sex itself is not abrogated, but fulfilled; or rather it is filtered through, all that is sexually limited, or
lustful, being left out. Beatrice, for whom such a disguise would be
impossible, is mentally nearer to man; these women are at once
more than women and womanhood in perfect flower.

In *The Merchant of Venice* more is involved. Portia's feminine
surrender of herself to Bassanio as an 'unlesson'd girl' (III. ii) is
followed by her assumption of male disguise as a Doctor of Laws in

order to solve problems too great for the men. The three caskets, gold, silver and lead, have already associated her with true value as opposed to false exteriors, and when she opposes Shylock in court she functions as the exponent of a Christian wisdom against Judaic legality.[1] Legal exactitudes may not apply when life in all its complex and organic interfusions is our subject:

> Tarry a little: there is something else.
> This bond doth give thee here no jot of blood;
> The words expressly are 'a pound of flesh' . . .
>   (IV. i.)

Justified in the small context, we may be condemned within the greater.[2] Here life and law are in conflict, the disguised Portia now corresponding across the centuries to the bisexual Athena in the trial of the *Oresteia*. Her speech on 'the quality of mercy' counsels the union of mercy with law, of the 'heart' with the 'temporal power' of the 'sceptre' (IV. i), of Christianity and kingship; and her assumed bisexuality may be said to correspond to the union of Church and State. Together Shylock and Portia constitute a peculiarly vivid expression of what is to be a recurring dramatic balance of human power and some person of bisexual or seraphic grace.

A rather similar contrast is dramatized in *All's Well that Ends Well* (1603–10),[3] but without disguise. Helena assumes male prerogatives as Diana's 'knight' (I. iii), attaining miraculous powers of healing through a combination of love and esoteric science, and on every front winning. Her powers are shown in strong contrast to the male powers of warfare typified by Bertram. It is Shakespeare's most forceful reading of female power, developing to the limit what was half present in *As You Like It*, where Rosalind plays the part of a miracle worker in collaboration with 'Hymen'.

In *A Midsummer Night's Dream* (c. 1596) the magic deepens. Sexual confusions on earth are caused by dissension in the spirit world arising from the fairies' love of an Indian boy. It is as though some strange, at once Dionysian and ideal, hinterland of earthly romance were being adumbrated.

---

[1] Harold Fisch in *The Dual Image* (1959), a study of the Jew in English literature, regards Shylock's reliance on his bond as a sound racial emphasis.

[2] This contrast of life and legality was first noted by Max Plowman in *The Adelphi Magazine*, New Series, II, vi; September 1931; and see my own discussions in *Principles of Shakespearian Production*, 1936, and *The Shakespearian Tempest*, 1932.

[3] The dating is difficult. Reasons supporting a late composition are given in *The Sovereign Flower*, 1958.

III

In actual life, however, there are few Portias or Helenas ready to counsel courts and heal kings, as Shakespeare's historical dramas, with their rivalries and tensions, only too clearly show. History is determined by men and in Shakespeare's historical dramas the women, so dominating in the comedies, play only background parts. These plays are patriotic, their patriotism flowering naturally from Elizabethan soil. A conflation and condensation of two speeches of George Peele (p. 59 above) gives us John of Gaunt's famous praise of England in *Richard II* (1595):

> This royal throne of kings, this sceptred isle,
> This earth of majesty, this seat of Mars,
> This other Eden, demi-paradise;
> This fortress built by Nature for herself
> Against infection and the hand of war . . .
>
> (II. i.)

From the height of Tudor accomplishment we look back on the various civil wars that succeeded the reign of Edward III. The three parts of *Henry VI* (c. 1592) and *Richard III* (c. 1593) reach the victory of Henry Tudor, later Henry VII, grandfather of Queen Elizabeth; and then we are taken further back, but with a developing historic conception, to the sequence from *Richard II*, through the two parts of *Henry IV* (c. 1597), to *Henry V* (c. 1599); the two sequences constituting an epic creation, a kind of Old Testament, in which a spiritual principle is felt working behind, or within, the action. This principle may be defined as 'royalty': the emphasis is mainly personal, the community being generally covered less by a direct projection than by the poetry of England's countryside disturbed, as are the women, by the turmoils of male power. To Shakespeare English royalty is rooted in English nature and both are sullied by civil strife. Kings may have the lustre of their office, but they are insecure: Henry VI is opposed by his barons, Richard II by Bolingbroke, Henry IV by Hotspur. The story of each in turn bears witness to the text: 'Uneasy lies the head that wears a crown' (*2 Henry IV*, III. i). Henry VI is a saint misplaced; Richard III is criminal; Richard II irresponsible; Henry IV a worried politician; the King in *King John* (c. 1596) unprincipled. Only Henry V succeeds, and his success, being the success of a warrior only, remains partial. Though the men are inadequate they are not ignoble; they have dignity and courage, and royalty as a poetical conception remains firm:

> For well we know, no hand of blood and bone
> Can gripe the sacred handle of our sceptre
> Unless he do profane, steal, or usurp.
> (*Richard II*, III. iii.)

The crown is both sacred and secular; it is God's medium; it is man's desire and man's burden; it is an engine for raising mankind. And the only enduring and substantial royalty exists not in the man but in the poetry, except in Shakespeare's last drama, *Henry VIII* (1613), which concludes with Cranmer's prophecy of the blessings to attend the reign of Elizabeth I.

Shakespeare's kings face opposition, and yet far more important than any Bolingbroke or Hotspur is the imaginative opposition of Falstaff, who in the two parts of *Henry IV* functions as a humorous and philosophic challenge not only to King Henry and Prince Hal, but to all our kings; indeed to society, in any age or place. The richest humour derives from the dissolution of accepted values by some nature force; man's moral or other presumptions are shown as inadequate; and we delight, momentarily, in the inadequacy. Comedy is said to have originated from the orgiastic, from surrender to the cosmic-physical powers in man outside reason; and certainly the rotund Falstaff, drinking and whoring, is the orgiastic incarnate. Morals and law he repudiates, making them appear ludicrous. He is always acting, buffooning. He enjoys arranging charades with himself as the King and next as Prince Hal. He is fully conscious of his role, seeing himself as 'not only witty in myself, but the cause that wit is in other men' (*2 Henry IV*, I. ii). In the first part his humour covers a wide range; in the second the impact is more serious, his own actions more dangerous and his criticisms of others more fiercely barbed. The change establishes the darker implications of his anarchistic personality; the implications, that is, of great humour.

Even those who most repudiate his moral nihilism must admit that the best things could not have come without it. Against Hotspur's honour cult stands eternally Falstaff's

> Can honour set to a leg? No. Or an arm? No. Or take away the grief
> of a wound? No. Honour hath no skill in surgery, then? No. What is
> honour? A word. What is that word, honour? Air. A trim reckoning!
> Who hath it? He that died o' Wednesday . . .   (1; v. i.)

Hal, the hero-king to be, he disposes of as

> A good shallow young fellow: a' would have made a good pantler,
> a' would have chipped bread well. (2; II. iv.)

But Hal is better than 'this same young sober-blooded boy', Prince John, who drinks no sack, and whose actions certainly bear out Falstaff's aspersions. This long speech on sack (2; IV. iii), which is said to make the brain 'apprehensive, quick, forgetive, full of nimble, fiery and delectable shapes', is Falstaff's gospel, witnessing to Dionysian powers greater than the stock-in-trade of such politicians as the King and Prince John. More, Falstaff has ingrained religious sympathies; religious phrases are constituent to both his humour and his graver moments; [1] his comprehensive mind has at least surveyed every ideal and every value, before taking its own way. Speaking from a deliberately assumed standpoint below conventions he attains as widely revealing a perspective or panorama as from a divine standpoint above. Comedy so expansive and so levelling naturally touches tragedy, and tragic moments are there, at least for the skilled actor. Against this 'true piece of gold' (1; II. iv) not only the heroic Hotspur and correct Chief Justice, but the dignified king and brilliant Hal, all have to fight mightily for our interest, and that they do not fail is the measure of Shakespeare's poetic artistry. Falstaff has humour, philosophy and wit, if scarcely poetry, though he has an eye for pictorial art and his gospel of sherris-sack is poetically conceived; and once, from the depths of sexual vice, the love he inspires in Doll Tearsheet touches, through a few words in a sordid scene, an intensity beyond romance. Falstaff must be rejected by Hal on his accession; afterwards he, not the others, lives on.

IV

In this there is nothing strange. Shakespeare's early work has many persons who radiate powers incommensurable with their environment. Faulconbridge in *King John* dwarfs his king; Bottom's self-assertion before Theseus in *A Midsummer Night's Dream* is a comical challenge; Berowne in *Love's Labour's Lost* and Mercutio in *Romeo and Juliet* (*c.* 1595) are examples in wit and Jaques in *As You Like It*

---

[1] These have been ably discussed in J. Dover Wilson's *The Fortunes of Falstaff* 1943. See also D. A. Traversi's *Shakespeare from Richard II to Henry V* 1958.

in satiric malcontent. Both Malvolio in *Twelfth Night* and Shylock in *The Merchant of Venice* assume disturbing powers:

> An oath, an oath! I have an oath in Heaven.
> Shall I lay perjury upon my soul?
> No, not for Venice.   (IV. i.)

Such persons are, within their dramatic contexts, power-bearers. The most powerful have, like Falstaff, religious or numinous apprehensions; Richard III always swears by St Paul; and they are entangled in various ways with evil. They need not have great gifts: Malvolio and Shylock are ordinary men, yet dramatically assertive. They are usually lonely people.[1] We may call them 'dramatic supermen'; they are the good acting parts sought by star performers. So, though Falstaff, like Satan in *Paradise Lost*, is rationally to be repudiated, we must nevertheless recognize that such larger conceptions, refusing confinement within rational and moral categories, force their way, assuming validity. The early 'dramatic supermen' point ahead. Both Shylock and Falstaff are tremors, or more, heaving up towards the great tragedies wherein the compressed power of Shylock bursts its bounds and the Falstaffian mountain becomes volcanic.

In the histories the central emphasis is on royalty, the opposers, though strong in their own right, acting as secondary though dramatically vital interests. In the tragedies there is a reversal, the emphasis falling on great individuals acting as rebels against order. The change might be said to forecast the historical change to come from monarchy to democracy. The hinge-piece is *Julius Caesar* (*c.* 1599), dramatizing the attempt to slay kingship in the cause of republicanism, and though the attempt fails, Shakespeare's drama for once preserves a republican tone by dividing our interest among four leading persons; the play is, as it were, technically democratic. Feminine interest is slight; here, as in the histories, women are background figures, suffering under the pressures of male ideals and endeavours. Brutus' rational self-sufficiency is contrasted with his marriage to Portia and also with the more emotionally compelling Cassius and Antony. Only to the boy Lucius does Brutus show love.

Man's reason lacks cosmic sanction; the female principle, which channels more of the Dionysian, cannot be ignored. It may be aligned with the humour of Falstaff: Berowne's praise of love as

---

[1] The loneliness of Shylock, Malvolio and Othello has been observed by Margaret Webster in *Shakespeare Today*, 1957.

psychic power in *Love's Labour's Lost* (IV. iii) corresponds directly to Falstaff's speech on sack. In the comedies women, like Falstaff, are witty and critical of the men, and control the action: it is *their* world. And now in the tragedies, as in the early revenge play *Titus Andronicus* (c. 1593) [1] and *Romeo and Juliet*, the feminine element is to be strong. We normally watch a hero of established royal or military repute thrown off balance by some torment to his Apollonian reason aroused by his relationship with women. The conflict expands and nature is disturbed, thunderstorms and supernatural phenomena witnessing the engagement of the Dionysian otherness with the daylight surfaces. In this conflict the hero is caught; forced himself, whether king or soldier, to become Dionysian and anarchic; until in death we feel a new unity, a remarriage of ultimate sexual or super-sexual principles greater than, yet working through, the experiences of man.

Troilus and Cressida (c. 1602) discusses government, war, passion, and disillusion, dramatizing a juxtaposition of romance and satire. *Measure for Measure* (c. 1604) is written from a dissatisfaction with ethical surfaces and a keen awareness of natural energies and instincts. The Duke in friar's disguise adumbrates the as yet un-achieved union of Church and State, and a wisdom, like Portia's, or that of Aeschylus' Athena, beyond the strictness of law. From this wisdom the great tragedies are composed: they are *Hamlet* (c. 1601), *Othello* (c. 1603), *King Lear* (c. 1605), *Macbeth* (c. 1606), and *Timon of Athens* (c. 1607). *Hamlet* with its baffling criss-cross of humane villainy in Claudius and death-impregnated virtue in Hamlet serves as a challenge to tidy systems; and thenceforward, though fierce ethical conflicts are contained, they are not final, the battling being best defined in more universal and semi-sexual terms. Hamlet is horrified by his mother's remarriage; Othello tortured by marital jealousy and Lear by his daughters; and Macbeth is plunged into crime by infernal and female powers acting in consort with his wife. Lear's inroads of sexual nausea, recalling the Dark Lady of the Sonnets, are organic to his story. The female principle may appear as good or as evil, but the general truth holds: man is, one way or another, attacked by, or through, it. Yet the conflict, the split, is not all destruction; the hero's courage allows the Dionysian powers to swill through him; they invade, cleanse, and recreate. Through

---

[1] I would draw attention to Alan Sommers's remarkable essay 'Wilderness of Tigers' in *Essays in Criticism*, X, iii, July 1960, as the first adequate account of the play that has appeared.

agony and madness Lear achieves self-realization: he is more royal on the storm-riven heath than in his petulant tyranny. From the womb of Hell in *Macbeth* rises the 'Child, crowned, with a Tree in his hand':

> What is this
> That rises like the issue of a king,
> And wears upon his baby brow the round
> And top of sovereignty?
> (*Macbeth*, IV. i.)

That this sovereign excellence which in its blend of nature, creation and the crown covers both principles, Dionysian and Apollonian, signifying the harmony of the greater powers and human ideals, should remain throughout intact, is symptomatic of a pervading optimism. For always, as the action accelerates, we are aware of an inrush of power; there is growth, in which the hero shares. The agony is part of a tension tugging him and us to a fuller realization, a deeper self-achievement. The men are noble and brave, based as firmly in soldiership or royal dignity as are the women in love; and, as tragedy encompasses them, from Romeo in the tomb onwards, the hero accepts his destiny, enters the numinous, the death-shadowed, area, becomes titanic. Richard III and Macbeth do not repent, and we should regret it if they did; Claudius' prayer in *Hamlet* shows precisely the kind of religious complexity in which Macbeth refuses to engage. Instead we find self-knowledge and an attunement to necessity. There is no final blame. Moral conflict is only part of a dynamism which itself owes sole allegiance to this fuller experience, this wider, more than human, insane or super-sane, comprehension: each hero towards the close has moments of supernal insight, Macbeth included.

Each whole, moreover, extends well beyond its hero; what it reveals is the tension existent between the hero and his human and cosmic environment; and in this tension the evil and the agony are symptoms of a necessary discrepancy and a necessary expansion. To call it a marriage of good and evil is inadequate, because 'good' and 'evil' are superficial appearances only and cannot be married on their own level. What we watch is the tug of creation, made of the relation of protagonist to environment, opening what was shut, for new powers and a new enlargement. Since throughout Western drama these powers, whether dark or light, flow more directly through the women than through the men we can say that the total tragic mystery or synthesis is bisexual. The marriage bond is an appallingly strong

Shakespearian value, and so in Shakespearian tragedy, as assuredly
as in Aeschylus' *Oresteia*—Lady Macbeth and the Weird Sisters
corresponding to Clytemnestra and the Erinues—we watch sexual
principles flowering out into the yet wider engagement and interlocking of human ideals with the numinous and the supernatural:
tragedy is a sublime marriage. These greater, super-sexual, principles
are symbolized in Shakespeare by music and tempests, corresponding
to what Nietzsche means by Apollonian and Dionysian; for in
Shakespeare music is used, as in any period it may be, for an Apollonian purpose. Perfected royalty would cover both principles and so,
were such a state achieved, would a superman. Shakespeare's
tragedies are a step towards the achievement of both.

Definition of the mystery is hard, but we can at least watch Shakespeare attempting what may be called incarnations of it; that is, the
creation of persons who are at home within and assimilate the tragic
mystery. This quality Romeo has as he enters the tomb. The Hebraic
Shylock has it; and so has Falstaff, from his at once comic and
cosmic viewpoint, his long speech on sherris-sack defining the more
than mental powers needed, together with his many references to
Death (e.g. the 'Death's-head' in 1 *Henry IV*, III. iii). After agony and
collapse Othello finally surmounts his suffering to become master of
a serene self-dramatization:

> Methinks it should be now a huge eclipse
> Of sun and moon, and that the affrighted globe
> Should yawn at alteration.   (v. ii.)

Such accents are our guide; we must, in these higher matters, not
only respond, but think, poetically. Othello with his exotic background and wondrous handkerchief has a rounded and magical
personality unlike that of Macbeth or King Lear, whose power is
less their own, as persons, than made of the powers generated by
their plays, as wholes.

We are still nearer a tragic personality in *Hamlet*. From the ghost
scenes onwards, Hamlet is death-shadowed; he is living tragedy,
moment by moment, and functions as a threat, a numinous and dark
force. And there is much else. He is in tension towards an integrated,
beyond sex, state, in his relationships with his mother and Ophelia
willing an idealism which alternates with revulsion, and is accordingly
insecure. Apollonian images of perfected man 'infinite' in 'faculty',
angelic in 'action' and god-like in 'apprehension' (II. ii), torment
him, draw him; and yet his only achieved success in poise and grace

is in the sphere of dramatic art, in the theory of which he is expert. Shakespeare's avenger and king-opposer is here no man of blood; he is to be contrasted with the male valuations of Laertes and Fortinbras. He is more delicate, an artist, aiming to 'catch the conscience of the king' (II. ii) with a play, precursor of our social dramatists, and of the artist heroes of Browning and Ibsen. Falstaff had dramatic instincts too, burlesquing the King and Prince in a charade, and Hamlet has much of the buffoonery and wit of Falstaff. Hamlet's personality covers the wider range: death and a ghost—though Falstaff was often thinking of death too—sexual or bisexual integration or purity, humour, dramatic art, satire, all are levelled by this strangely complex and vital ambassador of Death against the King. Even so, it is a tussle:

> There's such divinity doth hedge a king,
> That treason can but peep to what it would,
> Acts little of his will.   (IV. v.)

Though Hamlet and Claudius are far from perfect representatives, their opposition reflects in balance the two furthest Shakespearian quests, those 'mighty opposites' (v. ii.) of superman and royalty. The conclusion is acted out in ceremonial, almost ritualistic, manner; for great issues are involved.

    Timon of Athens takes us further. Less subtle than *Hamlet*, hewn in blocks, unsmoothed and perhaps unfinished, it yet has its own peculiar mastery. Timon, patron of art and bounteous giver, personifies, as did the chivalrous Theseus in *A Midsummer Night's Dream*, the best of Renaissance aristocracy; but there is folly in his lavish expenditure and trust. To him gold is, as *The Merchant of Venice* drives home, only valid when sacramental; he is guided entirely by his own emotional warmth and honesty of heart. Un-at-home in an avaricious society wherein 'usury' makes the government itself 'ugly' (III. v.), he obeys, and expects others to obey in return, the law of giving. If one personal emotion can be deduced from Shakespeare's dramas, it is hatred of ingratitude or disloyalty, and of this hatred *Timon of Athens* is the supreme expression. Timon's friends are male; the only women are those disguised as warrior Amazons for the masque (I. ii), and Phrynia and Timandra, who are denounced as prostitutes. To this extent we are close to the Sonnets. However we cannot call Timon homosexual, since sexuality as such is dissolved through its own expansion. He desires no 'power' (I. ii), nor is his all-embracing love possessive. Though formerly a soldier, he is now compared to the bisexual 'Phoenix' (II. i). That he as a person has a meaning beyond that of Hamlet, Othello, Macbeth, or Lear is clear from the absence of supernatural powers. At the reversal there is no thunder or earthquake, no supernatural symbols; no ghost or incantations; the whole action is summed in Timon's personality.

Leaving Athens he becomes prophetic. The first three acts, with their glittering, dream-ideal society, are Apollonian; the last two Dionysian. Naked, by the sea-coast and communing with the elements, Timon lives out by deliberate choice that return to nature to which earlier people in *The Two Gentlemen of Verona*, *As You Like It*, and *King Lear* were forced. If his denunciations of sexual vice, war, and all greed-engendered conflicts forecast the satires of Swift, his new setting is romantic, in line with his deliberate embracing of cosmic powers, Promethean and Byronic. With him we leave the glittering aristocracy of the Renaissance for another and later quest. Such is the span of *Timon of Athens*.

Assistance is accordingly needed in the staging, which demands a full employment of atmospheric effects. The 'woods' mentioned (IV. i) are not enough. We need a setting correspondent to the sea-coast poetry, using rocks, a recurring sound of surf, and lighting to give the protagonist's nakedness human and cosmic appeal. For Timon is more than a tragic hero: he has become Man; that is to say, pretty nearly 'superman'. The new gold which he finds renders him still supreme and sought for, but it functions now symbolically, a sign of his soul worth, as he flings it with his imprecations on those who visit him. Listening to the sob and surge of ocean, he is himself now within the eternal. Those fifth-act glimpses agonizedly attained by other heroes are possessed by him through two acts with full and enduring assurance:

> My long sickness
> Of health and living now begins to mend,
> And nothing brings me all things.
>
> (v. i.)

From this Nirvana-like apprehension his very curses are creative. Anarchic as Falstaff, he tells the bandits to thieve freely, since property is false and taking universal throughout nature and society:

> The sun's a thief, and with his great attraction
> Robs the vast sea; the moon's an arrant thief,
> And her pale fire she snatches from the sun;
> The sea's a thief, whose liquid surge resolves
> The moon into salt tears; the earth's a thief,

> That feeds and breeds by a composture stolen
> From general excrement. Each thing's a thief.
> The laws, your curb and whip, in their rough power
> Have uncheck'd theft . . .
>
> (IV. iii.)

And the poor bandits, staggered by these fantastic imaginative excursions, are stung to respond: 'He has almost charmed me from my profession by persuading me to it' (IV. iii). That is the way of all our great unmoral and anarchic dramatic persons, our Falstaffs, Macbeths, and Timons: *spurning morality, they nevertheless channel powers from which good, not bad, will spring.* Our dramatic transmutations are mysteriously creative. Timon is always well above his curses; pity is contained—his phrases burn with it—but surmounted; and he will not return. The repentant Senators approach, pleading with him to save them from the terrors of war. But their sin, the sin of putting legality before sympathy, money before the heart's gold it symbolizes, is unforgivable:

> Come not to me again; but say to Athens,
> Timon hath made his everlasting mansion
> Upon the beached verge of the salt flood;
> Who once a day with his embossed froth
> The turbulent surge shall cover.
>
> (V. i.)

No cause of Timon's death is given. Like Sophocles' Oedipus, of whom he is a reincarnation, he is gone. No cause is needed: properly understood, he is already there.

Timon of Athens has been a peculiar favourite of great writers, in Britain and abroad; and no Shakespearian work has had so great an influence on British drama.[1] Critics point to faults, and yet the play's technical crudities are the measure of its magnitude; and only the production which is sensitive to what is necessarily rough, and smoothes it, which collaborates with the great meanings, will serve.[2]

Must then our pseudo-superman, whether too idealistic like Hamlet or too universal like Timon, remain in effect non-sexual? The question arises in discussion of Christ and Nietzsche's Zarathustra: does integration preclude sexual union? As though to formulate a

---

[1] See my article '*Timon of Athens* and its Dramatic Descendants' in *The Review of English Literature*, II, iii, October 1961.

[2] My own productions were given at Toronto in 1940 and at Leeds in 1948; also the last scenes, in *This Sceptred Isle*, at London in 1941. Accounts appear in my 'Dramatic Papers' at the Shakespeare Memorial Library, the Reference Library Birmingham.

dramatic answer, Shakespeare wrote *Antony and Cleopatra* (*c.* 1607),
which reads and performs like an attempt to mate a superlative man
with a superlative woman, so bearing to *Hamlet* and *Timon of Athens*
the relation of *Much Ado about Nothing* to the comedies of disguise.
Like Benedick and Beatrice, our lovers are superb representations of
their respective sexes. Antony's strength is that of male soldiership,
exaggerated beyond all normal categories. Even Othello lags behind
this

> demi-Atlas of this earth, the arm
> And burgonet of men.
>
> (I. v.)

And yet there is nothing coldly inhuman about it, as there is in
Coriolanus (*c.* 1608); Antony has the warmth and rich-hearted
generosity of Timon. Cleopatra is woman in all her 'infinite variety'
(II. ii.). Each, like Benedick and Beatrice, subtly touches the other's
sex. Antony is criticized for betraying the warrior and political
values; he is now no more 'man-like' than Cleopatra, nor she 'more
womanly than he' (I. iv); he is shown as feasting, luxuriant, as 'the
curled Antony' (V. ii). Cleopatra, who once changed clothes with
Antony and 'wore his sword Philippan' (II. v), shares in Antony's
warring, commanding at sea, buckling on his armour. They neither
succeed: Antony's lost soldiership weighs on him as he dies and
Cleopatra flies from the battle. The interplay is presented with high
dramatic mastery to map the reciprocal interrelationship of these
two grand sexual beings.

Despite all countering negations of lust and jealousy, the poetry
points us to a transfigured humanity:

> Eros!—I come, my queen—Eros!—Stay for me:
> Where souls do couch on flowers, we'll hand in hand,
> And with our sprightly port make the ghosts gaze;
> Dido and her Aeneas shall want troops,
> And all the haunt be ours. (IV. xii.)

After his death her 'Emperor Antony' becomes to Cleopatra the
majestic universe itself:

> His face was as the heavens, and therein stuck
> A sun and moon, which kept their course, and lighted
> The little O, the earth.
>
> (V. ii.)

At her own death, more a dissolving than a death, Cleopatra attains
her end: 'Husband, I come' (V. ii). Dramatically the marriage must

be delayed, since there is, or appears to be, some inherent impossibility of realizing a marriage on earth corresponding to the completion envisaged; and that is why our greatest love drama necessarily dramatizes an illicit love.

Antony and Cleopatra celebrates a fusion not merely of the human sexes or of two cultures, oriental and western, but also a fusion of those yet greater dramatic principles, Dionysian and Apollonian. In it Dionysian substances assume an Apollonian and visionary poetry.

V

Shakespeare's world has throughout been saturated in the supernatural: the ghosts, the witches and apparitions; the amazing storms, thunderings, and distortions of nature; and mysterious music, conjured by the magic of Welsh Glendower in *Henry IV* or sounding a soldier's fall in *Antony and Cleopatra*. In his final period we have a victory for the musical over the tempestuous; and the supernatural is not dark, but light. The female principle is now assured, beneficent and sacred, with an idealization nearer religion than romance. In *Pericles* (c. 1609) and *The Winter's Tale* (c. 1610) the ladies thought dead, wife and daughter, come newly to life; after loss there is now reunion to 'the music of the spheres' (*Pericles*, v. i). This comes about through no explicit theological or esoteric beliefs. Shakespeare's darker phenomena were always newly imagined; the apparition scene in *Macbeth* has resemblances to mediumistic materializations, but the symbolic apparitions obey only Shakespearian law. Many a later seventeenth-century dramatic ghost is to be more scientifically apprehended and discussed than the strange hotch-potch of folklore and religious beliefs that makes the ghost in *Hamlet*; and yet Shakespeare's ghost, in part for this very reason, is more dramatically warm than any rivals. In passing to his last period, he uses his own dramatic experiences to create a drama beyond tragedy. The old happy-ending romance patterns are fused with tragedy to make a new form and Shakespeare may be said less to have had a vision of immortality, or to have learned of it from Florentine Platonists (p. 44 above, note) or some clairvoyant adept —though both may have played their parts, and the Christian tradition too—than to have created it. He works both from and through the dramatic incarnation, in close contact with human experience. In plot structure the nearest forerunner is probably the beautiful Inca drama, *Apu-Ollantay*, though of this Shakespeare is unlikely to have heard.[1] Profound racial experiences are certainly present. The sheep-shearing festival of *The Winter's Tale* is warm with poetic myth and rustic tradition; even the resurrected Hermione is 'warm' (v. iii); myth, folklore, drama, combine, and we are asked first rather to experience than to believe even though, having experienced, we may find our beliefs affected.

State affairs are still insistent. Under the new mode the union of Rome and Britain is celebrated in *Cymbeline* (*c.* 1610). At a thundering climax the Roman god, Jupiter, actually appears. Magical apprehensions cluster round the two royal boys, Guiderius and Arviragus, in their Welsh mountain retreat—Wales, the home of Glendower's spirit music and the Tudor dynasty [2]—where Imogen, disguised as a boy, comes too. It is a sacred, a faery, a magical spot, given magical poetry. In the princes, male power blends into the seraphic; they, and Imogen too, are 'angels' (v. iii; III. vi, p. 69 above). All three are of royal blood.

We have watched a recurring tension between king-opposer or society-opposer, and king or society: on the simple, heroic plane in Hotspur or Coriolanus; more subtly in Malvolio before Olivia, Shylock before the Duke, in Falstaff, in the studious Brutus and artistic Hamlet, rising to the prophetic Timon; and all may be distantly referred to the archetype of Christ before Pilate. What we want is to have king and superman identified; then all might be well. This is what Shakespeare imagines in *The Tempest*.

Of course our people have not been real supermen, but within the dramatic patterns they touch the needed quality. Though larger than their companions they are not necessarily better and may well be, or seem, from a moral standpoint, worse. What is needed is a protagonist at once sovereign, superman, sane, and good; and it is a lot to ask. Prospero in *The Tempest* (*c.* 1611) has these qualifications. That in consequence he lacks human warmth is true, but inevitable. Descending from the Duke in *Measure for Measure* and the saintly Cerimon in *Pericles*, he is Shakespeare's attempt at an achieved and royal superhumanity.

---

[1] A translation was published by Sir Clements R. Markham, in *The Incas of Peru*, 1910.
[2] That *Cymbeline* contains Stuart implications also is argued by Emrys Jones in 'Stuart Cymbeline', *Essays in Criticism*, XI, i, January 1961.

In Prospero, student of the 'liberal arts' (I. ii), many earlier heroes
are contained. The recurring return, or advance, to nature which
culminated in *Timon of Athens* and the Welsh scenes of *Cymbeline*
is here given new meaning. Prospero on his island is man commanding nature: like Christ, he can control the elements.[1] His empire is
wide, covering nature, man, spirit-phenomena, and a miraculous
music: in him the opacity between nature and supernature has
dissolved.

He has a daughter, Miranda. Such old and honoured persons
often do. The old Oedipus, sacred in suffering and accepted by the
gods, had his Antigone; Shylock had Jessica, Polonius Ophelia, Lear
Cordelia. Pericles' queen is less important than Marina,[2] though in
The Winter's Tale the positions are reversed. Daughters maintain a
creative reference without committing our patriarchal figures to
immediate sexual interests, so striking a balance between sexuality
and integration. In Prospero the numinous quality haloing Oedipus
and Lear is rendered explicit. He has in his service Ariel, a delicate
nature spirit nearer the seraphic than Puck, volatile and fiery, an
angel of judgement, yet boy-like in song and speech. But the island
society has its troubles, with Caliban as our new king-opposer, for
even here the tension persists. Caliban acts out a progress from black
magic, through nature and animal life, to human art and human
wickedness, and thence to 'grace' (v. i), and within our drama he,
rather than Prospero, has the mysterious warmth which such lonely,
thwarted, yet wondrous figures as our Shylocks, Falstaffs, Timons,
and Milton's Satan possess. Caliban and Ariel represent our balance
of power-man and seraph, Dionysian and Apollonian, and both are
controlled by Prospero, just as Plato's charioteer in the *Phaedrus* has
his two horses, fierce and docile, and Nietzsche's Zarathustra his
serpent and eagle.

Prospero is supreme among the countless avengers of Elizabethan
and Jacobean drama; he accomplishes his purpose by magic, by
bloodless power, like that which Bernard Shaw's Captain Shotover
aspires to and his Ancients have attained; and having utterly mastered
and subdued his enemies, he forgives. When he reveals himself in his
ducal robes the stage effect should be staggering, for this is no less

---

[1] Compare, from a modern work of esoteric philosophy: 'But a master filled,
for a brief time, with the Divine Creative Wisdom can alter the courses of the
winds . . . ' (Geraldine Cummins, *Beyond Human Personality*, 1952 edition;
XVII. 181).

[2] T. S. Eliot's poem *Marina* is a fine piece of listening in to the daughter
mysticism in Shakespeare.

than *religion, art, wisdom and goodness assuming secular authority*; in Christian terms, the return of Christ in power. So Prospero, like his ancestor the Duke in *Measure for Measure*, takes up again his ducal responsibilities. And he has renounced his magic. Why? Partly because such magic dominating Renaissance politics would be inconceivable; Prospero is of the future not of the present, and a basic contemporaneity and realism must be preserved. He is Shakespeare's rough indication of what might come from the religion and esoteric studies, the new science, and the poetry *with all those powers of evil which it transmutes,* and also the great music yet unborn, of Renaissance Europe, as he saw, or foresaw, them; and of what might be done for statecraft by such an achieved superhumanity, in which Church and State, spirituality and royalty, are at last identified, a theme to be taken up later by Henrik Ibsen. Categories beyond the normal are involved. Prospero, even more surely than Timon, lives in eternity:

> The cloud-capp'd towers, the gorgeous palaces,
> The solemn temples, the great globe itself,
> Yea, all which it inherit, shall dissolve . . .
> (IV. i.)

From this Nirvana comprehension we are 'such stuff as dreams are made on'. And yet, what are dreams? Or sleep? Prospero claims that graves have at his command yielded up their dead (v. i); the garments of those who should have been drowned are, through his or Ariel's magic, miraculously fresh and their ship intact (I. ii; II. i; v. i); and Ariel's song hints of death turning man into 'something rich and strange' (I. ii). Precise answers are not offered; *The Tempest* remains a sublime enigma; but it is a sublimity and an enigma towards which the race is advancing.

Shakespeare himself, like Prospero, returned to firmer ground, and wrote *Henry VIII* (1613).[1] It is a massive, ceremonial piece, in which kingship and religion are co-present and interaffective. It has strong king-opposers, Buckingham and Wolsey; a great woman in Queen Katharine, whose personality sums and contains those many earlier women who suffer under male statecraft; the romance of burly Henry and Anne Bullen; and Cranmer, for religious humility. Before her death Queen Katharine is visited by angels, calling her to Paradise. We conclude with Cranmer's prophecy addressed to the

---

[1] The authenticity of the disputed scenes in *Henry VIII* has been defended in *The Crown of Life*, 1947.

seething, Falstaffian, London crowd, spoken for yet another daughter, the child Elizabeth:

> This royal infant, heaven still move about her!
> Though in her cradle, yet now promises
> Upon this land a thousand thousand blessings
> Which time shall bring to ripeness . . .
>
> (v. v.)

It is fitting that Elizabeth, called 'the maiden Phoenix', should conclude our story. Lines are added for James I, and there is a forecast of Britain's future greatness. This is Shakespeare's final and royal statement.

Shakespeare gains as a dramatist by laying a primary emphasis on his royal or other protagonists as individuals whilst not omitting to relate them to the community and the wider universe, either directly or through symbolism: his mystique of royalty allows an artistic lucidity and condensation which have much to do with his dramatic pre-eminence. Later dramatists often blur their effects by tilting the balance too far either one way or the other; and they lack the royal essence. Drama must work first in personal terms, though its persons and their drama only attain full reality through the wider relation.

CHAPTER V

Jacobean

My soul, like to a ship in a black storm,
Is driven I know not whither.
JOHN WEBSTER, *The White Devil*, v. vi.

I

UNDER James I drama expands. Public theatres gain in strength; boys at the indoor Blackfriars theatre take on a semi-professional status; and court masques become elaborate. The prevailing tone is sombre, marking a reaction from Elizabethan confidence.

The seeds of reaction were always there, in Marlowe pre-eminently, and the transition may be watched in the life-work of Ben Jonson. *Cynthia's Revels or The Fountains of Self-Love* (1600) was a satire on Elizabeth's court and has an Elizabethan sparkle: there is fun from Cupid as a mischievous page and Gelaia or 'Laughter' as a girl-boy, and much general amusement. Jonson's critical intelligence was keen. In *The Poetaster* (1601) he levelled a stinging attack on contemporary dramatists.

He was a master of both comedy and satire. *Every Man in His Humour* (1598; revised 1616) is mainly concerned with follies and neuroses. The people are studied rather as units than as part of a dramatic society, and the jealous Kitely revealing his misery in asides may be contrasted with the more properly dramatic conception of Shakespeare's Ford at cross purposes with Falstaff in *The Merry Wives of Windsor* (c. 1600). Jonson's skill is prodigious, at its best in the bogus Captain Bobadill, fashionably moody, a critic of literature, a fighter adept in the latest Continental terms and in reminiscences of the battlefield; and bearing that signature of true dramatic creation when, his braggadocio exposed, he proves, in his own terms, invincible. But Jonson is not always so kind. *Epicoene or The Silent Woman* (1609) shows an old man who cannot stand noise being made by his scheming nephew to endure agonies from his newly married virago of a wife, until she is revealed to his relief to be no wife and a boy in disguise. The plot is brilliant but the fun cruel. *Bartholomew Fair* (1614) is a wonderful realization of London low life, its bawds, harlots and pickpockets, puppet shows and ballad singers, roast pig and beer, with a number of comic and satiric interweavings. When the puppet Dionysius is denounced by the puritan Zeal-of-the-Land Busy as a member of that wicked profession which engages in sexual disguises, the puppet answers that, though it recognizes that this is indeed an old argument of the puritanical attack on the stage, yet it cannot properly be applied to the puppets, who are 'neither male nor female'; and forthwith takes up its garment, drawing from its opponent the confession: 'I am confuted, the cause hath failed me' (v. v). The humour is the richer for the implicit commentary on the recurring sexual ambiguities of dramatic art.

These are comedies. At the other extreme are the two weighty tragedies, *Sejanus* (1603) and *Catiline* (1611). Dramatists were deeply concerned with government: the issues recently raised by Essex's rebellion, the problem of succession and the coronation of James I, all stimulated anxiety. In *Sejanus* the Emperor Tiberius, though pretending to be a liberal monarch, is unreliable, vicious and tyrannical. Sejanus is an ambitious schemer. The tone is throughout ominous, as in Arruntius'

> May I pray to Jove
> In secret and be safe? . . . May I think
> And not be rack'd? What danger is't to dream?
> Talk in one's sleep? or cough? Who knows the law?
> May I shake my head, without a comment?
>
> (IV. 300.)

Life has become an enlarged prison and 'Well, snore on, dreaming gods' (IV. 269) the right comment. When thinking himself near to the achievement of his ambition Sejanus is faced by Tiberius' ironically worded repudiation, and after his execution the mob, recently his applauders, enjoy a riot of sadistic fury, dismembering his body. The Emperor is a vicious tyrant, the hero a shameless villain, and the people stupid, bestial or worse. The only good appears in one spectacular suicide and the choric comments of Arruntius.

Catiline is more important. Sejanus was of low birth and aims at imperial sway; Catiline of noble birth and he plots against the republic. Catiline's plot is associated with liberation and the rights of the poor as against the ruling class, but his motive is in the main egocentric. He aims deliberately at destruction; he is a nihilistic, or satanic, force, to whom virtue is a sign of inward poverty (III. 150–1).

He is finely tempered and radiates scorn and power with a glamour never approached by Sejanus. He is one of our many protagonists who house fires lacking to morality. Caesar, for a while one of Catiline's supporters, knows that the judgement of history will depend on the outcome and that political reversals can only be compassed by violence and fraud (III. 490–518). Such are the appalling truths, or half-truths, with which dramatic thinking confronts us. In Catiline revolution is an egotistic, individualistic, aristocratic instinct, and since without such men we could not have successful revolutions, we must accord them a provisional respect.

Catiline is a dark and ferocious work. The conspirators' sacrament of blood, the plans for Rome's burning, the thoughts of hell and horror, the ghost of Sulla, the omens and hideous storm—all contribute to a fearsomeness of sombre power. In both *Sejanus* and *Catiline* we are aware not only of a sulphurous atmosphere in the fiction but also of a certain mental oppressiveness in the writing, as from a mind ungeared to human sympathies.

In his two most famous dramas, *Volpone* (1606) and *The Alchemist* (1610), Jonson's satiric, comic and tragic impulses work in unison. We take *The Alchemist* first. A rich man's servant uses his master's house in collaboration with a pseudo-alchemist to gull a varied assortment of avaricious people with promises of illimitable wealth. The action is compact yet varied, and the blend of satire and comedy is brilliant. One visitor, Sir Epicure Mammon, is a figure of grandiose sensuality:

> I will have all my beds blown up; not stuft:
> Down is too hard. And then mine oval room
> Filled with such pictures as Tiberius took
> From Elephantis, and dull Aretine
> But coldly imitated. Then my glasses
> Cut in more subtle angles, to disperse
> And multiply the figures, as I walk
> Naked between my succubae. My mists
> I'll have of perfume, vapoured 'bout the room,
> To lose ourselves in; and my baths, like pits,
> To fall into; from whence we will come forth,
> And roll us dry in gossamer and roses.
>
> (II. ii.)

Imaginative opulence is blended with an implicit repudiation.[1] Though near Marlowe's dangerous alignment of aesthetic positives

[1] The speech's ironic touches have been well indicated by L. C. Knights in *Drama and Society in the Age of Jonson*, 1937.

with damnation, the danger is avoided by suggesting a maximum of absurdity and a minimum of ridicule; the words have weight, including the strong, romantic connotation of 'roses'. Sir Epicure has poetic dignity. The relation of his downfall to the whole comic pattern is perhaps less satisfying since, though satire need have no limits, yet mockery of the aesthetic—and Sir Epicure is a prodigious aesthete—approaches artistic suicide. This is certainly Jonson's danger; he creates comedy so often—not always—from scorn, almost from scorn of human nature itself; as though a religious devotee were to construct his prayers from blasphemy.

The earlier *Volpone or The Fox*, though less well constructed, is more satisfying. Volpone is a Venetian magnifico who pretends to be dying in order to win gifts from his friends who expect advantage from his will. Thinking him deaf, one shouts abuses whilst fawning on him; another tries to force his own wife to succumb to Volpone's lust; the satire against avarice is withering. The comedy is cruel, but the people are nonentities: all depends on Volpone, and he is great.

Volpone is a philosopher. His followers include a dwarf, a eunuch and an hermaphrodite called Androgyno. These present a masque in which Androgyno is said to be a modern incarnation of 'the soul of Pythagoras', which came originally from Apollo and has since *descended* through various human and animal incarnations to the modern world, wherein it has chosen the form of an androgynous 'fool', not to gain the pleasures of both sexes but because the fool alone can now be called 'blessed' (I. ii). The speech may serve as a dramatic commentary relating comoedic wisdom to 'bisexual' disguise and both to Apollo. These alone now hold the elixir.[1]

Though he starts by addressing his wealth, like Marlowe's Jew, with an impressive poetry, Volpone is no simple miser. He glories 'more in the cunning purchase' of his wealth than in its possession (I. i). Besides, he has avoided all the respectable yet more dangerous ways of enrichment through oppression (I. i). His enjoyment is philosophic and satiric. 'What a rare punishment', he says, 'is avarice to itself' (I. iv.). His full-blooded stage dignity gives him every right to half mesmerize Celia in an Elizabethan speech of sensuous enchantments, packed with reference to jewels, rich foods, music and mythology (III. vii), and it is fitting that he should finally choose to ruin others at the suicidal cost of his own freedom, thereby attaining a near-tragic stature. He delights in being a denunciatory and

[1] Attention has been drawn to this speech, and its more satiric implications analysed, by E. B. Partridge in *The Broken Compass*, 1958; V.

moralistic force; his setting is sumptuous and he has grandeur. He is Jonson's one titanic figure; into him Jonson has poured his whole artistic self; his own skill in exposing folly and knavery, his preoccupation with avarice and lust, *together with his especial delight in such revelations*. By finding so brilliant and shameless an objective equivalent to his own evil—for to *delight* in revealing wickedness *is* evil—Jonson ceases to be a moralist and creates for once a pseudo-superman. That is why, while most of his work is of academic or literary interest only, *Volpone* can still, as Sir Donald Wolfit has shown, be triumphantly staged.

Jonson's two greatest works concentrate on gold,[1] but in so uncompromisingly damning man's lust for it he comes near to damning that spiritual principle of which gold is a reflection. Shakespeare, in both *The Merchant of Venice* and *Timon of Athens*, does not forget that gold has dual pointings. Shakespeare's Timon by the sea-coast with his new-found, symbolic gold is beyond Jonson's artistry. But Jonson could turn to poetic fantasy when he wished, as in his many brilliant masques, done in collaboration with Inigo Jones for the court of James I.

Jonson's Roman tragedies serve to show how deeply concerned was the Jacobean consciousness with problems of statecraft. Elaborate examples of state drama are to be found in the work of Sir Fulke Greville (composed *c*. 1590–1610) and Sir William Alexander (1603–1607). These follow the academic Senecan tradition, offering interminable arguments on the anxieties of monarchy and government, the miseries of revolution and disorder, and the torments of ambition and of greatness generally; and on the divine aspirations of man and the inscrutable yet overbrooding eternity which encloses his brief term. Every relevant thought is in these stately and static fabrications and many a noble chorus, but the matters handled are for the most part insoluble in terms of static categories and demand rather expression in that kind of thought-action which has a more popular appeal; for the compulsions of 'entertainment' have their place among the profundities. Our key problem is that of the great individual, such as Jonson's Catiline, as against king or society; and the human dynamic which gives rise in age after age to the opposition of ruler and opposer, must be itself dynamically rendered. Among such heroic challenges the dramas of George Chapman are outstandingly important.

[1] E. B. Partridge (p. 90 note) analyses Jonson's gold imagery well.

Ben Jonson's reading of human nature is pessimistic; his friend George Chapman's optimistic. Chapman is interested, like Marlowe and Peele, only more philosophically, in heroes of superlative gifts; and also in the occult, scientifically rather than imaginatively approached. His dramas are loaded with difficult but exciting thought.

He wrote comedies, with the usual sexual gaming: in *May Day* (*c.* 1600) both man and girl disguise themselves into the opposite sex; and in *The Gentleman Usher* (*c.* 1602) a majordomo, Bassiolo, is fooled by Vincentio's pretence of being passionately in love with him. Chapman's work perhaps shows a homosexual strain, his favourite concentration being, in the main, male.[1] His occult interests are important. In *The Gentleman Usher* Strozzi masters a deadly wound by a 'submission to Heaven' wherefrom the 'mind' spreads her 'powers' throughout the suffering organism to render the 'whole life' subservient to the 'soul', with knowledge of things 'hid from human sight' (IV. iii). In such abstruse matters Chapman's thinking is carefully and exactly phrased.

His greater dramas labour to define certain high types of personality. In *Bussy D'Ambois* (*c.* 1604) a robust hero at the court of Henry III of France arouses the jealousy of the King's brother Monsieur and the Duke of Guise, who take advantage of his liaison with Tamyra, wife of Montsurry, to encompass his death. From a context of intrigue and pride, Bussy stands out as a man of native if rough integrity well aware of his pre-eminence. He fights a victorious combat in defence of his honour:

> When I am wrong'd, and that law fails to right me,
> Let me be king myself (as man was made)
> And do a justice that exceeds the law.   (II. i.)

Being a law 'to himself' he is his own 'king'. Beyond all questions of revenge we are involved in the claims of greatness to that unfallen, golden-age, status ('as man was made') of which the King's office, as the King himself admits, is no more than a provisional symbol (III. ii), forced by human inadequacy:

> No envy, no disjunction had dissolved.
> Or pluck'd one stick out of the golden faggot
> In which the world of Saturn bound our lives,
> Had all been held together with the nerves,
> The genius and th' ingenuous soul of D'Ambois.
>   (III. ii.)

[1] The question is discussed by Havelock Ellis in *From Marlowe to Shaw*, 1950, 63–4, 85–6.

But Bussy is no king-opposer: he dare do anything but 'kill a king' (III. ii.).

He is no saint either. Renaissance drama exists to face afresh the heroic, the political and the sexual, and though heroically and politically D'Ambois is safe, he falls through an adulterous engagement. Sexual instinct is regarded as a force beyond control (II. ii) by a worthy friar who assists the liaison. Nature has its rights and we feel that D'Ambois would be less the man were he to withdraw. We have a vital discussion on nature: does it make 'souls' blindly? Or must not the 'wondrous fabric' of man have a purpose? What we should call the evolutionary problem is discussed without reliance on Christian concepts (v. ii). Beset by intrigues, D'Ambois enlists the Friar's 'learned holiness' to raise up 'good aerial spirits' (IV. ii), though they fail to prevent disaster.[1] In this interesting and likable friar sexual broad-mindedness and an enlightened spiritualism combine with an unquestioned goodness. Both as man and later as a ghost he opposes vengeful thoughts, speaking as an authoritative minister of 'our holy mother', the Church (v. i). Chapman's creative alignments are bold.

The poetry is tangled with labouring thought, and without colour. It has elemental force, using images of nature's vastness in sea, tempest, earth. Man is a tree before fierce winds, a ship in storm, his soul clouded from the sun. Nature is inexplicable and her purposes obscure. Nevertheless there are good if unavailing spirits, and the potentiality of a human greatness beyond all normal categories; even beyond, though not opposing, the King.

Bussy is loyal, but such self-conscious worth has its dangers. The two parts of *The Conspiracy and Tragedy of Charles, Duke of Byron* (*c*. 1608) dramatize the opposition of Byron and King Henry IV of France. Wars are over and the benevolent and conscientious king expects peace and order. We first see Byron, who has won fame as a warrior, on a crest of public acclamation and spiritual intoxication. Music sounds:

> What place is this? What air? What region?
> In which a man may hear the harmony
> Of all things moving? Hymen marries here
> Their ends and uses and makes me his temple.
>   (1; II. ii.)

'All things' are married within his integral being; in him lodges momentarily the universal meaning and harmony. The wars are over.

---

[1] For such 'good' spirits see my references on p. 44 and 82 above.

Can he now, in peace, hold this 'heaven'? (1; I. ii). His is a spiritualized ambition of swiftness and light, akin to the celestial (1; I. ii),
and France's enemies employ La Fin's skill in magic to seduce him,
for men who exceed 'human limits' are naturally attuned to such
arts (1; II. i). La Fin's Iago-like insinuations (1; II. i) start Byron
rationalizing his ambition into a beyond-good-and-evil and relativist
philosophy asserting the right of 'the free-born powers of royal man'
to repudiate convention; nothing is wholly 'good' or 'bad' (1; III. i).
The King, in a dialogue of subtle innuendo, warns him of the dangers
with which he is flirting and sends him on a mission to England.
Before he goes he interviews a magician who describes the torments
of second sight; we are told, he says, to imitate the divine, and yet
every advance—the analogy to Byron's ambition is clear—leaves us
worse off than those drowned by 'sensual affectations'. He prophesies
Byron's execution (1; III. iii). Here Byron is at his greatest, asserting
human free will as against the stars:

> Give me a spirit that on this life's rough sea
> Loves t'have his sails fill'd with a lusty wind,
> Even till his sail-yards tremble, his masts crack . . .
> (1; III. iii.)

No danger touches one who knows 'what life and death is'; the
warrior, like the occult adept, is death-friendly; his range outspaces
normal men and this 'knowledge' puts him above all laws; he is a
law to himself (1; III. iii).

Byron's visit to the court of Elizabeth I in England forces from him
the recognition: 'You make all state before utterly obsolete' (1; IV. i).
She explains the interdependence of sovereign and subject on which
her rule is based. A standard is set by which our play's action may
be judged.

On his return Byron is infuriated by the King's refusal to extend
his powers: 'Come, he dares not do't.' Byron's stupendous boasts
are met by the King's: 'Do not enforce your merits so yourself.'
Byron's egotism swells: 'I will be mine own king', 'None but myself',
'None but I', ' I alone'. At a marvellous climax the King suddenly
bursts into laughter and leaves him (1; v. i). Byron is staggered:

> What's grave in earth, what awful, what abhorr'd
> If my rage be ridiculous?
> (1; v. ii.)

He in all honesty *reverences* himself. Returning, the King with suave
and kindly wisdom explains to Byron that he cannot, in his present

mood, see things objectively. He *asks* for Byron's allegiance. Suddenly, whilst the King is speaking, Byron kneels. He confesses his 'short madness' and is forgiven (1; v. ii).

But he cannot stop. His warrior virtues, which are spiritualized virtues, find no outlet in 'sensual peace'. If society cannot place and use the supreme values he has touched, so much the worse for society. He sees it as a return to the time 'when the red sun held not his fixed place'. In failing to place and use what is highest, it reverses order:

> We must reform and have a new creation
> Of state and government, and on our chaos
> Will I sit brooding up another world.
> (2; I. ii.)

He is the type of all revolutionaries who pit their own greatness against the normal, or second best. Kingship, once celestially rooted, is failing through international dissension:

> By small degrees the kingdoms of the earth
> Decline and wither . . .
> (2; III. i.)

'The blaze of princes' is extinct. Byron has been justified by history. With uncanny insight Chapman probes into the final justification of what in its own context must in every age be repudiated. Such attacks against society ring, and will always ring, true. Byron feels himself the champion of a purer, more heroic, order: within his criminal egotism burns a high virtue.

Bitterly the good King meditates on the appalling responsibilities of his office with a Shavian forecast: 'He should be born grey-headed that will bear the sword of empire' (2; IV. ii). There follows the arrest, trial, and condemnation. Byron by turns 'doubts, storms, threatens, rues, complains, implores' (2; v. iii). To him it seems a universal, earth-disrupting injustice; his emotions terrify everyone. Being already rooted in 'heaven' he rejects, as many a protagonist of the Romantic period is to reject, the offices of the Church (2; v. iv). He is no dignified martyr. Every twist and turn of his agony is shown without somehow detracting from his stature. In him ordinary emotions are raised to gigantic proportions: he is not better than others, but bigger.

For his third delineation of a super-type Chapman returns to the period of his first in *The Revenge of Bussy D'Ambois* (c. 1611). 'Revenge' means 'avenging', and the avenger is Bussy's brother,

Clermont. In Clermont are qualities both human and religious: he could be called a 'chivalric saint'. Though urged by his brother's ghost and his sister to avenge Bussy's death, he is reluctant to meet 'villainy' with 'villainy'; to him a private wrong is no excuse for usurping the prerogative of law (III. ii). He is both an heroic scorner of an effete aristocracy and a man of spiritual wisdom and 'zeal' for righteousness (II. i). Sexual activity he rates low; his only love is his friend, the Duke of Guise. He regards marriage as the antithesis of love, preferring friendship 'chaste and masculine' (v. i). Man is a creature 'built with God's finger' (I. i), and Clermont an 'absolute', that is wholly integrated and so sexually independent, man (II. i).

His heroism is semi-magical. When during a review of troops his enemies try to arrest this 'more than man', he becomes 'air' and 'wild lightning' rather than 'flesh' and 'earth', scattering opponents as leaves and burning his captors' fingers like fire (IV. i). Clermont is stoically independent of fortune in a state which is called 'th' end of all skill, power, wealth, all that is' (IV. v). He is intended to represent an achieved superhumanity.

Revenge still confronts him. Chapman solves his problem by drawing on the occult, and with more than the conventional insight. When Clermont, after seeing his brother's ghost together with that of Guise of whose death he had not heard, observes that earthly actions all occur previously 'in th' other life' (v. v), he shows exact knowledge.[1] His brother's ghost has commanded him to execute the justice left unperformed by 'corrupted law' (v.i) and he obeys, though with a maximum of chivalric consideration, insisting on a fair duel. After that, wishing to join his loved Guise, he kills himself. Chapman's choice of such a conclusion is made clearer by Cato's defence of suicide in his *Caesar and Pompey* (c. 1613): the soul does not 'destroy' the body when it 'dislives' it; and in terms of the 'lighter nature' there is reunion with the body no longer 'concrete' but 'fin'd by death and given heavenly heat' (IV. v). The difficulties of commentators may be resolved by reference to the 'etheric' body and dimension of spiritualism. Chapman appears to know all about it.

In Clermont, Chapman attempts to blend Renaissance honour and the Sermon on the Mount to create a superman. As a person he is not wholly convincing and structural artistry suffers, but the discursive action must be accepted for its purpose. The insight is exact: were such a Nietzschean fusion of virtue and virility attained

---

[1] I have heard a spirit communicator assert that what happens on earth happens earlier in the 'etheric' dimension.

it would indeed radiate the powers poetically attributed to Clermont. The thought is working on the frontiers of human destiny. It is strange to think that these weighty dramas in all their tangled profundity were acted by the boy players of Paul's and the Queen's Revels.

II

Chapman has the Elizabethan tang and Jonson is a Protestant moralist. As though in reaction from an islanded and ephemeral confidence, other Jacobean dramatists concentrate on revenge dramas of European tone: the horrors of the European Renaissance have still to be faced. *The Spanish Tragedy* and *Titus Andronicus* had set the type, and the cult became vigorous and proliferating.

Comedies concentrate on intrigues and sharp practice among the middle and low classes of contemporary city life, tragedies on the wickedness of princes with revenges and sensational conclusions. In both, avarice and sexual lust accompany a fall from ancient pieties. A Catholic might call this the price paid for humanistic assertion. As John Marston puts it in *Antonio's Revenge*:

> Still striving to be more than man, he proves
> More than a devil.
>
> (III. ii.)

Religion lost, death is newly horrible: we have tombs, skulls, mouldering bodies and unhappy ghosts.

Lust troubles John Marston's highly sensitive intelligence. In *The Dutch Courtezan* (1605) he asks why sexual instinct, 'nature's highest virtue' (II. i), should be sin and 'the very music of life' become 'so unutterably hellish' (v. i). In *Parasitaster or The Fawn* (1606) the young hero is, like Euripides' Hippolytus, averse from such engagements, and Zuccone wonders why God could have devised 'no other means of procreation and maintaining the world peopled but by women' (IV. i). Women are man's torment, his 'opposite' (IV. i), his own rebelling, Dionysian self. In *Sophonisba* (1606) the lustful Syphax is deluded into satiating his desires on the hideously repellent sorceress and necrophilist Erichtho, whose pleasure it is to find a corpse and 'gnaw the pale and o'ergrown nails from his dry hand' (IV. i). We are spared nothing.

Yet Marston can create likable women provided that they have male attributes such as the witty and forceful Crispinella in *The Dutch Courtezan* or the heroic Sophonisba; and he is correspondingly attuned to the gentler qualities in a man. The bisexual ideal is implicit.

The Malcontent (1604), having as hero a social satirist who steers the plot towards a ritual judgement at a masque and dance, may be to the critical eye his most accomplished work; but the earlier *Antonio and Mellida* and its sequel *Antonio's Revenge* (*c.* 1600) have a greater warmth.

Antonio is at first an idyllic lover, so tenderly conceived that he can readily disguise himself as a woman, and yet on him falls the appalling responsibility of avenging the murder of his father by the tyrant Piero. In an atmosphere of tombs and gloom, but with exquisite and recurring impressions of silvery dawn, Antonio's terrible story unfurls in obedience to his father's ghost: 'Take spirit, gentle boy, revenge my blood!' (*Antonio's Revenge*, III. i). When, though fully conscious of the deed's piteousness, he sacrifices Piero's child to his father's spirit, a groan signifies some mysterious, cosmic suffering. And yet, after tasting blood, Antonio is strangely happy:

> Methinks I am all air and feel no weight
> Of human dirt clog. This is Julio's blood!
> Rich music, father: this is Julio's blood!
>
> (III. v.)

Now he accepts 'deep, deep observing sound-brain'd Machiavel' as his guide (IV. i); crime has forced crime, and as the horrible conclusion approaches he is 'all soul, all heart, all spirit' (V. v). As in *The Malcontent* we have a final ceremonial, here a banquet. Antonio exults in the torture of Piero, who is brought to tears before he dies. Though offered high office in the state, Antonio and his companion Pandulpho decide to retire to a religious order to purge their 'hearts of hatred' (V. vi).

Every psychological truth and relevant emotion of the revenge theme is sounded in this lucid play. Evil in high place forces youthful sweetness beyond inhibition to an only too horrible maturity. Marston's central intuition is of harmony and music within a world of meaningless horrors. He loves and uses music. Mellida is called 'the music of nature' (*Antonio and Mellida*, IV. i); at death 'all the strings of Nature's symphony are crack'd and jar' (*Antonio's Revenge*, IV. v); and yet a body after death may 'hold still a faint perfume of his sweet guest' while the soul bounds free in its new dimension (*Antonio and Mellida*, IV. i). Such refined intuitions are often closer, as is the heroic *Sophonisba*, to the dramatists of the Restoration than to Marston's contemporaries.

If Marston were called 'romantic', Thomas Middleton would be 'realistic'. In comedy he contributes a number of strong character interests from the amusing intrigues of *A Trick to Catch the Old One* (1604–6) to the repellent people and vicious atmosphere of *A Chaste Maid in Cheapside* (*c.* 1611). His efficient and emotionally uninvolved sense of moral corruption reaches intensity in his tragedies.

Hengist King of Kent or The Mayor of Quinborough (*c.* 1619) has a monstrous power-seeker who in disguise rapes his blind-folded wife and next accuses her of an impurity she cannot deny in order to be rid of her. Middleton's more usual targets are women, and his favourite theme is moral collapse, or descent:

> 'Tis her cunning,
> The love of her own lust, which makes a woman
> Gallop down hill as fearless as a drunkard.
>
> (II. iii.)

The Witch (*c.* 1610–16) has two unprincipled women apart from the witches themselves. In the appropriately named *Women Beware Women* (*c.* 1620) a worldly-wise widow, Livia, not only deceives her niece Isabella into enjoying an incestuous relationship with her uncle, Livia's brother, but also assists the Duke of Florence to seduce the happily married Bianca from her worthy middle-class husband Leantio. Led by vanity Bianca disintegrates rapidly, Leantio cynically observing that 'all preferment that springs from sin and lust' grows as easily as crops on 'the rotten'st grounds' (III. ii). These and various other complications are resolved in a final masque with revenges and counter-revenges, poisonings intended and mistaken, and wholesale death. The moral is:

> Sin tastes at the first draught like wormwood-water,
> But drunk again, 'tis nectar ever after.
>
> (II. ii.)

Nevertheless the people are not happy. The verse is lucid, often colloquial, sometimes forceful: innuendo and irony can be brilliant. There is little warmth, except in the cardinal's denunciation.

More exciting is *The Changeling* (1622) written in collaboration with William Rowley, who probably contributed the sub-plot. To avoid an unwelcome marriage the heroine Beatrice employs a detested admirer, De Flores, to murder her husband-to-be. When De

Flores proceeds to blackmail her into accepting his embraces she is morally shocked, but as he points out she is now what the crime has made her—'you are the deed's creature'—and is hardly in a position to talk of modesty (III. iv). De Flores has a semi-satanic fascination:

> Can you weep Fate from its determin'd purpose?
> So soon may you weep me.
>
> (III. iv.)

After marrying her true love, Beatrice, fearing that since she is no maid her relations with De Flores may be discovered, gets a waiting-woman to take her place surreptitiously on the bridal night. Now dawn approaches and the connubial sleep continues. De Flores, never at a loss, starts a fire and dashes about the place with the appropriate gadgets—with one of which he seizes the opportunity of murdering the servant-girl for safety—to everyone's admiration:

> VERMANDERO: That fellow's good on all occasions.
> BEATRICE: A wondrous necessary man, my lord.
>
> (V. i.)

In such ironic twists Middleton is a master. When the truth is revealed De Flores maintains his poise: his reward has been worth everything and he is content. He has purpose, efficiency and a semi-pathetic appeal. He is lit by a gleam from beyond morality and is not all unworthy of his romantic name. The play's action is brisk: it has narrative inevitability and a poignant verse. The psychology of Beatrice is acute, if nearer criminology than tragedy. Only once, in De Flores, does Middleton's sombre artistry touch glamour.

Middleton shared with his contemporaries a concern for state-craft: his *Game at Chess* (1624), devised as an attack on Spanish diplomacy, aroused trouble from the authorities. His early political ideal was the young prince of *The Phoenix* (c. 1604) who in disguise probes the evils of his father's realm and is finally given control of it as a 'miracle' of youthful wisdom (v. i). The name 'Phoenix' is natural, since only in such seraphic persons—the prince is once called a 'pretty whoreson' (II. ii)—can disillusioned Jacobeans like Middleton put any final trust.

We need not question the ascription from 1656 onwards of *The Revenger's Tragedy* (1607), to Cyril Tourneur, author of *The Atheist's Tragedy* (pub. 1611).[1] The pair, together with their dates, harmonize.

---

[1] See the introduction to Allardyce Nicoll's edition of Tourneur's works (p. xi above).

The first ranges from the serious-macabre to sheer burlesque, as though the author were concerned for the issues and dissatisfied with the conventions. Vindice, holding his love's skull, plans vengeance on the Duke whose lust caused her death. This Duke and his second wife have between them four sons, one a bastard, and the family is shown as guilty, variously, of adultery, rape, incest, and murder. They are ready to double-cross each other in pursuance of their atrocities, and miscarriage of intention can be comic, as when two of the brothers aiming at the heir get the wrong brother executed by a slip. When Vindice, who in disguise has murdered the old Duke, is commissioned in his own shape by the heir to murder his other self, he solves the problem by dressing the corpse in his former disguise. When at the concluding banquet and masque four of the villains are unobtrusively stabbed by four of the avengers, only to be next attacked by four more villains who find themselves unexpectedly forestalled, the game becomes riotous. The comedy is not that of *The Jew of Malta* or the fire episode of *The Changeling*; it is more like a deliberate burlesque:

> Is there no thunder left: or is't kept up
> In stock for heavier vengeance? (*Thunder*). There it goes.
>
> (IV. ii.)

The direction for thunder does not appear in the original text, but is clearly intended. Vindice's telling asides often expect laughs; so does the pretty remark of the bastard Spurio 'Old dad dead?' (v. i). The central murder has a more serious, macabre comedy. Vindice brings what he facetiously calls 'the bony lady', that is the skull, dressed up and with poisoned lips. This he pretends to the Duke to be a country girl for his lust, saying:

> Faith! my lord, a country lady, a little bashful at first, as most of them are; but after the first kiss, my lord, the worst is past with them. Your grace knows now what you have to do; she has somewhat a grave look with her—but—— (III. v.)

The Duke is next pinioned, his tongue pinned by a dagger and his agony increased by his having to die watching his wife in the seductive embraces of Spurio.

There are the usual attacks on lust and corruption, including the testing and fall of Vindice's mother Gratiana; there is genuine force in the will 'to blast this villainous dukedom vexed with sin' (v. ii); there are stabs, and some passages, of as caustic and man-blasting a poetry as we could wish. But the people, who all have label names, are as people less real than the 'bony lady'; Vindice is less a man than a personification of the revenge theme; and the comedy increases as the action develops. The play reads as a burlesque of the revenge theme; and that may be why Vindice is finally condemned.[1]

The Atheist's Tragedy follows naturally. It contains speculation on the causes of modern wickedness; a farcical treatment of conventional horrors; a serious inquiry into the nature of psychic phenomena; and a stoical-Christian opposition to revenge. Tourneur is trying to get things straightened out.

D'Amville's villainy proceeds from avarice supported by a philosophy of egocentric and atheistic materialism. His thinking is eminently logical. Having successfully arranged the murder of his brother, Baron Montferrers, he philosophizes insincerely on the mysteries of unfeeling nature, crime, death, and the victim's goodness, and then recapitulates to his accomplice each step of the 'sweet comedy' just concluded (II. iv). There is some excellent normal comedy: the promiscuous Levidulcia's playing off of two surreptitious visitors against each other in order to blind her husband as to the significance of both, is brilliant farce (II. v). But farce also invades the supposedly serious plot. The vastly amusing chaplain Languebeau Snuffe forgets himself so far as to take an attractive girl for amatory purposes to the graveyard, disguising himself for safety as Montferrers' ghost, but seeing Montferrers' son Charlemont, whose death had been reported, they fly terror-struck, dropping the disguise which Charlemont promptly assumes himself; then Charlemont retreats into the charnel house where his father had been buried and from which he emerges to terrify D'Amville who is trying to rape Charlemont's love, Castabella (IV. iii). The jack-in-the-box dodging in and out of the tomb, the sharp juxtaposition of the amorous encounters with a false-bearded ghost, the fun of Languebeau Snuffe's puritanical phrases and the philosophical D'Amville's subsequent soliloquy arguing with typical logic that a really efficient ghost should have waited for him to commit the new crime to increase his guilt, all constitute a comic deflating of conventional horrors. Death is opposed by sex comedy as in the conclusion to Byron's *Don Juan*. There is also a deflating of lust nausea, both in the worldly-wise acceptance of sexual instincts by Levidulcia and in that

---

[1] Professor A. G. H. Bachrach of the University of Leyden tells me that the Dutch version of *The Revenger's Tragedy*, which dates back to the travelling companies of Jacobean times, is in the nature of a burlesque.

forecast of Sheridan's Charles Surface, the attractive, warm-hearted, generous yet licentious, young Sebastian.

D'Amville himself begins to recognize that his loved 'nature', or materialism, is making him comic:

> Now to myself I am ridiculous.
> Nature, thou art a traitor to my soul,
> Thou hast abused my trust. I will complain
> To a superior Court to right my wrong.
>
> (v. i.)

He is a bundle of false premises and ludicrously logical conclusions. Having got the blameless Charlemont on trial for killing a man sent to murder him, he complains fussily to the court of the cosmic injustice by which his murders

> Of one, or two, or three at most; and those
> Put quickly out o' pain too, mark me . . .
>
> (v. ii.)

have proved useless, since his sons, for whose advantage he was working, have died. Being allowed to wield the axe for Charlemont's execution, he brains himself by mistake! Before dying he admits that 'nature' is a 'fool'. Rationalism has proved comically suicidal.

Interwoven with these amusing variations on the dramatic convention is another deeply serious reversal centring on Charlemont. While he is on active service his father's ghost appears telling of his murder and charging his son to

> Attend with patience the success of things;
> But leave revenge unto the King of kings.
>
> (II. vi.)

Charlemont analyses his experience: are such phenomena dreams? Is it his own 'genius', what we should call the 'subconscious mind'? Or his recent initiation into war? The analytic emphasis recalls Chapman's. The ghost reappears; a soldier shoots; it remains. It appears again later to keep Charlemont on the straight path of non-resistance, and also to D'Amville, saying: 'D'Amville, with all thy wisdom, th'art a fool' (v. i). Charlemont is baffled but maintains a Christian stoicism resembling that of Chapman's Clermont.

In *The Atheist's Tragedy* Tourneur simultaneously attacks the egotistic bases of avarice and murder, makes terms with sexual instinct, burlesques conventional horrors and shows us a convincing spirit messenger counselling non-resistance. Such are his dramatic answers to the problems posed by the earlier play.

Many of the constituent elements of Tourneur's two plays are
found in John Webster's *The White Devil* (1611–12) and *The Duchess
of Malfi* (*c*. 1614), though the effects are different. Seriousness is not
relaxed and irony strong and never comic. No contemporary dramatist except Shakespeare has left work so solidly based. Our world is
grim, but it is lit and mastered. Within it move villains of complex
fascination and heroines of indomitable courage.

In *The White Devil* Vittoria, wife of Camillo, commits adultery
with the Duke of Brachiano, who with the help of her brother
Flamineo has Camillo and his own wife Isabella murdered, thereby
bringing on Vittoria the wrath of Camillo's uncle, Cardinal Monticelso, and of Isabella's brother Francisco. Vittoria is brought to
trial while the chief criminals escape. Narrative links are not all
clear, since Webster's people, by an extension of the normal dramatic
tendency, are motivated less by surface events than from their
inmost being. Their motives are dramatically rather than logically
convincing. This is not always a weakness; sometimes they are the
more alive for it.

Flamineo, the agent of villainy, is by turns ironic, satirical, witty,
and troubled: he knows exactly what he is doing and the wickedness
of the society in which for his own advancement he does it. At the trial
he comments: 'Proof! 'twas corruption. O gold, what a god art thou!'
He is at once implement and chorus: religion is 'commedled with
policy', and indeed 'the first bloodshed in the world happened about
religion' (III. iii). The perpetrator of villainy is its most caustic critic:
he is a criminal moralizer. Entangled in good-evil he knows that
'best natures do commit the grossest faults' (IV. ii). His appalling
honesty makes him reluctant to claim what virtue he possesses:

> I have a strange thing in me, to the which
> I cannot give a name, without it be
> Compassion.
>
> (V. iv.)

Once, during a pretence of dying he indulges in a guilt-stricken,
serio-comic self-dramatization: the way is 'dark and horrid'; he
smells 'soot'—how homely-strong the impressions—and a scalding
agony is in his 'guts' (V. vi). When he is faced by actual death his
poise is maintained:

> GASPARO: Recommend your self to Heaven.
> FLAMINEO: No, I will carry mine own commendations thither.
>
> (V. vi.)

Moral condemnation is inept; looking to Heaven we only 'confound knowledge with knowledge'. Even so he knows that his life has been 'a black charnel'. Flamineo is well named: nurtured in a wicked society, he accepts his precarious place in it, but his personality flames.

Vittoria has vivacity, her husband is cold. The degree of her guilt is left vague. Though an adulteress and suspected murderess, she has intellect, conscience, and religion. At the trial her answers to the Cardinal are pointed and laconic:

> O poor charity!
> Thou art seldom found in scarlet.
> (III. ii.)

If guilty she would scorn to plead for life, but her faults have been only 'beauty', 'gay clothes' and a 'merry heart'. There is some truth in it. When condemned to a 'house of convertites' or 'penitent whores', she meets shame with scorn:

VITTORIA: O woman's poor revenge,
                 Which dwells but in the tongue! I will not weep;
                 No, I do scorn to call up one poor tear
                 To fawn on your injustice; bear me hence
                 Unto this house of—what's your mitigating title?
MONTICELSO: Of convertites.
VITTORIA: It shall not be a house of convertites;
            My mind shall make it honester to me
            Than the Pope's palace.   (III. ii.)

Her personality dwarfs her accusers and her cry that they have 'ravished justice' rings true, since the main criminals are passed over. With Brachiano's help she later gains her freedom and marries him, and after his death is rich; but religion now dominates her mind. When death comes she sees it as payment for sin. The conflict of sexual instinct and conventional morality has done its worst; as Flamineo says, 'Many glorious women' famed 'for masculine virtue' have been 'vicious' (v. vi); and anyway our central value here is not morality, but courage. She leaves us with the haunting:

> My soul, like to a ship in a black storm,
> Is driven I know not whither.
> (v. vi.)

Nor, if we have followed her course correctly, do we.

We watch people driven on by unruly and irrepressible energies; by sexual instinct, by scramble for advance, and by the temptations of high place. Thoughts on princes and the great abound: 'great men' work well with 'knaves', each breast containing 'three thousand' furies (IV. ii, iii). It is a world of violence, where 'horror' attends the fate of 'princes' (V. iii). Those who unleash war are responsible for its murders and lusts (IV. i). Instead of the age-old balance or conflict, we have a newly dangerous collaboration of Church and State neatly symbolized by the worldly Cardinal's ceremonial advancement to the Popedom (IV. iii). Divinity starts wars (IV. i). Worldly policy cohabits with an infected religion in a society where a man can take the Sacrament to bind him to an 'intended murder' (IV. iii). Among these grinding yet all-too-human energies the desires of a Vittoria are crushed and the brilliance of a Flamineo perverted. Only the young are unsullied: the 'noble youth' (V. ii) Marcello and the pathetic little Giovanni asking whether the dead 'hear music, go a-hunting and be merry as we that live' (III. ii).

Events are imaginatively, even fantastically, conceived. Brachiano is shown by a magical apparatus the murders being perpetrated for him; Cornelia enters in a fantastic madness like Ophelia's; Brachiano dies at the hands of avengers disguised as monks who reveal themselves gloatingly during their supposed prayers. Brachiano's wife, Isabella, returns as a ghost, and Brachiano's ghost visits Flamineo, whose ability to make the most of every occasion gives us:

> Pray, sir, resolve me, what religion's best
> For a man to die in?
>
> (V. iv.)

That the ghost preserves silence whilst simply showing a skull is typical. Webster's best effects are non-committal: thought is a subtle juggler and such appearances may have natural causes (IV. i). The poetry unites appalling power with an uncanny reserve; it is simultaneously both extravagant and condensed, flaming yet homely. We are aware of force compressed. Each person is a charged fire-piece: we admire them not morally but as we admire fire and detonation. The avenging Lodovico, proud of his murders, flings out: 'I limn'd this night-piece and it was my best' (V. vi). Horrors fertilize excellence, as in Flamineo's unforgettable because elucidatory line: 'A dead man's skull beneath the roots of flowers' (V. iv). The plot is untidy, and the strands intertwist confusingly, yet nowhere in our drama is the native force and pride of the human essence more compellingly presented.

The Duchess of Malfi is less energic. Good and bad people are more firmly divided, but the good are passive and the bad move cumbrously in pursuit of their dark purposes. Weight replaces fire; or rather wickedness smoulders and erupts. Philosophic gloom pervades, with an atmospheric toning that covers the territories of both *Macbeth* and *King Lear*. Atmosphere takes precedence over, almost clogs, the action.

The story is simple. The Cardinal and his brother, Duke Ferdinand, proud in their Castilian blood, oppose any thought of second marriage for their widowed sister, the Duchess, and when it is known that she has married her steward, Antonio, Ferdinand's wrath leads him to torment and murder her. As before, warm feminine instinct is thwarted against a background of statesmanship and religion in corrupt alliance. Ancient pieties have gone and princes' sculptures are nowadays shown looking earthwards instead of heavenwards (IV. ii). A dumb-show ritual (III. iv) in which the Cardinal exchanges his ecclesiastical insignia for the accoutrements of war symbolizes—as does too the 'fortification' made from a ruined abbey in the 'echo' scene (V. iii)—an important, Renaissance, transition. The use of music does not detract from the meaning, since music here accompanies the macabre: despite our horrors the prevailing tone is harmonious.

The Cardinal, a 'melancholy churchman' who missed the Popedom by a too impudent use of bribery (I. i), is a background figure of generalized significance until in the fifth act he is shown tormented by his crimes, meditating on Hell and seeing in his fish-pond 'a thing armed with a rake' (V. v). His death is ironic: having arranged with his guards not to be disturbed while he disposes of a corpse, he enjoys seclusion while he becomes one. Ferdinand is less sedate and more irascible. He has his brother's Spanish gloom, together with his own 'turbulent nature' (I. i). He shows a pathological distaste for gaiety and laughter: imagining the Duchess laughing he comments 'excellent hyena' (II. v); if ever he laughs himself it is 'like a deadly cannon that lightens ere it smokes' (III. iii). The Duchess's normal enjoyment of living sickens him. He can hitch religion to his anti-sexual disgusts, doubting if his sister's 'brats' have been 'christened' (III. iii). He has her imprisoned, mentally tormented, and murdered, and afterwards suffers revulsion and goes mad: 'I'll go hunt the badger by owl-light' (IV. ii). He digs up graves with his hands in his madness. He dies with a typically Websterian fling, saying that he will 'vault credit and affect high pleasures beyond death'. The suggestion of an incestuous love as his motive receives support from

his last cry: 'My sister, Oh, my sister, there's the cause on't' (v. v).
The brothers are adequately covered by Bosola's:

> You have a pair of hearts are hollow graves
> Rotten and rotting others.
>
> (IV. ii.)

Their religious antagonism to spontaneous love-joys forecasts
similar themes in twentieth-century drama, such as Sean O'Casey's.
Webster is often ahead of his age.

Bosola replaces Flamineo. Formerly a soldier and recently a galley
prisoner, he is brave but embittered, and allows himself to become
Ferdinand's implement. He is a 'speculative' man (III. iii), deeply
aware of human wickedness; man's form repels him. However he
recognizes the virtue he betrays with a curiously ambiguous appreciation. He torments the Duchess with a vivisectional curiosity,
testing her courage and religion. He can speak as a Manichean
moralist, disguising himself as the 'bell-man' sent to condemned
persons, seeing man's body as 'a box of worm-seed' (IV. ii) and
chanting:

> Of what is't fools make such vain keeping?
> Sin their conception, their birth weeping . . .
>
> (IV. ii.)

After the murder he probes Ferdinand's conscience, insisting on the
deed's wickedness. He himself repents and tries to save Antonio,
though he kills him, through another play of irony, in error. We are to
believe fundamentally in his better 'nature' (v. v.).

Antonio is of a stoic, philosophic turn. He has human insight,
caution, and integrity; he is a norm of sane judgement, agnostic and
wise. Ambition he despises. Though he can show religious belief, he
is once said to be an unbeliever who accounts religion as 'but a
school-name' (v. ii). Both he and the Duchess tend to think things out
on first principles for themselves; as dramatic types they might be said
to belong to a later century. We can call their thinking 'advanced'.

The Duchess is a bravely independent lady of grace and charm.
Like a Shavian heroine she woos and gets her man. Her marriage
compact, though first informal, she considers, in twentieth-century
manner, to be as firm as anything the Church could build, something
which it may 'echo' but not originate (I. i). The trust is in human
instinct, the instincts so flamingly revealed in *The White Devil*, as
opposed to all externals. She believes in happiness: why should her
'youth' and 'beauty' be 'cased up like a holy relic'? (III. ii). Natural

desires are contrasted with cold religion. As tragedy closes on her she becomes less a person than a tragic voice, supreme in all the dignities of grief. She and Antonio part:

> Your kiss is colder
> Than that I have seen an holy anchorite
> Give to a dead man's skull.
>
> (III. v.)

The quiet words are typical of our hushed poetry, its muffled music reverent before suffering. Imprisoned, she muses in silence. She is shown the supposedly dead bodies of Antonio and her children:

> I'll tell thee a miracle.
> I am not mad yet to my cause of sorrow:
> Th' heaven o'er my head seems made of molten brass,
> The earth of flaming sulphur, yet I am not mad.
>
> (IV. ii.)

In death she is brave:

> Pull, and pull strongly, for your able strength
> Must pull down Heaven upon me.
>
> (IV. ii.)

Her poetry may be too male, as that of Shakespeare's women never is: Webster's heroines are conceived as women of tragic prerogative and strength. But the Duchess is feminine too: before dying, she remembers the medicine for her little boy's cold (IV. ii). She and her children assert domestic innocence against the dark powers that crush them.

No easy solutions are offered. The dance of madmen sent to torment the Duchess (IV. ii) with their 'dismal' music and the attendant satire on middle-class professions—doctor, lawyer, priest, astrologer, tailor, farmer—suggests less a bad than an insane society, grading naturally into our sense of physical corruption in this 'pit of darkness' (v. v.). Death is dramatized in the cold hand and show of corpses offered to the Duchess; and beyond death is mystery, perhaps Hell, perhaps 'not-being' (IV. ii). We are 'the stars' tennis balls' (v. iv). Religious phrases are mostly ominous and superstitious forebodings abound. Yet the superstitions are half-realities only and medieval religion is decaying, like the abbey ruins of the echo scene, now a fortification:

> I do love these ancient ruins.
> We never tread upon them, but we set
> Our foot upon some reverend history . . .
>
> (v. iii.)

Antonio recalls the good men who gave their lives to the Church, and now its ruins only throw back as from a mouldering past the visitor's own unhappiest thoughts: 'like death that we have', 'thou art a dead thing' and so on. Is all evil but an echo of ourselves? Some wraithly unreality? Do Webster's horrors, depending so consistently on the superstitious, on the traditional fear and the irrational response, contain their own contradiction? Never were all the ingrained fears of Jacobean drama so thickly clustered, yet never constituent to a deeper harmony. Sounds accompany the action: the music for the Cardinal's ritual; the 'dismal' music of the madmen; the bellman's bell and dirge; and the marvellous echo. Worst evil is, as near as may be, aesthetically mastered, though it is done mainly by almost too weighty, too overloading, a poetry and not, as in *The White Devil* and in Shakespeare, by the people also acting in full energic collaboration; so that we are sometimes more aware of the extension of suffering into the poetic dimension than of the suffering itself. On a more rational level there is hope:

> O that it were possible we might
> But hold some two days' conference with the dead.
> From them I should learn somewhat, I am sure,
> I never shall know here.
>
> (IV. ii.)

To that Beddoes will have his answer. For the rest, we may wrench Bosola's famous words from their ironic context: 'Look you, the stars shine still' (IV. i).

The Devil's Law-Case (pub. 1623) has another strong heroine who defies convention. Two incidents are especially remarkable. By a neat stroke of Websterian irony an avenger in stabbing his sick and dying enemy performs the needed operation which his doctors had refused to risk, and saves him. The other occurs at a trial: the heroine tries to disinherit her son by falsely confessing that he is the issue of her adultery with a long-lost friend, who unfortunately for her turns out to be the judge.

Webster's imaginative extensions, however fantastic, work strictly, in both poetic reference and human delineation, from the normal, the earthly; he has no 'bisexual' persons; innocence is defined by ordinary children. But John Ford's *The Lover's Melancholy* (1628) shows a vivid apprehension of bisexual grace in the disguised girl Parthenophil, who appears as a youth of an 'excellence' beyond earthly 'creation' (I. i). Faith in human excellence runs as an elixir through his dramas. *Perkin Warbeck* (pub. 1634) significantly chooses to emphasize the pretender's innate royalty and admirable courage. This trust beats as a heart within his dark and militant tragedies, in which the reconciliations artistically established by Webster are rationalized and the case for instinct against convention reappears in greater force to stamp man's amatory desires, however questionable, with authority.

The desires of *'Tis Pity She's a Whore* (pub. 1633) are incestuous. Our sympathy for the loves of Giovanni and his sister Annabella is implanted from the moment when after confessing their feelings they kneel to each other and kiss, the stage impact of this *natural* marriage, recalling *The Duchess of Malfi*, saying more than words. Giovanni has, like Romeo, a friar for confidant and confessor, whose disapproval he meets with reminders of his teaching on the correspondence of the aesthetic and the moral. The Friar's case is weak. This is the best he can do:

> Indeed, if we were sure there were no Deity
> Nor Heaven nor Hell, then to be led alone
> By Nature's light—as were philosophers
> Of elder times—might instance some defence.
> But 'tis not so: then, madman, thou wilt find
> That Nature is in Heaven's positions blind.
>
> (II. v.)

The conclusion is trite; reason and the new learning supports Giovanni, but religion comes in with its fiat. The Friar is half on Giovanni's side:

> I know the baits of sin
> Are hard to leave; O, 'tis a death to do't.
>
> (III. vi.)

On the Friar's advice Giovanni's sister has for safety married Soranzo, and when her husband discovers the truth Anabella faces his fury with a passionate assertion of her devotion to her 'angel-like' brother: 'I dare thee to the worst—strike and strike home' (IV. iii). Though she subsequently repents, Giovanni pursues his course, still dwelling on the glory of 'united hearts' (v. iii), and when warned by the Friar—who is aware of the traditions of the revenge play—not to accept an invitation to Soranzo's birthday feast, answers:

> Not go! Stood Death
> Threatening his armies of confounding plagues,
> With hosts of dangers hot as blazing stars,
> I would be there: not go! Yes, and resolve
> To strike as deep in slaughter as they all;
> For I will go. (v. iii.)

He would 'be all a man' and assert his freedom from 'the curse of old prescription', or conventional morality. He parts with Annabella: they talk of their reunion in another life; he calls 'the spirits of the air' to bear record of his devotion. Now she, who is to 'fill a throne of innocence and sanctity in Heaven', must pray (v. v). She understands; he stabs her and joins the feast with her heart on his dagger, avenging himself and his sister on Soranzo before his own death.

Language and emotion tilt our sympathies in the lovers' favour. Giovanni admits that 'the laws of conscience and of civil use' may justly condemn their loves, but those who understand must sympathize (v. v.) The more normal opposition of instinct and society in Webster is expanded to a more challenging problem; the kind of sympathy so often *felt* in tragedy for some normally to be repudiated action is here both forced and formulated. Apart from certain subsidiary complications and ineffectual and irrelevant comedy, the main story moves swift and sure. The level poetry with its choice and lucid diction, without overtones and only blazing under pressure, is a perfect medium for this conscious and purposeful drama.

Love's Sacrifice (pub. 1633) presents a rather similar conflict turning on the cult of 'Platonic' love that was being encouraged at court by Queen Henrietta Maria. The middle-aged Duke Caraffa loves with equal passions his favourite, Fernando, and his wife, Bianca. Now the young pair fall in love, and though they preserve a 'Platonic' relationship the Iago-like D'Avolos, in scenes not unworthily reminiscent of *Othello*, raises the Duke's suspicions and wrath. Bianca's behaviour under accusation is the reverse of Desdemona's, showing a feminine defiance worthy of Webster's Vittoria. To Fernando she is outspoken:

> Why shouldst thou not be mine? Why should the laws,
> The iron laws of ceremony, bar
> Mutual embraces? What's a vow? A vow?
> Can there be sin in unity?
>
> (v. i.)

When after discovering them most compromisingly together the Duke again charges his wife, the interchanges are magnificent, she again on the attack, comparing him to his disadvantage with that 'miracle composed of flesh and blood', Fernando, to whom, she says, her response has been as natural as was the Duke's love of herself: the emphasis is again on the rights of natural instinct. The courage of her abandon is staggering and makes his murder of her appear inevitable (v. i). But changes come swift: the Duke is soon convinced of her innocence, for 'lawless courtship' (v. ii) is here allowable if it remains platonic; and he suffers agonies of remorse. At Bianca's funeral, done in high ceremonial with music and monks in procession, the Duke kneels. The sudden appearance of Fernando from the tomb symbolizes his right to Bianca in death; he takes poison and the Duke remembers his 'unmatched' friend (v. iii).

The uncompromising yet dramatically well-balanced emphasis on love's integrity in opposition to social law is strikingly modern. The new acceptance is supported by a noble ceremonial elevating our revenge themes and tomb horrors to a more serene plane. This happens again in *The Broken Heart* (pub. 1633).

The scene is Sparta. Orgilus is embittered because his loved Penthea has been made by her ambitious brother Ithocles to marry a peculiarly irritating nobleman, Bassanes. He sees this marriage of convenience, with a valuation pointing ahead to such modern sex dramas as those of Somerset Maugham, as no better than a 'rape'. Penthea knows herself 'a ravished wife widowed by lawless marriage' (III. iv; IV. ii). Ithocles himself regrets his conventional action, and is near despair when she calls herself a 'whore' living in 'adultery' (III. ii). He realizes his fault the better in that he now loves the King's daughter, Calantha. Meanwhile Orgilus, who pretends to have forgiven him, is arranging some revels to celebrate the marriage of his sister to Ithocles' friend. Penthea has just died. Before the revels he flatters Ithocles as his future sovereign. 'Take that chair', he says, and 'Sit there, my lord' (IV. iv). He sits; the chair closes on him, and Orgilus lets fly the stored furies of his anger. Ithocles' noble calm raises in Orgilus a chivalrous response and the assurance that he himself means to die too. There is mutual forgiveness and an interchange of respect. Revenge can be barbaric as in Marston or forbidden as in Tourneur, and here we have a third course: the act of judgement accompanied by courtesy and forgiveness. Thinking of Ithocles and the dead Penthea together, Orgilus murmurs: 'Sweet twins, shine stars for ever' (IV. iv).

This stately drama has also a new variation on the traditional revels scene. During a dance (v. ii), Calantha, after the first movement, hears of the King her father's death; after the second, of Penthea's; and after the third, from Orgilus himself, of her lover's murder. Each time she preserves her calm, merely calling for new, and finally brighter, music. Tragedy is being suffused with a strange serenity. Calantha is conceived as a princess of almost superhuman control.

Orgilus is quietly condemned without rancour and allowed to die as he chooses. In a final ritual (v. iii) the dead Ithocles, robed and crowned, is met by the crowned Calantha and her retinue of maidens, all in white, before an altar. They kneel to 'soft music', and with a ring she marries him. Hers is the 'broken heart' of the title. Ford's interest in the tragedy of blood is one with his acute sense of the heart's blood-feeling, rich but desecrated. Calantha carefully orders her realm and establishes her successor, and then follows her lover. Our interest in Calantha may not seem to have had adequate preparation, but after the violences of his predecessors Ford's stately heroine serves to crown our horror sequence with a welcome dignity. He lays heavy stress on feminine rights; on the softer yet invincible emotions of men, on the desecrated loves of women, and on the rights of both against convention. There can be no simple solutions:

> Mortality
> Creeps on the dung of earth, and cannot reach
> The riddles which are purpos'd by the gods.
>
> (I. iii.)

Webster is his predecessor and there is to be nothing quite like it again until our century.

III

We have noted some important tendencies of Jacobean drama: much has been omitted. Dramas ranged from realism and intrigue to fantasy and masque, and from gloom to gaiety. They are not all so fiercely coloured as those we have discussed. Thomas Heywood's *A Woman killed with Kindness* (1602) treats of marital jealousy in a middle-class setting with Christian good sense. Thomas Dekker maintains a simple and healthy, if rather external, approach to his various people and events. *The Honest Whore* (1604) covers prostitution and a mad-house sensibly presented and contains a lovely speech on patience of that Chaucerian or Tolstoyan type of literary simplicity that is always in danger of making our greater dramas appear neurotic:

> The best of men
> That e'er wore earth about him, was a sufferer,
> A soft, meek, patient, humble, tranquil spirit,
> The first true gentleman that ever breathed.
>
> (v. ii.)

Dekker's 'bisexual' ideal is characteristically found in the good-hearted Moll of *The Roaring Girl*, whose conception was probably his, though both he and Middleton were given as joint authors (1611). She rampages in male dress among high and low, setting complications right for everyone, as a saint of the underworld. Dekker's range is wide: *The Witch of Edmonton* (1621), written in collaboration with Ford and Rowley, blends human sympathy with demonology and crime. He was probably happiest in good humour, such as that of the rollicking *The Shoemaker's Holiday* (1600), a lively comedy about city apprentices and their irrepressible master Simon Eyre who, like George-a-Greene and Bottom, remains unabashed before royalty. This, with Beaumont and Fletcher's *The Knight of the Burning Pestle* (*c.* 1607), in which a London apprentice comically invades and dominates a stage burlesque of fantastic heroism and romance, are living reminders that beneath the surface of great poetry and its stock-in-trade of dukedoms and duplicity lay a city, despite Jonson and Middleton, of good humour and sound sense.

IV

And yet it would be wrong to regard kingship itself as a less realistic concern than middle or low class city life. The new Stuart monarchy raised many problems of divine right and state authority, of which dramatic records survive in the work of Francis Beaumont, John Fletcher and Philip Massinger.

Beaumont was the author of an interesting poem based on Ovid, *Salmacis and Hermaphroditus* (1602), in which the nymph Salmacis woos the beautiful Hermaphroditus, son—as the name implies—of Learning and Love, who rejects her advances. The gods turn them into a single person:

> Nor man nor maid now could they be esteem'd,
> Neither and either might they well be deem'd.

Henceforth all who bathe in the waters where the miracle occurred will enjoy a similarly bisexual state. Beaumont's collaboration with Fletcher grew from a close friendship and has left us three vivid royalistic dramas: *Philaster* (*c.* 1610), *The Maid's Tragedy* (1611), and *A King and No King* (1611). These are aristocratic and heroic, showing strong themes of love and friendship and a fine command of dramatic situation. The swift passage from climax to climax, the especially narrative urgency and appeal, may be in danger of substituting excitement for profundity, yet they all revolve on the important centre of kingship.

Philaster has a straggling story with a tyrannical usurper and a good if erratic hero-prince going rather too slickly through the paces of Hamlet, Orlando and Othello. There are pastoral adventures and a pathe'tic heroine becoming in disguise not merely 'the loving'st and the gentlest boy that ever master kept' but also a 'Hylas' and 'Adonis' of 'angel-like' form (I. i; II. i); and there is a revolution before the happy ending. The too rapid developments preclude a deep engagement, but kingship strikes a spark:

> KING: What! Am I not your King?
>   If 'ay', then am I not to be obeyed?
> DION: Yes, if you command things possible and honest.
> KING: Things possible and honest! Hear me, thou,
>   Thou traitor, that darest confine thy King to things
>   Possible and honest. . . .
>
> (IV. i.)

No one could improve on that: fortunately, the King learns better. Of more solid workmanship is *The Maid's Tragedy*, turning on the question as to what are the limits of loyalty to a tyrannical and licentious king. Intense situations, dialogues of masterly construction and a cunning use of delayed statement, expectation and suspense, all draw every possible advantage from this fiery centre. The hero, Amintor, forced to desert his love, Aspatia, who follows him in boy's disguise, is distracted. Though he calls the King to his face a 'tyrant', he yet recognizes his 'divinity': 'As you are my King I fall before you' (III). Eventually another wronged lady, Evadne, obeys the charge laid on her by Melantius, her own brother and Amintor's friend—the most powerful positive value here is friendship—to execute vengeance on 'this hated King' (IV). In *A King and No King*, our agonized hero and questionable king are the same person. Starting as a victor whose absurd boasting is openly criticized by the loyal but outspoken Mardonius, he is gradually made to realize that love is a greater power than high place, and is brought by a number of ironic twists in plot manipulation to the point where he is in ecstasies of joy to discover that he is no king after all and that the lady he has mistakenly thought to be his sister is the true sovereign, whom he can safely marry.

These three dramatic essays in royalistic criticism make a link between the royalism of Shakespeare and the coming revolution: they sound the dangers of personal monarchy.

Of the plays attributed to Fletcher alone, *Valentinian* (1613–14) has a story resembling that of *The Maid's Tragedy*. After a severe self-conflict, for nothing is more sacred in Fletcher's world view than friendship, Maximus sacrifices his friend Aecius in the course of his avenger's duty. Scene rises on scene in the usual series of compelling duologues, and there is a sensitive exposition of Roman nobility, though some strength has been lost by Beaumont's death. Fletcher's natural verse is limpid, with weak endings and falling rhythms, and he is fond of the dissolving emotion. *Bonduca* (1613) is a finely tempered heroic drama on the conflict between Rome and Britain, but it is from the general Caratach and his little nephew Hengo, close relation to Webster's Giovanni, that Fletcher draws his most original music. They are refugees, in hardship and hunger, firm in mutual devotion:

> HENGO: I know, uncle,
> We must all die; my little brother died,
> I saw him die, and he died smiling; sure
> There's no great pain in't, uncle. But, pray, tell me,
> Whither must we go when we are dead?
>
>   (IV. ii.)

Caratach assures him that it is 'the blessed'st place'. 'No Romans, uncle?' No one who lives by 'violence' and 'oppression', says Caratach. When near death the little boy hears a mysterious 'noise of bells' (v. iii). He dies bravely. Some of this may be too long drawn out, risking sentimentality, and yet the best moments hold an exquisite pathos.

He wrote other dramas. *The Faithful Shepherdess* (1608–9) is an elaborate exercise in symbolic pastoral. Like his contemporaries, he could move easily from extreme to extreme. In his comedies, of which *The Wild Goose Chase* (c. 1621) is perhaps the best, we meet outspoken women and irrepressible men in lively sex battle, together with an extravagant play of sexual disguise. His aristocratic tone, wit, and occasional licentiousness in comedy, together with his heroic valuations and delicate perceptions in tragedy, forecast the dramatists of the Restoration.

Philip Massinger's dramas are notable for their firm and severe handling of sociology, statesmanship, and religion. He succeeds in making living drama from weightiest themes, striking a happy balance of statecraft and stagecraft. In *The Virgin Martyr* (c. 1620).

written in collaboration with Dekker, religion is set against state. The Emperor Diocletian offers a firm defence of Roman imperialism and treats the vanquished with a fine clemency, but the Christian Dorothea suffers martyrdom under the persecutions of the cruelly conscientious Theophilus. Theophilus is, however, brought to realize his error, being shown a vision of Paradise by the heroine's mysterious page Angelo, a 'delicate' and 'young lad' upon whose eyes 'dance' a thousand 'blessings':

> It is, it is, some angel! Vanished again!
> Oh, come back, ravishing boy! Bright messenger!
> Thou hast, by these mine eyes fix'd on thy beauty,
> Illumined all my soul.
>
> (v. i.)

Angelo is no page but a real angel who has been manifesting as a boy. This identification of page and angel serves to point the meanings of seraphic equivalents elsewhere. Nor have we any better description of their spiritual effect on the beholder.

Massinger's dramatic thought is peculiarly honest. In *The False One* (after 1618), a work on Caesar and Cleopatra done in collaboration with Fletcher and for which Massinger seems to be mainly responsible, we are aware simultaneously of both the wickedness and the provisional justification of authoritative rule. State necessity crushes fine feelings and treachery is appalling. Caesar himself is great, ambitious, a blazing force in war and a scorner of underhand methods, whatever the dangers, though his record is far from stainless:

> Why does this conquering Caesar
> Labour through the world's deep seas of toils and troubles,
> Dangers and desperate hopes? To repent afterwards?
> Why does he slaughter thousands in a battle,
> And whip his country with the sword? To cry for't?
>
> (iv. iii.)

He has successfully broken his own country's laws. Why should not others do likewise? (v. ii). Such are the questions insistently raised. Massinger is quite fearless. Despite the contemporary fears of Spanish Catholicism written into Dekker's *The Whore of Babylon* (*c*. 1606) and Middleton's *A Game at Chess* (1624), he allows a Jesuit priest a sympathetic and controlling part in *The Renegado* (1624). But in *Believe as You List* (1631) his implied attack on Spain was so forthright that he was made by the authorities to mask it in terms of ancient history: from which we can see how easily a supposedly historic drama may contain contemporary meanings. Here

Rome's luxury and power are contrasted with the labour of the
subject nations on which her empire is built (I. ii); and though the
worldly wise Flaminius stills his conscience by thought of his duty to
Rome and the 'necessity of state' (II. i), our sympathies are with the
suffering prince Antiochus who is finally rescued from 'this devil's
paws' (v. ii) by the enlightened Marcellus who, despite Flaminius'
reiterated insistence that all fine feelings should be crushed in service
to state and empire (IV. iv; v. i), knows better. In this period all
dramatic tyrants must have seemed like warnings to the monarchy:
against a passage on taxation in the lost play *The King and The
Subject* Charles I wrote: 'This is too insolent and to be changed'.[1]
In *The Bondman* (1623) a rising of slaves is the occasion for a powerful plea:

> Equal Nature fashion'd us
> All in one mould: the bear serves not the bear,
> Nor the wolf the wolf. 'Twas odds of strength in tyrants
> That pluck'd the first link from the golden chain
> With which that Thing of Things bound in the world.
>
>   (II. iii.)

Cleora, a lady of high status, accepts the love of Pisander, disguised
as a slave. Here, as again in *The Great Duke of Florence* (1627),
Massinger's advanced sociology takes pleasure, as did Webster, in
dramatizing an unconventional alliance.

Massinger resembles John Galsworthy in his sense of balance: he
is never unfair, always judicial. The wicked emperor of *The Roman
Actor* (1626) behaves courteously to the hero-actor whom he condemns. Good sense abounds: in *The Duke of Milan* (pub. 1623)
Duke Sforza in a noble scene argues in such sound terms with the
victorious emperor for leniency and alliance in place of rape and
bloodshed, that he gains his point and keeps his crown. Women are
interesting, and may be strong. The narrative complications of *The
Maid of Honour* (pub. 1632) express numerous cross-currents in
valuation, which include the contrast of an enlightened and pacific
monarch, who yet at one point descends to trickery for state reasons,
with a virile heroism; conquest blended with clemency; and plighted
love in conflict with an ambitious match; all driven to a close
dominated by the gifted Camiola whose mastery of the occasion
leaves us content when satisfaction had seemed impossible. We are
not always so content. Loose ends and unmotivated actions can
annoy, but tidiness is sacrificed more often to some judicial interest

[1] F. S. Boas, *An Introduction to Stuart Drama*, 1946, 311.

than to entertainment. Extravagant plot and unconvincing psychology do not prevent *The City Madam* (1632) from being a valuable study in middle-class ambition, though the theme is better handled in *A New Way to Pay Old Debts* (pub. 1633).

Having grown rich by the most callous business methods Sir Giles Overreach aims to marry his daughter to Lord Lovell. His talk is crisp, business-like, and assured; his mastery exists in utter dissociation from any values beyond the one all-consuming desire. He is brave, and ready with his sword. His vigorous personality arouses in us an unwilling respect, as for a force of nature. Asked whether he is troubled by his victims' curses he replies:

> Yes, as rocks are,
> When foamy billows split themselves against
> Their flinty ribs; or as the moon is moved
> When wolves, with hunger pined, howl at her brightness.
> I am of a solid temper, and like these
> Steer on a constant course. (IV. i.)

He enjoys his grim techniques. But he is not mean-souled; the aristocratic lustre on which his eyes are fixed is the 'earthly crown' of Tamburlaine's desire (p. 55 above) in a new setting. At his downfall he resembles 'a Libyan lion in the toil' (v. i), and his greatness is dramatically defined by contrast with the jests of his miserable betrayer, Marrall. Sir Giles is a dramatic portent, channelling the old power quests for a new society, and nowhere can we see so clearly the danger of relegating such matters to economic terms alone. Societies and systems change; power and ambition persist.

Massinger's people are normally prosaic types, but in Angelo and Sir Giles Overreach he has left us admirable examples of our two recurring ideals of boy seraph and dramatic superman.

William Davenant shows affinities variously with Fletcher and Massinger. In both *Albovine* (1629) and *The Cruel Brother* (1630) a passionately loved and loyal young favourite is driven, despite strong mutual feelings, to act as instrument of judgement against his sovereign, the tragic complications being so devised that these romantic passions are half felt to be redeeming the horrors in which they are engaged. *Love and Honour* (1634) is a widely deployed romance reflecting the will towards a reversal of accepted values:

> Strange giddiness of war; some men must groan
> To further others' mirth. What fury rules
> O'er human sense, that we should struggle to
> Destroy in wounds and rage our life that Heaven

Decreed so short? It is a mystery
Too sad to be remembered by the wise,
That half mankind consume their noble blood,
In causes not belov'd, or understood.

(I. i.)

A complicated plot shows passions of revenge and jealousy giving place to self-sacrifice, mercy, and love. A strong idealism beats within *The Fair Favourite* (1638), in which, as also in *News from Plymouth* (1635) and *The Distresses* (1639), the problem of duelling receives a balanced handling and critique. Davenant's firmly written dramas work subtly towards a transvaluation of 'honour'; discontented with convention, he is always searching for the genuine in honour, love, and loyalty. In *The Unfortunate Lovers* (1638) tragedy is countered by a sense of spirit life beyond death. His favourite imagery is from flowers.

James Shirley's *The Traitor* (1631) and *The Cardinal* (1641) are little more than able exercises in the out-grown tragedy of blood, but his comedies *The Witty Fair One* (1626), *Hyde Park* (1632) and *A Lady of Pleasure* (1635) are attractive mirrors of contemporary high life. He and Fletcher are links with the comedy of the Restoration. Sir John Suckling's *Aglaura* (1637) is only noteworthy for a few flashes distantly reminiscent of Webster. *The Tragedy of Brennoralt* (1639) plays some highly complicated variations on the bisexual: Iphigene, disguised as a boy from birth, looks back as to a golden age to her Arcadian friendship with Almerin, when she herself, though a boy, played 'shepherdess' to his 'shepherd', both wishing that one—as in Lyly's *Gallathea*—could change his sex (I.). At the tragic climax she reveals her disguise; fatally wounded, she murmurs, 'I doubt which sex I shall be happier in' (v); and soon after she dies.

V

With Richard Brome the wheel of Elizabethan-Jacobean drama comes full circle. His peculiar blend of Elizabethan buoyancy and Jacobean realism develops into a mixture of satire, gravity and burlesque Utopianism reminiscent of Aristophanes. In *The City Wit* (1628) the shadowed territory of Jonson's and Middleton's satire is warmed and lit by memories of *Timon of Athens*; in its handling of money and ingratitude it is a close replica, in more modern terms, of Shakespeare's play. The hero of *The Antipodes* (1638) is cured of sexual impotence by being thrown into a society where all normality is amusingly reversed: men and women change functions, lawyers are honest, the disreputable honoured. Brome's social criticism registers the better for his good nature. *A Jovial Crew or The Merry Beggars* (1641) is on the wave-length of Autolycus' first entry in *The Winter's Tale*. Bird-song and spring invite us to leave the melancholy complexities of civilization for the beggars, whose carefree society, with its dances, songs and oracular priest or seer, appears in comparison Utopian. Knowing 'the benefit of a free state' (II) they are happy, like the banished Duke in *As You Like It*:

> With them there is no grievance or perplexity,
> No fear of war or state disturbances . . .
>
> (IV. ii.)

Riches are 'misery' (IV. ii). The general relevance to contemporary dangers is clear from the devising of a little play called 'Utopia', which is to show country, city and court at variance, Divinity and Law vainly trying to reconcile them and a soldier cudgelling the lot, until a beggar comes to bring them all to 'Beggars-Hall' (IV. ii). So poignantly and wistfully does this robust and good-hearted medley stand at the threshold of civil strife.

Similar and more gravely romantic impulses beat within *The Queen and Concubine* (c. 1635). The good Eulalia is banished by her husband, King of Sicily, to make way for the wicked Alinda. Destitute and with only a few followers she takes to the country, but is visited by her genius, or guardian spirit, who infuses into her the gifts of prophecy, healing, and wisdom (III. ii). Coming to a district named 'The Paradise of Love' she proceeds to use her new powers within an idyllic society where all wealth is 'communicable' (III. iv). Meanwhile the King's cruelty and suspicions have, as he thinks, caused the death of the young prince Gonzago, his punishment corresponding to that of Leontes in *The Winter's Tale*. The boy's posture in death is described as 'so sweet' that no marble could do it justice:

> I found his stretch'd-out fingers, which so lately
> Had clos'd his eyes, still moisten'd with his tears;
> And on his either cheek a tear undried,
> Which shone like stars.
>
> (IV. vi.)

The King's conversion follows; the wickedness of Alinda, driven mad by her 'brain-confounding ambition' (IV. viii), is unmasked, and the

King and Queen are reunited. In a final masque, offered to the King by the simple community of The Paradise of Love, the supposedly dead boy Gonzago is restored, 'dressed and crowned as Queen of the Girls' (v. ix).

In all our long story from Lyly to Brome, in dramas weighty or wistful, bloody or comic, one central ideal persists, in varying shapes: the ideal of innocent boys, girls as boys, or young men, an ideal of youthful purity and perfection.

They are dramatic fictions corresponding to Shakespeare's 'master-mistress' in the Sonnets (p. 67 above) and what Lord Tennyson saw in Arthur Henry Hallam's 'seraphic intellect', in whom manhood was 'fused with female grace' (*In Memoriam*, CIX). Against these stand our power-men, Tamburlaine, Shylock, Chapman's Byron, Sir Giles Overreach, souls of the necessary power while falling short of the perfection. For youthful grace is a reflection of what lies within the turmoils of maturity and what it lacks to render it sweet. The Socratic and Shakespearian soul sees in its seraph ideal a mirage of its own potential greatness; such greatness and attendant magic as Shakespeare attempted to rough out in Prospero.

CHAPTER VI

Milton

Methinks I see in my mind a noble and puissant nation rousing herself like a strong man after sleep, and shaking her invincible locks.

JOHN MILTON, *Areopagitica*.

AT the outbreak of the civil war the unrestful powers at work in Elizabethan and Jacobean drama erupted. The overthrowing of kings in Marlowe and Shakespeare, the challenge of Chapman's Byron, the aspersions on courts in Webster, the critiques of Fletcher and Massinger, took living form, with Charles I and Cromwell as king and king-opposer, the one for the divine rights of his office, the other as pseudo-superman. The King's execution was simultaneously history, ritual, and drama; and after it a lustre was lost to our dramatic tradition, now hard to recapture. State and Church had been temporarily fused into a theocracy; it could not last, but instead democracy was born. That the theatres should have been closed from 1642 to 1660 was proper enough: those who closed them had the real thing on their hands, and there was no need for histrionics.

The literary and dramatic voice of the revolution is John Milton, and his protagonists are made on a correspondingly gigantic scale. His early *Comus* (1634), written before the civil war, is a masque drama in descent from Peele's *The Old Wives' Tale*, *A Midsummer Night's Dream* and Fletcher's *The Faithful Shepherdess*. A lady of firm chastity is entrapped by Comus. The name 'Comus' comes from the Greek for 'revel', from which we derive our word 'comedy'. Comus is here called the son of Bacchus, or Dionysus, and Circe, and associated with Pan as a personification of orgiastic and Dionysian instincts. He is supported by a cosmic and elfin poetry of wide range and his arguments against chastity have point. His freezing of the lady, who resists his temptings, to a chair, may be taken to symbolize a static and inhibited state of being, forced by resistance to instinct; and the Attendant Spirit's assertion that her release should properly be accomplished by seizing and *reversing* Comus' magic wand is clearly a doctrine of sublimation. That proving impossible, the river goddess Sabrina is invoked, whose cool purity serves instead, though perhaps only as a second best. On virtue's side are all the seraphic powers covered by the attendant, 'aereal' (3), spirit, together with a number of virile arguments; and a higher state of super-sexual integration is indicated in the Spirit's epilogue, contrasting the sexually impelled sadness of Venus over the wounded Adonis with the celestial happiness of Cupid and Psyche, or the human soul, in union.[1]

But the powers symbolized by Comus are not easily stilled, as Milton found when, after serving during the war under Cromwell as a political propagandist, he returned to poetry at the Restoration. Like Marlowe, he endured conflicting loyalties to Renaissance humanism and Puritan morality, and in *Paradise Lost* (pub. 1667) these allegiances caused an artistic disruption similar to that of *Doctor Faustus*. In the opening books Satan and his followers are so titanically yet humanly heroic that the reader's sympathetic self-identification is forced, as for a dramatic protagonist. Satan is the supreme king-opposer in our literature. One of his speeches is said to have come from an earlier and originally dramatic draft, and the discrepancy between Satan as hero and the whole epic within which he is supposed to function as villain is best defined by saying that our response to the early books is *dramatic* while our response to the victory of the Messiah during the war in Heaven is *epic*. Drama and epic, Dionysian and Apollonian, wrestle for mastery.

Paradise Regained (1671), though still in narrative form, is mainly concerned with a semi-dramatic opposition of Church and State. Jesus as king-to-be is tempted by the counsels of Satan, whose arguments are nevertheless those which all cautious statesmen must in every age adopt. When these, together with the alternative of philosophic and literary wisdom, are uncompromisingly and scornfully rejected, Satan's reply is understandable:

> Since neither wealth, nor honour, arms nor arts,
> Kingdom nor empire pleases thee, nor aught
> By me propos'd in life contemplative,
> Or active, tended on by glory or fame,
> What dost thou in this world?

> (IV. 368.)

---

[1] Compare my remarks on Lyly's *Sapho and Phao* on p. 48 above. The myth of Eros and Psyche is discussed in *The Starlit Dome*, 301–4, and *Christ and Nietzsche*, 134–8; 1941 and 1948.

That sinks deep into our persistent problem: drama after drama
might have been composed around this as its text; indeed it is only
because our religious tradition is, or seems, sexually, militarily and
politically inadequate that great dramas exist to disturb our rest.

Milton's solution was dramatic. He had for long planned dramas
on biblical themes, and for long his imagination had been fired by the
figure of Samson. In *The Reason of Church-Government Urged against
Prelacy* (II; Conclusion) Samson's leonine strength is used as a
symbol of true royalty, his 'illustrious and sunny locks' corresponding to the monarch's 'laws' and 'prerogatives'; and in the *Areopagitica* a Samson figure becomes a symbol of the British nation
rousing itself 'like a strong man after sleep and shaking her invincible
locks'. Milton labours for the harmonization of virility and goodness,
and in *Samson Agonistes* (1671) makes a final effort to fuse human
and physical strength with divine meaning.

Comus studied sexual energies; *Paradise Lost* and *Paradise
Regained* the power impulse. *Samson Agonistes* relates the one to
the other.

Samson, blinded and imprisoned by the Philistines, is, or seems, a
wreck of his former self, God's warrior, who

> Ran on embattl'd armies clad in iron
> And, weaponless himself,
> Made arms ridiculous, useless the forgery
> Of brazen shield and spear, the hammer'd cuirass,
> Chalybean-temper'd steel, and frock of mail
> Adamantean proof . . .
>
> (129.)

See how the metallic clangours are built into this ironside poetry
celebrating a strength 'above the nerve of mortal arm' (639).
Samson's enemies are as powerless as Prospero's. Both Shakespeare
and Milton dramatize a more than metallic force; and so, once, did
Chapman. Milton's task was the easier for his firm belief in the Old
Testament and the aptness of Samson's story to his own interests.
Samson's strength depended on the preservation of one condition:
the 'holy secret' (497) of his hair,[1] which had been severed by the
treachery of Dalila, his Philistine wife. Hair is symbolic of virility
and Samson, vowed as a Nazarite to 'strictest purity', had not only
sought an 'unclean' bride but allowed himself to be tricked by her
'venereal trains' (319–21, 533). His power, like that of Chapman's

---

[1] See my discussion in *Chariot of Wrath*, 1942, 94–9; especially the quotation
(96) from *The Reason of Church Government*, II. iii.

Clermont, was one with a conservation of sexual energies, recalling the union of Cupid, or Eros, and Psyche at the conclusion of *Comus*. If too rashly misdirected and expended the power is lost. We are close to the psychology of other carriers of magical powers and magical wisdom, such as Shakespeare's Prospero and Nietzsche's Zarathustra. Meanwhile Samson has failed; enslaved, blind, useless, expiating his sin.

Though short and severely classic in the Greek rather than the Senecan form, *Samson Agonistes* is packed with material. God's ways are questioned, but the conflict of God and Dagon is never for long in doubt. There is a gripping dramatic progress and unfurling. Samson is first a figure of passive endurance; he resists any thought of a ransom, preferring expiation for his surrender to female allurements. Then gradually we become aware of an inward turmoil:

> Thoughts, my tormentors, arm'd with deadly stings,
> Mangle my apprehensive tenderest parts,
> Exasperate, exulcerate, and raise
> Dire inflammation . . .
>
> (623.)

At Dalila's entrance excitement grows. She adduces arguments to support her betrayal of him in terms of her duty as a Philistine to the 'public good' (867), so raising once again our persistent conflict of religion and state, and arousing Samson's scorn of such Machiavellian sophistries. His wrath gathers: like that of Sophocles' blinded Oedipus at Colonus, like Timon's, it burns from the seemingly inactive protagonist with rays more potent than material force. And next the taunts of the Philistine champion Harapha are met by Samson's ringing challenge inspired by a rising confidence in God's power to master the material order and its futile weapons:

> Then put on all thy gorgeous arms, thy helmet
> And brigandine of brass, thy broad habergeon,
> Vant-brass and greaves and gauntlet; add thy spear,
> A weaver's beam, and seven-times-folded shield;
> I only with an oaken staff will meet thee . . .
>
> (1119.)

Every sounding clangour serves a purpose; the new power is *no less* than armed force, which it can use and better for its own purposes. Milton's return to the Old Testament allows him to incorporate both the Jesus and the Satan of *Paradise Regained* within his new, and for him more inclusive, hero. Samson's challenge to Harapha comes from the old physical yet God-infused strength, re-awakening;

and Harapha, fearful of such an antagonist, retires. Hitherto Samson has been remembering the past; now he is rousing himself, like the great figure of Britain roused in the *Areopagitica*. The engendering and accumulation of excitement is wonderful.

And so to the conclusion when, during the public merry-making, Samson pulls down the pillared roof on the Philistine nobility. First he prays, and then:

> This utter'd, straining all his nerves, he bow'd;
> As with the force of winds and waters pent,
> When mountains tremble, those two massy pillars
> With horrible convulsion to and fro
> He tugg'd, he shook, till down they came, and drew
> The whole roof after them with burst of thunder . . .
>
> (1646.)

'Samson hath quit himself like Samson'; there is in it no cause for 'tears' (1709; 1721). *Samson Agonistes* is unlike other tragedies: it is a tragedy beyond tragedy, as assured, in its vastly different way, as is *The Tempest*.

The artistic harmony is faultless. Milton, who was presumably writing for a Puritan public, succeeded as has no other British drama-tist in aligning the Dionysian and destructive energies with a God who commanded unquestioned belief. No Greek drama shows a stronger, nor probably so strong, a religious impulsion. Behind it lies the Puritan revolution. The enslaved Samson's act is revolu-tionary; our other Samson figures (p. 126 above) are communal symbols; and here Samson's locks contain strength as of 'a nation armed' (1494). Contemporary and communal feeling beats within the words:

> Oh how comely it is, and how reviving
> To the spirits of just men long opprest,
> When God into the hands of their deliverer
> Puts invincible might
> To quell the mighty of the earth, th' oppressor,
> The brute and bois'trous force of violent men . . .
>
> (1268.)

Men, that is, who support 'tyrannic power', like that of Charles I.

In his mighty way and in his own terms Milton surpasses all dramatic rivals, since his religious assumptions enable him to create a semi-superman of appalling realism. That said, we must admit that many subtleties are by-passed; there is naturally no facing of Christian love, nor any involvement in the more complex problems of statesmanship; and the final emphasis is on wrath and destruction. France's left-wing religious dramatist Racine attempts to avoid this limitation in *Athalie* by preserving a fairer balance of Hebraic religion and pagan statecraft and inserting a New Testament prophecy. Gestures towards the superhuman in Sophocles, Shakespeare, Byron and Nietzsche show a delicacy and softness of sensibility in line with the New Testament and alien to Milton; and Ibsen remembers love. But perhaps they are all wrong and Milton right. Certainly his blend in Samson of British nation and biblical hero adumbrates the blend of state and superman forecast in Ibsen's *Emperor and Galilean*.

CHAPTER VII

Restoration

Nay, 'tis the hardest task perhaps of life
To be assur'd of what is vice or virtue.
NATHANIEL LEE, *Lucius Junius Brutus*, IV. i.

I

THE proper function of comedy is to assist the assimilation of instincts, especially sexual instincts. The Elizabethan period saw a grand attempt to assert the romance of marriage, of which Spenser's two marriage poems and the various Shakespearian emphases are outstanding examples. This was followed by the Jacobean concentration on criminal lust. Neither extreme meets the near-distance human problem: the darker comedies of the Jacobean period are scarcely comedies at all, or if they are they are comedies of a bastard sort, moralistic comedy being a contradiction in terms.

Now whatever might be true of southern Europe, or even of France, Protestant Britain had too firm a sense of sin to engage in any wholesale comic and communal relaxation. The medieval 'Feast of Fools' was not popular in England. And yet morality and convention alone are impotent; the stuff of life is there whatever we think of it, and it is comedy's business to face it. The next step is accordingly a facing not of the instinct alone as a simple force of nature, but of instinct recognized simultaneously as sin, as inevitable, and as honourable. For such subtleties the middle classes had neither the inclination nor the language. Clarification could only come through an aristocratic daring and a sophisticated expression. Hence the importance of the Don Juan myth, and in England the development under Charles II of the tradition of sex wit, running from Lyly through *Love's Labour's Lost*, *Much Ado about Nothing*, Marston's Crispinella, Fletcher, and Shirley, into what is known, by a pretty irony, as 'the Comedy of Manners'.

The conditions were excellent. The court had tasted the refinements of French culture. In London theatres had for long been closed, but now the puritanical element had little power, while its presence and recent supremacy lent a spice to daring. Two theatres were opened, the audiences were mainly aristocratic, and the rest followed. The play-pattern in favour is easy to define: what was wanted and supplied were dramatizations of adultery with the running game of a considered disrespect of marriage vows, which simultaneously depended for its effect on society's respect for them, a sense of sin being preserved, and the daring being the more acceptable in that aristocratic marriages had generally been arranged on social and financial grounds. This was the recurring theme of Restoration wit. There were difficulties: the scorn of propriety became itself a dramatic convention; shock tactics ceased to shock; there was the danger of sin becoming dull; indeed, within the dramatic convention, scarcely sin at all. However, what was accomplished was important. The challenge still lives; much of it has been more rationally developed by Bernard Shaw and other twentieth-century dramatists, and it would be idle to deny that the problems posed have been settled.

There were, it is true, comedies of a more Jonsonian kind. John Wilson's *The Cheats* (1663) develops an amusing balance of orthodox and unorthodox falsities in the casuistical Scruple as against the occultist Quack. *The Projectors* (1664), reminiscent of Jonson's *The Devil is an Ass* (1616), looks ahead, with advanced women planning a female 'commonwealth' (III) and some grandly comic schemes to elicit money from folly, including ships that sail 'in the air' (III) and a clockwork horse whose speed can be varied by mechanism (IV). Thomas Shadwell is also of Jonson's school, showing a clear-headed and sane handling of a varied material. The marriage approaches of two young people embittered by the falsities of society in *The Sullen Lovers* (1668) is excellently done (V), and there is a wide range of mainly satiric interest: national, military, dramatic, and poetical. Morality is firm: when Bellemon in *A True Widow* (1678) thinks that seduction has been made honourable for a man by custom, the lady's answer is neat: 'When a man of honour can turn coward, you may prevail upon me; the case is equal' (III). *The Squire of Alsatia* (1688) is a strong study in moral concern and educational psychology; and there is life in the bustling action of *Bury Fair* (1689).

Such well-varied interests are not present in the sexual concentrations of Sir George Etherege, William Wycherley and William Congreve. To introduce these we can do no better than turn to John Dryden. Dryden has a warm humour and an honest acceptance of the licentious. In *Marriage à la Mode* (1672) he interweaves two at first sight incompatible plots: one is a straight heroic romance, the other has two pairs of criss-cross seducers who show the usual scorn of marriage morality before finally submitting to it. We open with a song on the absurdity of preserving the marriage vow 'when passion is decayed'; there is no question as to this central emphasis; and yet there is the conventional romance too. Dryden's thought is on the *essence*, irrespective of *morality*; and in such terms, the terms of his tragedy *All for Love* (1677), the two themes may perhaps be harmonized.

The implications are developed in his *Amphitryon* (1690), adapted from Plautus and Molière. Jupiter plans to seduce Amphitryon's wife, disguised as her husband. He meets criticism on moral grounds by the claim that he does it 'for the good of humankind' and to beget a Hercules who will redress wrongs, conquer monsters, and reform the world (I. i). So a divine but illicit union is related directly to the central dream of Western drama: the creation of a superman. Having had his way Jupiter fears that Alcmena may have regarded him as no more than a 'dull' husband, and proceeds to contrast this 'common' or 'brutal' relationship with such love 'refined' as 'disdains a lawful title':

> No, no; that very name of wife and marriage
> Is poison to the dearest sweets of love:
> To please my niceness, you must separate
> The lover from his mortal foe—the husband.
> Give to the yawning husband your cold virtue;
> But all your vigorous warmth, your melting sighs,
> Your amorous murmurs, be your lover's part.
>
> (II. ii.)

What is wanted is something finer than lust yet not dulled by morality. We are close to the dangerous thought of Alexander Pope's *Eloisa to Abelard* (1717): 'How glowing guilt exalts the keen delight!' Jupiter's argument is deeply meant: 'There's mystery of love in all I say.' [1] This mystery it is which lies behind the cynical aphorisms of Sir George Etherege.

Of Etherege's three comedies, *The Comical Revenge or Love in a Tub* (1664), *She Would if She Could* (1668), and *The Man of Mode or Sir Fopling Flutter* (1676), the third is the most important. Its hero, Dorimant, resembles Don Juan in Molière's *Le Festin de Pierre*. His first words are: 'What a dull, insipid thing is a *billet-doux* written

[1] For an interesting analogy to the argument in terms of medieval 'courtly' love, see C. S. Lewis, *The Allegory of Love* (p. 30 above); I. 36.

in cold blood after the heat of the business is over!' (I. i). In breaking
with Mistress Loveit he is cool and controlled:

> LOVEIT: Is this the constancy you vow'd?
> DORIMANT: Constancy at my years! 'tis not a virtue in season. You
>   might as well expect the fruit the autumn ripens i' the spring.
> LOVEIT: Monstrous principle!
> DORIMANT: Youth has a long journey to go, madam. Should I have
>   set up my rest at the first inn I lodged at, I should never have
>   arrived at the happiness I now enjoy.
> LOVEIT: Dissembler, damned dissembler!
> DORIMANT: I am so, I confess; good nature and good manners
>   corrupt me . . .   (II. ii.)

The tone is superb:

> Love gilds us over, and makes us show fine things to one another
> for a time, but soon the gold wears off, and then again the native
> brass appears.   . (II. ii.)

Dorimant's arguments have truth. The cynical accent registers a
certain unease and even guilt and the aristocratic unconcern a
mastery of it. Our pleasure derives from a complicated poetic
recognition.

The cruelty is keen and dramatic fire is struck from the lady's
anguish. Dorimant's interest is temporarily transferred to Belinda,
and he has also been growing more seriously in love with the keen-
witted country heiress, Harriet. There are dialogues of excellent
verbal fencing. Deep feeling begins to show itself:

> I love her, and dare not let her know it. I fear sh'as an ascendant o'er
> me and may revenge the wrongs I have done her sex.   (IV.)

Like the ladies in *Love's Labour's Lost*, Harriet sees her lover's fault:

> When your love's grown strong enough to make you bear being
> laugh'd at, I'll give you leave to trouble me with it.   (IV.)

He is to leave the falsities of London and humbly continue his suit
to her in the country. We must face both the attraction of Dorimant's
first callousness and the concluding judgement.

Dorimant's reformation is brought about by a woman of intellect
arousing his own more generous and gentle tendencies. We may
suppose that marriage demands that each partner should have or
develop qualities beyond those normally attributed to their sex. In
The Man of Mode, as in *Much Ado about Nothing*, 'bisexuality' is
touched not by creating a central figure in disguise but by showing
each partner drawing towards such a state to meet the other.

William Congreve wrote later. The traditional grouping of his name with Etherege's and Wycherley's is, however, justified, since all three worry at the same problem. In Congreve we do not find the pungency of Dorimant's aphoristic skill, though in more extended passages he is a master, especially at pieces of self-dramatization, as when in *The Old Bachelor* (1693) Heartwell is being driven despite himself towards marriage:

> To enter here is to put on the envenomed shirt, to run into the embraces of a fever, and in some raving fit be led to plunge myself into that more consuming fire, a woman's arms. (III.)

'O', he cries, 'thou delicious, damned, dear, destructive woman!' In his wider deployments Congreve is less at ease. Of his four comedies only one, *Love for Love* (1695), is a satisfying whole. In it fun, satire and thought interweave while playing over the falsities, deceptions and self-deceptions of society, the unity of conception being personified in the hero Valentine, who avoids disinheritance by a pretence of madness through which he speaks, with an amusing burlesque of Hamlet, as 'Truth'. He addresses the comic Foresight, devoted to occult studies:

> VALENTINE: Hush!—interrupt me not: I'll whisper prediction to thee, and thou shalt prophesy. I am Truth, and can teach thy tongue a new trick:—I have told thee what's past—now I tell thee what's to come. Dost thou know what will happen to-morrow?—answer me not—for I will tell thee. To-morrow, knaves will thrive through craft, and fools through fortune, and honesty will go as it did, frost-nipped in a summer suit. Ask me questions concerning tomorrow.
> SCANDAL: Ask him, Mr Foresight.
> FORESIGHT: Pray, what will be done at court?
> VALENTINE: Scandal will tell you:—I am Truth, I never come there. (IV.)

Angelica, whom he loves, asks if he knows her:

> VALENTINE: You're a woman—one to whom Heaven gave beauty, when it grafted roses on a briar. You are the reflection of Heaven in a pond, and he that leaps at you is sunk. (IV.)

From the start Valentine has been shown as a philosophic and literary young man; he has been extravagant, yet no strong vices are imputed; and we can respond to his eventual acceptance by the astute Angelica, a girl corresponding to Etherege's Harriet, who has been testing him. The surrounding comedy is more varied than in Congreve's other plays, the characterization keen, and the situations amusing. Poetic delicacy cohabits with indecent innuendo without damage to the appeal of either.

The balance is not maintained: *The Way of the World* (1700) is less coherent. We are invited to enjoy satire against a sophisticated society, and it is hard to distinguish wit that is being satirized from the wit that satirizes. The heart of the trouble is the hero, Mirabell. He is regarded as a man of worth and fascination and we are expected to accept him as the voice of good sense. But whereas Valentine within his own play was sufficiently attractive, Mirabell's claims ring false. In pursuance of his love for the brilliant Millamant he has been pretending courtship under a false name to his ageing aunt, Lady Wishfort, and has on discovery aroused her anger. He next gets his servant to dress up as a supposed 'Sir Rowland' in order to re-awake for his purposes her amatory expectations. After making full allowance for comedy, we must regard Mirabell's fooling of a lady called 'the antidote to desire' (IV) as in dubious taste. His own life has been irregular; he has arranged Mrs Fainall's marriage to a bad man to cover the consequences of his liaison with her; nothing he *does* advances our moral or intellectual respect; and yet we are expected to admire him as one superior to his environment, who poses as a critic of society: the verbal and stylistic conception is contradicted by the action. Dorimant and Valentine are honest creations, Mirabell is not. *The Way of the World* is as an organism which, despite the brilliancy of its exterior and the grace of its limbs, suffers from a weak heart. The generally admitted inadequacy and obscurity of the plot springs from a deeper confusion.

Congreve is more successful with his women, Millamant and Lady Wishfort. Millamant's famous marriage compact with Mirabell is excellently phrased, and her conclusion, 'These articles subscribed, if I continue to endure you a little longer, I may by degrees dwindle into a wife', a happy touch; but she means it, regarding sexual intercourse as 'odious' (IV). Her last words are more promising:

> Why does not the man take me? Would you have me give myself to
> you over again?   (V.)

A sexual criss-cross is made by giving Millamant a name as forceful as Mirabell's is effeminate, so driving home the 'bisexual' impact which we found in *The Man of Mode*. In contrast Lady Wishfort— her name indicates as much—stands as a tower of sexual normality; this is our real though incoherently developed dramatic opposition. Lady Wishfort really exists as a challenge to that more cerebral attempt to *rationalize* sexual relationships which Bonamy Dobrée in his *Restoration Comedy* (1924; II. 23 and throughout) regards as the main purpose of these dramas. She is the most warmly conceived of our people, showing a peculiar blend of folly and dignity:

> LADY WISHFORT: And—well—and how do I look, Foible?
> FOIBLE: Most killing well, madam.
> LADY WISHFORT: Well, and how shall I receive him? in what figure shall I give his heart the first impression? There is a great deal in the first impression. Shall I sit?—No, I won't sit—I'll walk—ay, I'll walk from the door upon his entrance, and then turn full upon him—No, that will be too sudden . . .   (IV.)

The largeness of the comic creation is such that we move from it to her avenging fury with no sense of discrepancy. Her natural warmth dwarfs everyone but Millamant. Millamant's more esoteric brilliance is cold and brittle, like ice. It is nevertheless that brilliance, together with her gradual surrender to marriage, that has given the play its extraordinary reputation.

In comparison with Etherege and Congreve, William Wycherley is at once more powerful and less advanced, sex approach through wit or reason being thrown over in favour of the old expedient of bisexual disguise. The amusing intrigue of *The Gentleman Dancing Master* (1672) is dominated by a girl of fourteen, Hippolita, whose precocity and purpose drive the plot to the fulfilment she desires. To such a forthright and mentally alert young girl—a youthful equivalent to Harriet and Angelica—Wycherley can respond, but his feminine studies are more usually bitter. The hero of *The Plain Dealer* (1676; first version probably earlier) is a rough sailor, Manly, whose bitterness recalls that of Shakespeare's Apemantus and is fully justified by the treacheries of both his friend Vernish and his love Olivia. Olivia is slippery, lying, licentious and avaricious, and the attack driven home with a pounding insistence. The one light and hope is in the girl Fidelia, who serves Manly disguised as a boy whom Olivia tries to seduce. Loving her master, she is sweet, faithful, and finally victorious.

To make comedy out of such satiric loathing might seem impossible, yet in *The Country Wife* (1675), mainly through its shameless indecency, Wycherley succeeds. The hero Horner pretends to be impotent in order to blind husbands to his adulteries; among them is the jealous Pinchwife with his newly married country spouse, whom he tries to guard from the temptations of town life. Horner is a satiric voice; he resembles Volpone in simultaneously being and over-viewing what he satirizes. He is indecency incarnate, self-conscious and self-critical, and unrepentant. The fun is riotous but the satire savage. The mockery Horner incurs from the men is only less unpleasant than the loathing he at first inspires in the women: his very being is a comment on the lusts of a sex-ridden society. His own comments on women are fierce: 'Because I do hate 'em, and would hate 'em yet more, I'll frequent 'em' (III). Women, says Pinch-wife, 'have more desires' than men, 'more soliciting passions, more lust and more of the Devil' (IV). Though outwardly prim and shocked by the word 'naked' (II), the women are sexually shameless. When Horner pretends to have been giving Lady Fidget some china from his collection Mistress Squeamish wants some too:

> HORNER: This lady had the last there.
> LADY FIDGET: Yes indeed, madam, to my certain knowledge he has no more left.
> MISTRESS SQUEAMISH: O, but it may be he may have some you could not find. (IV.)

Woman of quality, we are told, never have enough of it. Horner apologizes, saying 'I cannot make china for you all'. It is both shocking and very funny. True, as opposed to dour, comedy is preserved by the daring and the indecency.

Mistress Pinchwife, the young country girl, has Hippolita's resource, and fools her husband gloriously. When for safety he has her disguised as a boy, she only becomes the more attractive. Horner's observation that 'love and wenching' really disgust him and that his preference is for 'good fellowship and friendship' (I) reflects the truth: his willingness in such a period to submit to the reputation of impotence itself marks a scorn of the sexual. Now the girl disguised as a boy at once arouses his only words of delight: 'I never saw anything so pretty in all my life'—'a glorious creature, beautiful beyond all things I ever beheld'. She is compared by another to 'a poet's first mistress of imagination'. Horner kisses her (III).

Wycherley shows a strong sexual disgust, but he can respond to the mischievous and astute Hippolita of Amazonian name, to the sweet and loyal boy-girl Fidelia, and to his young 'country wife' in male disguise. His work accordingly reflects a mind-structure similar to that which gave us the Dark Lady and Fair Youth of Shakespeare's Sonnets and all the various lust hatreds and bisexual idealisms of Jacobean drama. The sex issue cannot be settled without love, and love is a leaping of barriers, as Benedick and Beatrice leap theirs (p. 68 above), beyond the entrenched self; it is accordingly less sexual

than bisexual. In our present period, with its coldly external aspersions on marriage, the sexes are horribly separate. Approach is made
either by wit combat and sex duel, our Harriets and Angelicas and
Millamants reversing all sexual custom—as Congreve emphasizes
in his choice of names (p. 135 above)—by forcing the male, as in
Shakespeare's *Love's Labour's Lost*, into humility; or through such
more traditionally enigmatic young champions as Hippolita, Fidelia
as boy-girl and Mistress Pinchwife disguised as a poet's dream. The
change in this period from boy actors to actresses does not preclude
the continuance of such disguises.

On the relation of the bisexual ideal to homosexual instincts it
would be rash to dogmatize. Restoration comedy can on occasion
suggest the desire of male for male either real or by disguise. Such
suggestions are found in the work of Thomas Otway, Mrs Aphra
Behn and Sir John Vanbrugh. They are no more than peripheral,
but we have one comedy where the normal, the bisexual and the
homosexual are all skilfully interwoven: this is Thomas Southerne's
Sir Antony Love or The Rambling Lady (1691), in which our various
complexities are clarified under the authority of a dominating person
whose name and actions correspond to Wycherley's phrase on the
poetry of love.

The people are mostly English, in a French setting. The atmosphere
has a friendliness and good humour none too common in this period,
using quick repartee and a machine-gun, crackling dialogue. Sir
Antony is a lady disguised as a young man who controls the plot like
a refined version of Dekker's and Middleton's 'Roaring Girl': her
male talk is variously sprightly, brilliant, impudent, immoral, and
satiric. Coming from a woman her pretence of male licence is a
critique of it. She has achieved a character 'as the arrantest rake-hell
of 'em all' (I) and speaks of cuckoldom in England as 'more than in
fashion, sir, 'tis according to law' (II). She carries her disguise
brilliantly. She is no Viola inexpert at manly exercises, but a duellist
who can manage a quarrel:

> I am for universal empire, and would not be stinted to one province.
> I wou'd be fear'd, as well as lov'd; as famous for my action with the
> men, as for my passion for the women.   (I.)

She switches from male to female dress and back again, from the
bisexual dimension surveying and illuminating the whole field of
contemporary licence. She tells us that seduction may be more an
enjoyment of 'the accidents of the chase' than a matter of real desire

and is often enough driven no further (I). The conventional aspersions on husbands take on a sparkling life from her response to an
adoring lady:

> But, child, hast thou no more mercy upon my youth, my dress, my
> wit and good humour, than to make a husband of me?   (IV.)

Meeting a sanctimonious pilgrim she plies him with drink, and is
shocked to find him no hypocrite:

> Why, I begin to despair of thee: I took thee for a sanguine, sensual
> sinner, a man of sense, and an hypocrite. But I find thee a peaking
> penitent and an ass.   (III.)

Soon after he admits himself a rogue. Sir Antony is master-mistress
of every situation. In her we have a union of our two beyond-the-sexual
female types: those of intellectual wit and those of male disguise.

Homosexuality is also involved. She attracts an Abbé of homosexual propensities:

> ABBÉ: I know, you little rogue, your business is to be wicked. I love
> to be wicked myself too, sometimes, as often as I can decently
> bring it about, without scandal; and I will be as wicked—as wicked
> as I can be, for you, and with you.
> SIR ANTONY: You can do no more than you can do, good old
> gentleman.   (V).

She plays with him in dialogue. He grows excited:

> SIR ANTONY: If I should retire with you, you'll be disappointed——
> ABBÉ: No, no, don't talk of disappointment; I hate to be dis-
> appointed—We're very luckily alone, and should make a good use
> of our time; nobody will come to disturb us.
> SIR ANTONY: But I may disappoint you myself—
> ABBÉ: You will exceedingly, if you don't go along with me. Delays
> are dangerous, when opportunities are scarce; and we elderly
> fellows have 'em but seldom—I vow I'll teize you, and kiss you
> into good humour; I swear I will, if you won't go.
> SIR ANTONY: But 'tis not in my power to oblige you.
> ABBÉ: I'll put it into your power, I warrant you.
> SIR ANTONY: But that I doubt, sir. For, very unhappily for your
> purpose, I am a—woman.   (V.)

He drops her hand, staggered. After the first surprise he becomes
courteous, formal, dignified: the change is cleverly done. He is
deeply apologetic:

> ABBÉ. I don't use to take the freedom of being so familiar with the
> ladies—
> SIR ANTONY: I do believe you.

ABBÉ: Indeed I don't: I pay a greater respect to your sex; and had I
known you were a woman before, I had kept my distance——
SIR ANTONY: Fie, fie, fie, ceremony among friends! Tho' you know
me now to be a woman, you need not keep a distance. What tho'
I have disappointed you in your way, I may make you amends in
my own—— (v.)

But to this suggestion the Abbé does not respond. He is now terrified
of scandal, the more so since there have been watchers who, however,
promise not to cause trouble: 'Nobody shall betray you; we are all
friends' (v).

The prevailing tone is kindly, even warm; the outspoken impu-
dency of Sir Antony's talk marks a health; on her lips pretended
licentiousness is its own purification. She does nothing but good,
satirizing and serving the others: 'I love', she says, 'to bring things
to a good end' (II). The play's plot in itself is slight, the structure
weak and the intrigues over-complicated, but all depends on the one
central conception of Sir Antony Love:

Make one! thou mak'st all; thou'rt all in all; the whole company
thyself; thou art every thing with every body; a man among the
women, and a woman among the men. (II.)

She is the culmination of a century's concentration on the bisexual.
Everyone admires this youth 'so sweet' and of 'form so excellent',
one

so finish'd by the great Creator's hand, I worship him in thee. (I.)

Sir Antony is Love personified, corresponding to Southerne's
definition of love in The Loyal Brother (1682) as 'the seraphic flame
that warms the soul' (IV). With a humour drawn from the bisexual or
seraphic insight our comedy simultaneously uses and surveys the
brilliance and the falsities of the contemporary stage. For the bold
treatment of homosexuality, though the scene with the Abbé was
cut in performance,[1] suggests that what passes for sexual daring in
our theatre, in this and other periods, and in real life too for
that matter, may sometimes be little better than a prudish mask
for instincts of a less acceptable kind whose presence we may be
half recognizing whenever we distrust the artificiality of Restoration
wit.

In comparison with the subtleties we have been reviewing any too
facile a morality appears crude. The sardonic John Crowne tells us

[1] This is stated in a dedicatory address to Thomas Skipwith printed in the
collected edition of Southerne's plays published in 1774.

in *Sir Courtly Nice* (1685) that the name 'love' is merely the 'fig-leaf' to cover 'lewdness' (II). His condemnation is wholesale:

> I am no senseless person—I ha' more senses than yourself. I have a
> sense o' vanity, and of the nothingness o' the things o' this world—
> and a sense o' sin, and a sense o' the insinuating nature o' sin . .
>
> (IV.)

True, but unhelpful. Moral criticism was to continue. Sir John Vanbrugh's *The Relapse or Virtue in Danger* (1696) and *The Provok'd Wife* (1697) are plays of verve and enjoyment, offering 'Restoration' indulgence and moral observance in rather unconvincing juxtaposition. Reform and development were to follow during the next century, but only slowly and in terms no less intricate than the refinements of the Restoration; in terms not of moral precept but of a new warmth and greater sympathy; in terms of more, rather than less, love.

That the more famous Restoration comedies should be morally ambiguous is, given their subject, a sign of grace. Neither the good sense and comprehensive humanity of Shadwell nor the dark criticisms of Crowne have the life of Dorimant, Horner, Millamant and Lady Wishfort. Morality may often be shocked, not so much by any explicit teaching as by certain recurring assumptions. These, however, are really the same as the assumptions of courtly love in the Middle Ages; much of the profligacy can be defended as a protest against what Mrs Aphra Behn in *The City Heiress* (1682) calls the 'vile merchandise' of conventional marriages (IV. i); and the hero's reformation may often be glimpsed. Even so the problems are not finally resolved and it would be rash to define our response in moral terms. We do better to face that unmoral aristocracy of mind to which we respond whenever we praise 'wit' or 'style', even though these, if too far divorced from plot, as in *The Way of the World*, may be dramatically dangerous; and to observe a forecast of the marriage strictures advanced by Bernard Shaw and other dramatists of our own century. Despite much lewdness, some boredom, and a host of insincerities, the ruling spirit, which is a kind of poetry, is at its best not decadent but healthy. Unmoral it may be, or seem, but nevertheless may serve, as Dryden's *Amphitryon* suggests, some great if distant purpose. We must never forget that our greatest love drama, *Antony and Cleopatra*, dramatized *of necessity* an immoral relationship. Our many paradoxes are placed and resolved within the person and name of Sir Antony Love.

II

The two theatres of the Restoration were dominated by the aristocracy and its heavier drama was correspondingly heroic and aristocratic, with emphasis on magnanimity and self-mastery: the aim was in part to blend Renaissance and Christian values on the heroic level. Charles II's experience at the French court set a standard, and Spanish influence was strong; Spanish and French romances as well as Italian poetry were contributory; and our own dramatic tradition, in Marston's *Sophonisba*, in Fletcher and Davenant, provided an ancestry. But the achievement was new.

The great Pierre Corneille might be regarded as a near-distance godfather and prototype since, building on the will to an integration of Christian and Renaissance values in line with his Jesuit education descending from the teachings of St Ignatius Loyola, his greater dramas stand as colossal if at times extravagant expositions of the superself in action.[1] But what was authentic in Corneille's mounting alexandrines was to find no adequate correspondence in our own rhymed couplets and the peculiar confidence of Corneille was absent. In France the Cornelian assurance was followed by the darker powers of Racine, Apollonian by Dionysian; and in England the tendency to question any too extravagant an idealism was strong. The much used term 'heroic' scarcely serves as a period definition. There were heroics, certainly, especially at the start, but there was much else and many of our best so-called 'heroic' dramas do more to repudiate than to advertise the warrior-ideal; the so-called 'heroic couplet' is given over by each in turn in favour of blank verse; and we have a number of dark tragedies concentrating on the wickedness and insecurities of tyrannic rule. Emphasis falls less on outstanding individuals than on the complexities of statecraft. Horrors are now a matter less of personal revenge than of judicial executions, in various forms and with various torments. The execution of Charles I had cut the golden thread of royalism, yet there is still faith in human nobility and a striving for magnanimous solutions. Religion is often involved, reflecting the pressure of contemporary antagonisms and threats. Much might be called sensational, and so was life itself; it was a period of near disruption accompanied by the will to refinement and civilization. Romance was vivid. The new perspective

---

[1] See Lewis Mumford's account of the teaching of St Ignatius Loyola in *The Condition of Man*, 1944, 221–30.

staging now lent itself to epic actions in distant lands, the Orient, Spain, Africa and South America tending to replace the over-worked field of Renaissance Italy; and Charles II's banishing of the boy actors on moral grounds gave scope for new feminine interests. The seraphic intuition through boy-girl disguise is certainly still awake and spirit life accorded a scientific interest. In his *Saducismus Triumphatus or Full and Plain Evidence Concerning Witches and Apparitions* (1681; Part 2, 'Real Existence'; iii) Joseph Glanvill is at pains to repudiate any too sense-bound a rationalism which argues 'as if a man should define an Angel to be a creature in the shape of a Boy with wings, and then prove there is no such being.' [1] But now glamorous ladies, as ladies, have new rights; they too assume seraphic powers. As against kings, supermen and the bisexual we have a growing emphasis on the communal and the heterosexual. In and through all these dramas runs as a single elixir an exquisite perception, descending from *Antony and Cleopatra*, of romantic yet physical love—never far from the dangerous magic of Dryden's *Amphitryon*—as the true sovereignty beyond place and glory, just as in comedy it rises above morals; together with a peculiarly exact apprehension of spirit life beyond death. These beat together as one heart; and from this heart or centre radiate out into the world of tyrannies and torments many noble readings of heroism, endurance, and sacrifice. The worth of the aristocracy in this period may be questioned, and yet within its dramatic poetry there beats a spiritual aristocracy to which we may respond.

III

What might be called the 'straight heroic play', with its epic matter and appeal, appears to derive from Davenant's operetta *The Siege of Rhodes* done during the Protectorate in 1656. Davenant, as we have seen, had enlightened views on warfare, and this operetta, and its companion pieces *The Cruelty of the Spaniards in Peru* (1658) and *The History of Sir Francis Drake* (1659), though heroic show a deliberate softening of the warrior values. Magnanimity and love are primary ideals, Drake being drawn as a figure of enlightened and chivalrous warring as opposed to Spanish cruelties. The aim is to blend war and goodness, as in the codes of chivalry. One way of

[1] See also H. S. Redgrove and J. M. L. Redgrove, *Joseph Glanvill and Psychical Research in the Seventeenth Century*, 1921.

doing this was to regard British warring as good and the wars of other nations as bad, though the best full-size achievements in this kind did not appear till the next century.

A major attempt at the heroic was made by John Dryden, collaborating with Sir Robert Howard, in *The Indian Queen* (1664) and following up with his own *The Indian Emperor* (1665) on Cortez's conquest of Mexico. Battles, captures and escapes in rapid succession mingle with extravagant heroisms, consuming loves and exalted virtues. There is little attempt at local realism, everything belonging to the one fantastic world. Perhaps the only lines worth remembering are spoken by some aerial spirits in *The Indian Queen* on the experience of human lives after death

> When leaving bodies with their care
> They slide to us and air.
>
> (III. ii.)

No other period could have given us 'slide'.

On such etherealities Dryden writes as an adept. When in *Tyrannic Love or The Royal Martyr* (1669) the Emperor Maximin tries to force the Christian saint Catharine into submission by condemning her mother to death on the wheel, the situation is saved by an angel-'youth', 'all heavenly fair' (v. i), who arranges an easier death for both to the sounds of 'ethereal music' (v. i). Elsewhere a lady assures her lover of her presence after death:

> I'll come all soul and spirit to your love.
> With silent steps I'll follow you all day,
> Or else before you, in the sunbeams, play . . .
>
> (III. i.)

She will visit him in 'gentle dreams' until he joins her:

> And when at last in pity you will die,
> I'll watch your birth of immortality.
> Then, turtle-like, I'll to my mate repair,
> And teach you your first flight in open air.
>
> (III. i.)

Such occult penetrations are of the authoritative sort found in Chapman; and we are now in a more scientific age, the age of John Glanvill's occult studies. Spirit raising is given a semi-scientific phraseology:

> And, thy full term expired, without all pain,
> Dissolve into thy astral source again.
>
> (IV. i.)

Dryden is deeply interested in the occult. Writing in the essay 'Of Heroic Plays' prefaced to *Almanzor and Almahide or The Conquest of Granada* (1670) he observes that all ages have believed in spectres; discusses the nature of their 'aerial'—we today should call them 'etheric'—bodies; and claims that such matters are the province rather of poetry than of theology or philosophy since the 'fancy', or imagination, 'being sharper in an excellent poet than it is likely it should in a phlegmatic, heavy gownman, will see further in its own empire, and produce more satisfactory notions on those dark and doubtful problems'. It is true, and at such moments Dryden has a feather-light touch. In *The Conquest of Granada* a dying man speaks:

> 'Tis gone; that busy thing,
> The soul, is packing up, and just on wing,
> Like parting swallows, when they seek the spring . . .
> (2; IV. ii.)

In the next scene the hero's mother returns as a ghost to describe her failure at death to pass the 'crystal walls', her falling back—'I flagged, and fluttered down, and could not fly'—and the subsequent direction from an angel to wait in readiness for the time when she is to warn and guide her son. Meanwhile her home is in the half-way region or state symbolized by 'the mountains of the Moon', where heaven and nature meet and souls are 'prepared for light' (2; IV. iii). Dryden is happier as poet and occultist than as dramatist.

In *The Conquest of Granada* Almanzor is a super-hero in the style of Homer's Achilles, Shakespeare's Coriolanus, and Chapman's Byron. But his assertive valour, inordinate claims and 'flashy behaviour are countered by none of the darker shadings necessary, at least in British drama, to any convincing depiction of such a hero, unless indeed we rank him with Coleridge's Andreas with whom his story has something in common (p. 225 below), though he has nothing of Andreas' youthful magic. When Maximin in *Tyrannic Love* cries

> And shoving back this earth on which I sit
> I'll mount, and scatter all the gods I hit . . .
> (v. i.)

we can accept the grotesquerie. But Almanzor is supposed to be admirable. His 'Stand off; I have not leisure yet to die' (1; I. i) may pass; 'She must be chaste, because she's loved by me' (2; IV. iii) is comic.[1] Almanzor's switching from side to side to turn defeat into victory is unconvincing. Nothing about the war-action, its armies, peoples, Moors, Christians, cities, has reality. There is a queer sense of activity without progression, as the people dance in and out of their repetitive successes and failures, speaking rhymed couplets; artistically it is all of a piece, event and language are in similar vein. In such peculiarly horizontal and oscillatory terms Dryden vainly attempts to touch the heights.

For he has a purpose. He is deliberately trying to present human essences as positive powers without any deeper and darker traffickings. His themes, following—sketchily—*Coriolanus* and *Antony and Cleopatra*, are love and honour. Almanzor surrenders his warriorship to love and next has to subdue his love to a higher honour, or virtue. His magnanimity has been so far 'a miracle of virtue'; will he, asks his lady Almahide, now sacrifice honour 'for one tumultuous minute'? Neither Dryden—we may remember *Amphitryon*—nor Almanzor are really sure as to whether such virtue is worth while. But the lady wins, saying:

> There's pride in virtue, and a kindly heat;
> Not feverish, like your love, but full as great.
> (2; IV. iii.)

Perhaps. In such terms Dryden tries to realize an 'august' and 'godlike' virtue (2; IV. iii), and the success is fragile.[2]

What might be called the 'dance' technique is developed more coherently in *Aureng-Zebe* (1675). Through a number of reversals of fortune, battles, and fallings in love, the people chase each other in a kind of cyclic motion. There is a dark dignity in Queen Nourmahal and the reformation of Morat has drama. There are passages of exquisite poetry. Our prevailing impression is admiration for the artistic if not specifically dramatic technique which so skilfully makes its people's fortunes and emotions dance within the geometric design; the kind of admiration which we might give to a decorated vase.[3] *All for Love or The World Well Lost* (1677) replaces rhyme by blank verse and adapts Shakespearian influence to classic form.

---

[1] Douglas Jefferson has argued for a deliberately comic intention ('Aspects of Dryden's Imagery', *Essays in Criticism*, IV, i, January 1954). In his preface to *The Indian Queen* Scott refers to 'the glowing language which, though sometimes bordering on burlesque, suits so well the extravagant character of the Moorish hero' (*The Dramatic Works of John Dryden*, edited by Sir Walter Scott, revised George Saintsbury, Edinburgh, 1882, II. 225).

[2] For an acknowledgment relevant to this paragraph see p. x above.

[3] Bonamy Dobrée's vivid appreciation of Dryden's plays in his *Restoration Tragedy*, 1929, is couched mainly in aesthetic terms.

Despite human insight and some fine poetry, the result is still cold. We are again involved in a conflict of love and honour, and again the action, being limited to a succession of alternating decisions and re-decisions by Antony as to whether he shall or shall not part with Cleopatra, is in effect static and leaves the spectator unrewarded. We have no sense of that gradual accumulation of power so impressive in *Samson Agonistes* and Matthew Arnold's *Merope* and so peculiarly important in dramas of classic form. The climax of the jealousy aroused in Antony by the really loyal Cleopatra, being caused by a deliberate pretence, has no depth of meaning. Nor have we any aura of mystery, any atmosphere: we are simply shown a human relation-ship on the key problem—the relation of wife and mistress—of Restoration comedy, rationally discussed and poetically delivered.

Don Sebastian (1689) is a straggling and at times powerful dramatic narrative in blank verse, more or less in the heroic and superman vein:

> He looks as man was made; with face erect,
> That scorns his brittle corpse, and seems ashamed
> He's not all spirit . . .
>
> (I. i.)

We have the usual brilliant insights into spirit life:

> Life is but air,
> That yields a passage to the whistling sword,
> And closes when 'tis gone.
>
> (III. i.)

Cleomenes (1692) gives us a strong contrast of Spartan nobility and Egyptian decadence; it is a firm and dignified work, arousing sym-pathy in the pathetic dialogue of the starving boy Cleonidas with his father, a copy of Fletcher's Hengo in *Bonduca*. From any normal dramatic standpoint Dryden's best accomplishment is perhaps *The Spanish Friar* (1680). Interest converges on the guilty but naïve Queen Leonora. Complexities of plot support and draw excitement from the central guilt, nemesis and recognition; and Leonora, through a series of poignant situations, grows up during the action. The entanglement of love and evil is dramatically worked out and it is the kind of entanglement that needs drama to work it out. The sub-plot contains some amusing anti-ecclesiastical farce, and a delightfully comic friar.

Dryden has both poetry and thought. He understands rulers; on love in all its insinuating magic he writes as a devotee and on spirit life as an expert; in dramatic debate he is excellent. But his exquisitely apt similes and extended metaphors are rather epic than dramatic; his thinking is a daylight, Apollonian thinking, by itself too rational for drama, giving us glitter but not glory: it is all too external and, at the worst, factitious. And yet he alone among his contemporaries writes from a happy recognition that there is in man 'a mounting substance made of fire' (*Don Sebastian*, IV. i); he alone ambitiously and uncompromisingly, if over-confidently, wills the romantic, the superman, quest. And those deeper and darker undercurrents absent from his plays are found in his greatest work *Absalom and Achitophel* (1681) which, though in narrative form, is essentially dramatic. In Achitophel, 'resolved to ruin or to rule the state', we have a worthy companion to Milton's Satan. Here the volcanic forces active in contemporary London are felt working at high pressure.

IV

Our other main dramatists are more realistically concerned with politics and religion and less with heroics. The soldier statesman Roger Boyle, Earl of Orrery, wrote of nobility and magnanimity in rhymed couplets; starting with *The General* (c. 1661) he continued with *Henry V* (1663), *Mustapha* (c. 1665), *The Black Prince* (1667), and *Tryphon* (1668). Against a background of heroism, he concentrates on personal relationships and recurring conflicts of love and friendship, the balance being tilted in favour of the latter. There is little action; speech is quiet; courtliness, high ideals and devotion prevail. Disputation—as never in Dryden—can be dull, but the couplets have grace and sometimes poignancy. Like his contemporaries he is master of the feather-light touch in the poetry of love or immortality. A lover in *Mustapha*, asked to describe his experience, replies:

> As quietly as day does vanquish night,
> I heard no noise, but saw resistless light.
>   (II. ii.)

Such gems are found throughout this period.

The tragedy of *Mustapha* is comprehensive and important. The Sultan Solyman is made by his wife Roxolana to suspect the allegiance of Mustapha, his elder son by another woman, because she knows that her own son Zanger will be killed, according to Turkish custom, on his brother's accession. Meanwhile the conquered Isabella, Queen of Hungary, who has brought her child as a peace-offering to Roxolana, unwittingly arouses the love of both the princely half-brothers whose ardent friendship conflicts with their rivalry. The main persons endure severe conflicts: none, except for Roxolana's Machiavellian assistants, are bad; some are faultless. But they are tangled in a web of divergent interests and mutual mis-understanding. Nothing is exaggerated; discussions on paganism and Christianity, State and Church, arise naturally from the action, and the tragic conclusion is inevitable and moving.

Solyman is a humane sovereign baffled by circumstance and his persecution of Mustapha forced upon him. Roxolana is by nature generous, and yet maternal instinct plunges her into plots against a good prince, which she detests: 'What sin of mine, oh Heaven! incenses thee?' (IV. v). Isabella is likewise trapped by various com-plications in regard to the safety of her child and the embarrassment of the princes' love in this hostile environment. Her Christian valua-tions contrast with the noble paganism of the rest. Christians, who think no war just unless defensive (I. i), should stand for a virtue beyond politics, and yet we have a cardinal whose political trickery raises in her a sense of universal religious frustration:

> Zeal against policy maintains debate;
> Heav'n gets the better now and now the state.
> (III. iii.)

Always religious controversy persists, with no settled conclusion; though 'the priestly office cannot be deny'd', it yet seems unfair that humanity should be punished 'when all our guides dispute which is the way' (III. iii).

Complexities abound. The princes' mutual love survives their rivalry, Mustapha magnanimously renouncing his claims; and when his father's persecution drives him to death the younger Zanger fulfils a vow by dying too. The distraught Roxolana realizes that she has in effect slain the son she has been trying to save. Great tragic power is generated, the more impressive for the gradually increasing and well-dramatized threat of the army's insurrection, personal actions being felt within a communal context. The conclusion is dignified. Solyman is merciful and remains content with Roxolana's banishment. He is now alone in solitary and unhappy state; for 'Love, the ornament of Power, is gone' (v. ix). As an interweaving of nobility, passion, and weakness with the calls of religion and statesmanship within a well-realized historic community, *Mustapha* can have few rivals.

Orrery's other pieces are less richly woven. The compact and powerful *Herod the Great* (c. 1671), reminiscent of *Othello*, adds nothing to Jacobean drama. In *The Tragedy of Zoroastres* (1675) we meet a magician tyrant and a number of spirit spectacles elaborately directed. Advances in staging gave opportunities for such spectacles.

A similar control of weighty material is shown in the two parts of John Crowne's *The Destruction of Jerusalem by Titus Vespasian* (1677). He follows his source with a close regard to the various historical and cultural implications. Within the city are Matthias, high priest and governor; the treacherous John, leader of a revolutionary party aiming to draw advantage from the siege; and the heroic Phraartes, a Parthian king temporarily driven from his kingdom and in love with Matthias' daughter. On the Roman side is the emperor, Titus Vespasian, and his ruthless adviser Tiberius. Titus loves and is loved by Berenice, Queen of Judea. The ghost of Herod appears. All have exact historic significances.

Portents are especially well handled and discussed. Aerial combats appear above the city:

> Through all the air they scattered rays so bright,
> As if their prancing steeds were shod with light.
>
> (1; III. i.)

There is an earthquake and a mysterious voice prophesies 'woe'. The Veil of the Temple opens to reveal the Sanctuary and an angel 'all clad in robes of fire' (1; III. i) pronounces doom. Now will the thousand beasts slain in sacrifice have their revenge:

> And this once blessed house, where angels came
> To bathe their airy wings in holy flame,
> Like a swift vision or a flash of light,
> All wrapt in fire, shall vanish in thy sight.
>
> (1; III. i.)

The portents are exactly reviewed and analysed, and the argument warm with historic and local feeling. Surely this temple, the very heart of the universe, cannot be doomed? Its very 'oil' feeds the sun,

> And all the order which in nature dwells
> But dances to the sound of Aaron's bells.
>
> (1; III. i.)

Besides, are they not expecting their king for the new 'golden age', the Messiah? But to the practical, Hotspur-like Phraartes these portents are no more than pretty novelties. If, he says, lightning came seldom it would be regarded as miraculous, and no doubt looking-glasses were once thought prodigies. There must be a rational explanation: perhaps the aerial figures are indeed related to blood sacrifices, which have somehow helped human souls to 'get for the present some thin rags of air'; that is, to materialize themselves. Or they may be independent entities. Why should the 'sky' be empty? Nature dislikes a vacuum and there may well be unseen existencies 'of a more fine complexion', beyond normal sense perception (1; III. ii). Phraartes' approach is scientific and spiritualistic rather than religious. The heroic manner, Almanzor's manner, is exactly and delightfully used for a purpose when the stalwart young hero, after agreeing that all this may be well enough for so spooky a spot as Jerusalem, adds:

> But what bold spirits durst so saucy be
> To try these damn'd experiments on me?
>   (1; IV. i.)

After our terrifying phenomena the heroic accent comes as a blast of fresh air. And yet Phraartes' healthy-mindedness does not dispose of the facts. There is also the earth-bound and grimly impressive ghost of Herod the Edomite, who traces his descent from 'abandoned Esau's line' and comes now to gloat over those 'damn'd tormentors of mankind', the sleeping Sanhedrim. A long, Old Testament past is behind his rage. Joying in the prospect of blood, he will, as 'a malicious tortur'd ghost', help to call down 'all the ills' which in life he could not accomplish on this proud city. He will act as a possessing power:

> Lash me, ye furies! blow th' infernal fire!—
> Fill me with rage, that I may now inspire
> My nation with the spirit on't refin'd,
> And pour it scalding into every mind.
>   (1; IV. i.)

The conception is Aeschylean; it is also true to occult science.[1]

John and his rebels are also called 'Esau's sons' (1; IV. i). They rise and disrupt the city; Matthias is saved by Phraartes; but they rise again. From out of this grim chaos shines the love of Phraartes for the saintly Clarona, Matthias' daughter, who wishes to preserve her virginity in obedience to a religious vow. The virile Phraartes

[1] For a modern doctor's study of possession by earth-bound spirits see Carl A. Wickland, *Thirty Years Among the Dead*, London, 1947.

sees such a religion as 'the jail of fools' (1; v. i). Miracles he again
attributes to great nature whose ocean depths elude sense perception:
'We only see what on the surface swim'. As for a future life, 'a state
unknown' fails to arouse his interest; at the best it serves 'like
poetry' as a recreation 'in idle intervals of active joy'. Born at no
request of his own, he will resign his being willingly, without anxiety
as to the future (2; iii. i). At Clarona's death he is distracted. Momen-
tary loss of reason shatters his philosophy:

> Where are those lying priests that hang the graves
> With maps of future worlds?—Shew me, you slaves,
> These lands of ghosts!—Where is Clarona gone?
> Aloft!—I see her mounting to the sun!—
> The flaming Satyr towards her does roll,
> His scorching lust makes summer at the Pole.
> Let the hot planet touch her if he dares—
> Touch her, and I will cut him into stars,
> And the bright chips into the ocean throw!—
> Oh, my sick brain!—Where is Phraartes now?
> Gone from himself!—Who shall his sense restore?
> None, none, for his Clarona is no more!
>
> (2; v. i.)

After the third line a stage-direction tells us that he 'grows mad', yet
his madness is visionary. Distrust of religious belief is followed by
vision and that by a human and heroic opposition to the cosmos,
with a final admission of distraction. Heroic extravagance is en-
woven with psychological and visionary truth. Phraartes dies fighting
magnificently to save the city, assisted by 'voices' and 'visions' in the
air. He is 'something more than man' (2; v. i).

Titus, the besieging Emperor, is by nature kind; but, dominated
by his general Tiberius, he agrees that captives should be crucified
to strike terror into the city, though he is distraught by their pleas.
Hearing that 'crucified bodies cover all the plain' he complains that
his advisers 'distort' his 'nature' (2; i. i; iii. i). There is no easy
solution; he calls on Heaven to witness that his actions are not his
fault (2; iv. i). 'That tedious death' (2; v. i), his imperial office,
demands that he sacrifice his love for Berenice.

Personal, religious, and communal forces interrelate within this
drama of hideous destruction, ruthless cruelty and enigmatic
providence. Much converges on the problem of death,

> that dark and fatal door
> Which once locked on us, never opens more.
>
> (2; v. i.)

And yet, perhaps,

> When dead, we shall behold within the scenes
> What this dark riddle of destruction means.
>
> (2; v. i.)

In *The Destruction of Jerusalem* historical drama attains a new realism and a new depth. The archetypal yet historical event is handled with exact regard to both local colour and universal meaning.

The hero of *The Ambitious Statesman* (1679), Vendosme, is the medium for a bitter denunciation of society. He who cuts throats 'for glory' is 'a vain and savage fool':

> In short, I know not why he should be honour'd,
> And they that murder men for money hanged.
>
> (II.)

A 'triumph' is merely 'a public sacrifice to insolence'. Wronged by intrigues he rejects the court and its falsities with a Timon-like contempt. He imagines himself becoming a scarcely human creature of lonely anguish in the wilderness (IV.). Imprisoned under false charges he concludes that if we did not look beyond this world we should have to believe it 'the bloody slaughter-house of some ill power' (V). Reason is an arrow fixed in the brain and pleasure only exists 'when wine rots the arrow or the moon pulls it out' (V). Vendosme's wicked father with some truth urges that only the bad are consistent, since 'in a damned world' the good are unavoidably a mixture of good and bad (V). Vendosme is given to the rack; he survives to prove his loyalty and save the king; but the end is tragic. Despite his bitterness Crowne can express in *Darius, King of Persia* (1688), a sweet and simple resignation:

> Gods would not suffer so much misery
> In their poor creatures, but for some great end.
>
> (IV.)

His peculiarly bare blank verse is at its best in such simple utterances as this or 'The Gods sit at the table of the poor' (V). Darius' conqueror, Alexander, is magnanimous; Darius dies blessing him and after death reappears 'brightly habited' to demonstrate that 'life is a false light' (V). Such assurances recur: in *Regulus* (1692), a study of heroic martyrdom, light comes from the eyes of a lady's ghost 'which brightly shone thro' the dim mists of death' (II).

Caligula (1698) is a subtle diagnosis of tyranny. The young emperor engages in absurd pomp and ugly cruelties, but he is no fool.

Like Vendosme's father, he accepts wickedness and folly, and builds from that. Hearing that a lady loves him 'to madness', he replies: 'Oh, you are mad no doubt, for who is not?' Cowards fear death, which may well be a good; the brave die for a useless fame; the learned, the religious, laws, states, kings—all are mad. Thumping repetitions on the word 'mad' culminate in:

> The vicious are all mad, by laws confin'd,
> The virtuous are more mad, themselves they bind.
> And Jove was mad when he made mad mankind.
> There's one great flaw runs through the earth and sky;
> And every god and man is mad, but I.
>
> (IV.)

Comic though it sounds, this is a profound commentary on the solipsist nature of human reason and its logical development in tyranny.

Crowne's is a sombre contribution; Elkanah Settle is more fiery. The interest of his *Cambyses, King of Persia* (1671) lies less in its intrigues and villainies than in some elaborately devised shows, including a council of spirits; and *The Empress of Morocco* (1673) need be remembered only for a remarkable speech on departed spirits who, in their 'airy walk' stealing as 'subtle guests' into human minds,

> There read their souls and track each passion's sphere,
> See how revenge moves there, ambition here . . .

These dark passions, the origins of murders and wars, they will labour to replace:

> We'll blot out all those hideous droughts, and write
> Pure and white forms; we'll with a radiant light
> Their breasts incircle, till their passions be
> Gentle as nature in its infancy.
>
> (I.)

Such exact intuitions recur and recur in this period. They are found throughout *The Conquest of China* (1675), which has thoughts of an earth-bound ghost, lovers in the spirit world, and a departed father half in Heaven and half active within his son, in the manner already described. Love and chivalry are contrasted with tyranny and bloodshed, and even assert themselves above patriotism. There are two 'bisexual' figures. The heroic and Amazonian Amavanga in male disguise engages her lover Zungteus in single combat; he wins, thinks her dead and discovers her identity. After further complications he is at the point of suicide but is preserved by another girl in male dress, and Amavanga enters, safe after all. The compact and Racinian *Ibrahim the Illustrious Bassa* (1676) generates great force; it was closely adapted from the French and contains nothing of importance beyond intrigues and passions of an easily recognizable kind.

Settle's most important achievement is probably *The Female Prelate* (1680), on 'the History of the Life and Death of Pope Joan'. Joan is a legendary person who was supposed to have attained the popedom in disguise. The play is a compact and ferocious attack on Catholicism. The Duke of Saxony, set on avenging the murder of his father, accuses the Cardinal of Rheims, really the disguised Joan. Drama is fierce:

> SAXONY: Lord Cardinal of Rheims, for to that name
> Your prodigal stars have called you. Oh that spectre!
> JOAN: Young Saxony, go on.
> SAXONY: Yes, Cardinal,
> Hither I come to wake your drowsy conscience,
> And tell you, that this scarlet mantle shrouds
> That canker'd fiend that stung my father dead.
> JOAN: How, my young lord!
> SAXONY: Yes, my young poisoner.   (I.)

Joan admits the murder before the Consistory, claiming that it was necessary in order to prevent an insurrection against Rome, and to Saxony's fury her action is approved. Settle's verse is finely accented for stage speaking:

> SAXONY: Is this your doom? Churchmen you call yourselves.
> Is this a Church reward for murder'd majesty?
> Oh, I could rave; but, lords, I'll reason calmly.
> Grant those false libellers, and this poisoner, honest;
> Yes, grant my father that lewd thing they paint him;
> Nay more, suppose th' Almighty Rome has power
> To judge a King and doom a sovereign Head—
> 1ST CARDINAL: Suppose it, Saxony!
> SAXONY: Yes, suppose it, priest:
> Were he a criminal, why were not all
> Those intercepted letters sent to Rome,
> And he as an offender fairly tried,
> Call'd to the Bar, to Rome's king-killing bar,
> And his accusers met him face to face?   (I.)

Saxony is arrested and excommunicated, and Joan made Pope.

To her accomplice and lover Lorenzo she confides the story of her various intrigues and wickedness, which originally sprang from her thwarted love of the Duke, whom she murdered. Curtly she dismisses her recent evidences as 'Cheat, artifice, all trick' (III), but on Saxony's entrance guarded by officers she at once assumes a compelling sanctity and authority:

> Shall we
> Who from immediate Heaven derived have right
> To make or unmake saints, want power t'enthrone
> Or depose kings, dispose of crowns above,
> And yet not place 'em here! Command eternity,
> And have mortality control us?
> But do I talk like a descending god,
> Stoop to converse with poor and humble dust.
> Dull slaves, away.
>
> (III.)

Notice the abrupt lift on 'us' and the curt dismissal: the language lives and stings; it is as much gesture as language. As Saxony denounces her and her Church a new passion rises in her. We are fascinated by her asides: 'Ye gods, his father's shape, his face, his mien'; and ''Tis bold, 'tis bravely bold. Where am I going?' (III). When she intrigues with Lorenzo to gain the young Duke's love, the interchanges of these two double-dyed villains are vastly entertaining.

Saxony is taken to the prison where heretics are being tortured by taunting priests:

> SAXONY: Where am I brought? T'a Roman prison. Death!
> Is this the place! Hold, minister of horror,
> Why all this cruelty?
> 1ST PRIEST: Ask when you feel it.
> SAXONY: Bold slave, is this an answer for a prince?
> 1ST PRIEST: Bold prince, is this an answer for a priest? (III.)

In no drama does the great conflict of Church and State strike so fiery-fierce as in these sharp interchanges. Though we have more torture scenes, and violent denunciations of the Church's cruelty, Saxony is saved and by a trick made to lie, unknowing, with Joan, thinking her his own love Angelina. But the prison has been set on fire by the prisoners; there is a smell of burning; and in the bedchamber the ghost of the old Duke appears with a taper writing 'Murder' on the walls in fiery letters. The ghost has frightened Joan, whose conscience is at last aroused. Must she now add her new love's murder to her other crimes? 'Is't not barbarous?' she asks Lorenzo, who reminds her of the wholesale slaughters of war, generally

allowed to be glorious. Why bother over 'one poor gasping slave'?
(iv). Dramatically a woman in male dress is nearly always a saving
power; Joan is an exception; and we find the more normal use in the
girl Amiram who in page's dress reveals to Saxony that Angelina has
been simultaneously tricked into lying with Lorenzo. At Angelina's
distracted entry Saxony cries out against the gods, asking why they
should destroy their own achievements, why 'strike the masterpiece of their creation', dashing 'the shining crystal globe to pieces'
(v). Restoration dramatists are peculiarly sensitive to the delicate
fabric of human, and especially feminine, excellence.

Saxony is burned at the stake, cursing the Church. Joan has had a
miscarriage in the streets, her disguise is publicly divulged and the
cardinals agree that such a scandal must not recur. The end is
ironic, almost comic. *The Female Prelate* was addressed to the Earl
of Shaftesbury as statesman and bulwark against Rome.

Settle has also left a strongish work on religious martyrdom. In
Distressed Innocence or the Princess of Persia (*c.* 1691) a Persian king
is misled by the dangerous princess Orundana in collaboration with
the ambitious and intriguing Otrantes to suspect his Christian general
Hormidas, who is in consequence reduced to slavery. The King's
ruthless attempts to extirpate the Christian faith in his kingdom are
unavailing; the martyrs' sufferings serve only as propaganda; he is
deeply troubled. In a world of cosmic harmony human statesmanship appears to him, in contrast, as rotten: whilst great Time 'beats
not one pulse uneven' our 'distemper'd state' and 'crazy sway' is
'sickly' (v). And soon he discovers how he has been deceived regarding Hormidas and recognizes his injustice. Otrantes' own ambition
causes him to reveal that Orundana is not the real princess at all, but
though exposed and degraded she remains great; whatever her birth,
her soul, she says, was of 'unbounded grasp' ready to wield 'the
sceptre of the universe' (v). She has her place among our many
dark dramatic persons whose wickedness appears to be the obverse
of a thwarted good. In this period such powers are more likely
to appear in women than in men. Settle's women are peculiarly
powerful.

Nathaniel Lee has both the mordant judgements of Crowne and
the dramatic fire of Settle, and his subtlety and realism in psychological diagnosis is in advance of either.[1] His *Nero* (1674) is a lurid

---

[1] Apart from Malcolm Elwin's praise in *The Playgoer's Handbook to Restoration Drama*, 1928, Lee has scarcely received his due of honour during the present
century.

study in the perverted logic of tyrannic egotism. Nero maintains himself in rage on principle, fearing good, but in a brilliant stroke of theatre he is finally brought to his knees by 'mighty love' (v. iii). Lee is an expert in the pathology of tyranny and understands the occult. His conception here of the ghost of Caligula as an earth-bound spirit in part Nero's own 'genius' and in part Caligula himself coming to the 'aid' of Nero's cruelty to make him act 'what can't be done by me' (IV. iv) is as psychically interesting as Crowne's similar ghost of Herod. And there are happier intuitions too. The hero Britannicus in half madness through loss of his love Cyara is fascinated by that same Cyara, supposed lost, in boy's disguise. She befriends and soothes his distraction: ''Tis a pretty boy—Cyara's image!' (IV. i). After she has been killed when interposing herself between him and Nero, Britannicus meditates on death:

> Is there an end of thought? No further care?
> No throne of bliss nor caverns of despair?
> No dens of darkness, nor no seats of glory?
> Then all our grave discourse is but a story . . .
> (IV. iii.)

Such beliefs are merely the fabrications of priestcraft: 'Death's nothing'. Afterwards, with one of those swift transitions so character-istic of madness, and corresponding exactly to the great speech of Crowne's Phraartes—Crowne may have been indebted to Lee—Britannicus' agnosticism is suddenly reversed:

> My boy is dead.
> To Heaven's bright throne his brighter soul is fled.
> Yonder he mounts on silver burnish'd wings,
> Each god immortal sweets around him flings.
> Now, like a ship, he cuts the liquid sky;
> His rigging's glorious and his mast is high,
> Fann'd with cool winds his golden colours fly.
> (IV. iii.)

Lee is a master in the use of rhymed triplets at a climax: we can hear the actor's voice ringing them out at many a noble conclusion. 'Cool' here is used in opposition to Lee's favourite impression of human passions as heated. Nowhere can we more clearly see the point of our bisexual disguises, and in this vivid realization of the ethereal or seraphic newly swift and triumphant Lee outrivals all contem-poraries. Returning as a spirit, Cyara warns Britannicus against submitting to Poppaea's 'sorceress' arms' (IV. iii). Cyara functions as an angelic being in contrast to Nero, following the usual contrast of seraph and power-man. Lee's *Caesar Borgia* (1679) has a pathetic and lovable boy called Seraphino.

The Tragedy of Sophonisba or Hannibal's Overthrow (1675) is a widely deployed heroic—and that among our present group means pretty nearly 'anti-heroic'—drama on the Roman-Carthaginian conflict earlier dramatized by Marston. Scipio is a stern and unde-viating Roman, assisted by Massinissa, King of Numidia; Hannibal, for Carthage, is primarily a patriot anxious to save his country from disaster.

Massinissa, formerly heroic, has now, through love, seen deeper, abhorring ambition and power lust and denouncing its supposed glories as 'highest sin':

> For when to death we make the conquer'd yield,
> What are we but the murd'rers of the field?
>
> (I. i.)

This preludes our main action which further underlines the horror of war by a scene recalling the cauldron scene in *Macbeth* with many of its gruesome implications related to war instead of murder. We are in Bellona's temple with an altar, two priestesses, Aglave and Cumana, holding daggers, and a soldier ready for blood sacrifice:

> The dire oblation thus we drain,
> And with his blood our temples stain.
> The screech-owl warns us with her note,
> Strike your dagger in his throat,
> Gash him deep and suck his blood,
> Prepare his frighted ghost a shroud.
>
> (IV. i.)

They see war coming; the goddess will feed on 'thousands'. Hannibal enters, like Macbeth. Cumana in trance is possessed by the goddess and sings:

> Hark hark, the drums rattle
> Dub-a-dub to the battle . . .
>
> (IV. i.)

Warned, as was Macbeth, not to press for further knowledge, Hannibal insists and is shown 'visionary horrors' indicating the death of his love Rosalinda. Hannibal has good sense and for his country's sake plans to arrange terms with Rome. He will warn Scipio of the suicidal nature of imperial ambition, but if he insists on

behaving like 'Sol's offspring' and remains deaf, then—with another
of Lee's glorious triple rhymes—

> Like Jove we'll toss him from his glistering chair,
> Singeing the clouds, hissing through liquid air—
> And darting headlong, like a falling star.
>
> (IV. i.)

Scipio remains cold to all offers. Rosalinda in male disguise follows
Hannibal to the war and is killed. Hannibal fights lion-like, and after
defeat remains calm, reserved yet still determined. In Hannibal Lee
depicts a praiseworthy and rational heroism.

Meanwhile King Massinissa has fought for Rome in order to
rescue and join his love Sophonisba. Rome he thoroughly despises,
scorning all her glory and pride. Knowing that the implacable Scipio
will take Sophonisba back as a captive, he determines, with reminders
of *Antony and Cleopatra*, that they shall 'be one spirit as we are now
one heart'; and together they plunge into eternity. Love has an
'empire and eternal bliss' unknown to Scipio's Rome (v. i).

Gloriana (1676) on the reign of Augustus is less successful, but
The Rival Queens or Alexander the Great (1677) is a remarkable
study. Alexander, traditionally as in Lyly, Sir William Alexander
and Crowne a figure of magnanimous heroism, is by Lee submitted
to a scalpel-like analysis. He is loaded with three loves: two ladies,
Statira and Roxana, and the 'darling' of his 'soul' (II. i), Hephaestion; and he is himself in a state of semi-permanent confusion.
Critics call him 'cruel as a devil'. He has tortured Philotas:

> Ye saw him bruis'd, torn, to the bones made bare;
> His veins wide lanc'd, and the poor quivering flesh
> With pincers from his manly bosom ript,
> Till ye discover'd the great heart lie panting.
>
> (I. i.)

Without altogether denying Alexander's generally accepted greatness
Lee's drama is mainly concerned with his weaknesses. The blunt and
honest captain Clytus is disgusted at his effeminacy and refuses to
flatter him. Alexander always feels insecure. When the loyal Lysimachus will not renounce his love for the girl Parisatis in favour of
Hephaestion he fumes and mistakes a challenge addressed to his
favourite for one against himself:

> Against my life. Ah! was it so? How now?
> 'Tis said that I am rash, of hasty humour;
> But I appeal to the immortal gods . . .
>
> (II. i.)

He insists, splutteringly, on his good humour, a mixture of Tamburlaine and Cloten, and has to be stopped by Clytus' 'Contain yourself, dread sir'. He is always swerving from self-defence to threats. If anyone tells him that the absent Statira is dead he will have him impaled and 'glut' his eyes on 'his bleeding entrails'. His amatory sensations are expressed as only this period of our poetry can express them:

> My soul and body both are twisted with her.
> The God of Love empties his golden quiver,
> Shoots every grain of her into my heart.
>
> (II. i.)

There is far more weakness than strength in his loves. At one moment he is a child, crying 'O Mother, help me, help your wounded son'; and the next shouts that his word is 'destiny' (II. i.). He decides that Lysimachus must be given to a lion. The honest Clytus comments: 'This comes of love and women; 'tis all madness'. Alexander feels suddenly sick. Why was he born a prince? There is no joy nor liberty in it (II. i.). He is a mass of nervous contradictions. His warring is denounced:

> Thou torment of my days,
> Thou murderer of the world; for as thy sword
> Hath cut the lives of thousand, thousand men,
> So will thy tongue undo all woman-kind.
>
> (III. i.)

Alexander is drawn not as bad but as a man of mediocre abilities hopelessly confused by his position as world conqueror. He is always trying to live up to a destiny which he cannot understand.

Our climax is a feast. The honest Clytus, whose criticisms arise from a genuine friendship and loyalty, has under the influence of drink become more outspoken than usual. He refuses to wear a Persian robe:

CLYTUS: O vanity!
ALEXANDER: Ha! what says Clytus?
Whom am I?
CLYTUS: The son of good King Philip.
ALEXANDER: No, 'tis false.
By all my kindred in the skies, Jove made
My mother pregnant.
CLYTUS: I ha' done.

> (IV. i.)

There is a dance; the robe is offered him again; tormented and angry Clytus sits apart like Shakespeare's Apemantus, and takes more wine.

Ceremonial and adulations increase. When talk turns to war, Clytus deliberately deflates Alexander's boasting, raising in him a querulous anger:

> Lysimachus, Hephaestion, speak, Perdiccas,
> Did I e'er tremble? O the cursed liar!
> Did I once shake or groan? or bear myself
> Beneath my majesty, my dauntless courage?
>
> (IV. i.)

Renewed boasting rouses in the drink-fumed Clytus a truly maddening bluntness:

> 'Twas all bravado, for before you leap'd
> You saw that I had burst the gates asunder.
>
> (IV. i.)

Alexander's fury rages. They rise:

CLYTUS: What, do you pelt me like a boy with apples?
     Kill me, and bury the disgrace I feel.
     I know the reason that you use me so,
     Because I sav'd your life at Granicus;
     And when your back was turn'd, oppos'd my breast
     To bold Rhesace's sword; you hate me for't,
     You do, proud prince.

ALEXANDER: Away, your breath's too hot.
     [*Flings him from him.*

CLYTUS: You hate the benefactor, tho' you took
     The gift, your life, from this dishonour'd Clytus;
     Which is the blackest, worst ingratitude.

ALEXANDER: Go, leave the banquet: thus far I forgive thee.

CLYTUS: Forgive yourself for all your blasphemies,
     The riots of a most debauch'd and blotted life;
     Philotas' murder—

ALEXANDER: Ha! What said the traitor?

LYSIMACHUS: Eumenes, let us force him hence.

CLYTUS: Away.

HEPHAESTION: You shall not tarry: drag him to the door.

CLYTUS: No, let him send me, if I must be gone
     To Philip, Attalus, Calisthenes,
     To great Parmenio, to his slaughter'd sons,
     Parmenio, who did many brave exploits
     Without the King—the King without him nothing.

ALEXANDER: Give me a javelin.

HEPHAESTION: Hold, sir.

ALEXANDER: Off, sirrah, lest
     At once I strike it through his heart and thine.

LYSIMACHUS: O sacred sir, have but a moment's patience.

(IV. i.)

Alexander cries out that he is being murdered and quite absurdly orders his trumpets to sound the alarm, to arouse the whole army to save him from treason. Suddenly he stabs Clytus, who in death, the drink driven from his brain, admits his fault and asks pardon. Alexander is struck with grief. The failure of this festive occasion, the psychology of pride, the clash of honesty with flattery, the appalling *littleness* accompanying greatness, the silliness of the debating points on both sides, all speak of the pathos within human glory. There is no more masterly scene of its kind in our drama: all humanity is in it.

The rivalry of the two queens, Roxana and Statira, is well developed, if less exciting. Poisoned by his enemies Alexander dies in delirium, disjointedly giving battle commands with a pathetic and ambiguous heroism corresponding to his life:

> He bleeds, with that last blow I brought him down;
> He tumbles, take him, snatch the imperial crown:—
> They fly, they fly—follow, follow—Victoria, victoria,
> Victoria—O! let me sleep.
>
> (v. i.)

Somehow his whole career is in this last, delirious speech.

Lee understands the psychology of power. In *Mithridates, King of Pontus* (1678) tyranny is countered by attempts at self-conquest. Despite himself the tyrant sins, is conscience-stricken and repents, finally recognizing that 'there's a thorn call'd conscience' (IV. i); and at his death he denounces all temporal glory. Such a concern with the ethics of temporal rule led naturally to a concentration on that key period of the impingement of religion on state, the newly Christianized Roman Empire. In *Theodosius or The Force of Love* (1680) we have a Christian ruler of 'soft, young, religious, god-like qualities' (IV. i) handing over power to his fierce and unprincipled sister Pulcheria and being accused of inefficiency by the manly, Clytus-like Marcian, who prefers the heroic values of the empire to Christian meekness (II. i). Nero's crimes were at least those of a Roman (IV. ii). Christianity is allied with an enervate irresponsibility as against the old virilities:

> Alas, good man,
> He flies from this bad world, and still when wars
> And dangers come, he runs to his devotions,
> To your new thing, I know not what you call it,
> Which Constantine began.
>
> (II. i.)

We are aware that our problem is not simply one of Christianizing our rulers; Christianize them too successfully, and they become useless. Lee is at the heart of post-Christian history. Much more, including a sub-theme contrasting true love with social aspiration, is contained in this complex and deep play. In Theodosius' grimly active sister we have yet another of the dangerous women so active in Restoration drama. Lee's search next takes him back to Constantine himself in *Constantine the Great* (1683). The Emperor is caught between his conversion to Christianity and his amatory instincts. Silvester is his Christian counsellor:

SILVESTER: Be not too hasty in your answer, sir,
                 If I should ask, What then?—What then must
                 follow?
CONSTANTINE: Death certain, on the instant; imminent death;
                 Death; and I swear not all the gods shall save him.
SILVESTER: Ruin of piety! Not all the gods!
                 That your religion?
CONSTANTINE: O forgive me, Saint,
                 I am caught up with passion: so o'er-wrought
                 With racking love, I knew not what I said.
                                                   (IV. i.)

Like Mithridates he is guilty of an inordinate love. He is all nerves; he thinks that he hears his dead mother's voice (v. ii). With Silvester's support he gradually attains the self-conquest demanded by the new faith: 'I'll try to win in this Olympic race' (v. ii). Old virilities are being painfully replaced by a new power. The theme is announced at the start by angels who sing over the sleeping emperor of the sufferings which he is to endure.

Lee has every sort of subtlety: broken verse, colloquial touches, innuendo, psychological twists, and all in service to the greatest and most crucial themes. 'Crucial' indeed, for his obsession is judicial torment. In *Mithridates* a Roman prisoner is condemned to die by having molten gold poured down his throat (I. i) and in *Constantine* torment becomes poetically spiritualized:

        Confess? No, as he urged, bring forth the rack;
        Wire-draw my limbs, spin all my nerves like hairs,
        And work my tortur'd flesh as thin as flame . . .
                                                   (II. i.)

Lee writes from the nervous strain of a period of internal conflict when fear of such horrors was widespread. His recurring theme is the instability, the wickedness yet pathos of tyranny, great men at the mercy of egocentric lusts, and all the appalling concomitants of government. At every turn we are baffled. Christianity is needed to humanize an emperor; and yet again, it may weaken him. But why have an emperor? Is not a republic safer? This solution is surveyed in *Lucius Junius Brutus, Father of his Country* (1680).

Brutus has saved Rome from King Tarquin and the Republic is established. Of Brutus' two sons, one, Tiberius, is for counter-revolution, the other, Titus, loyal to his father. Tiberius expresses the case for royalism as against law:

> A king is one
> To whom you may complain when you are wrong'd;
> The throne lies open in your way for justice.
> You may be angry and may be forgiven,
> There's room for favour and for benefit . . .   (II. i.)

Laws themselves are 'cruel, deaf, inexorable', knowing no 'pardon', nor differences of status. The 'accidents and errors' of existence cannot be adequately met by so inhuman a rigour. A republic is too logical to be safe.

Titus, hearing that his lady Teraminta is to die if she does not win him for the royal cause, distractedly agrees (III. iii). The counter-revolutionaries hold a blood sacrifice; the scene discloses a burning and a crucifixion; blood is drunk (IV. i). Meanwhile Titus has repented and enters to demand back the paper he has signed, but he is too late; the brothers are arrested and Brutus appalled to find both his sons' names among the signatories. On receiving evidence of Titus' essential innocence he forgives him and is pleased at the young man's determination to die. However, he dishonestly decides to take what advantage he may from the occasion to establish the Republic's fame. As consul, he will himself take pride in condemning both his sons and have Titus publicly lashed before execution 'without one pitying tear' as a grand example to future ages. In vain Titus pleads: 'Is this a father?' (IV. i). But Brutus is firm: it is a glorious martyrdom for Rome. Others are aghast:

> HORATIUS: What, Titus too?
> VALERIUS: Yes, sir, his darling Titus:
> Nay, tho' he knows him innocent as I am,
> 'Tis all one, sir, his sentence stands like Fate.
>   (v. i.)

Titus was technically guilty, and legality is being *used* for a further and inhuman purpose. Brutus is now 'no more a man' (v. i): he obeys only his vision of Rome's future greatness.

Titus enters driven and whipped by the lictors. Teraminta calls
for him:

> Where is he? Where, where is this god-like son
> Of an inhuman, barbarous, bloody father?
> O bear me to him.
>
> (v. i.)

Tiberius comes next, denouncing his father with scalding invective:

> Enjoy the bloody conquest of thy pride
> Thou more tyrannical than any Tarquin . . . .
>
> (v. i.)

It goes on—'Sit like a fury on thy black tribunal'—and concludes:

> Away; my spirit scorns more conference with thee.
> The axe will be as laughter; but the whips
> That drew these stains, for this I beg the Gods
> With my last breath, for every drop that falls
> From these vile wounds, to thunder curses on thee.
>
> (v. i.)

In the Senate Brutus proudly points to 'the difference betwixt the
sway of partial tyrants and a free-born people'. The new commonwealth will establish equality before the law, repudiate favouritism
and idleness, cherish virtue, industry, and trade. So much for male
reason; but against it are lifted the voices of two women, Teraminta
and Sempronia. Sempronia's cry 'Speak to him, oh you mothers of
sad Rome', urging them to save their young ones from Brutus,
counters his coldness with fire. Titus before dying prays for 'the
glorious liberty of Rome'. When all is over Brutus too prays for the
Utopia he so confidently expects of 'harmless labour', 'endless
peace', safe shipping, rich harvests, calm seas, and perfect weather
(v. ii).

What then is our conclusion? Simply this: that commonwealths
no less than kingdoms may be built on appalling horrors and that
there are opportunities for tyranny in both. Brutus acts in good
faith:

> Nay, 'tis the hardest task perhaps of life
> To be assur'd of what is vice or virtue.
>
> (IV. i.)

Apart from the main persons, the common people of Rome are
vividly presented and dramatized. The range, complexity and

understanding brought by Lee to the gravest social, political, and religious issues of his or our time, will be apparent.

Turning to Thomas Otway's *Alcibiades* (1675) and *Don Carlos* (1676) we find the usual intuitions of spirit life—the first has a scene in Elysium—together with some poignant situations and a fine poetry of distraction. Otway is concerned mainly with individuals and is a specialist, like Fletcher, in pathos and situation. *The Orphan* (1680) manipulates an extraordinary situation which generates keen suspense and strong feeling from the friendship and rivalry of two lover-like brothers. There is little general implication: individuals are convincing, but there is no dramatic soil. Otway's greatest success, *Venice Preserved* (1682), wherein a likable young hero joins, and next for his love's sake betrays, a revolution, is the richer for the communal issues involved. A revolutionary's defence of bloodshed on the grounds that 'there is nothing pure upon the earth' and that 'the most valued things have most alloys' (III. ii) has realism. The people on both sides are hard and some are treacherous. We are in a grim society, and in it the innocent Jaffier is torn by rival and incompatible claims on his heart till he is in tears before the scorn of his condemned friend, Pierre: 'What whining monk art thou, what holy cheat . . .' (IV. ii). On the scaffold Pierre forgives him. Agony and pathos dominate, and they are as the agony and pathos of this whole period of our drama, torn by agonizing allegiances. There is little of Lee's nobility, and no grandeur: the suffering is purposeless. The difference between Lee and Otway may be pointed by imagining the action of *Lucius Junius Brutus* accompanied by such a comic sub-plot as Otway uses in *Venice Preserved*.

John Banks wrote 'heroic' plays. *Cyrus the Great* (1695) opens with a scene of dead bodies on a battlefield to drive home the horrors. But his main contribution is in his tight dramas of English history converging on famous executions. Feminine interests dominate. Banks's heroines are in turn Queen Elizabeth, Mary Queen of Scots, Anne Bullen, and Lady Jane Grey. In both *The Unhappy Favourite or The Earl of Essex* (1681) and *The Island Queen or The Death of Mary Queen of Scotland* (1684) Queen Elizabeth is shown as a distraught woman suffering acutely under the complexities and compulsions of sovereignty. Banks's people have dignity and the clash of personalities is well conveyed. The motivation and gradual unfurling of Essex's self-assertion is so skilfully handled that his suicidal boldness becomes completely convincing, if not forced. So

168 THE GOLDEN LABYRINTH

are the Queen's actions, her love of Essex being made, through a neat use of misrepresentation and a play of jealousy, to work against him. Banks has a keen eye for the interweaving of human passions with affairs of state.

Our last is Thomas Southerne. *The Loyal Brother or The Persian Prince* (1682) has a spectacular execution scene with a distraught queen-mother pleading passionately for a son condemned by his tyrannic brother. The attack against brutality is characteristic, Southerne's tendency being to stress the warmer, gentler, emotions. His poetry is richer in nature reference than that of his contemporaries; it has warmth and colour. Its emotional disposition is indicated by the good Tachmas' expression of willingness to 'offer the scarlet treasure of my heart' (III. iv). His brother's brutal nature is eventually softened; he is now a 'man' again, 'as the first' (III. iv); that is, as before the Fall, with the implication that our hideous and sadistic executions are unnatural to man. *The Spartan Dame* (c. 1688) is a substantial, exciting and in parts powerful drama, more or less in the Fletcherian style. Southerne's achievement is varied: *The Fatal Marriage or The Innocent Adultery* (1694) shows a social sensibility and pathos pointing ahead to nineteenth-century melodrama and *Oroonoko* (1695), dramatizing a rebellion of slaves under an enslaved but heroic African prince, is our first strong drama on the slave trade. The iniquities of the masters, together with their elaborately described tortures, are strongly exposed and man's plea for natural liberty given full voice. The balances are justly held: the Europeans are not all bad and we are glad to discover that 'a Christian may be yet an honest man' (v. iv). The heroic prince and his inevitable love are rather too conventionalized for full conviction and *Oroonoko*, like *Venice Preserved*, is spoiled by an unfortunate sub-plot.

V

Restoration drama replaces the old revenge plots and fifth-act blood-baths with a greater concern for communal issues and their hideous expression in public torments and executions: the wheel, the stake, burnings, molten metal, crucifixion, impaling, lions, the rack, whipping. That the horror is now one of judicial or semi-judicial punishment rather than private murder or revenge only makes it the more fearful. The obsession is sensational, yet it is found as far back as Aeschylus (p. 9 above) and was, and is, central to Christianity. No scene in Restoration drama shows a more emphatic use of torture than the staging of the Crucifixion in the York Mystery Cycle. It is likely that these later dramas have themselves done much towards the gradual humanizing—in so far as they have been humanized—of our penalties.

Closely allied are the various questionings on politics and religion, natural enough at such a time, for the Stuart monarchy was insecure, religious controversy rife, and plots and counter-plots active. In Restoration drama tyrants are shown as insecure and sometimes as absurd. There is the will to counter war with chivalry, rising to a sense on occasion of the inadequacy and even wickedness of the warrior ideal. The great positive is romantic love, the love of Dryden's *Amphitryon*, conceived as an enthralling, dissolving, paradisial experience, at once physical and spiritual and too compellingly sweet for any but a poetic definition, and far superior, as in Shakespeare's *Antony and Cleopatra*, to glory and empire, this peculiar superiority corresponding to its superiority to morals in the comedies; though Dryden can also show us a Cornelian surmounting of it, in terms of honour, and Lee in terms of Christianity. In close association are the intuitions, like Antony's expectation of Elysium (p. 81), only more scientifically phrased, and pastel replacing oils, of spirit life beyond death, sometimes assisted by the advances in staging which gave new scope to age-old beliefs. Friendship is a high value and there is still, despite the loss of boy actors, a free use of the bisexual and its old seraphic connotations, though now women as women are the more usual theme of dramatic idealization. The superman quest fires a number of heroic speeches, but the only full-scale attempt is Dryden's. We have strong individuals, though they are always so closely enmeshed in communal interests and compulsions that none have the autonomy of the people in Marlowe, Shakespeare or Webster, nor—except perhaps for Dryden's Almanzor—the will to break these communal obstructions shown by Chapman's Byron. The most powerful personal units are now the many dark and dangerous women, typified for ever in Congreve's *The Mourning Bride* (1697) by the famous lines:

> Heaven has no rage like love to hatred turn'd,
> Nor Hell a fury like a woman scorn'd.
>
> (III. i.)

The new actresses had nothing to complain of; nor for that matter had the great Thomas Betterton, whose range of parts, tragic, heroic and comic, was extraordinary. And yet no really great tragic role seems to have been created, unless Settle's Joan might so qualify. These dramas are sublime problem plays rather than tragedies. They leave us unrestful; evils were too near and too appalling for acceptance, enjoyment and catharsis, and that is why, despite the greatness of the achievement, they have suffered neglect.

CHAPTER VIII

Augustan

He who disclaims the softness of humanity,
Aspiring to be more than man, is less.
GEORGE LILLO, *The Christian Hero*, III.

I

THE reigns of William III and Queen Anne saw a change in moral tone. Licentiousness was countered by morality. Protestantism joined with patriotism under a new monarchy guarding national and individual liberties from Continental threats. Both comedy and tragedy were affected: we shall turn first to the comedies.

Jeremy Collier's attack on the immorality of the stage in 1698 was symptomatic of a general tendency. But we are to witness less a new severity than a new loosening, a new fluidity and warmth, and a new variety. Life again flows through the nation, the country holding equal rights with London; and this flow means sympathy, and sympathy leads to morality, for licence is cruel. Augustan comedy strives for a peculiar blend of warmth and morality.

The note already sounded in Southerne's *Sir Antony Love* recurs in the Irish humour of George Farquhar. His prevailing gaiety is personified by Sir Harry Wildair in *The Constant Couple* (1699), a man 'entertaining to others and easy to himself' (I. i), turning passion to fun and spreading, despite all failings and follies, friend-liness and good humour. When in a gloriously comic situation he is faced by the scorn of a fine lady whom he has been fooled into thinking a prostitute, he remarks: 'This is the first whore in heroics that I have met with' (V. i). Vice and morality are wedded by humour.

Fresh airs blow through Farquhar's writing. The action of his two best plays is set in the country: we are no longer prisoned by London. *The Recruiting Officer* (1706), though loose in structure and by innuendo in morals, is a healthy and invigorating work. Farquhar is deeply concerned about unhappy marriages, which he attributes to a lack of pre-marital intimacy. 'I'm resolved', says our hero

Plume, 'never to bind myself to a woman for my whole life, till I know whether I shall like her company for half an hour' (I. ii). Our chief interest here is the fascinating and forward girl, Silvia, a sylph-like creature who believes that a man should in youth have a varied sexual experience. She is regarded by others as herself half male and as one who, had she been a man, would have 'been the greatest rake in Christendom' (I. iii). Rakery is provisionally accepted; yet we are faced rather with humour than with doctrine. Silvia dresses as a man, and becomes a soldier, dominating in the manner of Sir Antony Love, and like her being the centre of homosexual innuendo (IV. i). She wears a uniform of 'white trimmed with silver' (v. vi), and her brilliant insight, or rather wit-sight, plays lightly above our sexual anxieties. Of the rough Bullock, married 'by the articles of war', she comments:

> He means marriage, I think—but that, you know, is so odd a thing, that hardly any two people under the sun agree in the ceremony. Some make it a sacrament, others a convenience, and others make it a jest; but among soldiers 'tis most sacred. Our sword, you know, is our honour; that we lay down; the hero jumps over it first, and the amazon after—leap rogue, follow whore—the drum beats a ruff, and so to bed. That's all—the ceremony is concise.   (v. ii.)

As the action matures her pert and telling attacks spare no one. She is not herself involved in any laxity. We expect no logical answers; our solutions must be looked for in the humour; and through Silvia-as-Wilful we seem to glimpse some new and happier way through which sexual instinct and moral precept might cease to torment each other.

The Beaux' Stratagem (1707) has action and life. The opening in a country inn and an atmosphere of highwaymen and robbery breathes picaresque adventure, and the amatory escapades of our two young adventurers are highly entertaining. More seriously important is the problem of Mistress Sullen, married to an impossible and surly husband. In comparison with such 'radical hatreds' a 'casual violation' would be nothing. 'Nature is the first law-giver', and that has been desecrated (III. iii). Farquhar unwaveringly refuses to forget 'nature'. When Mistress Sullen, tempted, commands her lover to go, muttering 'If he denies, I'm lost' (v. ii), the humour is one with our identification; we are with her, there is no coldly external approach. And on such sympathy we can build. Farquhar does not legislate, but he reveals the spirit in which our difficulties might be resolved.

He probably helped to inspire Charles Johnson's *The Country*

Lasses (1715), which has two young adventurers from town in Farquhar's style. Here the satire on city life is direct. Freehold, the stern guardian of the two girls, condemns it:

> MODELEY: This may be the picture of a saint; but for the character of a fine gentleman, 'tis as unlike it, my dear——
> FREEHOLD: As you are. Your love is lust, your friendship interest, your courage brutal butchery, your bounty usury, your religion hypocrisy, your word a lie and your honour a jest. (IV. ii.)

Strong language, however, does not solve the problem. Our dramatic solvent is again a boy-girl, the vivacious Aura, pretending to be her own brother and challenging Modeley, with a delightful mock irascibility:

> AURA: ... Know, sir, that what I want in nerve and bone I make up in vigour and youth. What are your weapons?
> MODELEY: Nettle-tops, infant, nettle-tops. (v. i.)

She offers 'country diversions' such as flails, cudgels or scythes; or for 'town gallantries' rapier, dagger, pistol, or even 'blunderbuss, demi-cannon, culverin, howitzer, mortar-piece or barrel of gunpowder'. The implicit mockery of duelling is exquisite. Her mischievous wrath in the cause of 'the reputation of a lady' is countered by his 'Cool thyself, Narcissus, cool thyself, child' (v. i). The touch is light but telling. In *Caelia* (1732) a callous seduction leads to disaster, the case against the prevailing code being pointed with great force.

Farquhar and Johnson develop the earlier comedy, giving it new twists. Colley Cibber is more obviously making a break. His plays are deeply engaged in the antagonisms of the sexes, and strive for a clarification. He knows that it is not all simple. Though the man be at fault, the wife may not be blameless; sympathy and affection may do more than jealousy. Lady Townly in *The Provoked Husband* 1727), a reworking of an unfinished play by Vanbrugh, is admirably drawn. He can use a 'bisexual' disguise for a controlling figure, though without any particular fascination. He is happiest with a straight deployment of sexual antagonisms and most of what he has to offer is covered by his best known work, *The Careless Husband* (1704).

Sir Charles Easy, a pleasant man of irregular behaviour, is made to realize the wrong he is doing to his patient and gracious wife. Meanwhile Lady Betty is gradually made to cease her coquettish tormenting of the good if colourless Lord Morelove. Lord Foppington is a conventional beau of wit and licence, presented objectively and half comically.

Morelove discusses with Foppington his shameless life. Is he not afraid of rebuffs? Foppington scorns the thought of a lady presuming on 'a little pride that she calls virtue'. He recounts one of his approaches:

MORELOVE: . . . Well, but how did she use you?
FOPPINGTON: By all that's infamous, she jilted me.
MORELOVE: How! Jilt you?
FOPPINGTON: Ay, death's curse, she jilted me.
MORELOVE: Pray, let's hear.
FOPPINGTON: When I was pretty well convinced she had a mind to
    me, I one day made her a hint of an appointment: upon which,
    with an insolent frown in her face (that made her look as ugly as
    the devil) she told me that if ever I came thither again her lord
    should know that she had forbidden me the house before. Did you
    ever hear of such a slut?   (II. ii.)

Every phrase counts, Foppington's self-revelation serving to reflect the suicidal, self-contradictory quality of his behaviour. But his rights are dramatically maintained, his self-confidence persists, and at the conclusion he bears his rejection by Lady Betty with an innate courtesy. The handling is subtle and this interplay of new morality with old cynicism gives the creation a truth neither alone could possess.

Lady Betty's cruelty is admirably diagnosed. Her main delight is power; in her wit duels with her lover she shows strength; however, she fights a losing battle. The plot arranged to overthrow her pride is rather heavily handled by the dramatist, though dialogue and characterization are throughout brilliant.

The reformation of Sir Charles is our main interest. From the start he is self-critical, we are aware that his love-affairs are giving him little satisfaction, and he can see and denounce the faults in Lady Betty. When at the climax his wife finds him sleeping beside the servant-maid with whom he has been carrying on an affair, Cibber by a brilliant stroke allows her a moving utterance in broken verse:

> The ease of a few tears
> Is all that's left to me—
> And duty, too, forbids me to insult
> Where I have vowed obedience. Perhaps
> The fault's in me, and nature has not formed
> Me with the thousand little requisites
> That warm the heart to love.
> Somewhere there is a fault:
> But heaven best knows what both of us deserve.
>   (V. v.)

'Somewhere there is a fault'; that is the text of Cibber's kindly genius.

Without losing himself in false sentimentality or moral doctrine, he adds a new dimension to the tradition, weaving the sympathetic virtues into the old fabrics of cynicism and licence.

Sir Richard Steele is less concerned with the sexual problem, but he has strong convictions, especially on duelling. In *The Lying Lover* (1703) the hero, thinking that he has killed his friend in a duel, is shown in prison struck by remorse. Hitherto a young man of carefree irresponsibility, his heart melts into pathos and repentance. *The Conscious Lovers* (1722), with a hero whose 'religious vow' (II. i) prevents his marrying without his father's consent, drives ethic to a dangerous extreme. Disguising his love, young Bevil is content just to serve his lady, claiming that such selflessness is the highest happiness; which, though it may be true, needs a greater power than Steele commands if it is to convince us. However, his readiness to accept and emphasize moral values is one with his ability to give us a firm story. In those Restoration dramatists who refused morality its rights, wit had to do the work of action. Plot they never mastered. Steele's social interests include the country as well as the town and the middle class as well as the aristocrat. He opens up new freedoms, pointing on to Cumberland and Sheridan.

II

The Augustan world-view was in danger of self-satisfaction. Internal warring having been replaced by peace and patriotism, the more acute minds turn to satire, aiming to reveal the poisons over-filmed by social pretence. Satire and mock heroics become a natural medium. So does opera: poetry, wanting the Dionysian inwardness, elaborates its drama with music. These tendencies are found in Gay and Fielding.

In his little burlesque *The Mohocks* (1712) John Gay shows the gangsters of the underworld turning the tables on the watch, or police, and his farce *The What D'Ye Call It* (1715) blends satire against the penal system with song. *The Beggar's Opera* (1728) celebrates a union of merriment and horror. We are in the lowest society: informers, blackmailers, thieves, double-crossers, an underworld of iniquity. Nevertheless it is more than mockery and the humorous extravagance is a means, not an end. Gay is trying to relate contemporary society to heroism.

The hero is Captain Macheath, a noble-spirited highwayman in danger of hanging. The semi-heroic robber, of which Robin Hood is an archetype, has perennial appeal, as a rebel against society. To be heroically effective he must be brave, chivalrous, and loyal to his comrades: 'There is not a finer gentleman upon the road than the Captain' (I. iv). Such figures serve to blend the darker virilities with virtue.

His companions do not recognize the civil order; they win by the law of arms, are above fear and claim to be more loyal to each other than courtiers. The topsy-turvy attributing to the gangsters of a sense of honour denied to the aristocrat is a comic and cutting social stroke. High life is vicious and society unjust:

> We are for a just partition of the world, for every man hath a right
> to enjoy life. (II. i.)

Macheath is a miniature Napoleon, willing a better order: the avaricious are the true robbers, 'for money was made for the free-hearted and generous' (II. i). He has a generosity unknown to high life where, when one's resources are gone, people are ready enough with pity and advice, 'but shift you for money from friend to friend' (III. iv; Air XLIV). Gay probably has *Timon of Athens* in mind, and Brome too perhaps. Like Timon, the hero is brought up against ingratitude, being betrayed by his associates. Perhaps the thieves are no better than the courtiers after all, and except for the two ladies who love him, Macheath is finally alone.

The gallows stands over the action: after the various judicial torments of seventeenth-century drama, the fascination is now narrowed to hanging. In this period it functions as a public entertainment, at once punishment, ritual, and sacrifice. To the women the condemned man is a hero:

> Beneath the left ear so fit but a cord
> (A rope so charming a zone is!)
> The youth in his cart hath the air of a lord,
> And we cry, There dies an Adonis!
> (I. iv; Air III.)

This prepossession pervades the opera, using a mixture of judicial horror and lyric gaiety that is to recur in the operas of Gilbert and Sullivan.

Despite the light treatment substances are contained harking back to the origins of drama. The fun and music are the terms in which the superlative and liberating hero, Adonis or superman, can be glimpsed; 'But we, gentlemen, have still honour enough to break through the corruptions of the world' (III. iv).

In the sequel, *Polly* (1728), Macheath has sadly deteriorated into a villainous pirate in the West Indies. The native Indians are noble and good; European planters and pirates wicked. The satire against Europe, where wisdom is only esteemed as a step to wealth which 'raises ourselves and trips up our neighbours' (III. xi), is comparatively crude. Our only real hope is in Macheath's girl-wife Polly, who has followed him in boy's disguise, and from this bisexual dimension contrasts with the other Europeans 'like a gem found in rubbish' (III. iii). More successful is *The Distress'd Wife* (prod. 1734), a straight comedy wherein a husband is tormented by his wife's extravagance. Confronted by the bills that are ruining her husband she cries: 'Give me your hideous papers, then' (V. vi), only to fling them away. The psychology is excellent.

Gay is more worried about money than about sex, and this particular anxiety, which existed as a minor theme in earlier comedy, from now on becomes emphatic. We find it in Henry Fielding.

Like Gay, he wrote both straight plays and extravaganzas. The former are characterized by a close and caustic concern with both the sexual problem and money. Morality does not come easily to him. Modesty is 'a flaming sword to keep mankind out of Paradise' and an honest woman may be 'a greater plague to her husband' than a loose one (*Love in Several Masks*, 1728; IV. iii; *The Universal Gallant*, 1734; V. i). In *The Wedding Day* (comp. 1731) love gradually wins over licence, though it is a stiff tussle. 'Rakery', we are told, must be accepted, being 'a disease in the blood, which every man is born with' (II. xi), and the poetry of sexual delight—'We'll wind our senses to a height of rapture' (III. x)—is exploited. But gradually the opposing logic is driven home and Millamour admits the absurdity of a code which makes it 'infamous for women to grant what it is honourable for us to solicit' (V. iii). Fielding is honest; he knows human nature; the victory for morals does not, cannot, come easily.

He is in little doubt regarding more general corruptions. His dramatic genius is instinctively satiric, much of it in the tradition of *Timon of Athens*. The prevailing interest of *The Modern Husband* (1731) is money. Lord Richly, who holds a levee like Timon's while despising his flatterers, is an ogre of vice; and we are warned against fawning friends who will disburse nothing to save a man from ruin

(II. v). Gambling dominates. The plot turns on a hundred pound note that changes hands again and again with dramatic results. Stronger, if less subtle, is *The Fathers or The Good Natured Man* (comp. c. 1734; discovered and produced posthumously), a satire on avarice, wherein Mr Boncour, a man of simple Timon-like trust and generosity, is warned by his brother that were he in need no friends would help him. He agrees to his son and daughter marrying into the family of old Valence, a distrustful and mean-minded man. Boncour's pretence of ruin reveals the nastiness of the Valence family, though his own children stand the test and his warm-hearted philosophy is to this extent justified.

Fielding's satiric genius finds further scope in operetta and farce, attacking avarice, corruption in justice and politics, hypocrisy, oppression, and indeed all the rampaging iniquities of society. He is never far from the wave-length of Timon's curses: the poet Spatter in *Eurydice Hissed* (1737) has a drama on the *Timon* pattern. The attack on Sir Robert Walpole in *The Historical Register for the Year 1736* (1737) resulted in the Licensing, or Censorship, Act of 1737. But such satire is by itself either too ephemeral or too obvious; what we need is some positive aim or aspiration, and if we cannot have it direct the contact must be made, as in *The Beggar's Opera*, by burlesque. The burlesque of poetic drama in *Tom Thumb the Great* (1730) has probably enjoyed a greater reputation than it deserves, its effects depending on the too simple expedient, so often found in bad burlesque acting, of doing badly what the original has done well. The reminiscence of *Othello* in 'Oh Huncamunca, Huncamunca, oh' (II. v) is neither good poetry nor good burlesque; and we have only to turn to the extravaganzas of J. R. Planché (p. 274 below) to see how such things should be done. However, *Pasquin*, 'a dramatic satire on the times' (1736), is a delight. The rehearsal of Trapwit's *The Election* leads to a remark worth the whole of *Tom Thumb*:

> FUSTIAN: 'Dreamt', sir? Why, I thought the time of your comedy had been confined to the same day, Mr Trapwit?
> TRAPWIT: No, sir, it is not; but suppose it was, might she not have taken an afternoon's nap? (III. i.)

Fustian's tragedy *The Life and Death of Common Sense* follows, with an amusing introduction of stage ghosts to mark a discrepancy between the Augustan consciousness of the supernatural and that of previous and succeeding periods.

The relation of Augustan common sense to these deeper intuitions of our tradition is again brought to mind by one of the farces of Samuel Foote, *The Orators* (1762), where the ghost of a certain Miss Fanny that had been disturbing and exciting London is put on trial; she insists that she can only be tried by her peers, and though it is argued that her tappings were material it is finally ruled that she is 'unquestionably entitled to a jury of ghosts' (II). Issues not so very dissimilar have in all seriousness arisen, and it is interesting to find such an issue being dramatized, however farcically, in Augustan London.[1]

The second half of the century saw a deluge of light drama in farce, operetta, and extravaganza. To these the actor David Garrick contributed as a minor dramatist of a keenly critical intelligence and a terse and pointed style. An outstanding playlet is Isaac Bicker-staffe's comic operetta *Lionel and Clarissa* (1768), in which a licentious father is made the unwitting and highly amusing accomplice of his daughter's elopement.

III

Meanwhile a new warmth was being brought to high comedy. In it humour was to be one with sympathy, and sympathy involves respect for the softer, more humane, at the limit the more moral, valuations. Such warmth liberates the dramatist, loosening the joints of dramatic technique, and gives us action. And the action is meaningful; it is not over-complicated by intrigue, nor simply narrative; it has significances from within. Wit and brilliance assume less importance. Much of this was forecast by Steele, but now it is to be done with more assurance.

George Colman was a leading dramatist, covering the usual themes, including inevitably one on finance, a young spendthrift and 'hollow' (II) friends, called *The Man of Business* (1774). *The Clandestine Marriage* (1766), in which he collaborated with Garrick, is notable for the clever study of the old beau Lord Ogleby.[2] His best is *The Jealous Wife* (1761).

Here what we may call 'the new comedy' appears in strength. The

[1] For the famous 'Cock-Lane Ghost', also referred to in Garrick's *The Farmer's Return from London*, 1762, see the Letters of Horace Walpole to Georg Montagu, 2 February 1762; and Elizabeth P. Stein, *David Garrick, Dramatist*, New York, 1938, 161–4.

[2] Elizabeth P. Stein regards Garrick's as the major contribution.

story, which owes something to Fielding's novel *Tom Jones*, is exciting, the character studies varied, and the situations telling. The psychological insight is keen as Cibber's, while relying more on stage-craft and less on literary brilliance. Mrs Oakly torments her husband like a Cibber heroine. Persuaded by his brother, Major Oakly, to assert his rights, the poor man agrees:

> I believe you're in the right, Major! I see you're in the right. I'll do't,
> I'll certainly do't . . .   (I.)

He fears distressing her, true, but he works himself up to it: 'I will have my own way, I am determin'd'. He is 'adamant'. He is to go out on his own initiative to dine with the Major, who doubts his courage:

> OAKLY: I will. I'll be a fool to her no longer. But hark ye, Major!
> My hat and sword lie in my study. I'll go and steal them out, while
> she is busy talking with Charles.
> MAJOR: Steal them! For shame! Prithee take them boldly, call for
> them . . .   (I.)

Mrs Oakly catches him, crushes his scheme, walks away and turns at the door: 'Mr Oakly!' He replies, 'O, my dear', and follows her.

A wide canvas gives us the country squire Russet, whose daughter has run away to avoid marrying Sir Harry Beagle, to whom a girl is a creature inferior to horses and hounds; the unprincipled town aristocrats Lady Freelove and Lord Trinket who are satirized survivals from the older comedies made to strike repellent figures in the new; the Irish adventurer Captain O'Cutter; and the young and irresponsible hero Charles. Charles is likable, though wild. Our new comedies are to offer a succession of such virile young men, descendants of Fielding's Tom Jones, whose instincts lead them to drink or sexual laxity but who are guilty of nothing more than high spirits and warm hearts.

We are in a wider world. Denial of the softer values had for long been a stifling limitation. Now in *The Jealous Wife* Mr and Mrs Oakly do not suffer because the wife itches for power or the husband is licentious, but simply because they love each other: 'What a strange world we live in! No two people in it love one another better than my brother and sister, and yet the bitterest enemies could not torment each other more heartily' (IV). That is our new, more hopeful, note; nor is it false to human nature.

A yet greater warmth inspires the dramas of Richard Cumberland. His rich talent covered both tragedy and comedy, and in comedy he is equally at home with sentiment and satire. *The Natural Son* (1784) offers a revealing contrast of nature and town life:

> Nay, if you talk sentiment to me, Blushenly, you'll set me a-crying; hands off from that edg'd tool if you love me. Sentiment in the country is clear another thing from sentiment in town; in my box at the Opera I can take it as glibly as a dish of tea, down it goes and there's an end of it; but in walks of willows, and by the side of rivulets, there's no joke in it. I'm undone if I hear it by moonlight— Of all things in the creation I hate pity.   (I.)

His surface style is as pointed as anyone's, when he wishes, but his main concentration is on the human heart. He is fond of dour, apparently man-hating, disillusioned types who have within hearts of gold. Such is Mortimer, the caustic, Apemantus-like critic of the extravagant Lord Abberville in *The Fashionable Lover* (1772) who is yet the agent of final happiness; such again is Penruddock in *The Wheel of Fortune* (1795).[1] Cumberland is aware of a warmth, a generous love, instinctive but thwarted; and his most vivid dramatic statement of it is *The West Indian* (1771).

The aptly named young Belcour comes from the West Indies to a London merchant whom he thinks his guardian and who is really his father, watching his son's extraordinary behaviour with some anxiety. The young man's reckless ways lead to most amusing complications. Closely interwoven is a story of true love and poverty contrasted with the hypocrisy and avarice of a sanctimonious lady who refuses to help a penurious relative and descends finally to fraudulency.

All converges on Belcour, the most fascinating of our many wild young heroes. He has 'strong animal spirits', 'honour', and 'benevolence' (III. v); his amatory passions are exuberant and promiscuous, and the reverse of cynical; he is generosity personified and as happy in relieving distress as in an amatory conquest (II. vi). In him you cannot easily distinguish sexual instinct from Christian charity, since his actions are all impulsive, from the one emotional centre. Such qualities are brought sharply up against 'the cunning and contrivances of this intriguing town'—London (IV. x). Our usual contrast of country simplicity and town vice is here extended by his having come from Jamaica: the sun was vertical at his birth (III. i) and it is still active in both his passions and his kindliness. That 'blessed' torrid zone has quickened his nature into benignity, whereas the northern latitudes are made rather for politics and philosophy than

---

[1] This, together with *The Jew* (1794), we shall discuss later (pp. 242–3). For Cumberland's tragedy *The Battle of Hastings* see pp. 197–200.

for 'friendship' (III. vii). To him London appears an overgrown, noisy and chaotic place where 'the whole morning is a bustle to get money and the whole afternoon is a hurry to spend it' (III. vii):

> What evil planet drew me from that warm sunny region, where naked nature walks without disguise, into this cold contriving artificial country?   (IV. x.)

'He is, simply, too 'honest' (v. i) for it.

In strong contrast is the sanctimonious but mean-minded Lady Rusport, daughter of a puritan who never laughed nor 'allowed it in his children' (I. vi). Despite her religion, says the kindly Irishman, Major O'Flaherty, she is 'hard-hearted as a hyena'; indeed no animal is so savage as a human being 'without pity' (II. xi). She thinks only of money.

The plot is both lively and amusing. It is organically harmonious, at once meaningful and convincing. The £200 on which the action turns is as artistically used as are the references to nature and the sun; money and the cosmos confront each other. Belcour's irregularities are finally forgiven and he is accepted by the girl Louisa, to whom he promises fidelity. Such a work as this has universal pointings and we may suppose that instinct and fidelity are to be regarded as compatible; so too, when the money expected by Lady Rusport comes instead to her deserving nephew, Charles, it is as 'the justice of Heaven' (v. vi); and as for the various discoveries and recognitions, 'O my conscience', says O'Flaherty, 'I think we shall be all related by and by' (v. viii), a truth of human brotherhood similarly conveyed at the conclusion of Cumberland's *The Jew* (p. 243).

What is our conclusion? Charity is 'a main clause in the great statute of Christianity' (I. vi). Belcour has it, by instinct. His uninhibited self-expression appears to condition alike his failings and his virtues, whereas the puritanical and cold-hearted Lady Rusport descends to fraud to prevent her nephew getting his legacy. Does some degree of sexual freedom condition virtue? Belcour 'would not be so perfect, were he free from fault' (III. i). He is conceived as a new type of man who 'does nothing like other people' (IV. x), he is one who 'comes amongst you a new character, an inhabitant of a new world' (v. iii). Whereas in most of us 'the soul grows narrower every hour' (III. vii), Belcour has preserved a child-like innocence into sexual maturity and sexual activity; and this innocence is contrasted with the money-greedy and sanctimonious society of London. Belcour points on to Byron's Sardanapalus and recalls Berowne's equation of 'love' and 'charity' in *Love's Labour's Lost* (IV. iii). After completing *The West Indian* Cumberland made an adaptation of *Timon of Athens*.

A different reading of generosity was given in Oliver Goldsmith's rather heavily manipulated *The Good Natured Man* (1767), which pivots on the psychological study of Young Honeywood, a benevolent spendthrift whose benevolence is in part to be attributed to lack of judgement and weakness of disposition. We have an interesting contrast to our many studies favouring youthful benevolence: Goldsmith is cautious.

She Stoops to Conquer (1773) has a greater richness. The farcical action is set in motion by the rollicking Tony Lumpkin, redolent of village life, whose supposedly dull wits succeed in throwing everyone into a salutary confusion. The trick by which Hastings and Marlowe are made to take Mr Hardcastle's house for an inn leads to one of the most amusing situations in all our comedy. It also enables the shy Marlowe's free manner with girls of an inferior status to assist him despite his social inhibitions to a genuine marriage. Tony's practical joke on Mrs Hardcastle, whereby she thinks herself stranded among highwaymen, though she is in her own back garden, may be read as an apt retribution for her foolish respect for social glitter. Country is set against town, instinct against conventions, simplicity against sophistication. The country-house atmosphere is well realized; we feel the surrounding country, its by-lanes and slow life. These are our ruling powers, with the old family retainer Diggory as a symbol and Tony Lumpkin, functioning like Shakespeare's Puck in the wood near Athens, as presiding genius.

Our account is crowned by the plays of Richard Brinsley Sheridan. *The Rivals* (1775) offers less a particular reading of human affairs than a comprehensive embodiment of them. Life's abundance is before us, as in Homer or a Tolstoy novel. We know the society of eighteenth-century Bath, its walks and parks, its libraries; we know its people, the romantic novel-reading Lydia Languish, descending from Steele's *The Tender Husband* (1705) and from Colman's *Polly Honeycombe* (1760); the attractively comic country squire Bob Acres and our best Irishman, Sir Lucius O'Trigger; and some delightful servants; and Mrs Malaprop's misused vocabulary. Each is strongly individual and yet typical, original and yet normal. Goldsmith may have more warmth, an earth-contact outside Sheridan's artistry, but in terms of his artistry Sheridan gives us a created world.

Events are rapid, exciting, and amusing. The action is not over-complicated by intrigue, nor reliant on descriptions, nor dominated by sex talk, nor wit. It is, simply, dramatic. Just as stage gesture precedes speech, so we are not asked to think or know anything that we have not a split second before been made to experience; only so much information as can be *acted* is given us at any one time. The opening dialogue between the servant Fag and the coachman is a masterpiece of dramatic exposition. Here is another:

> LYDIA: Well, I cannot blame you for defending him. But tell me candidly, Julia, had he never saved your life, do you think you should have been attached to him as you are? Believe me, the rude blast that overset your boat was a prosperous gale of love to him.
>
> (I. ii.)

The facts are insinuated, they grow into us, as a side issue; we find that we know them without having had to think.

The surface appears unintellectual, but there is really more, not less, mental activity at work. There are no Jonsonian caricatures: we simply watch the normal springing to life under comic emphasis.

We are used to attacks on tyrannic parents and arranged marriages. Here Captain Absolute, after being promised a fortune by his father, hears suddenly that a wife is involved:

> CAPTAIN ABSOLUTE: Sir! Sir! You amaze me!
> SIR ANTHONY: Why, what the devil's the matter with the fool? Just now you were all gratitude and duty.
> CAPTAIN ABSOLUTE: I was, sir—you talked to me of independence and a fortune, but not a word of a wife.
> SIR ANTHONY: Why, what difference does that make? Odds life, sir! if you have the estate, you must take it with the live-stock on it, as it stands.
>
> (II. i.)

That is not satire; humour dominates; yet satiric thought is contained. The psychological realism of Sir Anthony's subsequent rage, fuming through his protestations of calmness, is delightful; so is that of his son's unloading of his anger on to a servant afterwards; and of that servant's doing the same to a page-boy, in his turn. The truth, or thought, is within the dramatic action, and humour its circumference, or aura.

The jealously sensitive Faulkland's love for Julia touches neurosis. After solicitously inquiring as to her health, he is soon pervertedly worrying at the thought of her gaiety, and ends up as a dynamo of self-torment, his agony being exquisitely capped by Bob Acres's 'The gentleman wa'n't angry at my praising his mistress, was he?'

(II. i). The Faulkland–Julia relationship is driven to a near-tragic intensity:

> JULIA: Oh! You torture me to the heart! I cannot bear it.
> FAULKLAND: I do not mean to distress you. If I loved you less, I
> should never give you an uneasy moment.   (III. ii.)

Jealousy is an old enough theme, but never was the torment given a stage artistry more intimately, absurdly and yet pathetically, convincing. Perhaps no dramatist but Shakespeare draws level with Sheridan in this ability to think and work so closely in terms of dramatic experience. We are asked to take nothing on trust.

Duelling, so persistent an anxiety from Davenant down, especially strong in Steele and in Hugh Kelly's *The School for Wives* (1773), is neatly handled through the characters of Sir Lucius O'Trigger and the worried Bob Acres, trying despite himself to be fierce, though uncertain as to the rights of it all:

> SIR LUCIUS: What the devil signifies *right* when your honour is
> concerned? Do you think Achilles or my little Alexander the
> Great ever inquired where the right lay?   (III. iv.)

The artificiality of Acres's attempt at anger suggests a similar absurdity in the code which prompts it, and the critique expands to the whole heroic tradition, with an extension to imperial and international affairs. The humour has ignition quality; it illuminates a wide field, and is more effective than volumes of argument.

Perhaps Sheridan's most typifying trick is his way of showing people being amused at a situation wherein the audience knows that it is they themselves who are being fooled. The 'Ha! Ha!' of the printed page (as in III. iii) conveys little of the stage effect, though the relevant thought-extensions are many. The comic opera *The Duenna* (1775) is made almost entirely from this type of dramatic irony.

Sheridan is the richer for his free use of earlier dramatic themes: *The School for Scandal* (1777) is a studied, patterned work, summing up a long comic tradition. In the scandalmongers' wit talk and the marital relationship of the oldish Sir Peter Teazle and his young and all but seduced wife we have the world of Restoration comedy under satirical and moral control. In the contrast of Charles Surface as wild-libertine-with-a-heart-of-gold against his puritanical and hypocritical brother Joseph we are in the world of the 'new comedy'. There is not here the vivacity and tang of *The Rivals*; the careful patterning precludes that. It is a distillation of a century's comedy, rather as *The Tempest* is a distillation of Shakespeare's life-work.

Lady Teazle descends from a line of tormenting ladies of country origin caught up by pleasures of the town, Gay's heroine (p. 177 above) being perhaps the nearest; and her quarrelling with Sir Peter is vastly amusing. She refers to her 'elegant' expenses:

> SIR PETER: 'Slife, madam, I say, had you any of these little elegant
> expenses when you married me?
> LADY TEAZLE: Lud, Sir Peter, would you have me be out of the
> fashion?
> SIR PETER: The fashion, indeed! What had you to do with the
> fashion before you married me?
> LADY TEAZLE: For my part, I should think you would like to have
> your wife thought a woman of taste.
> SIR PETER: Aye—there again—taste—Zounds! madam, you had no
> taste when you married me!   (II. i.)

That is not, as literature, subtle, yet though it is far from easy to put across it is potentially a piece of brilliant theatre. The 'wit' is not in the people, but in the manipulation of dramatic dialogue. The people are tangled by their own talk and actions, controlled expertly by the dramatist, who forces them to self-revelation. The famous screen scene (IV. iii) is Sheridan's most consummate exploitation of stage irony. We watch Sir Peter having fun with Joseph Surface about the 'little French milliner' behind the screen, whilst we await the climax of his discovery that it is his own wife. As always, the comedy is based on matters of deep human concern. Within this one situation we have compacted the shock given Sir Peter, the shame fallen on Lady Teazle, and the disclosure of Joseph's hypocrisy. The economy is extraordinary: it is in this loading of dramatic action rather than in speech as such that Sheridan is pre-eminent. His language is, in comparison with some of his predecessors, less rapier-like, the wit less quick-silvery—Cumberland's *The Natural Son* has more of that —but it is better as stage talk. The literary consciousness is not stimulated; it rests, letting drama awake.

Charles Surface recalls *The West Indian* and also, inevitably, *Timon of Athens*. Charles is 'the most dissipated and extravagant young fellow in the kingdom' (I. i); he loves 'wine and women' (IV. ii); but he is generous, endeavouring to raise money 'in the midst of his own distresses' for a penurious relative (III. i) and refusing to sell his uncle's picture for an exorbitant price (IV. i). We see him, like Timon, at a feast, praising drink like Byron's Sardanapalus. Conversely the puritanical and hypocritical Joseph receives a request for financial help in the manner of Timon's friends (V. i). This contrast we have met before and shall meet again: it is one of the main themes in our dramatic tradition.

The new comedy is deliberately balanced against the old. Wit of immoral innuendo has as its spokesman the unamiable Joseph Surface: 'for when a scandalous story is believed against one, there certainly is no comfort like the consciousness of having deserved it' (IV. iii). For the rest, it is the preserve of the scandalmongers, whose choric tattling becomes finally a satanic horror: 'Fiends! vipers! furies! Oh, that their own venom would choke them!' (v. ii). It is typical of Sheridan that the worst condemnation falls on the hypocrite, Joseph, whereas an obvious villain such as Snake has his own dignity. Having been bribed to betray his employers he implores secrecy since 'if it were once known that I had been betrayed into an honest action, I should lose every friend I have in the world' (v. iii).

The Critic (1779), our best burlesque of heroic drama, is a natural flowering of Sheridan's dramatic genius. We have seen that he himself never relies on laboured information, or second-hand description. Here is his burlesque:

> SIR WALTER RALEIGH: Philip, you know, is proud Iberia's king!
> SIR CHRISTOPHER HATTON: He is.
> SIR WALTER RALEIGH: His subjects in base bigotry
> And Catholic oppression held—while we,
> You know, the Protestant persuasion
> [hold.
> SIR CHRISTOPHER HATTON: We do.   (II.ii.)

Again, for narrative:

> PUFF: Hey, what the plague! What a cut is here!—why, what is become of the description of her first meeting with Don Whiskerandos? his gallant behaviour in the sea fight, and the simile of the canary bird?
> TILBURINA: Indeed, sir, you'll find they will not be missed.   (II. ii.)

So too with another description, 'one of the finest and most laboured things' (II. ii) cut, wisely, by the players.

These are tangible excellences; less tangible is the excellence of the verse lending itself beautifully not to that anathema the burlesque voice but to a subtle vocal projection, as good as may be, until the moment when, following the suggested lilt, the ever so faint ineffectuality, the whole edifice crashes. As for Burleigh's silent entry, his gravity, his shaking of the head all without a word and yet intended to be so fraught with meaning—well, what questions of dramatic art and literature in collaboration or opposition does it not raise?

Our recent discussions have treated what may be called the golden age of our national comedy, for which much of the credit goes to Ireland. From Farquhar to Goldsmith and Sheridan a large number of our dramatists were of Irish extraction. The later comedies especially appear far richer, at once more dramatic and of more human value, than the old comedies of sex wit and literary finesse. This new comedy has its own peculiar strength: the strength of what we might call 'normality'. It is sex friendly and sex warm, as the other was not. Consider even how obtrusive would be one of our pert or seraphic boy-girls or girl-boys in *The West Indian*, *She Stoops to Conquer* or *The Rivals*: acceptance of youthful licence followed by an expectation of marriage fidelity appears to render such bisexual solutions no longer necessary. The new comedy has both more morality and more sympathy than the old. It is, however, arguable that a certain essence is being shirked, and that these warm comedies have bought their warmth at a cost. If so, it was a fair bargain.

IV

In tragedy and heroic drama too the eighteenth century shows a new morality and a new softening. The emphasis is a daylight, Apollonian emphasis; Dionysian and numinous effects are less frequent; ghosts are unwanted and spirit life neglected. We have few examples of violent sexual passion—one of the most powerful occurs not in a play but in Alexander Pope's dramatic monologue *Eloisa to Abelard*—and many of heroism; and this heroism is not, as in Dryden, a matter of personal honour, but patriotic. The communal horrors of the past century give place to a communal purpose. War and imperialism are criticized whereas Protestant Britain is regarded as the bearer of freedom, peace, and commerce across the world. Contemporary patriotism shines through historical stories; ancient Rome may be felt either as the bearer of stoical virtues or as a too ruthless imperial power, like contemporary France; and many dramas are composed on British history.

Nicholas Rowe illustrates the transition. *The Ambitious Stepmother* (1701) is in the older vein with a restless and violent queen and a rescue at the cost of her own life by the 'sweet saint' Cleone in boy's dress (IV. iii). Next *The Fair Penitent* (1703) balances strong evil against softer and redemptive powers. The gay seducer, Lothario, has fascination, and the seduced Calista is assertive in sin; both gain our respect in their refusal to be other than they are. Though in her distress she is forced by Lothario's faithlessness and her father's wrath to anguish, her very repentance has a Websterian dignity:

> Thus torn, defac'd and wretched as I seem
> Still I have something of Sciolto's virtue ...
> (IV. i.)

At the last Calista is softened, hard though it be for her imperious nature, by her father's and husband's forgiveness. We have a remarkable balance and interpenetration of Jacobean self-assertion and the softer values. A new dimension of moral warmth, already forecast in the pathos of Otway, is apparent.

Such an expansion has its dangers, since it can so easily lead to sentimentality and platitude. Rowe steers his course skilfully. In *Jane Shore* (1714), set in the reign of Richard III, a heavier emphasis falls on penitence. Richard is brutal, the guilt of the fiery Alicia drives her mad, but Jane has the dignity of repentance. Rowe is strong in religious feeling and also in patriotism. The strange contrast in his early *Tamerlane* (1701) of the Scythian conqueror as a man of humility hating war and the villainous Bajazet was intended to shadow a contrast of William III and Louis XIV. *The Royal Convert* (1707), dramatizing a conflict of pagan Saxon and Christian Britain, ends with a prophecy of Queen Anne, who, though she delights most 'in peaceful arts', will oppose tyrants and free the 'groaning nations' (v). More subtle is *Lady Jane Grey* (1715), concerned with the rivals for succession to the sick boy-king Edward VI: Jane and Mary. Lady Jane is a Protestant and a student of Greek philosophy; Mary a Catholic. Lady Jane is pre-eminently the patriot: against the threat of 'bloody zeal', 'priestly power', and 'idol' worship (I) stands 'fairest Albion', famed for liberty, whose rights and laws must be preserved (III). Though the end is tragic it is suffused by a sense of omnipotence active beyond the petty dealings of man.

The most interesting of John Dennis's dramas is *Liberty Assured* (1704), on the rivalry of the French and the British in Canada. From an intricate yet naturally unfurling plot arise some intense situations. The dominating contrast is of Britain as preserver of liberty and justice against the French tyranny which has brought 'impious war' to these 'happy groves' (v). But the propagandist bias does not preclude a generous humanism asserting that 'every brave man's country is the universe' (II. ii). Patriotic feeling comes from the conviction that Britain is supporting 'the dignity of human nature' (II. ii). We end happily with a fusion of parties. The verse is heavy, but the handling of imperial issues able. Dennis's severe and semi-Roman interests found a congenial theme in *Appius and Virginia* (1709). That Roman nobility aroused a contemporary response can be seen from the success achieved by Joseph Addison's *Cato* (1713), which is, however, little more than a one-way study of stoic virtue serving to underline the dangers attendant on a moralistic drama.

Some interesting thoughts on imperialism enliven Ambrose Philips's *The Briton* (1722). How far we are to align the Roman conquerors with France is not clear; the rights of both Romans and Britons are neatly expressed and British imperialism too may be in question. Valens claims that Rome has changed the ancient Britons from 'barbarians' to 'men'; Vanoc, for Britain, answers that they have been turned into 'servile beasts' gaining at the best a certain material comfort in exchange for liberty. When he calls Rome with all her arts and laws the true 'protectors of mankind' Valens arouses a withering response:

> Came you then here, thus far, through waves, to conquer,
> To waste, to plunder, out of mere compassion?
>
> (III. viii.)

Valens, however, has a case: though 'lions in spirit' the Britons had been horribly cruel, their altars reeking with human sacrifice. Later on he observes that their 'native fierceness' will in turn 'ripen into virtue' (IV. iv). These arguments alone lift Philips's drama to importance.

His verse is more pliant than Dennis's. His use of a vivid stabbing utterance, jerked out by pressure of situation and emotion, is well exploited in *Humfrey, Duke of Gloucester* (1723), a powerful expansion of incidents handled more briefly by Shakespeare in *Henry VI*. Humfrey and his wife Eleanor have Wycliffian religious views; against them is the wicked Bishop Beaufort, whose evil schemes culminate in Gloucester's murder in a nightmarish atmosphere reminiscent of *Macbeth*. The contrast of religious enlightenment and Catholic wickedness is driven home with the usual Augustan emphasis. Praise must be accorded the rapidly advancing action, the nervous dialogue and the powerful if derivative atmospheric effects.

Patriotism again fires James Thomson's *Sophonisba* (1729). The
public-spirited Carthaginian heroine sees the Romans as vexers of
the world, their prided justice as a pretence and their civilization as
slavery:

> Against her tyrant power each generous sword
> Of every nation should be drawn.
>
> (III. iii.)

All Carthage—or Britain—asks is commercial freedom to carry the
blessings of 'plenty', 'letters', 'science' and 'wealth' across the
globe. That was the Augustan ideal; in its cause personal passions
must be sacrificed, as Sophonisba sacrifices hers. Both sides have
communal virtues. Sophonisba's lover Massinissa is urged by the
Roman Scipio to put heroism above passion. The speeches are over-
long and talk smothers action, but the conception of Sophonisba-as-
patriot is powerful. *Edward and Eleanora* (1739), on the Crusades, is
well filled with anti-imperialistic thought. Possession creates a right
and there is no excuse for the Crusaders' 'rapine' and 'slaughter'
(I. iii.). The Sultan, who magnanimously risks his life for Eleanor,
speaks out well:

> You call us bigots—O! Can'st thou with that
> Reproach us, Christian prince? What brought thee hither?
> What else but bigotry?
>
> (V. iii.)

The attack is, of course, against Christians in a Catholic period.
The Sultan is heroically conceived. Our Augustan dramatists have a
clear conception of heroism usually felt as constituent to some
universal, because humane, cause. Thomson's masque *Alfred* (1740)
contains a vision of Edward III and Elizabeth I, with especial
praise accorded William III as opposer of superstition and supporter
of law and freedom, and with thoughts on Britain's victory over
France and supremacy on the sea and in commerce. It contains the
lyric 'Rule, Britannia'.

A simple and all-good heroism, however enlightened, does not
really demand dramatic expression; drama is only powerful when
facing the complexities; and once Thomson faced them, in *Tancred
and Sigismunda* (1745). The newly crowned young king, Tancred, has
been tricked by the patriotic statecraft of his old adviser Siffredi into
appearing in public false to his love Sigismunda, Siffredi's own
daughter, in order to satisfy certain necessary conditions of his
election. Intense and complex situations develop fast, with strong

reversals and poignant emotions. No one is basically at fault. An astringent idealism inspires Siffredi's trickery:

> Few get above this turbid scene of strife.
> Few gain the summit, breathe that purest air,
> That heavenly ether, which untroubled sees
> The storm of vice and passion rage blow.
>
> (I. iv.)

Tancred is urged to think beyond himself, of the State, of the dangers of civil war; of all the simple people, the labouring masses (II. viii); to these, as king, to sacrifice personal integrity, renounce his love and marry the daughter of his father's murderer. The conflict of allegiances is torturing. Whichever way he turns 'dishonour rears her hideous front'; 'virtue' opposes 'virtue'. But he decides that private integrity conditions public virtue and becomes fiercely set on dispelling the lie (II. viii). When he learns that Sigismunda, believing him faithless, has herself been forced into a marriage, his wrath against her father is withering. For has he not, while talking of 'rights' (IV. iv), trampled all human values underfoot?

The rapid developments within a compact, classic form, recall the French dramatists: we have the idealism of Corneille blended with the passionate subtleties of Racine. The accepted civic virtues are thrown into sharp conflict with the most sacred personal values; virtue is not so simple after all. Perhaps nowhere else in British drama is so fierce an action made from the clash of virtuous interests, and this particular conflict of personal and political values is certainly of first importance. The conclusion is that to tyrannize over the heart is to 'betray' the 'great ties of social life' (v. viii): the public weal is not an absolute. *Tancred and Sigismunda* may be accounted our finest drama in the neo-classic mode.

We have been surveying works representative of contemporary idealism. With Edward Young's *Busiris, King of Egypt* (1719) we return to a sombre tone reminiscent of the Jacobeans and pointing on to the Romantics. Busiris is a ruthless yet not despicable tyrant. The historic context of ancient Egypt is well realized. A popular revolution is rising and there is a strong, perhaps contemporary, sense of social repression. But the main interest is personal. The prince, Myron, loves Mandane, daughter of his tutor in war and fast friend, Nicanor. Since her love is given elsewhere he is tempted to force her; in a state of self-conflict bordering on distraction he resists the temptation; they are by chance thrown together; the revolution is rising and it seems that she is one of the rebels; he forces her. His

fall appears almost inevitable. So many accidents, he says, concur
to work

> My passions up to this unheard of crime
> As if the gods design'd it.   (III.)

So was it in *Macbeth*. Like Macbeth he is fully aware of the horror:

> Lo, I come
> Swift on the wing, to meet my certain doom:
> I know the danger and I know the shame!
> But, like our Phoenix, in so rich a flame   .
> I plunge triumphant my devoted head
> And doat on death in that luxurious bed.
>   (III.)

Afterwards he knows that he is bound for 'perdition' and that
repentance would be blasphemy (IV). Like Macbeth, like the Gothic
heroes of a later drama, he faces, loathes, and accepts his guilt, his
very sensitivity precluding penitence.

It is typical of the Augustan period that this strong personal action
should be related to social issues. Though the revolution, aiming to
free the masses from slavery and toil, succeeds, Busiris fights bravely
and accepts defeat with dignity; he has had complete faith in his
tyrannic rights, recalls his great deeds and knows that his fame is
bound for posterity. The balance is at once unethical and dramatically just. Young is not subdued to his age: he has a sense of the
numinous, the overwatching dead, of vast stretches of time and of
historical atmosphere. He is less rational, less of a daylight dramatist,
than Thomson.

The Revenge (1721) is a compact piece, derivative from *Othello*, in
which a royal and enslaved Moor, Zanga, tricks a European, Don
Alonzo, into jealousy and crime. The reversal of nationalities serves
a purpose since Zanga's revenge is given, in the Augustan manner, a
more than personal motivation. He glories in knowledge that he,
'an abject beaten slave'—Young may be thinking of the slave trade
—has triumphed over a European:

> Let Europe and her pallid sons go weep;
> Let Africa and her hundred thrones rejoice . . .
>   (V.)

As for the morality of it:

> If cold white mortals censure this great deed,
> Warn them, they judge not of superior beings,
> Souls made of fire and children of the sun,
> With whom revenge is virtue.   (V.)

As in *Busiris* we have a sense of the numinous. The spirit of Zanga's father is with him (II); in the world of death our forms are 'transparent' and thought naked to thought (II). Earthly life is trivial:

> This vast and solid earth, that blazing sun,
> Those skies through which it rolls, must all have end.
>
> (IV.)

As for death, it merely 'joins us to the great majority' (IV). From such a height good and evil assume a new guise. Zanga reminds Alonzo, when he realizes how he has been tricked, that trouble is man's inevitable lot. Why complain?

> Heroes and demi-gods have known their sorrows.
> Caesars have wept . . .
>
> (v.)

Daring as are his metaphysical excursions, Young is master, when he needs it, of a classic simplicity and reserve.

Both sides of the contrast between Young and Thomson are found within the dramas of George Lillo: he has two strong studies of evil and two of public virtue. In *The London Merchant or The History of George Barnwell* (1731), a tragedy of middle-class life, we watch an innocent apprentice, George Barnwell, being seduced by the unprincipled prostitute Millwood, who so plays on his sympathies that he robs his kindly master and ends by murdering his uncle. His very kind-heartedness, developing through love to a frenzied infatuation, forces him into crime. No horror of the coming execution is spared us, but the young man's repentance, with full reliance on religious counsel, is serene. The study is convincing, the doctrine clear and the power great.

Even more interesting is the prostitute, Millwood. She is conceived as a woman of beauty and intellect at enmity with men and their false standards; men, who cause women to fall and despise them afterwards. Condemned with Barnwell she, like so many a tragic protagonist, maintains her dramatic dignity by refusing to repent. More, she becomes the channel for a terrifying indictment, reminiscent of the curses of Lear and Timon, against the whole social order, including those pillars of it, priests and magistrates:

> I hate you all, I know you and expect no mercy; nay, I ask for none.
> I have done nothing that I am sorry for; I followed my inclinations,
> and that the best of you does every day.   (IV.)

Men, like animals, simply 'devour or are devoured, as they meet with others weaker or stronger than themselves'. She is 'not fool enough to be an atheist', but believes that religion as practised does as much harm as good, and that hypocrisy is a greater evil than 'war, plague, and famine'. Laws are simply a 'screen' to villainy 'by which you punish in others what you act yourselves, or would have acted had you been in their circumstances':

> The judge who condemns the poor man for being a thief had been a thief himself had he been poor. Thus you go on deceiving and being deceived, harassing and plaguing and destroying one another: but women are your universal prey. (IV.)

At the gallows, though in a frenzy of agonized guilt expecting torments in Hell, she, like Young's Myron, still cannot or will not repent. When Barnwell offers to pray for her, in the last paroxysm and paradox of a noble selflessness rising from the very strongholds of evil, she cries: 'If thou wilt pray, pray for thyself, not me' (v). Millwood exists as a rationalization and placing of that strong feminine evil so active in high drama from the Greek tragedies to the modern world; and her crushing religious and social indictment does much to illuminate the psychology of crime.

Lillo brings a clear, Augustan, analytic consciousness to bear on these dark problems. He knows that we are all on a precipice:

> There's nought so monstrous but the mind of man
> In some conditions may be brought t'approve.
> (III.)

The lines come from *Fatal Curiosity* (1736), a grimly powerful little drama of Greek severity set on the Cornish coast in an atmosphere of foreboding and nightmare. An old married couple have fallen into poverty. At the limit of their distress the proud and embittered Agnes works on her husband to murder a stranger guest for his money, only to discover that it is their own son, returned from abroad to put everything right. There is a stern morality and an even sterner dramatic irony. They sin through distrust of Providence.

Less gripping, but no less significant, are Lillo's heroic dramas. *The Christian Hero* (1735) follows its title in delineation of the royal young Scanderbeg, 'a Christian and a soldier' (II) leading Albanians against Turks, who sacrifices personal love to public duty. He is descended from a line of constitutional monarchs (II); 'the detested growth' of 'despotic power' only thrives through human folly and crime, and cannot establish itself in a society wherein 'public virtue' flourishes (IV). Our hero is a 'patriot king' who prides himself on enjoying the unlimited powers of popular consent: 'This is to reign; this is to be a king' (V). At one point a lady in boy's dress performs, according to the time-honoured dramatic tradition, a saving function (IV). There is little dramatic subtlety, but the religious and political alignments are important. We have a companion piece in *Elmerick or Justice Triumphant* (1740), wherein a king of Hungary on leaving for a crusade makes Elmerick his deputy, charging him to execute justice without fear or favour. The Queen descends to such villainy that Elmerick in strict pursuance of the King's directions has her put to death in the name of justice. On his return the King is furious. Elmerick replies:

> Sir, I resign my life without reluctance.
> Take, if you please, my head. But know, your fame
> Is in the balance, and your conduct now
> Must fix your character to all posterity;
> Must place you in the list of lawless tyrants,
> Or kings, whose virtue dignified the office,
> And honoured human nature.
>
> (V.)

It is all quite simple: 'The Queen transgress'd—and I have done my duty' (V). The King recognizes Elmerick's rectitude. Such public virtues are not easy to handle with full emotional conviction, but Lillo succeeds. It could have been done in no other period.

The plots and intrigues, the villainies and heroics, of Jacobean and Restoration drama are by Lillo pointed, more clearly than ever before, to the Augustan ideals of Christian warriorship, public rectitude and constitutional rule. There is not the complexity of Thomson's *Tancred and Sigismunda*, and the prostitute Millwood's impassioned denunciation has a dramatic impact denied to Christian heroes; but that is not Lillo's fault.

With John Home, one of our few Scottish dramatists, we break new, more romantic ground. He has his Augustan patriotism, but he likes best splendid young men, tragic mothers, and wild scenery. *Agis* (1746) is a Spartan story of nobility and public virtue and *The Siege of Aquileia* (1760) a study in youthful patriotism and maternal grief. In *Douglas* (1756) we have a tragic mother and a splendid son. Set in Scottish mountains, and a surrounding atmosphere of castles, forests and caves, it is weighted with gloom. The supposedly dead son of Lady Randolph has been nurtured by a hermit in the wilds, but there is recognition and reunion before the tragic conclusion

forced by a villain's machinations. Narrative and verse are rather
heavy; the strength lies in the atmosphere of gloom, rugged nature,
moonlight and mystery, together with the splendour of the young
Douglas, of kin to the princes in *Cymbeline*, and his mother's love.
In *The Fatal Discovery* (1769), an action of ferocity, with two rival
lovers and a passionate heroine, has a rugged setting of woods,
caves and sea, and is heavy with thoughts of ghosts. This is typical,
spoken of the recluse Orellan:

> In early youth he kill'd the fair he loved,
> Then left mankind, to live alone with sorrow.
> Bare is his bosom to the howling winds,
> And wet his hoary head with foam that flies
> From the resounding surges of the main;
> The coot, the cormorant are his companions.
> Sometimes, he says, his cries bring from her cloud
> The pallid image of the murder'd maid!
>
> (IV.)

That has the note of the 'Gothic' dramas shortly to dominate our
stage. Nature is a haunting presence, a power.

Alonzo (1773) drives Home's delight in splendid and almost
magical young heroes to an extreme. The boy Alberto, reared like
Douglas in the wilds, speaks with the authority of 'an angel's voice'
(II). He is a 'wondrous youth' of amazing valour, 'sublime above the
level of mankind'; one not to be judged by 'common rules' but
'irregular like comets in their course' (II). Great nature has been his
foster-parent, giving him a more than human stature. As in *Douglas*,
the new-found hero's relationship to his mother is dramatically
central: he risks his life for her and she, at an intense climax, dies for
him. We shall find a similar story pattern in Coleridge's *Zapolya*.
These last plays are more romantic than Augustan, but the patriotic
note is again sounded in *Alfred* (1778). Alfred has a dream vision of
a noble youth sacrificing his life for him, and yet another tragic
mother 'majestic in her grief' (I). Alfred is a national hero in whose
soul shines 'the light of ancient times' (I). The heroine prays to
perfected spirits, once human and now among the seraphs (v).
Wild nature impregnates the action.

We conclude with Richard Cumberland's noble drama, *The Battle
of Hastings* (1778). Harold has his throne unrightfully, the true king
being young Edgar, a youth of beauty and prowess such as Home
might have drawn, who has been brought up as an orphan and is
now told of his royalty by the patriotic Edwin, who insists that

he renounce his love for Edwina, Edwin's own sister, and marry Harold's daughter Matilda, to consolidate the realm. Edgar, like Thomson's Tancred, refuses. He speaks love poetry of a Shakespearian ease:

> By heaven, I love thee
> More than the sun-burnt earth loves soft'ning showers,
> More than new-ransom'd captives love the day,
> Or dying martyrs, breathing forth their souls,
> The acclamations of whole hosts of angels.
>
> (I.)

Cumberland's poetry has nature quality, felt both in its references and in its unforced, natural, unfurling.

A Scottish soothsayer, Duncan, warns Harold of his guilt: as a 'man of sin' he is told to conquer his ambition before any talk 'of setting England free'. He is warned not to fight 'till Edgar's found', and there is a hint regarding Matilda (III). Harold soliloquizes on the trammels of ambition, and the way evil is brought on by evil; the moral insistence grows, is inevitably, almost reluctantly, squeezed from the situation; there is morality without moralizing. Though he is anxious to compound with his sin by arranging the match with Edgar, Harold, when he and Edgar meet, finds the young man adamant. Love, he insists, 'owns no law but of the heart' (IV). In a speech of magnificently sustained poetry he asserts his willingness to endure the worst fury of battle while still refusing to 'save my country at my soul's expense' (V). Cumberland's balancing of love and patriotism throws back light not only on Thomson, but on all our many earlier Shakespearian and other dramas of love in contrast with glory: without emotional integrity, even patriotism is valueless.

The hour of battle approaches. As warrior and patriot king Harold, despite his guilt, has his nobility. Indeed his status is somehow the greater for this very burden, far beyond that of Lillo's Christian hero. He watches the sun rising:

> Lo, in yon red'ning cloud I see thee mount;
> Not as thou'rt wont with odour-breathing gales,
> Serene and marshall'd by the dancing hours
> Up to the laughing east; but warrior-like,
> With rattling quiver and loud stormy march,
> And bloody ensigns by the furies rear'd
> Aloft and floating in the flecker'd sky:
> So shall the day be suited to its deeds.
>
> (V.)

The resource is Shakespearian; great images roll out, surge and subside, effortlessly, as from a natural voice. Harold goes to battle like Macbeth, sin-trammelled, but with a difference:

> Come forth, bright sword; hence, nature from my heart.
> Now take me, England. I am all thine own.
>
> (v.)

It is typical of Cumberland that 'nature', kindly feeling, must be crushed; never does he forget such feelings. There had been no such convincing patriotic drama since *Henry V*.

Nor have we anywhere at all so finely realized a battle. Neither stage fights nor messenger speeches are properly dramatic. But see Cumberland's method. The battle is acted by one man, in one speech: notice its sharp, dramatic discontinuities and contrasts, gifts to the actor. Northumberland enters, wounded:

> A little onward yet—Enough, enough!
> Good fellow, hold thy kerchief to my side.
> Run one of you and bring me speedy word
> What troops those are which wilfully maintain
> A dying kind of combat; if there's hope
> Make signal with your hand and shout—staunch, staunch my wound—
> My curse upon that Norman boar Fitz Hugh,
> His tusk has ripp'd my heart-strings; yet I cleft him,
> Did I not, soldiers?—Soft, for mercy's sake.
> Jesu Maria, what a pang was that!
> Look out; no sign of hope?—None, none, all's lost—
> He smites his breast with anguish. Hence, stand off.
>   [*He breaks from the soldiers who support him.*
> Wide as the grave I rend this bleeding breach.
>   [*He tears open his wound.*
> Fall England! fall Northumberland!—'Tis past.
>   [*He falls into his soldiers' arms and expires.*
>   (v.) [1]

The horrors of war have been denounced by Edgar, as they have been in play after play, for a century or more, but never have we been so made to feel them, dramatically. Stage suicides have been frequent, but even in Dryden's day drew laughter. Cumberland's answer is, following one grand principle of dramatic art, to make of what is dangerous an especial, an elaborately acted, point. Northumberland's death is the drama's climax.

In nobility of emotion, since all the people rise above themselves

---

[1] Texts vary. 'He smites . . . anguish' is in one given as part of the stage directions.

to a far from easy magnanimity; in avoidance of sentimentality, since every movement is controlled by a severe reading of human nature; and in its successful projection of the relevant values into an action historically and nationally important; in all this Cumberland's drama serves more than adequately as a crown to our sequence. Cumberland touches the highest level of the eighteenth century in both comedy and heroic tragedy; and we shall have cause to refer to him again.

Dark tragedy, despite our chosen examples, is rare in this period. Augustanism at its best was a surmounting of the tragic energies, and its central record the dramatic psychology, doctrine of sublimation and living ethic of Alexander Pope's *Essay on Man* and satiric dialogues. It was a culture nearer the Socratic than the Dionysian. Dr Johnson, whose moral drama *Irene* (1749) was, despite David Garrick's efforts, a failure, might, with Boswell as his Plato, be called its Socrates.

PART 3

PART 3

CHAPTER IX

Gothic

That man was never born whose secret soul,
With all its motley treasure of dark thoughts,
Foul fantasies, vain musings, and wild dreams,
Was ever opened to another's scan.
                    JOANNA BAILLIE, *De Monfort*; I. ii.

I

WE HAVE been discussing dramatists of clarity and purpose. We now revert to nihilism and nightmare. The output of comedies, farces and extravaganzas continues, but we shall concentrate on the centre.

The romantic age was one of social, psychological and metaphysical eruption, of which the French Revolution with its unleashing of passions and horrors was a grand-scale symptom; so was the Marquis de Sade, who is said to have discovered six hundred sexual perversions. This widening of experience, this extension of consciousness, was also a deepening; through the horrors new realms were half glimpsed, dimensions beyond reason. Terror and sublimity are, as Edmund Burke records, close partners.

Imaginative literature is now fascinated by what has come to be known as the 'Gothic'. Respect for ancient Greece and Rome gives way, following the Faust myth, to the claims of Medievalism as a source of fear and insight; the pressure of Augustan discipline is relaxed and power pours in from the grotesque. The cult, which has been well described by Bertrand Evans in his study of Gothic drama,[1] favours ruined castles, with secret passages and dungeons; wicked barons tormented by unrevealed, generally sexual, crime; wild

---

[1] Bertrand Evans, *Gothic Drama from Walpole to Shelley*, University of California, 1947, a work which has helped my understanding of the period. My own earlier studies on the dramas of Wordsworth, Coleridge, Shelley, and Keats appeared in *The Starlit Dome*, 1941, reprinted 1959.
A valuable account of the Gothic novel is D. P. Varma's *The Gothic Flame*, 1957.

scenery of rough coasts and dark forests; and supernormal effects which may or may not turn out to have a rational explanation. As the movement, which starts in the last quarter of the eighteenth century, continues, there is an accretion of new elements: Faustian effects of devilry and black magic come in, under German influence; Schiller's *The Robbers* (1781) gives new impetus to the old theme of the sympathetic bandit; and secret tribunals strike terror.

Religion is ambiguous. Convents and monks recur; tolling bells sound a summoning note, and death is close. Religion is a ghostly complex of good and evil shadowing mysteries of the supernatural. The guilty tend, like Marlowe's Faustus, to reject religious offices. Gothic drama may perhaps be related back to some of the more heretical doctrines and secret cults of the Middle Ages.

Much of this was in the old drama. Shakespeare has his friars, *Macbeth* its weird phenomena, *Hamlet* its graveyard, and *The Duchess of Malfi* its ruins. Nor were the numinous powers ever for long forgotten. Restoration tragedy has them, though with a more ethereal touch and usually beneficent, the worst dangers being political until they in turn are pointed to patriotism by the Augustans. But there too we have the criminologists Young and Lillo, and Home with his dark secrets and rugged settings. Even so the new mode has its differences: there is now a rebound from politics and society to a newly emphatic concentration on the individual in dissociation from his communal context. Nor does evil function as a stimulus to strong action, to revenge. There are tormented heroines and worthy young men, but, as Bertrand Evans observes, they are dramatically weak—their weakness forecast by the comparative ineffectuality of Ophelia and Hamlet—and judgement comes, if at all, from some extraneous, human or providential, source. The dark figure is central and our interest is one of fascination rather than repudiation. Sympathy, though it appears early, can be said, on the whole, to grow as the dramatic movement unfurls. There is a long wrestling with personal, usually sexually impelled, evil and dark powers, without either the medieval placing or the Renaissance stimulus to action. Our dramas draw apart from Aeschylus' *Oresteia* to follow Sophocles' *Oedipus Tyrannus*, concerned rather, Ibsen-wise, with an irrevocable past, of which ruins act as a symbol, than with remedial action; with a guilty state of soul and inward torment; and with the vaguely apprehended mysteries that attend such experiences.

II

We shall notice first some characteristic dramas at different stages of the movement, starting with Horace Walpole's *The Mysterious Mother* (1768), the tragedy so admired by Byron in his preface to *Marino Faliero*. The Countess of Narbonne is devoting her life to good works while remaining tortured by a secret guilt. She refuses the offices of the priest Benedict, arguing 'that minutes stamp'd with crimes are past recall' (I. v). In return the fanatical priest, who regards such rationalizing as dangerous to his Church, having guessed her secret, wickedly expedites the marriage of her newly returned son to the child of that son's past union with his mother. For that was her crime: in a moment of distraction she had, years ago, without his knowledge replaced in darkness one of her son's earlier lovers. The double incest is now hideously revealed.

The treatment is controlled, the verse simple and the power generated great. The Countess's dead husband overshadows the action as a spirit of condemnation. He is said to sit by the church porch 'with clotted locks, and eyes like burning stars' (II. ii). The Countess senses his presence in a fearful storm, riding in the whirlwind and directing its bolt against the cross which her penitence has raised (II. iii). At the grim climax she thinks she sees him, torch in hand, awaiting her. Walpole knows how to use the terse but loaded comment for an awful occasion:

> Globe of the world,
> If thy frame split not with such crimes as these,
> It is immortal!
>
> (V. v.)

The secret is perhaps too long withheld and much would depend on the acting. There are opportunities for a strong actress.

Of more popular sort, and more representative of the crudities that attended the cult, is *The Castle Spectre* (1797) by M. G. Lewis, author of the famous Gothic novel *Ambrosio or The Monk* (1796). Osmond, living in a ruined and haunted castle, is a gloomy and ferocious earl whose brother and his wife Evelina were mysteriously attacked and both supposed killed sixteen years ago. The young hero Percy is trying to win Evelina's daughter Angela, who is suffering under the violent advances of the wicked Osmond. Much is made,

sometimes humorously, of the castle's haunting, and the language is
sensational:

> Osmond was his brother's heir—His strange demeanour!—Yes, in
> that gloomy brow is written a volume of villainy—Heavenly powers!
> an assassin then is master of my fate!   (I. ii.)

Osmond is violent:

> No! Rather than resign her, my own hand shall give this castle a
> prey to flames; then, plunging with Angela into the blazing gulf,
> I'll leave these ruins to tell posterity how desperate was my love,
> and how dreadful my revenge!   (III. ii.)

But his villainy lacks confidence. He knows that 'conscience, that
serpent, winds the folds round the cup of my bliss' (III. ii). He describes a fearful nightmare in which the murdered Evelina visits him
as a dying and mouldering horror. Her ghost actually appears to
save her daughter and reappears at the conclusion after Reginald,
Osmond's supposedly dead brother, is discovered alive in a gloomy
subterranean dungeon where he has been secretly hidden for years
by one of Osmond's accomplices, 'his hair hanging wildly about his
face and a chain bound round his body' (v. iii). The action is assisted
by music at key moments, bells sound, the heightened prose lends
itself to the stage, and there is some good comedy, some of it pro-
.vided by Father Philip, a kindly and useful ecclesiastic.

Lewis wrote a number of plays. His *Adelgitha* (1806) is a powerful
study of crime and mental agony in strong verse. We shall refer to him
again.

Our next is William Sotheby's *Julian and Agnes* (1801), set in 'the
environs of the Great St Bernard' amid 'the wildest Alpine scenery
of ice mountains and precipices covered with snow' (I. ii). Though
action and thought are pitched on a passionate level matching the
scenic grandeur, the echo which 'heaves back the slow clang of the
convent bell' (I. ii) is ominous.

Attached to the convent is a mysterious man who has become
renowned for his courage in saving travellers lost in 'the howling
night-storm' (I. i). It is clear that some 'strange, unexpiated guilt
harrows his soul' (II. i):

> When all within
> Shake at the barr'd out blast,
> Singly he ventures forth, his dog sole guide,
> At starless midnight or when drifted heaps
> Have hid the pass.
>
>   (II. i.)

He is implored by the Confessor to unburden his soul to the visiting
Provost. But, like Walpole's Countess, he for long refuses, though
eventually the Provost prevails and we hear how Julian has married
bigamously and killed the husband of his second wife in a duel. He
can justly claim that guilt was alien to his nature, a succession of
temptations and chances having drawn him despite himself from
innocence (IV. i). However, and this is typical, he gains no relief from
confession and goes off in distraction, regarding himself simultaneously as an outcast from society and as an accuser of all lustful
wickednesses throughout the world.

On the heights he comes on Agnes and Ellen, the two women he
has loved, and saves them from assassins. Agnes speaks with sweet
accents to soothe his misery, but his suffering persists: 'the fiend
that tends on evil deeds is busy with my soul' (v. ii). The half-crazed
Ellen blesses him before she dies from her wounds. He too dies and
the Provost says that Heaven will hear Ellen's interceding prayer. We
have an emphasis on the hero's innate goodness, his will to expiation
and on the surrounding powers of mercy and forgiveness.

Vast nature is majestic:

> It will not be concealed! Death! death! release me!
> Ye mountains! on whose heights, when first ye tower'd
> Coeval winter stood! hoar cliffs! where time
> From the first stretch and waving of his wing
> Shed everlasting snows! Hear, hear my voice!
>
> (II. ii.)

Though the note is Promethean, self-assertion is one with remorse,
awaiting the 'appointed hour' when 'each secret sinner' hears his
doom (II. ii). *Julian and Agnes* is interesting for its pervading sympathy; for the hero's nobility and association with agents of blessed-
ness; and for the snow-clad heights which replace mouldering castles
or graveyards as the companions of guilt.

Here the evil is almost dissolved into good. Resolution can also
come by allowing evil to assert its own peculiar rights, but then the
evil itself must be less tangible. This happens in C. R. Maturin's
Bertram (1816), a sensational drama wherein the hero's original
torment derives not from any actual crime but from an embittered
and revengeful state of mind: the contrast with the old revenge plays
is vivid.

We open with a convent and monks terror-struck by a fearful and
unearthly storm, the scene changing to a rocky coast, a wild sea, and
a vessel in distress. The convent bell tolls. A stranger is cast up,

bearing the well-known marks of a Gothic protagonist such as 'inward mutterings' and a 'fixed eye' (I. iii), and is taken to the convent. The Prior watches him in a sleep disturbed by 'feverish tossings and deep muttered groans', observing

> How the lip works, how the bare teeth do grind—
> And beaded drops course down his writhen brow . . .
>
> (II. i.)

The Prior urges the sufferer to reveal 'the horrid tenant' of his heart (II. i). What is it?—wrath, hatred or revenge? It is all three.

Bertram, whose ambition was dangerous, had been banished by the local lord, St Aldobrand, who had subsequently married Bertram's love, Imogen. Bertram has become a bandit chief and has now been cast up near his enemy's castle, which he proceeds to visit, meeting Imogen, whom he fiercely denounces for her disloyalty. We have a succession of strong dialogues between the Prior and Bertram, Bertram and Imogen, and Imogen and Lord St Aldobrand. Emotional violence and dramatic pressure are only relieved by scenes set within the eternal calm that pervades the convent.

The main stress is on Bertram's 'wild and terrible grandeur' (II. iii). No one is more impressed by it than the Prior:

> High-hearted man, sublime even in thy guilt,
> Whose passions are thy crime, whose angel-sin
> Is pride that rivals the star-bright apostate's—
> Wild admiration thrills me to behold
> An evil strength, so above earthly pitch—
> Descending angels only could reclaim thee . . .
>
> (III. ii.)

While making the usual pleas, he recognizes that the Church fights a losing battle. Bertram is haloed with a 'fiend-like glory' (IV. i). When he openly admits having killed St Aldobrand, the Prior's wonder is unbounded: 'This majesty of guilt doth awe my spirit.' He is positively 'sublime in guilt'; over his 'stormy grandeur' plays a dazzling light, a struggling beam that 'dazzles, awes, and vanishes'; our very 'curses' are blended with 'wonder' (V. ii). Eventually, the stage effect underlining Bertram's satanic dignity, the Prior kneels, imploring him to relent and soften. But Bertram is not touched till Imogen appears in madness. Then he sinks down: 'Am I not weak? Am I not humbled now?' (V. iii). Stabbing himself, he exults in that he dies a warrior's death. The only positive power is love.

Bertram is notable for its vivid delineation of the satanic hero and the Church in opposition, though according to an earlier code Bertram's vengeance would be scarcely criminal. Personal vengeance is now replaced by a not very secure sense of human or divine justice. In *Manuel* (1817) Maturin shows us a distraught father, descendant of Kyd's Hieronimo, trying to bring to justice the murderer of his son, an unrestful and self-tortured villain of the usual sort. There are some interesting advances, particularly in thoughts of 'the voice of by-gone time' and 'unearthly' tenants in an 'ancient Gothic apartment' (v. i), and in Manuel's insistence that both he and another have heard his dead son's voice, denying that such clairaudience is an insanity:

> Must all ears
> That hear the sounds *I* hear be phrensy-struck?
>
> (v. ii.)

The treatment of psychic power is convincing and the agony of Manuel has throughout pathos and poignancy. It is a more complex and subtle work than *Bertram*.

We have noticed a few representative dramas, to which we might add that strange study of remorseful frenzy, H. H. Milman's *Fazio* (1815). Such themes were effective and popular: *The Castle Spectre* was an outstanding stage success and Edmund Kean played in *Bertram* and *Manuel*.

These dramas are symptomatic of a newly introverted self-consciousness arousing a sense of guilt without there being any acceptable solace from religion. There is now also the further suggestion that those whose experiences have probed deeply into this dimension are of a greater than normal stature.

The dramas of Joanna Baillie were deliberately devised to illustrate the workings of various passions. Her *De Monfort* (1798) has a remark that serves as a text for Gothic drama:

> That man was never born whose secret soul,
> With all its motley treasure of dark thoughts,
> Foul fantasies, vain musings, and wild dreams,
> Was ever opened to another's scan.
>
> (I. ii.)

De Monfort is a study of envious hate working up to a typical accumulation of gloomy forest, night time, owls, Gothic convent, tolling bell, monks and corpse. De Monfort, despite his proud heart, has 'bursts of natural goodness' (I. i). Though more averse than most men to inflicting pain, he conceives to his horror the thought of murder, and carries it out. After the murder he is in torment, fearing 'things unutterable' beyond death (v. iv), while the attendant monks hear voices 'on the dark midnight winds' (v. v). It is a strong and psychologically coherent study of the human paradox. Joanna Baillie has always a stern control: sensationalism never clogs psychology or drama. *De Monfort* was acted, and her other plays are stage-worthy.

The two parts of *Ethwald* (pub. 1802) form an elaborate study of ambition. Ethwald is a warrior of Mercia, happy in war and, like Chapman's Byron, uneasy under 'cold, blasting peace' (1; II. iv). He engages in more battles while asserting his loathing of cruelty and claiming that his sword is for protection rather than destruction (1; III. v). But his actions falsify his claims. The soldiers prefer him to the weak King Oswal. Like Macbeth he solicits occult assistance, visiting Druid mystics in a great scene of incantation and super-natural pageantry, including spectres of the dead. This is done for the audience, while the author's stern psychology arranges that Ethwald himself, who hears sounds, sees nothing. Where is the 'mighty master' they have invoked?

> 1st Mystic: Above, around you, and beneath.
> Ethwald: Has he no form to vision sensible?
> (1; iv. iii.)

Eventually he sees a crown and sceptre which he recognizes as objectifying 'the inward vision of my soul', and though he also fore-sees his own future tyranny and dismal end he accepts the conditions and seizes sovereignty. To extend his people's sway, labouring as he thinks or pretends for the general good, he engages in more wars described as horrible; and, while half hating what he does, he cannot stop. His friend Edward, the rightful heir, he has murdered. He endures torments, is sleepless, is loathed by others and a torment to himself. Though the theme is not new, there are new subtleties in the psychology of self-deception and the exact gradations of the hero's rise and fall: much of it reads like a commentary on Napoleon.

From this grim world the good Edward has an intuition of a more beauteous existence beyond the invisible veil of death (2; III. i): such psychic intuitions are deliberate and exact.

Orra (pub. 1812) studies fear. The young heiress Orra is simul-taneously fascinated and frightened by ghost stories, finding 'a joy in fear' (II. i); she is psychically sensitive, feeling the presence of her

dead father (II. iii). Trading on these qualities, her relative and
guardian meets her refusal to marry according to his wishes by
placing her in a half-ruined Gothic castle supposed to be haunted by
a huntsman once murdered by an ancestor of the family. The legend is
kept alive for their own purposes by a company of bandits who enact
the ghostly hunt round the castle; and Orra is driven mad by terror.

The realization of fear is extraordinarily powerful. Through the
'dark arches' of the old castle 'the sound of time long past', by a fine
use of the mystique of Gothic drama, is felt murmuring, as from a
grave (III. ii): 'The very air rests thick and heavily' (III. ii). Alone she
meditates on the terror of spirit communication. The hunter's horn
is heard and the yell of hounds. Surely, she thinks, she should trust
God who rules not only the living but also the dead 'in their dark
state of mystery' (IV. iii). She senses the 'awful bond' existing
between the two states (IV. iii). Driven by fear she once flies to the
warm humanity of the evil Rudigere who acts as her jailer; and when
her lover enters the castle to save her, she goes mad with terror. Her
thought in madness is penetrating:

> I'll tell thee how it is:
> A hideous burst hath been: the damn'd and holy,
> The living and the dead, together are
> In horrid neighbourship.—'Tis but thin vapour,
> Floating around thee, makes the wav'ring bound.
> Poh! blow it off, and see th' uncurtained reach.
> See! from all points they come . . .
>
> (v. ii.)

She sees the dead rising in their grave clothes, mouldering and bony.
She is psychologically limited to a Websterian experience of death
as death, but from that materialistic angle hits near a truth. From
the start she has been attuned to the other world: her error is to see
it clouded by earthly horrors.

Fear is again central in *The Dream* (pub. 1812). Monks in a Swiss
monastery have been warned by dreams to stop a division of the
imperial army and choose by lot a man who must spend the night
with them to expiate a crime. The lot falls on General Osterloo and
his crime of murder is revealed. The Prior, in part motivated by
personal revenge since the victim was his own brother, condemns
Osterloo to immediate death. An attempt at rescue made through a
secret passage from a neighbouring castle fails, but the imperial
authorities are just in time to stop the execution, only to discover that
the general has died of fear.

There are the usual effects, with an especially emphatic use of the recurring bell. Suspense is keen. Here is Osterloo's guilt showing itself at an early stage:

> OSTERLOO: The stranger's burying vault!
> PRIOR: Does any sudden thought strike you, Count?
> OSTERLOO: No, no! Here's your health, Fathers; [*drinking*] your wine is excellent.
> PRIOR: But that is water you have just now swallowed: this is the wine. (I. iii.)

Osterloo confesses and asks to be made to undergo a severe expiation. He, the brave soldier, is now in terror of the next life, sensing 'an unseen world' of 'spirits' and 'the invisible dead' (II. iii). At his sentence fear of divine judgement drives him to distraction. He questions one of the monks as to whether we are conscious immediately after death, and is told:

> It is indeed my belief. Death is but a short though awful pass; as it were a winking of the eyes for a moment. We shut them in this world and open them in the next: and there we open them with such increased vividness of existence, that this life, in comparison, will appear but as a state of slumber and of dreams. (III. i.)

Such intuitions gain in clarity as our dramatic history develops. *The Dream* is the more gripping for its brevity and the precision of its prose. The moral is, that 'the bravest mind is capable of fear' (III. iii).

Joanna Baillie's strength is in her firm sense of psychological and psychic truth. Her avoidance of actual ghosts—except in *Ethwald*, where they are invisible to the hero—marks no disbelief in the other world but rather a reluctance to commit herself to any superstitious forms. Without ceasing to be dramatic her work is diagnostic and scientific; she aims at no such theatric grandeurs, such tragic positives, as we find in Shakespeare, and which both Sotheby and Maturin attempt, and this is certainly a limitation. However, her intellectual quality serves peculiarly well to link the Gothic mode with the dramas of our greater romantic poets. To these we shall now turn.

III

The fascination of evil is given a metaphysical formulation in William Wordsworth's *The Borderers* (1796). What drama so often makes us feel, here we are forced dangerously to think. As a young

man Wordsworth tried unsuccessfully to get it produced, and there-
after let it remain unpublished until near his death. The play's
movement is heavy and laboured, on occasion obscure: its importance lies in the intricacy of its thought, certain impressive dialogues,
and its bleak Wordsworthian atmosphere.

We are in wild country on the borders of England and Scotland.
Marmaduke is the young leader of an independent border-band
admitting no political allegiance. Oswald, a man of travel and
experience, gives him evidence that the blind old Herbert, whose
daughter Idonea Marmaduke loves, is not really her father and is
planning to prostitute her to 'that cold voluptuary' (I. 279), Lord
Clifford, who in his 'shattered castle' is busily employed with
'infernal orgies' (II. 660). Though he does not actually appear,
Clifford serves as a link with the Gothic tradition. So does the
prevailing atmosphere. Here is a neat direction:

> A desolate prospect—a ridge of rocks—a Chapel on the summit of
> one—Moon behind the rocks—night stormy—irregular sound of a
> bell—Herbert enters exhausted.   (IV.)

One could ask for nothing better as a setting for our two main
themes. These are: (i) the rights of rough justice; and (ii) the value
of crime.

Marmaduke is persuaded that he must murder Herbert both as a
punishment for his past and to prevent worse in the future. Does not
the border-band claim to 'guard the innocent'? (I. 63). Here, independent of social bonds, 'justice has indeed a field of triumph'
(II. 598). That question, active from Aeschylus to the Renaissance,
is again before us: a situation is devised where action can be independent of society, of law; and murder appears to be justice. After
all, says Oswald, benevolence that cannot use 'the wholesome
ministry of pain and evil' (II. 619) is contemptible and the 'nightmare conscience' (II. 866) must be mastered. Do we not kill a worn-
out horse, or withered tree? Why worry unduly about an old man?
Such weakness merely obscures 'the moral shapes of things' (II.
1083). As for exact proof, passionate conviction may be a better
guide than 'the spiritless shape of fact' (III. 1157). Gradually, though
at the first opportunity Marmaduke is prevented by conscience from
committing the murder, Oswald's insistence wins. Moreover, in a
society where a king whose wars slaughter thousands is a hero and
one who enjoys himself idly is called decadent (III. 1228–39), what
test can there be of right or wrong except personal judgement? In a

scene of grim power wherein the personality of the innocent Herbert takes on an awe-inspiring grandeur, Marmaduke leaves the blind old man to Providence, alone on a desolate heath. Herbert dies.

Oswald congratulates Marmaduke on his self-conquest while further driving home the horror of what he has done. He has rightly obeyed his own 'independent intellect'; the squeamish will no doubt reject him as a 'murderer', but 'the eagle lives in solitude', and if good spirits fail there are others ready. Great action and suffering go together; compassion and pity are false. As for remorse, it cannot co-exist with clear thought: in our chance-ruled world where a cat's sneeze may alter everything, responsibility is meaningless. Besides, all is a struggle for power: we control the brutes, just as our rulers for their own ends control us; Marmaduke has overleaped the 'flimsy barrier' (III. 1470–1590). The dialogue is subtly fraught with irony and un-ease; it is ominous.

Oswald tells Marmaduke how he as an innocent youth was once made an accomplice in a murder which he thought justice, only to discover his error. He travelled 'a dim and perilous way'; learned to see that any action whatsoever 'might lead to good'; grew in 'intellectual' stature through communion with nature's 'mighty' works; and concluded that there was no worse curse on man than self-consuming conscience. So he broke through—Wordsworth may be thinking of the French Revolution—into a realm of 'futurity' and 'freedom'; merit is directly proportional to the 'obloquy' of society and those who would truly 'serve' the world must disregard its 'hate' and 'scorn'. He became as a 'monarch' and the religion of priest-craft no longer meant anything to him. Those who had deceived him into crime had wrought a 'liberation' (IV. 1684–1844). Crime is identified with highest virtue. It enlarges 'man's intellectual empire' (IV. 1856).

The ground has been prepared for admitting to Marmaduke that he too has been deceived. Oswald, who may be read as a profound study of the satanic impulse lying behind the creation of all our Iagos, wanted companionship in crime, to make Marmaduke a replica of himself. And there is a clear gain for Marmaduke as well:

> But what is done will save you from the blank
> Of living without knowledge that you live.
> (IV. 1870.)

Crime registers an advance in consciousness. Marmaduke receives the appalling news with an icy calmness more effective than any

raging: 'You have betray'd me—I have done—I am content . . .'
(IV. 1846). There is a Wordsworthian placidity over the whole action
and Marmaduke's concluding words are calm. He will hold no
further converse with human kind,

> but over waste and wild,
> In search of nothing that this earth can give,
> But expiation, will I wander on.
>
> (v. 2348.)

The voice is quiet. Despite our knowledge that 'the mind of man
upturned' is a 'strange' and often 'hideous' spectacle (III. 1168) and
that until the 'mystery of all this world' is solved he remains less
happy than the 'worm' (IV. 1796), yet beyond good and evil is
another, perhaps deeper, recognition:

> In terror,
> Remember'd terror, there is peace and rest.
>
> (III. 1468.)

On the 'frozen heart', we are told, 'the extremes of suffering meet in
absolute peace' (v. 2216). The paradoxes are driven home with a
fearless and fearful insistence.

Problems of evil and justice are given a different if no less paradoxical formulation in Percy Bysshe Shelley's *The Cenci* (1819).
Count Cenci ranks among such dramatic 'ogres' as Volpone and Sir
Giles Overreach. His wickedness is defended by close and disturbing
argument. All men, he says, have sensuous and revengeful instincts
and most derive a 'secret peace'—we may remember Wordsworth's
'peace'—from the sufferings of others. His own actions arise merely
from his peculiar 'taste' which causes him to 'feed' his 'soul' on
the mental anguish of those under his power (I. i). Incest as such is
not our central problem. He conceives the idea of forcing his
daughter simply as a means to torturing her, feeling a physical thrill
in it:

> My blood is running up and down my veins;
> A fearful pleasure makes it prick and tingle;
> I feel a giddy sickness of strange awe;
> My heart is beating with an expectation
> Of horrid joy.
>
> (IV. i.)

His surrender to this sexual-sadistic excitement is no cold wickedness
but has the thrill and 'awe' of obedience to a great power. He
feels his soul as a 'scourge' wielded by Providence (IV. i.). Hearing

of a mysterious voice that said 'Cenci must die', he is flattered,
thinking he is 'favoured from above'; and he believes that his
curses have especial power (IV. i). The life to come he leaves to
God, his thoughts working within the orthodox scheme and regarding repentance as 'an easy moment's work' (IV. i). In Cenci evil has
pretty nearly become good: his whole mental and physical self ratifies
it. He is the channel for a cosmic force. He performs the hateful
action (v. iii. 79–80).

Against him is Beatrice. Though good, she has all the dramatic
power that one associates with a dangerous woman; her very gaze is
'awe-inspiring' (I. ii); and prevention of her father's persistent
wickednesses being unattainable from the authorities, she plots with
her mother and brothers to murder him. That the murder scene, in a
Gothic castle, has many Shakespearian reminiscences, with Beatrice's
courage and control as close replicas of Lady Macbeth's, only the
more firmly drives home our paradox. When she proudly asserts her
and her relatives' innocence, we have the extraordinary experience of
witnessing and approving such protestations from a good woman
whom we know to be guilty:

> My lord,
> I am more innocent of parricide
> Than is a child born fatherless.
>
> (IV. iv.)

She actually calls on God to hear her oath (v. ii). Finally, the others
having given way under torture, she regards God himself as the guilty
one who removed all redress save

> That which thou hast call'd my father's death . . .
> Which is or is not what men call a crime,
> Which either I have done or have not done;
> Say what ye will. I shall deny no more.
> If ye desire it thus, thus let it be,
> And so an end of all.
>
> (v. iii.)

Fact is not, as Oswald too insisted, everything; if too irrelevant to
the values engaged, it vanishes. No doubt many a murderer on trial,
if with less obvious excuse, feels like this.

For Cenci evil becomes a good sanctioned by cosmic and human
powers; for Beatrice good forces her into the position of a Lady
Macbeth. The old problem of the Book of Job and Aeschylus is with
us still: is God just? Our play has three fathers: Cenci, the Pope,

God. The Pope accepts Cenci's bribes; and it is because he himself
holds a paternal office that he will not tolerate any complaints against
a father (II. ii). What is Beatrice to think? The two fathers whom she
knows are terrible. What of the third?

> If there should be
> No God, no Heaven, no Earth in the void world;
> The wide, grey, lampless, deep, unpeopled world!
> If all things then should be . . . my father's spirit,
> His eye, his voice, his touch surrounding me . . .
>
> (v. iv.)

Are death's laws 'unjust, perhaps, as those which drive us now'?
(v. iv). Her own life has known no justice: what reason have we to
expect it of God?

The verse is bare, eschewing colour and flashiness; the suspense is
throughout maintained; and the problems posed are, as in *The
Borderers*, disturbing. Wordsworth and Shelley are worrying in the
main about evil rather than death, but the poetry of death is sensitive in 'Barry Cornwall' (B. C. Procter) and T. L. Beddoes is a
master of it. In Barry Cornwall's *Mirandola* (1821) a duke has
married his son's love, thinking him dead. The son returns.
They decide to part, but before he goes, the Duke's suspicions are
aroused and he condemns his son, only to discover his error. The
poetry has a deftness of touch which handles with equal ease
psychological intuitions and dark grandeurs. The Duke is parting
with his son:

> We will meet—hereafter:
> In the world, never. In the grave perhaps—
> In the dark common chamber of the dead
> We'll visit, where upon his shadowy steed
> (Pale as a corpse) the speechless phantom rides,
> Our king and enemy; there, friends and foes
> Meet without passions, and the sickly light
> That glimmers thro' the populous homes of death
> Will be enough to find us. We shall know
> Each other there, perhaps.
>
> (IV. ii.)

It recalls the great Jacobeans, though with a certain refinement of its
own. At the end the Duke pronounces judgement by night in the
garden where the supposed love-making has been discovered. His
mind is unbalanced, blending inconsequence with sublimity. He will
sit 'beneath the stars' and commands that the 'curtains' which
obscure the moon be rolled back. The order for execution is given.

He is still, in solitary state: 'He looks like marble with those fixed eyes' (v. ii). Then he speaks:

> My heart is cold as lead.
> I should have had a cloak to cover me—
> A tomb, a tomb, to keep the wind out. Ha!
> I love this lonely pomp. My lamps are hung
> All round a mighty dome; and music, like
> The noises bursting from Aeolian caves
> Come round me like a charm. Oh! I have been
> Betrayed; ay, and revenged—All silent?—How!
> Come, talk, Sirs, talk.
>
> (v. ii.)

His son's innocence is revealed and a reprieve sent, too late; the musketry sounds; the Duke dies in a paroxysm of remorse. There is no deep meaning, but the poetry is superb.

Crime and death are the central interests of T. L. Beddoes's *The Bride's Tragedy* (1822), in which a young man, Hesperus, murders his wife. An 'indistinct' purpose forms with 'a depth of wickedness' at once 'hideous' and 'inevitable' (II. iii), 'deeper than sight', beyond sense perception, yet appallingly real and even 'wildly sweet' (II. iv). Dark spirits are considered, and yet it seems rather a replica of himself, though not his 'perfect self', that takes control; and yet again he feels newly integrated, with a tingling vitality and a strange courage (II. vi). Surrender to crime is accompanied, as in the development of poetic power throughout *Macbeth*, by an access of living; or is it—the thought is suggested—spirit possession? (III. iii). This state, as in Aeschylus' Clytemnestra, continues a while after the murder. Though convicted, Hesperus will not at first repent, and claims, like Wordsworth's Oswald, that crime is the measure of daring and flings out scorn and insults, like Lillo's Millwood; but, unlike her, finally softens.

What is strange in this appalling study is the optimism with which the horrors are countered. We move through evil to strangely sweet apprehensions. Hesperus' father and the victim's mother are kind; there is little bitterness. The victim's death is regarded as a sweetness, 'the sugar' of life's 'draught' (III. iii). Ghostly thoughts are pervasive, leading to vivid apprehensions of an after-life, sensed through flowers, which are said to be impregnated by the souls of the dead. Birds too are its witnesses (v. iii). Spirits are close: 'Some say they hang like music in the air' (IV. iv). We are invited to expect a world of 'rainbow-girt pavilions' and 'rivulets of music' beyond death (v. iv). In no other dramatist have we quite this extraordinary co-presence of horror and serenity, this strange sense of some sweet otherness impinging through earth's nature on mortality.

Of a more normal sweetness is the boy, reminiscent of the Jacobeans, whose innocent mind in sleep is said to be with the seraphs of Paradise (II. i) and the attractiveness of whose 'silken limbs' (II. ii) in part precipitates the tragedy.

Beddoes's greatest work, *Death's Jest-Book or The Fool's Tragedy* (1826; often revised, and published in 1850), suffers as drama from its own imaginative superabundance. Its poetry and metaphysics are fascinating, but action and psychology are confusing and the plot rambling. Much is in the Websterian tradition, though the untidiness is greater. There is the same macabre grip, though ironic fatalism is replaced by deliberate jocularity. Beddoes attempts to develop deathly horrors through a grim humour to *a dramatization of the breaking down of the barrier between life and death.* He does not rely merely on intuitions of spirit life; rather he plants himself firmly in the sense world of Jacobean horror, and from there aims to expand Webster's scattered hints of a beyond (pp. 104–10) into a solid, earth-based reality, reminiscent of Webster's earth dirge, 'Call for the robin red-breast and the wren' (*The White Devil*; v. iv). As in *The Bride's Tragedy* death speaks through fecund nature, especially flowers (v. iii).

The story's skeleton is this: Duke Melveric has murdered his friend Wolfram and now moves about his dukedom disguised as a pilgrim. Wolfram's brother, Isbrand, caustic descendant of Webster's Flamineo, is an avenger who joins with the Duke's son Adalmar in planning a revolution. The Duke wishes to raise up his dead wife, but since Isbrand has put Wolfram's body in the tomb he finds instead that he has resurrected his victim. After this the resurrected Wolfram takes a full part in the action.

The drama is saturated in the thought of communication with the dead, and this abnormal comprehension tends to make action paradoxical: people are liable to murder freely and accept condemnation to death with gratitude. The Duke comforts his conscience with the thought that his victim Wolfram is not really dead: the body 'falls away from light' like the turning globe, while the true life remains, like the sun, 'triumphant' (II. i). He is in part a moralist, murmuring

> Thou art old, world,
> A hoary, atheistic, murderous star.
>
> (II. ii.)

Being incognito, he thinks of joining the revolution as a traitor against himself, since 'there may be good in it' (II. ii). Contradictions abound; nothing is firm; the world of mortality is rotten and out of joint; the thing to do is to press beyond it.

Ghoulish, yet merry, horrors accumulate. The conspirators meet in 'a church yard', by 'the ruins of a spacious Gothic cathedral' on the walls of which is painted 'the Dance of Death' (III. iii); and the 'Deaths' come from their walls 'to a rattling music', singing that Death is a 'merry' fellow, while 'the wind howleth through the ruins bravely' (v. iv). The title *Death's Jest-Book* is a true pointer: we are asked to see the joke, the joke of even death's physical horror; and, since Death is merry, we should expect communication.

Isbrand thinks that his murdered brother ought surely—like the Ghost in *Hamlet*—to return. But he is counselled to be patient. What do we know of Death's laws,

> What seas unnavigable, what wild forests,
> What castles, and what ramparts there may hedge
> His icy frontier?
>
> (II. iii.)

Perhaps the dead do not return as they did in the past because their world is no longer lonely, being now perhaps full; soon they may be shutting us out (III. iii). The Duke too wants to make contact with his dead wife:

> She died. But Death is old and half worn out:
> Are there no chinks in't? Could she not come to me?
> Ghosts have been seen . . .
>
> (III. iii.)

A magician, Ziba, claims the power of raising the dead, and though his attempt fails comically, the Duke himself succeeds, except that, through Isbrand's transference of the bodies, he raises Wolfram and not his wife. Henceforward the murdered Wolfram moves about, taking various disguises, seeming as solid as the others. He introduces himself to his love, Sibylla:

> I am a ghost. Tremble not; fear not me.
> The dead are ever good and innocent,
> And love the living. They are cheerful creatures,
> And quiet as the sunbeams. . . .
>
> (IV. ii.)

They are 'the new-born of mankind' (IV. ii). Voices in the air sing

of death's wonder, whereby we 'rise to be' (IV. ii). There is no firm
distinction between the two states:

> ISBRAND: But how came you to die and yet be here?
> WOLFRAM: Did I say so? Excuse me. I am absent,
> And forget always that I'm just now living.
> But dead and living, which are which? A question
> Not easy to be solved. Are you alone,
> Men, as you're called, monopolists of life?
> Or is all being, living?
>
> (v. iv.)

All 'living' is a physical wearing down and what we call 'life' is
rather the 'sparks of spirit' continually shot from the ever-decaying
body (v. iv). Elsewhere the spirit world is regarded as this 'hard old
rocky world' melted into fluidity, to give us blue sea, music, flowers,
and other Elysian intimations (IV. ii); (see pp. 233–4, 285, 290).

Poetic drama has two main directions: (i) the relating of human
affairs to the powers beyond, and (ii) the heroic, at the limit the
superman, quest. Beddoes alone among our dramatists presents
both in juxtaposition. To Adam, says Isbrand, life was new and
exciting, but to us it has grown dull:

> And man is tired of being merely human;
> And I'll be something more: yet, not by tearing
> This chrysalis of psyche ere its hour,
> Will I break through Elysium. There are sometimes,
> Even here, the means of being more than men . . .
>
> (IV. iv.)

He would be 'heavenly in my clay' (IV. iv). As man is to a beast, so
the new man on 'the way to godhead' should be to man as he is,
as yet only 'half created'. What is needed is a power to direct the soul
as the soul directs the body, a will above the will:

> What shall we add to man,
> To bring him higher? I begin to think
> That's a discovery I soon shall make.
>
> (v. i.)

Beddoes forecasts the philosophy of Nietzsche.

At his death in 1849 he left two unfinished dramas, *Torrismond*
(1824) and *The Second Brother* (1825). Each has a figure of riotous
extravagance or indulgence and the second has also one who is lonely
and embittered, in contrast. Both the bright and the sombre aspects
of *Timon of Athens* are covered.

IV

Our lonely romantic heroes are not all persons of darkness, and when they are not Timon is their prototype. M. G. Lewis's *Alfonso, King of Castile* (1801) provides a good example. Orsino, wrongly suspected of treachery by his friend the King, lives apart among forests, rocks and waterfalls. His first speech, moving as it does from natural grandeurs to repudiation of civilization, is a close replica of Shakespeare's opening to the second half of *Timon of Athens*. Alfonso visits him, only to be bitterly repudiated. Hate is now Orsino's one consolation:

> And would'st thou rob me
> E'en of this last poor pleasure? Go, sir, go,
> Regain your court! resume your pomp and slendour!
> Drink deep of luxury's cup! be gay, be flattered,
> Pampered and proud, and if thou can'st, be happy.
> I'll to my cave and curse thee!
>
> (II. ii.)

Yet when his son solicits his help in a revolution he is staggered. To others the King has been good: 'What are my wrongs against a monarch's rights?' Or 'a nation's blessing'? (III. ii). Even so, it is not till the King spares the young man's life for his father's sake that Orsino's heart melts: 'My pride is vanquished' (v. i).

Romantic drama can on occasion draw near the optimism more characteristic of romantic lyric. In Lewis's *Adelmorn* (1801) the hero thinks he is guilty, when he is not, and the final happiness is sung by a chorus of spirits. The great romantic statement of revolt-with-virtue followed by a happy conclusion is Shelley's *Prometheus Unbound* (1820), where an apprehension of living nature and awakened Earth is housed in the old myth. Prometheus and Faust are close, and both are precursors of the Romantic movement. For the Gothic horrors are all, properly understood, to be regarded as preliminaries to a brighter statement; and the move from the one to the other is peculiarly clear in S. T. Coleridge's two plays, *Remorse* (1813; first version as *Osorio*, 1797) and *Zapolya* (1815).

In the first Don Alvar returns disguised as a Moor to arouse remorse in his treacherous brother Don Ordonio, who had arranged, as he thinks successfully, to have him murdered. It is natural in this period that the will to arouse remorse, recalling Hamlet with his mother, should replace revenge. Ordonio's accomplice, Isidore, is now on Alvar's side.

Dramatic dialogues are intense, playing over Ordonio's highly susceptible conscience. He is deeply shocked to hear from Isidore of the supposed murder, for was not Alvar 'his Maker's image unde-fac'd'? (II. i). He is a sensitive villain, lonely and unhappy, with a searching and uneasy mind. His self-diagnosis is Byronic:

> All men seemed mad to him!
> Nature had made him for some other planet,
> And press'd his soul into a human shape
> By accident or malice. In this world
> He found no fit companion.
>
> (IV. i.)

He has to undergo a severe test when Alvar, disguised as a magician, produces before the assembled company a spectacle of staggering power—again recalling *Hamlet*—culminating in an illuminated picture of his own supposed murder. The miserable Ordonio is thrown off his balance and half confesses to his father, Valdez. If one reptile stings another, where is the crime? Is not everything transient? Must it bring on 'the idiocy of moist-eyed penitence'? Besides, a corpse breeds insects, multiplying life (III. ii). He has the macabre logic of Wordsworth's Oswald. He murders his treacherous accomplice Isidore in a peculiarly dank and gloomy cavern after an intense dialogue gradually revealing his hideous intention. He also visits Alvar in the dungeon where he is now imprisoned, and offers him drink. Alvar points to an insect:

ALVAR: Saw I that insect on this goblet's brim
            I would remove it with an anxious pity!
ORDONIO: What meanest thou?
ALVAR: There's poison in the wine.
ORDONIO: Thou hast guessed right; there's poison in the wine.

> (V. i.)

Though Alvar denounces him as a 'blind self-worshipper' of 'shallow sophisms', Ordonio persists in rejecting remorse and all religious consolation, since 'not all the blessings of a host of angels' can serve to 'blow away a desolate widow's curse' (v. i). And when Alvar reveals himself as his brother, he cries: 'Touch me not. Touch not pollution, Alvar! I will die' (v. i). His sensitivity has throughout been his torment.

Our surrounding atmosphere is one of hostility to the Inquisition

and belief in spirits. Orsino is haunted by the words: 'He that can
bring the dead to life again' (II. ii). The dead are part

> Of that innumerable company
> Who in broad circle, lovelier than the rainbow,
> Girdle this round earth in a dizzy motion,
> With noise too vast and constant to be heard.
> Fitliest unheard! For oh, ye numberless
> And rapid travellers! what ear unstunn'd,
> What sense unmadden'd, might bear up against
> The rushing of your congregated wings?
>
> (III. i.)

Coleridge's intuition is probably happier with the paradisial than
with the satanic. He is happier still with more earthly, martial, and
yet spiritualized splendours. We end with a magnificent and resounding speech by Alhadra, the Moorish warrior-wife of Isidore, who
strikes a Fortinbras note of militant health and liberation after
inward corruption, threatening 'the kingdoms of the world' and
'foundations of iniquity' with destruction until all who have in them
'the spirit of life' are united in song.

It is precisely this richer, at once human and spiritualized, note
that is embodied in *Zapolya*. Celebrating a universal good rather
than evil, it follows Alhadra's speech in having a firm communal
reference: we are no longer among the lonely agonies. We first see
the noble general Raab Kiuprili opposing the tyrant Emerick's
usurpation of the Illyrian throne: in a fierce and blazingly dramatic
dialogue we have the claims of a 'commanding spirit' against both
law and the patriot's will to guide the flood of constitutional royalty
'in its majestic channel'. The tone is splendid on both sides, rich in
words radiating power: 'triumph', 'oracular', 'sovereign', 'glory',
'imperial' (Prelude, i). Raab Kiuprili, the queen Zapolya and the
boy child Andreas, the rightful heir, escape. Sixteen years elapse.
Andreas, now separated from his mother, has been brought up as
'Bethlen', son to an old mountaineer, his mother and Raab Kiuprili
still hiding in the wilds.

Nature is fierce, with wolf, tiger and eagle, but also sweet with
roses, bird-song and 'the bright blue ether' (I. i). A lovely lyric
imagines a brilliant bird in a shaft of light slanting from 'sky to
earth' (II. i). Here each dew-drop is 'an orb of glory' (I. i). Strength,
sweetness, splendour, are emphatic. Raab Kiuprili looks like 'some
god disguised' (III. i) and a lady has 'angel-eyes' and 'regal forehead'
(III. i). Even the tyrant Emerick, splendid on his 'pawing courser'

(IV. i), shares the pervading glory. A 'golden' casket (I. i) and a gold-inlaid helm and breastplate found in an oratory (III. i) tone with the divine humanism. Our vision must be firmly distinguished from a simple morality or sanctimony, and from the anaemic young semi-heroes of Gothic tragedy who pale before the satanic protagonists. Now the element of *uncanny* fascination in those dark persons is— the tyrant Emerick shows the transition—*itself being incorporated into a new excellence, beyond ethic, sounding and resounding the note of divine humanism to which all tragic drama points.* Shakespeare has it, in the royal boys of *Cymbeline*; Dryden reached for it; Home's young heroes are a gesture, and perhaps too Keats's Ludolf in *Otho the Great* (1819); but our most elaborated delineation is Andreas. He, like earlier heroes, is shown discovering his high birth; like Dryden's Almanzor and Home's Douglas he experiences reunion with a mother. The more universal implications of these themes are by Coleridge rendered explicit.[1]

As the young huntsman 'Bethlen'—a name as evocative as 'Andreas' itself—Andreas knows nothing of his birth. His thoughts and acts are noble. He is splendid, chivalrous, powerful, sweet, and in anger an Apollo:

> So looks the statue, in our hall, o' the god,
> The shaft just flown that killed the serpent!
>
> (I. i.)

Himself 'mysteriously inscribed by nature' (I. i) he has an implanted impulse to uncover his descent, corresponding to all who pine for what Wordsworth, in his ode on *Immortality*, called 'that imperial palace' of our true origin and home:

> Blest spirits of my parents,
> Ye hover o'er me now! Ye shine upon me!
> And like a flower that coils forth from a ruin,
> I feel and seek the light I can not see!
>
> (I. i.)

Hearing that his mother was last seen near a dreaded cave said to be haunted by the 'war-wolves' and 'vampires' he determines to search for her, though only one with a 'glory' burning from his head and 'eagle' wings dare undertake such a task (I. i). He will confront the worst horrors of bestial or infernal evil desecrating

[1] D. G. James was, I think, the first to isolate and emphasize the imaginative importance of the discovery of royal birth in Shakespeare and make the comparison—which I make below—with Wordsworth's *Immortality* ode. See *Scepticism and Poetry*, 1937, 216–24.

this to him 'sacred' (I. i) spot. Andreas is defined by his courage to face and master those abysmal horrors saturating our darker dramas.

He stands before the cave and blows his horn; and again. The voice of Raab Kiuprili is heard from within, warning of danger. Andreas' spear trembles in his hand but he answers this mysterious 'voice of command', this 'hidden Light', soliciting direction. The oracular voice replies:

> Patience! Truth! Obedience!
> Be thy whole soul transparent! So the Light
> Thou seekest may enshrine itself within thee.
>
> (II. i.)

It is an initiation, with universal meanings. His mother comes and there is reunion, yet the 'full orb of his destiny' (III. i) is not ready and she does not disclose her and his royalty. Soon after he discovers it himself: 'The light hath flashed from Heaven, and I must follow it' (III. i). He opposes the tyrant and during the conflict is rescued by his love Glycine, who shoots his would-be murderer, acting as a 'sword' leaping 'from a bed of roses', or as a 'falcon-hearted dove' (IV. i). Zapolya is Andreas' 'heroic mother' (IV. i). Such is our bi-sexual blend, of sweetness and virility, of right and power, to make true royalty.[1] Andreas, victorious, will yet await 'the awful sanction of convened Illyria' (IV. i).

Dramatic action, apart from the great moments, is loose, and the plot poor. We should expect no more from an unpractised dramatist at work on so demanding a task. *Zapolya*, despite its failings, is unique. How shall we understand it? We may contrast this cave 'overhung with ivy' (II. i) where the young hero braves horrors to find his mother and establish his royal heritage with that other slimy and crevassed cavern in *Remorse* where Ordonio commits his miserable and useless murder. Cave for cave; depth for depth; and the facing of the one may be the price for the realization of the other. *Remorse* and *Zapolya* together witness a transformation of evil mystery into magical humanism.[2] Apart from Shakespeare, we have nowhere else so fine a royalistic poetry, and nowhere at all have we

---

[1] An interesting bisexual emphasis occurs in Coleridge's poem *The Destiny of Nations*; and also in Shelley's *The Witch of Atlas* and 'Fragments' to *Epi-psychidion*. See *The Starlit Dome*, 141–2; 228, 241–2.

[2] In a note to his poem *Religious Musings* Coleridge writes: 'Our evil passions, under the influence of religion, become innocent, and may be made to animate our virtue.' See *The Starlit Dome*, 133.

so powerful a realization of virtue and virility, Apollonian and
Dionysian, in concord.

Gothic drama touches that positive essence within evil which is
felt in all great tragedy. Writing in his introduction to *Gregory VII*
(1840; p. 261 below) R. H. Horne observes:

> Whatever the crime, there is always something grand and solemn in
> exploring the depths of human nature. The wisest or the shallowest
> sitter-in-judgement would tremble and be mute were the criminal's
> thoughts and passions all laid bare to view. In the worst acts, it is
> probable, we might find within the individual something excul-
> patory, if not redeeming; something which, *under the circumstances,
> seemed right*; something, at heart, the very opposite to his one fatal
> act. . . .   (xvi.)

Though our tragedies naturally concentrate on sensational actions
their meanings correspond to the soul lives of us all. In Gothic drama
we have a fusion of the Faust myth and the Don Juan myth. The
protagonist's crime is generally related to the sexual—that is why
the settings are mostly, like those of Shakespeare's love tragedies,
southern—and for many of the authors, and some spectators or readers,
we may suggest the trouble was probably homosexual: W. Beckford
(author of *Vathek*, 1786), George Colman the Younger, whose *Iron
Chest* we shall notice in due course, and Byron all had homosexual
propensities. So probably had Beddoes: and perhaps Shelley, whose
'fragments' related to *Epipsychidion* describe the Socratic love
there celebrated as giving birth to a 'naked seraph' (*The Mutual
Flame*; 210–15; *The Starlit Dome*, 241–2). The regular dramatic
association of sin and occult insight may be usefully related to the
recurring association of male youth and seraphs. Our central Gothic
document is M. G. Lewis's famous novel *Ambrosio or The Monk* (1796),
in which the hero is seduced into wickedness by the mysterious girl-
boy, Matilda or Rosario, whose magic causes Lucifer himself to appear:

> At the same time the cloud disappeared, and he beheld a figure more
> beautiful than fancy's pencil ever drew. It was a youth seemingly
> scarce eighteen, the perfection of whose form and face was un-
> rivalled. He was perfectly naked: a bright star sparkled upon his
> forehead, two crimson wings extended themselves from his shoulders,
> and his silken locks were confined by a band of many-coloured fires,
> which played round his head, formed themselves into a variety of
> figures, and shone with a brilliance far surpassing that of precious
> stones. Circlets of diamonds were fastened round his arms and
> ankles, and in his right hand he bore a silver branch imitating
> myrtle.   (VII.)

That at the start, like a Greek Eros. On his second appearance to claim Ambrosio for Hell he is hideous; the process is interesting. The beauty which was the heart of Greek culture has become the signal of damnation.

Some high and fiery excellence becomes under moral condemnation evil; penitence must be put aside, as our Gothic heroes put it aside, since the subject knows the instinct to be an inalienable part of his created self. The only course is forward, using dramatic or religious ritual to transmute it, as Coleridge transmutes it in *Zapolya*, to the original excellence. This is the way to a wisdom attainable only through self-knowledge. Beyond self-knowledge lies self-realization.

CHAPTER X

Byron

You who condemn me, you who fear and slay me,
Yet could not bear in silence to your graves
What you would hear from me of good or evil;
The secret were too mighty for your souls.
         Lord Byron, *Marino Faliero*; v. i.

I

IT IS probable that full self-realization was more nearly attained by
Lord Byron than anyone else of modern times. He is drama personified. As a boy he inherited a baronetcy together with the half-ruined
Newstead Abbey, as described in *Don Juan* (XIII–XVI). In early manhood he played the Gothic villain, drinking from a skull and gaining
a reputation for mysterious wickedness. Shortly after, showing a
chameleon adaptability to circumstance, he was mixing in high
society with the bearing of Etherege's Dorimant, while retaining the
good heart of Charles Surface. But his interests ranged far wider.
Shakespeare was in his blood, and his prose and poetry are scattered
thick with Shakespearian quotations. In challenge to the Regency and
the dynastic monarchies of Europe he played Hamlet to their
Claudius, from his own apparent ineffectuality admiring Napoleon
much as Hamlet admired Fortinbras. As patron of poverty and
aspiring genius, he was a Timon, suffering a similar reversal and
removal, and turning to vast nature in his bitterness. In quality of
humour he ranges from Shaw to Falstaff, and from time to time he
put on flesh to suit the part; in macabre reputation, dreams, and
stories he was Richard III, suffering like Richard from a deformity,
and Macbeth. Adventuring in the east, returning to make a conventional and ill-fated marriage, and then off east again, he was Antony.
His poetry shows a Shakespearian feeling for the sea and every time
he went to sea he fought successfully a tempest of Shakespearian
fearsomeness. Like Othello, he believed himself to be royally

descended with Stuart blood in him, though his political opinions were nearer to Cromwell. He was an aristocratic revolutionary.

His life shows a balance of satisfying homosexuality and tormented heterosexuality, like Shakespeare's Sonnets. A visionary 'seraph' was his ideal (*Childe Harold*, IV. 121): the Greek boys who aroused his instincts he saw as seraphic equivalents or 'sylphs' (to Hobhouse, 23 August 1810), and the Cambridge chorister John Edleston was 'a dream of Heaven' (*If Sometimes in the Haunts of Men*, 1812). These ideal beings were reflections of himself. Though his powers as a man of action were as male as his prose, to his friends he appeared half feminine: he is our greatest recorded example of bisexuality, resembling his own Don Juan who is on one occasion dressed as a girl and on another an Eros in uniform like '.Love turn'd a lieutenant of artillery' (*Don Juan*, v. 6; ix. 44). Byron recognized both the mystery of sexual difference and the need for a bisexual 'Tiresias' to solve it (xiv. 73). In him dualisms are difficult to disentangle. He appeared strange, supremely physical yet touched by unearthly qualities. He and others often saw him as a fallen angel, a Lucifer, Milton's Satan; but he as often gave the impression of sweetness, radiating such beauty and power that ladies fell before him and strong men gave him their souls' allegiance. In religion he was a deist with Catholic sympathies and a strong, at times superstitious, sense of the occult. As both thinker and man of action he came near to blending the values of a Renaissance gentleman and those of the Sermon on the Mount, labouring in himself to solve this all but insoluble dramatic conflict of Caesar and God, of State and Church. He was by instinct attuned to the thought-valuations of ancient Greece, and in dying for Greece he became a personified symbol of the Western tradition, cultural and political. He was often compared to Napoleon, yet spirituality shone through him with more than Napoleonic radiations. Looking back on our dramas, we can say that he covers our two main ideals of sylph and power-man; as poetic symbols of aspiration, his mountains and sun forecast both Ibsen and Nietzsche; and despite an ingrained humility he all but claimed for himself a superman status. What centuries of drama had been, and still were, worrying over in ink and mimicry, Byron lived. He is western drama personified.[1]

---

[1] My readings of Byron's work and personality have appeared in *The Burning Oracle*, 1939; *Lord Byron: Christian Virtues*, 1952; *Lord Byron's Marriage*, 1957; and *Byron's Dramatic Prose*, University of Nottingham, 1954. To these I intend to add a final volume entitled *Byron and Shakespeare*.

Byron's Letters and Journals are saturated in dramatic feeling. Here is his comment dated 9 April 1814, on a key moment in European history. The quotations are from Otway's *Venice Preserved* and Shakespeare's *Antony and Cleopatra*:

> Napoleon Buonaparte has abdicated the throne of the world . . . What! wait till they were in his capital, and then talk of his readiness to give up what is already gone! 'What whining monk art thou— what holy cheat?' 'Sdeath!—Dionysius at Corinth was yet a king to this. The Isle of Elba to retire to!—Well—if it had been Caprea, I should have marvelled less. 'I see men's minds are but a parcel of their fortunes'. I am utterly bewildered and confounded.

On 19 April he quotes Macbeth's

> And all our yesterdays have lighted fools
> The way to dusty death

and proceeds, with quotations from *Romeo and Juliet* and *King Lear*:

> I will keep no further journal of that same hesternal torch-light; and, to prevent me from returning, like a dog, to the vomit of memory, I tear out the remaining leaves of this volume, and write, in *Ipecacuanha*, 'that the Bourbons are restored!!!'—'Hang up philosophy!' To be sure, I have long despised myself and man, but I never spat in the face of my species before—'O fool! I shall go mad'.

The accents are the accents of the theatre; there is the smell, the immediacy, of stage soliloquy. European history is given a dramatic focus, with Byron as protagonist.

II

To turn from such a personality to written drama is inevitably a descent, but Byron's dramas are nevertheless pivotal. In them many of our complications are found placed, clarified, and purposeful. The satanic nihilisms of Wordsworth and Maturin, the near atheism of Shelley's *Cenci*, the grotesque paradoxes of Beddoes—all receive justification in the light of Byron's subtle transvaluations and piercing insights.

As a young man he acted Penruddock in Cumberland's *The Wheel of Fortune*; in London he was a keen theatre-goer; and he became a member of the Drury Lane Committee. After breaking with England, he wrote a number of plays.[1] In these he deliberately avoided the more extravagant elements of Shakespearian and Gothic drama, following Walpole, whose *Mysterious Mother* he greatly admired, and aiming at a neo-classic clarity and condensation. Some of Byron's verse even runs better if printed as Shavian, or Jamesian, dramatic prose. Thought, symbol and pattern are very exactly interrelated. Such daylight control leads naturally to loss as well as gain; we cannot expect a Maturin's hurly-burly of stage excitement, nor a Shakespeare's surging rhetoric, but for once great drama becomes rational, and that is much.

Werner (1822) stands apart. It is a successful stage-piece, with dark irony, a mysterious murder and a father's peccadillo bearing horrible fruit in his son's crime. Moral values are given a good plot and some fine poetry and situations, but there is little more. However, it has the honour of being the first murder mystery of the British stage.[2] Of the rest we shall discuss five works, dividing them into two groups: (i) metaphysical and (ii) political.

Manfred (1817) is a condensation of the myths of Prometheus, Faust and Don Juan, showing affinities to the Gothic.[3] The hero is a baron who has delved deep into occult science, and his settings are a castle and Alpine heights. He communes with his own soul, nature, and spirits. He is a man of more than normal stature, of 'no common order' (II. iv), the more impressive as embryo superman for containing in himself both good and evil. A mysterious blood-crime of *Macbeth* quality haunts him, though he has not himself shed blood. He is guilty of some sin in love, though its exact nature is left undefined. He has the reputation of communing with departed souls, and with the help of spirits calls up Astarte, an ambivalent figure symbolic of love's desire and desecration, at once ideal and accuser. Statesmanship is also involved: Manfred had the will to be an 'enlightener of nations' (III. i), but has failed through refusal to seek advancement by intrigue and flattery. He is the successor to all dramatic king-opposers, such as Chapman's Byron, and the type of all noble revolutionaries. In metaphysics he has sinned through no

[1] See William Gerard, *Byron Restudied in his Dramas*, 1886; Samuel C. Chew, *The Dramas of Lord Byron*, Göttingen and Baltimore, 1915; G. Wilson Knight, 'The Two Eternities' in *The Burning Oracle*, and also 'Shakespeare and Byron's Plays' in the *Shakespeare-Jahrbuch*, 1939 and 1959; together with university theses by B. Taborski, at Bristol, and Patricia M. Ball, at Leeds, 1952 and 1953. Mr Taborski gives valuable details on the stage record of Byron's dramas during the nineteenth century.

[2] Observed by M. Willson Disher in *Melodrama*, 1954, VII. 50.

[3] Bertrand Evans (p. 203 note) regards *Manfred* as the crowning justification of Gothic drama.

Faustian compact, but rather, like a modern spiritualist, claims to have re-established 'by superior science' an age-old tradition of communication with

> The dead but sceptred sovereigns, who still rule
> Our spirits from their urns. (III. iv.)

He refuses the Abbot's solicitations. He knows that no hell could add to his remorse and that the issue must be fought out within the mind's own immortality (III. iv). The infernal powers are boldly repudiated, since 'the mind, the spirit, the Promethean spark' in himself is as potent as theirs (I. i). Unsoftened yet self-condemned, he strikes the balance held by Shakespeare in *Macbeth*. And he has also a Timon's grandeur: 'The lion is alone and so am I' (III. i). Communing with vast nature, addressing the Sun, he speaks, like Timon, as from a pinnacle of consciousness. Though 'extreme' in deeds of both good and evil (II. ii) he has, like Beddoes's superman, a 'will' that controls his own self-conflict (II. iv). He draws near some great revelation, feeling at certain elusive moments

> The golden secret, the sought 'Kalon', found
> And seated in my soul. (III. i.)

'The golden secret', the wisdom or wise-being of Socrates, or Nietzsche's Zarathustra.

In *Cain* (1821) Byron relates the romantic impulse to biblical mythology. Religious counsel has been by hero after hero rejected, and the relation needs clarifying. Cain is embittered by the apparent senselessness of Jehovah's tyranny and the curse of Death fallen on man for Adam's disobedience. Death is our dominating thought. Lucifer appears and answers Cain's questions, denying on biblical authority that he was responsible for the Fall and defending his cosmic rights with logic. Standing as 'Lucifer' or 'light-bringer' for the post-Renaissance intelligence as opposed to ecclesiastical condemnation, he takes Cain on two explorations corresponding to the scientific and spiritualistic quests of Renaissance, Faustian man. The first is set in space and we have a space voyage through the illimitable blue ether, Cain wondering at the multitudinous lights and myriad other worlds, the earth seen as a tiny glow-worm in the vast distances. Next he is taken to the other infinity of time, a dimension in which the past lives, though with a different being which will only make full sense to Cain after his own death (II. ii). Gigantic phantoms of a past world are vivid in a shadowy realm of blue and purple lights, the waterish yet ethereal element being Byron's definition of what we today should call the 'astral' or 'etheric' dimension. Staggered by these revelations as was Hamlet by his father's ghost, and only the more unrestful for Lucifer's enlightened arguments, Cain returns. Abel asks what he has seen:

> The dead—
> The immortal—the unbounded—the omnipotent—
> The overpowering mysteries of space—
> The innumerable worlds that were and are—
> A whirlwind of such overwhelming things,
> Suns, moons and earths, upon their loud-voiced spheres
> Singing in thunder round me, as have made me
> Unfit for mortal converse: leave me, Abel.
>
> (III. i.)

He is European man over-burdened by his own accumulating yet unsatisfying knowledge.

Animal suffering has been one of Cain's most insistent torments, and now Abel's sacrifice of a blood-offering, a horror 'shaming creation' (III. i), is accepted, while Cain's of fruits is rejected. Jehovah, not Lucifer, is the bloody god. The quarrel rises, Abel is killed. Cain the gentle-hearted becomes the first murderer, ancestor of all our Gothic heroes. Most skilfully and without falsifying the myth, Byron relates the Faustian and Gothic quests of Renaissance and Romantic Europe to traditional theology. Finer values are in the making.

In Part 1 of the lyrical drama *Heaven and Earth* (1821) biblical legend is used to dramatize what we have called the 'seraphic' intuition. The two 'daughters' of Cain are loved by two Seraphs. Though condemned by both Noah and the Archangel Raphael as an unnatural sin, this seraphic love is stoutly defended as in tune with man's creation in God's image (iii. 477). To avoid the coming flood the Seraphs take their loved ones to 'a bright world' of 'ethereal life' (iii. 820–1). Their exact destiny is left unsettled, since Part 2 was not written. It seems that Byron planned a tragic end, saying, 'It is not easy for the imagination to make any unknown world more beautiful than this' (quoted by E. Hartley Coleridge, Byron's *Works; Poetry;* V; 321). Part 1 concludes with the oncoming flood and the slaughter of men and animals under God's appalling judgement. The surrounding action is stern, but framed within it burn old memories of Satan's unfallen splendour and Cain's strength as imaginative supports to the wondrous though unhallowed mating of Cain's descendants to the seraphic. These seraphs from the 'angelic choir' (iii. 532) may have reminded Byron of Cambridge (p. 230 above).

Elsewhere the romantic torment is expanded to cover world affairs. In *Marino Faliero* (1820) Byron has a theme corresponding to his own political discontents as a revolutionary aristocrat. True sovereignty is being replaced not by a just commonwealth but by a ruling clique, as surely in nineteenth-century England as it was in medieval Venice. Traces of the Shakespearian royalism are in the autocratic Doge, a fiery old man loving and loved by the people but intolerant under the insults of the Senate. No drama ever had a finer opening than this, with the restless and impatient Doge waiting to hear what sentence has been given the calumniator of his domestic honour. When, wrathful at lack of redress, he is tempted by a former comrade-in-arms from the working classes to join a revolution within the state of which he is himself the sovereign, we have a social and dramatic situation of inexhaustible meaning. Personal passions join with political idealism to force him into treason. Before the tombs and statues of his ancestors he invokes their 'spirits' to bless his actions (III. i). Or must they not rather condemn them? He meets a fellow conspirator:

ISRAEL: Let us to the meeting,
            Or we may be observed in lingering here.
DOGE: We *are* observed, and have been.
ISRAEL: We observed!
            Let me discover—and this steel—
DOGE.   Put up;
            Here are no human witnesses: look there—
            What see you?

                                                          (III. i.)

He points to a statue, an ancestor, saviour of Venice.

ISRAEL: My lord, these are mere fantasies; there are
            No eyes in marble.
DOGE: But there are in Death.
            I tell thee, man, there is a spirit in
            Such things that acts, and sees, unseen though felt;
            And if there be a spell to raise the dead,
            'Tis in such deeds as we are now upon.

                                                          (III. i.)

Byron's habitual mystique of the past dramatizes death without reliance on superstition or Gothic extravagance. The numinous is concrete, the spirit world revealed in and through the dramatic pressure. Symbol rests on a firm basis of local and historic realism. Venice is before us, its moonlit palaces and gondolas, a world of stone and water; and the great bell of St Mark's. The action draws life from the created whole; man, city, cosmos, all cohere.

Marino Faliero has a mass and weight, and on occasion a majesty of language, comparable with Shakespeare and Milton; its subtle handling of state affairs, as profound an interpenetration of public idealism and personal passion as Tennyson's *Becket*, points ahead to the great Victorians; and its drawing of the Doge as one above normality, a man shadowed by 'eternity' (II. i) and in touch with a secret 'too mighty' for the souls of his accusers (v. i), points yet further. The Doge links Shakespeare and Chapman to Ibsen and Nietzsche: the drama is saturated in the advancing political and psychological thought of Europe. Outwardly, as an art-form, calm, it is yet loaded with a smouldering passion. Many speeches are over-long and must, as Byron himself insisted, be pruned for performance. That granted, we have a masterpiece.

The Two Foscari (1821), again set in Venice, is slighter. Here our Doge is a Cornelian figure of self-surmounting who has in duty to approve his son's torture by the State. Primary emphasis falls on the horrors attending State intrigue and State justice, the secret tortures being shown to be as horrible within a supposedly liberal republic as under any old-style tyrant or priestly inquisition. There are for once no spirit contacts. The fragmentary *The Deformed Transformed* (1822) has a powerful vision of phantom heroes of the ancient world on the battlements of beleaguered Rome.

Marino Faliero depicts a revolutionary sovereign; its twin master-piece, *Sardanapalus* (1821), a pacifist emperor. These paradoxes are weighted with import. The aim is to incorporate the royal essence within a liberal and humane society. On Byron's drama pivots the swing from Shakespeare to Shaw.

Sardanapalus is a pleasure-loving emperor of ancient Assyria who like Shakespeare's Antony has deserted his wife for a mistress. We see him at his love-making, feasting and conviviality, central in a glittering world. He is as rich-hearted as Timon, and a man of wit and enlightenment. His apparent scorn of the obvious manly virtues descends from a long series of seventeenth and eighteenth-century dramas rating love beyond glory and attacking the horrors of war. His famous ancestress Semiramis, whom he is expected to revere, he scornfully repudiates for the bloody deeds by which she expanded the empire. (I. ii). War he loathes, preferring 'ignominy' to such 'glory', the gist of Falstaff's 'honour' speech being repeated in deadly earnest (I. ii). His lenience to the subversive elements in his state leads to a revolution, which he faces with a magnificent heroism reversing expectations: like Shakespeare's Hal, he is shown to be greater than the conventional hero. But now, since he has engaged in bloodshed, his ancestors' spirits try to 'drag' him 'down' yet further to their level. In sleep, and so half in the world of death—the impingement is exactly noted—he has met Nimrod and Semiramis:

> Hence—hence—
> Old hunter of the earliest brutes! and ye
> Who hunted fellow creatures as if brutes!
> Once bloody mortals—and now bloodier idols . . .
>
> (IV. i.)

Like Cain, he sympathizes with the animal creation. In contrast to his Apollonian enlightenment, Nimrod and Semiramis here symbolize that drag of dead valuations covered by Aeschylus' Erinues and Ibsen's *Ghosts*.

Sardanapalus' aim to make his reign 'an era of sweet peace 'midst bloody annals' (IV. i) is met by base ingratitude. He is, like Timon, a man of boundless goodwill and golden bounty; and, like Cumberland's Belcour, conceived as a *new type* of man, unwise through the very warmth of his spontaneous feeling. He is from the start regarded as half feminine, while his Greek mistress Myrrha is, like Coleridge's heroines, an Amazon in war. Bisexuality dominates, as in Byron's *Don Juan*. So does the Sun, invoked at length in noble passages (II. i; V. i). We end with fire, as Sardanapalus and his loved Myrrha go, like Antony and Cleopatra, to their imperial martyrdom.

Byron's dramas sum up a long Shakespearian and post-Shakespearian tradition. Unfaltering selection and exact control give new and contemporary relevance to traditional themes while pointing them ahead to Ibsen and Nietzsche. The numinous is handled with an impressive critical understanding. The Faustian and Gothic agonies with their attendant crimes at last bear rational fruit in a number of ethical transvaluations asserting liberality and warmth against the established orderings of society and religion. Some form of irregularity is necessarily involved, for transvaluation is transvaluation, the human substance is limited, and all new virtue demands moral payment. But there is nothing dogmatic; all the dualities are preserved; it is a matter, not of any one-way doctrine, but of balance and emphasis. Construction, especially in *Sardanapalus*, which has no unduly long speeches, is admirable; and each drama, in Shakespearian wise, shows its people and action in a natural, human and cosmic context. Only one so saturated in the dramatic as Byron could have made so purposeful and Apollonian a drama without loss of contact with the Dionysian sources of dramatic power. Three of our heroes are embryo supermen, though nowhere do we find the magical poeticizing, the aura, of Coleridge's *Zapolya*. For that we must look rather to Byron's personality than to his writing, the writing being only a part of his dramatic challenge.

III

Goethe admired Byron's dramas, and in conclusion we glance at his *Faust*, that life's drama whose composition spans the romantic period.[1] The hero is both Don Juan and Faust, less a man within a myth than a man made of myth; what we may call a 'myth man'. Put otherwise he is the soul of Europe. From The Prologue in Heaven we learn that Mephistopheles is allowed by Providence to tempt man in order to keep him awake: he is a companionable creature ranging from cynical rationalism to fiery disruption; he does not arouse awe. The vast drama is comparatively bright. Mountains and great nature dominate.

In Part 1 Faust is a romantic seducer and the moral is clear: man's erotic instincts, if too directly expressed, lead to disaster. Sublimation is a large part of civilization and in Part 2 we watch Faust as the myth man of Europe enacting the purposes of the Renaissance era. As entertainers at the Emperor's court he and Mephistopheles are associated with masque and pastoral, though luxury and greed spoil the short-lived, in British terms 'Elizabethan', splendour. Their prompting of the Emperor to engage in dishonest and inflationary finance symbolizes the birth of modern capitalism. But meanwhile Faust has his vision of Helen, the myth lady of ancient Greece, and undertakes his Hellenic quest. In this he is helped by Homunculus, symbolizing the furthest advance of medieval science now enlisted by the Renaissance; and Faust is in medieval dress for his union with Helen. Their child is Euphorion personifying the Romantic Revival, explicitly equated with Lord Byron and shown meeting an early death through too unrestrained an aspiration.

The poem now advances beyond Goethe's own time; great conflicts arise, caused in part by the Emperor's financial policy; a rival authority—Goethe had Napoleon as a prototype—supplants him,

[1] My more extended commentaries on *Faust* have appeared in *The Christian Renaissance*, 1933, and *Christ and Nietzsche*, 1948.

and has to be met and defeated. When the war is won the Emperor returns to his vices. Ruthless men are about and active. In all this twentieth-century warring is forecast. Faust strives finally for a more selfless good and dies labouring frantically for humanity. Beyond death he is raised to a paradise in which Christian and pagan conceptions blend.

Throughout there is a strongly humanistic and erotic emphasis. In the masque poetry is personified by a boy in a winged chariot, half feminine, a kind of Eros; in the classical Walpurgis Night Homunculus, described as both beautiful and hermaphroditical (Pt 2; II), reaches self-expression in a semi-suicidal orgasm accompanied by a paean to Eros as universal lord; the boy Euphorion is given a blazingly Apollonian and seraphic description, aureoled with intellectual fire and every limb athrill with the eternal music (Pt 2; III; Phorkyas' speech). That the angels' song-music at the end should be to Mephistopheles a 'boyish-girlish botchwork' [1] only marks his blindness to the bisexual powers. Beyond death Faust, splendid in recaptured youth, is assisted by the company of Blessed Boys—boys who had passed over before knowing earthly contamination—and by Gretchen (Pt 2; v). Behind Faust's quest for Helen were the mysterious 'Mothers' (Pt 2; I), and now the boys and Gretchen are agents of Faust's ascent: 'the eternal womanly draws us above'. Beyond is the Virgin, Mother of God and Queen of Heaven (Pt 2; v).[2]

Though Faust's actions can often be called wrong, the moral judgement is only indirectly relevant. He is more myth than man, and we are primarily aware of a titanic striving optimistically toned and throwing up visions of man and nature in harmony, sometimes of men-gods or supermen. There is no simple moral; Mephistopheles is lightly drawn. Apart from the mountains our two main symbols are water and fire, for creation and disruption, and both together are needed to lift the poem. Goethe has little insight into abysmal evils and does not engage in the ethical transmutations of which Byron is our great exponent. He is content with titanic aspiration countered by a moral conclusion. *Faust* accordingly helps the student of British drama to place our romantic quest within the soul history of Europe and to show it dissolving into the more moralistic and communal problems that dominate the Victorian stage.

---

[1] I am following the Everyman translation by Albert G. Latham.
[2] This final scene is excellently analysed by Alexander Gillies in *Goethe's Faust*, 1957.

CHAPTER XI

Victorian

This long-tugged-at, threadbare worn
Quarrel of Crown and Church.
Alfred Lord Tennyson, *Becket*; II. ii.

I

DESPITE its mass and variety we find within Victorian drama a cluster of related characteristics: a change from internal to external excitements; a strong money complex, the villains wielding various forms of financial tyranny; favour shown to the socially inferior and the simple; or the savage, after the manner of Rousseau; no doubts regarding sexual morality; domesticity in personal affairs and liberalism in politics; and, among the greater exponents, statecraft, especially the interaction of Church and State. Except in our last group, virtue and villainy are in sharp contrast, virtue usually triumphant.

'Melodrama', a term deriving from the use of music to support emotion, covers a vast output of sensational plays, sometimes said to start with Holcroft's *A Tale of Mystery*, from the French of Pixérécourt, in 1802. Throughout the century French influence and adaptations are as strong as are the Germanic affinities of the Gothic. But disentanglement is impossible. Melodrama could also be called a development both from the more inward sensationalism of Gothic drama and from the heroic tradition, with Sheridan's *Pizarro* (1799) adapted from the German of Kotzebue as a transition piece, of the seventeenth and eighteenth centuries. Sir Walter Scott wrote Gothic plays. *The Doom of Devorgoil* (c. 1800) has a good title and *Auchindrane or The Ayrshire Tragedy* (c. 1800; prod. 1830) has something more; and there were numerous adaptations from his historical novels. It was a patriotic age and patriotism gave rise to a number of lively naval pieces. Prose melodrama contained elements from the poetic tradition, employing cruder and more sensational effects for the wider and less refined audiences and music at high moments to accompany or replace words, a usual climax being a succession of actions mimed to a musical crescendo and ending in a tableau; which, though sounding crude to the literary intelligence, demanded nevertheless a technique close to the inmost essence of dramatic art; and what was actually experienced may on occasion have been drama of quality.

Effects might involve mystery and supernature, as in Edward Fitzball's *The Flying Dutchman* (1827) and *Thalaba the Destroyer* (1836); or conscience, as in W. T. Moncrieff's *Eugene Aram* (1832). But the countering tendency to externals was strong and this joined to social unrest to make a worthy group in D. W. Jerrold's *The Rent Day* (1832), on the sufferings of a farmer-tenant under an oppressive and vengeful agent; his *The Factory Girl* (1832); John Walker's powerful *The Factory Lad* (1832); and G. F. Taylor's *The Factory Strike* (1838); and other such dramas of social challenge at the more popular theatres.[1] The brutality of naval discipline was exposed in Jerrold's *The Mutiny at the Nore* (1830). Social criticism had entered drama as early as Mrs Elizabeth Inchbald's attack on prison conditions in *Such Things Are* (1787) and Thomas Morton's powerfully constructed *Speed the Plough* (1800), with its emphasis on the nobility of labour; and it was to make strong melodrama in Tom Taylor's *The Ticket of Leave Man* (1863) and Charles Reade's *It's Never Too Late to Mend* (1865), both concerned with prisons. These sociological criticisms grow from a soil of accepted valuations found throughout the century opposing low-born simplicity and virtue to a villainous squirearchy, tyrannic landlords and legal cruelty. There is an implicit criticism of a system dominated by financial power supported by law. The social effect of such dramas, which included many adaptations from the novels of Charles Dickens, cannot be exactly assessed, but their value to us remains limited. Most melodramas have even less claim to our interest. True, though they could sink to G. Dibdin Pitt's *Sweeney Tod or The Demon Barber of Fleet Street* (titles vary; 1847), they could also rise to Henry Arthur Jones's and Henry Herman's *The Silver King* (1882), but the black-and-white morality in general favour was seriously lacking in dramatic depth. That is why, when we are amused at melodrama, we think first of the villains and their too obvious asides, recognizing a falsity.

[1] M. Willson Disher writes: 'For ten years the theatre was brave, which is more than it has been ever since' (*Blood and Thunder*, 1949; IX. 158).

The implied psychology is superficial. As the years passed, emphasis in the supernatural gave place to a sensational realism, made possible by advances in stage trickery, based on the externals of travel and invention, on fearsome effects drawing on explosions, fires, floods, shipwrecks and railways, intermixed with amazing feats of stage athleticism and the requisite villainies and rescues. Reliance on such stage tricks led to an unconvincing result, for the externals alone accomplish little, and the attempt to make popular drama of tragic affinities from the thought-world of a moralizing and scientific age inevitably failed.

To its credit, we can say that melodrama kept alive people's interest in terror and evil and in certain of the more supernatural mysteries too. In an unimaginative age it did what it could to preserve the tradition.

II

There were, however, many typical prose dramas which, though not of highest status, remain worthy of attention. Most are dominated by the prevailing money complex in descent from the *Timon* themes of the previous century, and we shall accordingly include in this chapter some pre-Victorian dramas, starting with Thomas Holcroft's *The Road to Ruin* (1792), where a generous hero in want is turned down by one whom he had helped to gain his wealth, and *The Man of Ten Thousand* (1796), which is pretty nearly a rewriting in contemporary terms of Shakespeare's opening acts. This interesting piece is far more than a simple Shakespearian rehash: it is a purposeful reinterpretation. Though we have the same old extravagance and entertainment criticized as folly, the hero Dorington is aware of what he is doing, and accepts disaster and ingratitude with a delicate irony. Some of his generosity has been well placed, and all has been done according to principle. 'Do good and receive good' (II. vi) is his motto, and his equanimity is never disturbed. When he gets his fortune back after all, it is no less than he deserves. The play might have been written to prove that Shakespeare's Timon was not so foolish as he looks. Holcroft was a man of revolutionary principles and these new principles, with some amusing satire on a city financier, are felt at work beneath the surface.

The large-hearted Richard Cumberland reversed the conventional attitude to Jewry in *The Jew* (1794),[1] wherein old Shiva, supposed a miser, is really a man of secret bounty who helps two young lovers, remarking that 'there is but one man in the world poorer than he was and he is going out of it, and there is a couple a great deal happier and they are coming into it'. After all, this is good business, 'two for one, cent per cent' (IV. ii). Seldom has a moral been driven home by so simple yet profound a logic. More substantial is *The Wheel of Fortune* (1795), which corresponds in more romantic fashion to the *falling* action of *Timon of Athens*. Here the deeply wronged and embittered Penruddock—the part played by the young Byron (p. 231 above)—comes from his hermit's retreat to take up his new-found fortune; he has the opportunity of acting according to his injuries, but after a severe self-conflict surmounts his bitterness and proves, unlike Shakespeare's hero, magnanimous. Faced by the palatial gaudiness of his new home he asks how one who has 'looked nature in the face' can turn to 'these symptoms of insanity' (III. iii). Here is his conclusion:

> I am weary, sick, discomfited. This world and I must part once more. That it has virtues, I will not deny; but they lie buried in a tide of vanities, like grains of gold in sand washed down by mountain torrents. I cannot wait the sifting.   (IV. ii.)

'The true use of riches', we are told, is 'to share them with the worthy' and 'the sole remedy for injuries', forgiveness (V. i). *The Jew* has weight at least of conception and *The Wheel of Fortune* an imaginative density which commands respect.

George Colman the Younger was a mid-level popular dramatist whose work is reasonably well loaded. He had abilities ranging from tragedy to farce, from high poetry to nonsense rhymes, and used them freely if rather haphazardly. His views are humanitarian and his dramatic thinking again in the *Timon* tradition.

The Heir-at-Law (1797) is a satire on wealth, snobbery and false friends in contrast to the simple and humble who have instincts of generosity and benevolence lacking in their superiors. Kindness is logical: 'Rich or poor, great or small, we all form one chain' (III. i). Lighter amusement comes from the absurd scholar Dr Pangloss, always introducing himself as 'A double S', for '*Artium Societatis Socius*'. *John Bull* (1803) contains a many-pointed satire against rich seducers, town fashions, marriages for money or rank, city finance— 'the constant habit of ruining one another teaches us temper' (II. i)—

---

[1] On *The Jew* see Louis I. Newman, *Richard Cumberland: Critic, and Friend of the Jews*, New York, 1919; and also Harold Fisch in *The Dual Image* (p. 70 note).

together with perversion of justice and betrayal by a friend. Job Thornberry is an honest brazier on the brink of financial disaster caused by the treachery of a friend, till a rich stranger whom he had helped as an orphan arrives to relieve him and disprove the general charge of man's ingratitude.

The Iron Chest (1796) is a verse drama in the Gothic tradition of secrecy and guilt. Despite the usual concomitants, it is strong with an acute psychology in the style of Joanna Baillie. Sir Edward Mortimer's exaggerated respect for his own honour has involved him in crime and secrecy developing into an atrocious accusation against another; and the action is pushed to an emotional climax of great power. The verse, rather like Cumberland's in *The Battle of Hastings*, wells up naturally from the thought to flow with Shakespearian ease. The girl Helen speaks to her troubled lover:

> I'd have each hour, each minute of thy life,
> A golden holiday; and should a cloud
> O'ercast thee, be it light as gossamer,
> That Helen might disperse it with a breath,
> And talk thee into sunshine!   (III. ii.)

Among our many post-Shakespearian masters of dramatic verse, this particular Shakespearian fluency and unstrained flowering of imagery is comparatively rare, and found elsewhere perhaps only in Cumberland and Albery (pp. 198-9, 305).

Colman's dramatic thinking ranges widely. His dominant emphasis is humane, with attacks on imperialistic tyrannies and an honouring of primitive man in the manner of earlier dramatists such as Southerne and Gay, further popularized by Rousseau. Here is a European explaining himself in *Inkle and Yarico* (1787):

> We were not born to live in woods and caves—to seek subsistence by pursuing beasts—we Christians, girl, hunt money, a thing unknown to you.   (III. iii.)

As usual in Colman, gratitude is again the preserve of the simple. He was still•on the *Timon* wave-length much later in *The Law of Java* (1822), a rich rambling play on business imperialism in the Dutch trade. The young and unsullied Hans Gayvelt has come out to his uncle in Java, who regards his warm sense of gratitude as a little rash: 'Aye, aye, you're a young man, but, for the purposes of life—however, we'll talk of that by and by' (I. i). Hearing from his uncle how the Europeans offer friendship to the natives as a preliminary to setting them against each other and finally gaining power over

them, Hans can only reply: 'Curse me if I ever heard of such a
parcel of knaves!' (I. i). The treatment is balanced. Hans's uncle is no
ogre, and Hans himself knows that he has come out to make money
for his mother at home, and can hardly afford to choose. The complexities gather round him: 'Plague on this Machiavellianism! It
claps a kind of professional extinguisher upon a man's conscience'
(I. i). The native Emperor is himself tyrannical. When Hans wishes to
help one of his victims but is told by his uncle that such 'a matter of
sentiment' is irrelevant to the Dutch trade, he replies:

> True, true. The Dutch trade and sentiment, as you say, are very
> different things.   (II. i.)

A more poetical interest is introduced in the hermit-priest Orzinga,
once betrayed by a friend whom he had trusted 'as a brother' (III. i)
and now a Timon of the solitudes, muttering how man 'befriends and
stabs you' (III. i). His denunciation touches the grand manner:

> Well—let our globe of peopled perfidy
> Roll on, while here I ruminate.
> (III. i.)

He is not wholly dedicated to hatred; rather he is akin to Cumberland's Penruddock and Lewis's Orsino (p. 222 above); he has religion,
and disapproves of suicide. *The Law of Java* is colourful. It has
grandeur and spectacle, and oriental magnificence for the Emperor,
and a barren and rugged nature for Orzinga. It and *The Iron Chest*
are Colman's two most impressive dramas.

Some of the others are slight in comparison. In *Blue-Beard or
Female Curiosity* (1798) a lively exposition of arbitrary justice under
a Turkish tyrant is presented with a comic and musical treatment and
a free play of Colman's skill in light verse, as in this, on the decapita-
tion of a wife:

> How many there are, when a wife plays the fool,
> Will argue the point with her, calmly and cool;
> The bashaw, who don't relish debates of this sort,
> Cuts the woman, as well as the argument, short.
> (I. iii.)

The thinking belongs to that peculiar vein of light-opera executions
found in *The Beggar's Opera* and Gilbert and Sullivan. There is the
pretty duet of the two sisters before the forbidden blue room:

> Say, shall we? Yes. Say shall we? No!
> What is it makes us tremble so?
> (II. iii.)

They enter: it is a chamber of Death and Horror. Comedy, music, and horror blend. Of Colman's other plays, *The Review or The Wags of Windsor* (1800) is notable for the comic conception and extraordinary flow of nonsense rhymes of the civic factotum, Caleb Quotem.

Colman helps to establish a number of valuations to be worked and reworked throughout the century. So, for that matter, does Joanna Baillie in two well-wrought social dramas: *The Trial* (pub. 1798), on a girl's refusal to accept a lover with a taint on his character, and *The Election* (pub. 1802), developing a finely balanced contrast of old aristocrat and new-rich careerist. Morals and politics, with money as a pervading force, are to be recurring Victorian concerns. One of the best-known straight plays of the century is Bulwer Lytton's *Money* (1840). Neither his *The Lady of Lyons* (1838) nor *Richelieu* (1839), both in verse, is, despite its contemporary reputation, of much interest now; but the prose satire *Money* has a symptomatic if not absolute importance. The workmanship is skilled, but the drumming on the now hackneyed note begins to irritate. The hero is poor and embittered, becomes wealthy and popular, tests everyone by pretending ruin and attempting to borrow and proves to his own dissatisfaction that society is rotten: 'Above, Vice smiles and revels—below Crime frowns and starves' (III. i). The attack has pungency:

> Three days ago I was universally respected. I awake this morning to find myself singularly infamous. Yet I am the same man.   (V. ii.)

Despite its clever elaborations, it remains a too-obvious *Timon* rehash, like D. W. Jerrolds's *The Golden Calf* (1832). Timonic satire without the vast nature of Shakespeare's later acts, or the romantic assertion developed by Cumberland, Lewis and Colman, grows tedious.

Victorian drama likes fresh air, and this is well provided by J. B. Buckstone. *Luke the Labourer* (1826) has a strongish revenge action in a country setting. In *The Green Bushes* (1845) the hero Connor O'Kennedy leaves Ireland and his wife Geraldine for fear of arrest, and associates in America with a wild huntress, Miami, of aristocratic French descent. His wife follows him, and Miami in jealousy shoots Connor, who as he dies implores her to befriend Geraldine. Miami inherits wealth and returns to Europe, and Geraldine eventually returns to Ireland to find Miami as a grand lady, helping Geraldine's and Connor's family. The play has human interest and a spacious action. In *The Flowers of the Forest* (1847) a gipsy lad, Lemuel, whipped for poaching by a landowner, shoots his enemy from an ambush whilst he is at a duel, with the result that the other duellist is arrested. The gipsy Cynthia, driven by love for this man, informs against Lemuel, who is convicted and to be hanged. Cynthia is condemned to banishment by her tribe unless she kills the man she loves; instead she commits suicide. Wild north-country scenes and gipsy customs support a passionate story, open air and vigour of action reinforcing each other.

Similar qualities enliven the Irish dramas of Dion Boucicault. He first won distinction with a social comedy, *London Assurance* (1841), which has dialogue of wit and pith and a racy movement. His gift of pregnant satiric language is Jacobean in resource. Here is his commentary on the falsities of the age in *The School for Scheming* (1847):

> Awful contemplation! A man, whose individual occupies a remote and obscure corner of his person—oh—but it is the same everywhere—all unreal. Facts exist no more—they have dwindled into names—things have shrunk into words—words into air—cash into figures—reputation into nothing. This is the reign of Nothing; to possess it, is the surest foundation of fortune in every walk of life. Examine the pocket of the capitalist—*nothing*!—penetrate the skull of the politician—*nothing*!—value the credit of a free and enlightened state—*nothing*!—or your own—*nothing*! Thus ridiculed, despised, calumniated, *nothing* is the philosopher's stone of our age, it turns all it touches into gold—to fame—to beauty—and all the other cardinal virtues. Scepticism is our faith, and this is our creed—trust a stranger never; your friend when you cannot help it, and yourself as little as possible. Even seeing is no longer believing. Thus you admire that girl's blushes. Bah! her modesty came last week from Paris, and was stopped for duty at the Custom House; and with it arrived a packet of wit for that author—this man gets his opinions from that critic, who never had an opinion in his life—this lady falls in love with that lord's fortune, while he is ensnared by her luxuriant figure—when the lady discovers that the lord has not enough to pay the bill in which her *embonpoint* is a large item—horror!—there's no great feat in nature but a dinner, and I put no faith in that, till I have eaten it. (I.)

Such thoughts are here peculiarly appropriate since the action is to show two people marrying each on the mistaken supposition that the other is rich. Satiric strokes are happily pointed: we hear of Cupid 'with one of his own quills stuck behind his ear' functioning as a book-keeper to demonstrate 'that £ s. d. means love, sincerity, devotion' (III).

Boucicault's abilities were various. He was a master of innovation, of which the cleverest example occurs in *The Octoroon* (1859), a work on the colour problems of the southern states of America, where a murder is by chance committed before an exposed camera-plate which eventually reveals the criminal. His Irish dramas are probably his best. *Arrah-na-Pogue* (1864) turns on the escape of a rebel leader wanted by the British. Even more gripping are *The Colleen Bawn* (1860) and *The Shaughraun* (1875).

Irish country is more than scene and setting; it is entangled at every point with the stories; rocks and caves, sea and lochs, boats, storms, chapels, all contribute. The usual melodramatic elements of simplicity and distress against blackmailing villains turning on the screws of rents and mortgages are present, but they are only a part and take on a new tone and colour from the terrain, and from the Irish brogue, characterizations and humour.

In *The Colleen Bawn* wild country is masterfully dramatized:

> DANNY: D'ye see yonder light upon Muckroos Head? It is in a cottage windy; that light goes in and out three times winkin' that way, as much as to say, 'Are ye comin'?' Then if the light in that room there (*points at house above*) answers by a wink, it manes No! but if it goes out entirely, his honour jumps from the parlour windy into the garden behind and we're off. Look! (*Light in cottage disappears*). That's one. (*Light appears*). Now again. (*Light disappears*). That's two. (*Light appears*). What did I tell you? (*Light disappears*). That's three; and here it comes again (*Light appears*). Wait now and ye'll see the answer (*Light disappears from window L*). That's my gentleman (*Music change*). You see he's goin'—good night, ma'am.   (I. i.)

Distance is packed on to the stage and emotions entwined with locality in mutual reinforcement. The action is as wild as its setting, dramatizing Danny's attempt at murder and subsequent misery, thinking wrongly that he has been successful; and we have a vivid study of a strong woman in Mrs Cregan, willing to sacrifice herself for her son. Passions run high, wild as their surroundings.

The Shaughraun has a less inward conflict and less intensity. Conn, 'the Shaughraun', is a kind of Tony Lumpkin, though his resource and trickery are more seriously engaged to save his master from the authorities. When two signal shots for a ship at sea cannot be given he appears above the rocks to draw the fire of the Constabulary, who in effect give the needed signal. Boucicault is more interested in his people than in the national cause, but horror is aroused against the informers, a grim retribution falling on one of them, who only escapes the enraged relatives of those he has had condemned by leaping to his death from a precipice.

Tom Taylor is typically Victorian in his high rating of the domestic emotions in contrast to personal ambition. In *Helping Hands* (1855) the blind and destitute violinist, hearing how his daughter has been wearing herself out to support him, allows the one remaining symbol of his past greatness, his treasured violin, to be sold; and in *The House or the Home* (1859) the politician hero has to learn not to let his ambition spoil his marriage. A similar conception is at the heart of the peculiarly powerful *Payable on Demand* (1859).

In Frankfort in the year 1792 the Jew Reuben and his Christian wife Lina save the Marquis de St Cast from the republican soldiers. Before escaping he leaves bills of exchange and assignats with Reuben, who gives him a receipt which St Cast puts in a portable desk. Hearing afterwards that St Cast has been killed, Lina insists on honesty, though Reuben is tempted. But they fail to trace St Cast's relatives. Lina dies, leaving Reuben with another Lina, his daughter. Twenty-two years later he is in London, having used the money to make himself a financier of power. He is devoted to his money:

> Gold, Lina—gold of all countries and coinages—doubloons—pillar dollars—spade guineas—louis d'or—Napoleons. The pretty goldfinches—they all fly London way, Lina. Dip thy hand in, child—isn't it pleasant? I love to feel their smooth hard glossy faces under my fingers [*plunges in his hand and lets a stream of coin flow through his fingers*]. (II. i.)

Now stocks are fluctuating violently, because of the war with Napoleon. Reuben—the specialized excitement is extraordinarily well conveyed—is playing with vast sums, and though he may at any time be ruined, enjoys his skill, his genius, firm as a ship's captain in storm; he is less miser than financier, and in his element when playing with hazards.

His daughter has brought a present for her French music-master fiancé; an old portable desk, which he discovers to be his father's. She tells Reuben, who recognizes his own receipt in the secret drawer. Shall he explain everything to his daughter and her fiancé? It comes at the very moment when the sum concerned makes the difference between triumph over his rivals on the market and ruin; he must have it for his last triumphant stroke; not merely money, but his inmost, artist's genius is involved. The dramatic pressure is strong. He addresses his wife's picture:

> I have found the orphan, and to keep my oath is ruin! Oh, what shall I do? You see me, you hear me, Lina! Look down and give me strength to conquer in this sore struggle! Lina, Lina—help me,

help me! [*He falls on his knees before the portrait, stretching out his arm towards it.*] Eh? Tell all to our child! I will, I will. She shall be to me what thou wouldst have been—my better angel!   (II.)

The truth is revealed; the young man is now rich, they poor, but he agrees to let Reuben have the money for his last stroke; and knowing through his personal agents of Napoleon's defeat, he wins.

So this hero too has to conquer his own ambition or genius for a less spectacular, more homely and domestic, end. Love is involved, since by revealing the truth Reuben resolves his former doubts as to whether his daughter is being wooed for her money. It is a relief to find a powerful drama on that great agent of European civilization, finance, without reliance on *Timon of Athens*. But whenever we find a man in loneliness brooding over his money, or remember Charles Reade's melodrama of Australian mining in *Gold* (1853), we can think of Timon, and the gold he digs from earth; for that is an important part of Timon's story.

W. S. Gilbert has satiric force. *Engaged* (1877) makes brilliant comedy from a supposedly doll-like girl who nevertheless has an eye to the main financial issue; *The Fortune Hunter* (1897) is a bitter attack on marriage for money; and *Brantingham Hall* (1888) contrasts the simple goodness and lack of money sense in an untutored girl, a convict's daughter, with the very different values of the all-but-ruined nobleman, father of her dead husband, whom she wants to help. Judicial horror has fierce impact in *The Hooligan* (prod. 1911), wherein a condemned man's agony reaches its climax when he falls dead, like Joanna Baillie's General Osterloo, at news of a reprieve.

Dan'l Druce, Blacksmith (1876) is a strongish play set in the seventeenth century during the civil war. The seduction of his wife has made Dan'l, once a man of great generosity, an embittered Timon, living alone by the sea and refusing to return to 'the hollow lying world' and its 'den of thieves' (I). He makes fishing-nets and is miserly over what he earns. Gold, recalling Timon's new-found gold, takes the place of the child he wanted: it is 'the best thing in the world', 'my beautiful golden bairn' (I). Now a gentleman and a sergeant, refugees from the Puritans, steal his gold and leave instead a child, before putting to sea. Seventeen years elapse. Under the Restoration Dan'l is back at his old trade, happy with his supposed daughter, for so he calls her, till he recognizes in a local baronet, Sir Jasper Combe, returned from abroad, the very man who stole his money. Complications follow; there is the possibility of Sir Jasper claiming the girl; old Dan'l resists, gaunt and terrible in his anger.

But it transpires that Sir John was his wife's seducer, and that Dan'l
and not Sir John is the father. Dan'l would be a fine part for a strong
actor; so would Taylor's Reuben; old men with daughters in the
time-honoured tradition. These two plays stand as solid achievements of popular Victorianism at its best.

III

Poetic dramas too showed a strong moral tone. Despite some rich
poetic colourings, the only really gripping scene in C. J. Wells's
Joseph and His Brethren (1823; revised 1876) is that of Joseph's
resistance to Potiphar's wife. The more usual interest is political,
the moral tone taking the form of liberalism against tyranny, after
the manner of Robert Southey's *Wat Tyler* (1794).

In Sheridan Knowles's *Virginius* (1820), the subject already
handled by Webster and Dennis is given a strong political fervour,
Virginius standing for Roman liberty against the tyrannical Appius.
Knowles is an accomplished dramatist, master of the intense situation and a stage verse well salted with colloquial accents and inter-
jections, which acts itself as we read:

> Friends ever are provisionally friends—
> Friends so far—Friends just to such a point,
> And then 'farewell'!—Friends with an understanding—
> As 'should the road be pretty safe'—'the sea
> Not over-rough', and so on—friends of *ifs*
> And *buts*—no friends! O could I find the man
> Would be a simple thorough-going friend!
>
> (III. i.)

Caius Gracchus (1823; early version 1815), in a similar vein, is more
subtle, recognizing inadequacies on the revolutionary side. *William
Tell* (1825) shows us heroic enlightenment resisting tyranny, and
Alfred the Great (1831) a just monarch whose 'throne' is his people's
'hearts' (II. ii). In dramatic verse, development of action, stage
power, firm characterization and enlightened outlook, Sheridan
Knowles is very able. What he lacks is ethical complexity and
atmospheric weight: valuations are obvious and the imagination
scarcely distended.

R. L. Sheil's best achievement is the conclusion to *Evadne or The
Statue* (1819), wherein the heroine invokes the moonlit chastity of
her marbled ancestors to subdue the bad intentions of a royal

seducer. Collaboration with John Banim produced another success in *Damon and Pythias* (1821), in which the readiness of one of its two heroes to die for the republican ideal and of both to sacrifice themselves for friendship is vividly portrayed. In Damon's ecstasy of relief on finding that he is in time to die instead of his friend we have a rare instance of goodness becoming passionately dramatic. The 'scaffold' is for one glorious moment Damon's 'throne' (v. i). His passion converts the cynical tyrant Dionysius: 'Almighty virtue, now do I own and worship thee!' (v. i).

Of a similar compact force and a kindred sense of nobility is Sir Thomas Noon Talfourd's *Ion* (1836). Ion, a youth of unblemished virtue, offers to obey an oracular message by braving and slaying the tyrant Adrastus whose crimes are causing a plague in Argos. From a moving dialogue wherein youth condemns and counsels age, a subtle relationship is established, leading at the moment of fearful action to the paralysing revelation that Adrastus is Ion's father. However, he falls by another hand. Ion is now acclaimed king, but since the oracle's command was that all Adrastus' line must fall, he dies for his people. The verse may be better as literature than for stage speaking but the human interest, especially during the dialogues between Ion and Adrastus, is intense. The atmosphere of ancient Greece is well realized and the depiction of youthful virtue convincing.

In *The Athenian Captive* (1838) a central emphasis falls on the friendship of the young Prince Hyllus of Corinth and an enslaved captive who has saved his life in the war, the Athenian Thoas. Urged by the much wronged Queen Ismene to kill the tyrannic King, Hyllus' father, Thoas refuses, but is eventually made to do so by a ruse. When unjustly accused of the crime, Hyllus is ready to die to save his friend. Thoas, now again commander of the Athenian army, refuses to accept his sacrifice and instead elects himself to die by Hyllus' hand. A Greek nobility breathes from it, as from its predecessor *Ion*.

In contrast *Glencoe or The Fate of the Macdonalds* (1840) takes us to the mist-wrapped Scottish mountains, ancestral voices prophesying doom and clouds forming into ghostly figures of people still living as a vague forecast of the massacre shortly to follow (II. i). Dark nature sets the stage for a drama involving the noble-hearted hero in the hideous recognition that his loved younger brother is guilty of treachery to his clan. Powerful emotions are woven into the grim story of betrayal and massacre. All three of Talfourd's dramas pivot on youth, ideal or desecrated, and all have central occasions where the hero is faced by the obligation to engage in a semi-judicial but hateful killing: Talfourd was by profession a judge.

Talfourd's liberal sympathies are evident and in the two parts of Sir Henry Taylor's *Philip van Artevelde* (1834), on the revolt of Ghent against the Lords of Flanders, the denunciation of tyranny attains great power. Philip is the ideal liberator saving the people from oppression; a keen historical realism combines with many fine human insights; and the verse has excellence.

A speech of Philip's is as impressive an example as we shall anywhere find of a long speech so technically modulated that its dramatic hold is never loosened. When, he says, 'liberty' and 'justice' ordered the 'commonweal', and government was in the hands of those holding 'supremacy of merit', revolution was a crime; but now political states have become 'a treason against Nature'. The speech rises with cumulative, not merely sequential, force:

> The hand of Power doth press the very life
> Of Innocency out! What then remains
> But in the cause of Nature to stand forth
> And turn this frame of things the right side up?
> For this the hour is come, the sword is drawn,
> And tell your masters vainly they resist.
> Nature, that slept beneath their poisonous drugs,
> Is up and stirring, and from north and south,
> From east and west, from England and from France,
> From Germany and Flanders and Navarre,
> Shall stand against them like a beast at bay.
> The blood that they have shed will hide no longer
> In the blood-sloken soil, but cries to heaven.
>
> (2; II. i; 1877 ed.)

This might well be our climax, yet it continues with a new and different power:

> Their cruelties and wrongs against the poor
> Shall quicken into swarms of venomous snakes
> And hiss through all the earth, till o'er the earth,
> That ceases then from hisses and from groans,
> Rises the song—How are the mighty fallen!
> And by the peasant's hand! Low lie the proud!
> And smitten with the weapons of the poor—
> The blacksmith's hammer and the woodman's axe:
> Their tale is told; and for that they were rich
> And robb'd the poor, and for that they were strong
> And scourg'd the weak, and for that they made laws
> Which turned the sweat of labour's brow to blood—
> For these their sins the nations cast them out,

> The dunghills are their death-beds, and the stench
> From their uncover'd carrion steaming wide
> Turns in the nostrils of enfranchised man
> To a sweet savour. These things come to pass
> From small beginnings, because God is just.
>
> (2; ɪɪ. i.)

The speech moves in waves, accumulating in Shakespearian manner, and ends softly. In his introduction the author notes: 'It was believed that entire success on the part of Ghent would bring on a general rising, almost throughout Christendom, of the Commonalty against the Feudal Lords and men of substance'. The historic action is contemporary with Wat Tyler's rebellion in England, but nineteenth-century implications are clearly present.

Westland Marston's poetic dramas present strong situations based on an advanced social thinking. *The Patrician's Daughter* (1842) is a drama of modern life, written, as the author tells us, 'when the fierce class animosities excited by the first Reform Bill had by no means subsided'. Mordaunt is a low-born but advancing politician who thinks that he has been scorned by the daughter of an earl and when later on he has been knighted and the marriage is desired, he repudiates the suggestion in public:

> My father was a man of toil;
> I mean real toil, such toil as makes the hand
> Uncouth to sight, coarse, hard to the touch;
> There are none here who would have clasped that hand
> Save at our borough contests, when all fingers
> Grew marvellously pliant.
>
> (ɪv. ii.)

He delights to speak out plainly 'here where your robes of blazoned memories thickly fold you in'. Repudiating personal vengeance, he claims to be acting on principle to show that when 'convention' dares to 'tread down man', then 'man shall arise in turn and tread it down' (ɪv. ii). Both sides are proud; Mordaunt is not sentimentalized, and he gets no satisfaction from his revenge. The balances are just.

In *Strathmore* (1849) the hero is by duty bound to condemn the father of his betrothed and a fierce conflict of loyalties is well and inwardly developed. *Anne Blake* (1852) satirizes the snobbery of the new rich and *The Favourite of Fortune* (1866) is a satire on money. Much is on period lines. However, at his best Marston has a fine sense of values and a keen dramatic instinct. He was performed by the best actors of his day.

IV

We have reviewed various attempts to interpenetrate society with virtue. In personal affairs, the domestic values all enjoying autonomy, morality may rule; in politics and in world affairs solutions are less simple. Revolutionary exemplars are not enough and liberalism is only a beginning. Can we align goodness with politics? Church with State? This problem was faced by our greater Victorian dramatists.

As the century develops we find ourselves forced to ask: Who and what is a tyrant? And what do we mean by freedom? As young men Coleridge and Southey had written their *Robespierre* (1794) with a protagonist blending revolutionary leadership and bloody tyranny; and Shelley's dramatic poem *Hellas* (1822) pronounces woe upon both tyrant and avenger, forecasting continual bloodshed and leaving the solution to metaphysics and symbolism. In Mary Russell Mitford's *Rienzi* (1824; prod. 1828) the liberator faces accusations of tyranny and an appalling choice: liberalism alone solves nothing. Her *Charles I* (1825) strikes fire from royalism:

> Tell him the crown
> On an usurper's brow will scorch and burn
> As though the diamonded and ermined round
> Were framed of glowing steel.
>
> (III. i.)

In *Otto of Wittelsbach* (c. 1826) blood-descent from 'the great founders' of 'thrones imperial' is given its poetry:

> From their ashes bursts
> The living fire, whose sacred halo plays
> Round each heroic son's anointed brow
> To latest time.
>
> (II. iii.)

These are as 'giants who walk the earth, rejoicing'. A liberalism which denies human greatness is as dangerous as tyranny. Meanwhile Byron had set a standard in precision and purpose. Such is the setting for the State dramas of the Victorian age.

Matthew Arnold will be our introductory choice. In his dramatic poem *Empedocles on Etna* (1852) the Greek philosopher plays a Promethean and Timon role among the mountains in a 'fierce man-hating mood' (I. i), ruminating on the persecution of 'greatness' because its very 'simplicity' rebukes 'this envious, miserable age'

(II). Beyond this life, our minds will no doubt persist, perhaps still earth-bound in desire and still failing to make contact with 'our only true deep-buried selves'. Intellectual warfare shuts us from 'warmth and light' (II); and craving those, Empedocles plunges into the volcano. Throughout the hero's meditations are dramatically countered, in the manner of so many earlier contrasts of protagonist and seraphic youth, by the harping and choric songs of the loved boy Callicles of girl-like attraction (I. i), who brings the light of various myths to bear on the protagonist's gloom.

Arnold faces state affairs in *Merope* (1858). The form is classic, with fine choruses; the tone and spirit of Greek drama were never better revivified; but the thought is modern.

Merope's husband King Cresphontes had been assassinated by Polyphontes, who has now for many years been established as a good ruler. He tells Merope that his bloody and unconstitutional act was forced because Cresphontes' liberal views were endangering the public good. Though a man of statecraft, he is at heart kindly. His defences to Merope recall Racine's Athalie and Claudius in *Hamlet*; all pose the same problem. Polyphontes is convinced that his action saved the realm.

In contrast, Merope pleads beautifully the wisdom of her husband's desire to unite conqueror and conquered 'into one puissant folk' as the only practical way to a 'safe supremacy' (290, 305). Polyphontes' thought is authoritarian, Merope's democratic. Polyphontes can be fearfully convincing:

> Dizzy the path and perilous the way
> Which in a deed like mine a just man treads,
> But it is sometimes trodden, oh! believe it.
> Yet how *canst* thou believe it? Therefore thou
> Hast all impunity . . .
>
> (368.)

In an elaborate movement the Chorus analyses the problem. The heart of man is obscure and motives are never single. Provided that it is really done for virtue's cause and the public good it is perhaps right that the best man should carve his way by force; even a long tradition may have to be overthrown; and yet who can ever claim with assurance to be the elect of God? Their conclusion is that Zeus condemns a self-asserting violence in the guise of 'Heaven's destined arm' (697).

Merope's son Aepytus, who, like Orestes in the Greek plays, has been living abroad, now arrives in secrecy, bent on revenge. But the steady reversal of the revenge motif by the Romantics has not been accomplished for nothing and within the Greek form the new spirit asserts itself in Merope's refusal:

> From the first-wrought vengeance is born
> A long succession of crimes.
> Fresh blood flows, calling for blood:
> Father, sons, grandsons, are all
> One death-dealing vengeful train.
>
> (1266.)

Merope has heard Polyphontes' defences; she has been moved by his kindness and consideration; she may even be near love for him. She tells Aepytus of his 'serious statecraft' and calm rule (1504–6). Her son, true to the old order, cannot understand her. Others support him. Do not justice and wisdom demand revenge? The pressure is strong.

Aepytus' identity is kept secret: it is reported that the prince has died; and in a scene of wonderful irony Polyphontes, whom we now know to be marked out for assassination, implores Merope to marry him and forget the past, since all possibility of revenge has now gone. Though she has been 'injur'd past forgiveness', cannot all personal feelings be put aside for 'the public weal'? The crimes of a ruler may sometimes leave him, as a man, 'guiltless' (1721–30). Merope cannot divulge her son's plot; she can only, in a speech of suppressed sympathy veiled as anger, urge Polyphontes to fly: 'Cut short thy triumph, seeming at its height' (1757). He thinks she must be mad.

The choric interludes have been steadily rising, reinforcing the dramatic power, and now as the climax approaches they reach a crescendo of triumph. Polyphontes' body is brought in. Merope meditates on the 'inscrutable' face still bearing its 'aspect of majestic care':

> What meantest thou, O Polyphontes, what
> Desired'st thou, what truly spurr'd thee on?
>
> (1994.)

Was it 'policy of state' or merely 'ambition'? She can neither triumph nor mourn over one who had in him both 'worth' and 'badness'. No man has a 'fix'd condition'; 'a two-fold colour reigns in all'. All she can do is to pray that her son may make the 'one colour' prevail (1996–2011).

Merope expresses the highest consciousness yet dramatized on all the old problems of revenge and statecraft. In Polyphontes we have not only a helpful commentary on Shakespeare's Claudius; all our dramatic tyrants, however grim, receive in this exquisitely handled figure some degree of justification. Until statesmanship becomes Christian, we cannot bring moral absolutes to the condemnation of those on whom the appalling responsibilities of government rest. Of this drama's capturing, for its new purpose, of the Aeschylean foreboding and irony; of its gathering power; of its deep recognition, which Dryden, but not Milton, missed, of the dynamic potentialities of classic form; of all these little need be said. Once the insights which they exist to reveal are recognized, the rest is self-evident.

Robert Browning too concentrated on statecraft. *Strafford* (1837) deals with the troubles arising between Charles I and Parliament. His loyal servant Strafford the weak King both uses and, for fear of Parliament, betrays, but Strafford's loyalty remains firm, even though he is forced to pretend responsibility for decisions not his own. Pym, who regards himself as providentially appointed to destroy Strafford, gets Parliament, when legal means fail, to pass a Bill of Attainder. Arbitrary action is used not by a tyrant but by the people's self-appointed leader. Evils that cannot be pinned down by law must be met by other means:

> RUDYARD: But this unexpected course—
>   This Bill . . .
> PYM: By this, we roll the clouds away
>   Of Precedent and Custom, and at once
>   Bid the great light which God has set in all,
>   The conscience of each bosom, shine upon
>   The guilt of Strafford . . .
>
>   (IV. ii.)

However illegal, it is 'England's manifested will' (IV. iii). Pym is in no stronger a position logically than Arnold's Polyphontes. The reluctant King finally signs the death-warrant. Pym sees himself as having sacrificed a once loved friend to his country's good: 'Have I done well? Speak England!' (v. ii). Strafford, hearing the sentence, foresees Charles's own execution:

> Oh, my fate is nothing—
> Nothing! But not that awful head . . . not that!
> Pym, save the King! Pym, save him! Stay—you shall . . .
> For you love England!
>
>   (v. ii.)

Both sides invoke England. We feel that not only Charles, who uses the term, but rather that all are 'in a net' (IV. iii). The issues at stake are beyond human adjustment.

King Victor and King Charles (1842) makes a fairly simple comparison of Victor's bad and tyrannic government and the more enlightened and democratic methods of his son Charles to whom in his difficulties he hands over sovereignty. Told by his father that he will now understand the reasons for the 'shifts', 'dissimulation' and 'wiliness' that rulers resort to, Victor answers boldly that with 'Truth helping' him he will go 'straight on' (*King Victor*; II). He succeeds, though the difficulties are baffling enough:

> Here, blindfold thro' the maze of things we walk
> By a slight thread of false, true, right and wrong;
> All else is rambling and presumption.
>   (*King Charles*; I.)

A neat text for a period of political change watching, like King Victor, 'the mad and democratic whirl' to which 'all Europe' is hastening (*King Charles;* I). Browning's dramatic thought is in advance of his dramatic projection. We know enough history to appreciate *Strafford*, but *The Return of the Druses* (1843) could scarcely grip an unprepared audience. To help the Druses rise against the oppressive Knights of Rhodes, their leader allows his followers to believe him an incarnation of their sect's semi-divine founder. The symbolism, which covers in general the art of all demogogues, is neat. The ethics are questionable, yet it is necessary:

> Ah, fool! Has Europe then so poorly tamed
> The Syrian blood from out thee? Thou, presume
> To walk in this foul earth by means not foul?
>   (IV.)

Some excitement springs from the congested action, and the poetry on occasion has fire.

Browning strove for clarification, and *Colombe's Birthday* (1844) is lucid enough. The heroine, Colombe, Duchess of Juliens and Cleves, is a wholly good, beneficent and beloved ruler. The softer virtues of good government are best 'embodied in a woman's form' (II), and though her title is justly disputed by Prince Berthold, we are assured that he cannot take her place in her subjects' hearts (III). Valence, representative of Cleves, loves Colombe, yet since such a marriage would reduce her status he denies himself for his townsmen's sake. However, though offered a marriage of expedience by Prince Berthold, Colombe is woman enough to take Valence and renounce her duchy. *Colombe's Birthday* has delicacy of feeling, strong situations and a neat construction.

Luria (1846) is again neatly done. The victorious Moorish general Luria, servant of Florence, hears that charges are already being made out against him in Florence as a precaution against his expected ambitions. When urged to respond with military force, he refuses and kills himself. Profound issues and divergent counsels are involved. Florence is to Luria 'mankind', his whole world (II). He is advised that the State cannot consider the individual, however noble; the State is itself the supreme Man (III). But again, he is told by another that the State's greatness was originally created by great individuals like himself. Such must come first, if human advance is to be safe-guarded: ''Tis man's cause'. All futurity is at stake:

> The chiefs to come, the Lurias yet unborn,
> That, greater than thyself, are reached o'er thee . . .
>   (IV.)

And yet for Luria, if beautiful Florence should be destroyed by him, what would be left? He decides to die. The rights of the great man are balanced against those of the many, the mediocre, the State: and there is no easy answer.

In *Strafford*; in Charles, son of Victor; in Colombe; in Luria; in all these we have types of greatness or virtue confronted by the complexities of State. Such subjects do not make easy drama, and we must not assess 'dramatic' merit without regard to the nature of the task in hand. When Browning attempts a personal and passionate action in *The Blot in the Scutcheon* (1843) he succeeds with ease. In reading our Victorians we might think back to the overweighted State dramas of Sir Fulke Greville and Sir William Alexander, and be thankful.

Our greater nineteenth-century dramas descend from the medieval conflict of Pope and Emperor. Catholicism had been a ghostly presence throughout Gothic drama, and sometimes, as in R. L. Sheil's sensational indictment of tortures under the Inquisition in *The Apostate* (1817), a macabre thrill. Now it becomes a closer, more realistic, concern. It still often arouses distrust. In Sir Henry Taylor's *Edwin the Fair* (1842) a likable English king is shown at grips with ecclesiastical power; and in his *St Clement's Eve* (1862) we meet a wise hermit and a saintly novice who pits her saintliness against a king's suffering like Shakespeare's Helena, in contrast with two peculiarly villainous 'Augustinian' monks. Westland Marston's *Marie de Méranie* (1856) dramatizes the clash of a French king and a strongly criticized Pope. These are natural period themes. The problems at issue sooner or later tend to involve Catholicism. W. E. Gladstone's first book was on the relationship of Church to State, and Cardinal Newman one of the century's symbolic figures.

The central conflict is dramatized in R. H. Horne's *Gregory VII* (1840). Gregory is of humble birth but ambitious. After having his predecessor Pope Alexander murdered he gains the Popedom and claims final authority for the Church:

> We live in a time
> When lion-mouthed war with brutalized force prevails,
> And monarchs bathe in most abhorrent glory:
> The which, not sanctioning—but from my soul
> Loathed as man's self-made pestilence—I denounce.
>
> (II. iv.)

It is now for mankind to choose between the Church's 'lofty ordinances' and 'sworded kings' (II. iv). His actions are considered, even defensible. Good men have hitherto relied entirely on their own implanted virtues, so leaving their 'tasks undone' and dying in martyrdom, whereas he, who knows mankind, will pursue a stronger course till kings become subservient to the 'high Pontiff' (IV. ii). He will match his enemies with their own weapons. He has a conscience set above worldly valuations, despises infernal 'terrors' when great desires are at stake, and repudiates the self-conflict of 'remorse' (IV. ii). Such is our 'great Artificer', building a throne for God and reducing 'militant kings' to servitude (IV. ii). His gospel sounds wonderful, but his supporters get frightened when they see him 'in actual work' (IV. ii). For he is quite ruthless: he becomes 'an iron bell tolling men's dooms' (V. i).

The Emperor, who has been forced in public to humble himself before the Pope, subsequently rises against him. Gregory answers the Emperor's charge that he maligns 'necessary and ennobling war' whilst himself using it by pointing to his record of artistic, intellectual and social achievement. War is engaged. Gregory confronts the Emperor, boldly charging him with having dared to advance 'with armed bands and homicide looks of war' and standards commemorating

> The glorious battles of immortal fools
> Who drove out mercy from the human heart,
> And with red Furies filled the steaming fields . . .
>
> (v. iii.)

The paradox of Gregory, though sharp, is no more baffling than that of any governmental bloodshed claiming Christian allegiance. When the lady Matilda, formerly Gregory's supporter, goes mad, the well-worn stage device is given a new relevance, since her confusion in thinking that Gregory is the Emperor disguised as his antagonist makes an all-too-neat correspondence to the equally mad confusions of Europe in Horne's day, or our own.

Gregory's end on the field of battle has magnificence. The Vatican's hopes, he says, will not fall with him, they have not failed:

> GREGORY [*faintly*]: Approach thou perfect hero, who hath ruled
> This day of swords! Approach me with thine ear—
> Stoop nearer—I wax faint.
> EMPEROR [*stooping to listen*]: What wouldst thou say?
> GREGORY [*raising himself*]: Kiss thou the dust from off thy master's feet!
>
> (v. iv.)

With that the fierce drama ends. The verse is perhaps too literary, nearer Talfourd's than Knowles's or Marston's, but the action, following the *Richard III* and *Macbeth* curves, is effective if at times straggling. The importance of its conception and general purpose can scarcely be exaggerated: it probes deep into the paradox of Christian Europe.

Horne's other dramas are less important. His *Laura Dibalzo or The Patriot Martyrs* (1880), on the ghastly tyranny of King Salomba of Naples, is dedicated to 'the illustrious memory of Washington and to the equally pure patriotic names of Kosciusko, Kossuth, Mazzini and Garibaldi'. It belongs among our dramas of liberation. Horne was unfortunate: Talfourd, Browning and Tennyson saw their work performed by leading actors, while *Gregory VII* remained unacted.

Within English history the grand conflict of Church and State was fought out in the life of the great archbishop portrayed in dramas by D. W. Jerrold and George Darley entitled *Thomas à Becket* (1829;1840), and in Tennyson's *Becket* (1879). Of the two first Darley's is the stronger. The emphasis falls on Becket as a psychological study rather than on any subtly developed conflict of State and Church, though this is remembered and well staged when king and archbishop meet with the two 'sacred wands' of Sceptre and Crozier opposed (IV. ii). The main opposition is personal. The King, who has a strong case against a dissolute and dangerous clergy, thinks that after he has appointed Becket to the archbishopric 'both Church and State are now beneath our rule' (II. v). But Becket is a man of easily inflated egotism who on advancement feels his soul swelling and brain swimming. He wonders, with reason, if a truly great man would so delight in self glory. He deeply wants to be great and meditates like Beddoes's Isbrand on the possibilities of man adding to himself a 'stature' beyond any previously known (II. iii). In this self-diagnosis his motivation is deliberately defined for us as a self-conscious desire to be a superman without being cut for such a role. And what follows bears it out. Comments on Becket's anger such as 'the wolf's dog-mad' (IV. ii) detract from his dramatic dignity. He gives himself away. 'Me!—Me!—most violently trampled down' (IV. ii). His face is said to look awful, like a felon's stuck on a gate; he is a man to 'spit venom' (V. iv). We do, certainly, hear of 'wrestling Titans' engaging in 'this fierce struggle between Church and State' (III. i), and Becket can speak finely for his office, refusing to make the mitre a mere appendage to the crown (III. vi), but we are mainly aware of the ugliness of his pride. The diagnosis is Marlovian. The dramatic construction is episodic and rambling, but there are strong scenes. Darley's best psychology and poetry are compacted in a single line spoken by Becket to the Bishop of Norwich: 'Touch not my hem with thy Iscariot kisses' (III. vi).

Lord Tennyson's *Becket* followed two other major studies dealing with England's history in relation to Rome. *Queen Mary* (1875) is weighted with theological controversy, to which the central human story of Mary's marriage to Philip of Spain is closely related. National resentments and fears are aroused alike by the Queen's repressive Catholicism and the dangers of Continental domination. Perhaps the most interesting figure is the Protestant Cranmer, the report of whose martyrdom is a model of reserved yet gripping dramatic narrative:

> PETERS: Then Cranmer lifted his left hand to heaven,
> And thrust his right into the bitter flame;
> And crying, in his deep voice, more than once,
> 'This hath offended—this unworthy hand!'
> So held it till it all was burn'd, before
> The flame had reach'd his body; I stood near—
> Mark'd him—he never utter'd moan of pain:
> He never stirr'd or writh'd, but, like a statue,
> Unmoving in the greatness of the flame,
> Gave up the ghost; and so past martyr-like—
> Martyr I may not call him—past—but whither?
> PAGET: To purgatory, man, to purgatory.
> PETERS: Nay, but, my Lord, he denied purgatory.
> PAGET: Why, then to heaven, and God ha' mercy on him.
> (IV. iii.)

Manipulation of action or dialogue is never unduly biased, though Protestant sympathies win. Both sides have been cruel and a specifically *sadistic* element is once admitted as part of man's 'fallen' psychology (III. iv). Mary sinks to her end, deserted by Philip and still concentrating on burnings and ever more burnings to salve her diseased conscience. From this 'world of fools' (IV. iii) what most vividly emerges is a pride beyond all theologies, in England, strong in the Catholic Lord Howard and even in Mary herself. Not till her death is the nightmare dispelled. Elizabeth speaks:

> I left her lying still and beautiful,
> More beautiful than in life. Why would you vex yourself,
> Poor sister? Sir, I swear I have no heart
> To be your queen. To reign is restless fence,
> Tierce, quart and trickery. Peace is with the dead.
>
> (v. v.)

As a whole *Queen Mary* remains necessarily heavy, though a masterly use of dialogue joins with keen insight into theological controversy and statesmanship to make this reading of a troubled reign a valuable dramatic commentary on England's relationship to Catholicism and the continent of Europe.

Tennyson is looking for origins, asking how Great Britain came to greatness. *Harold* (1877) searches back to the Norman Conquest. We have England's native stock in the manly and honest Harold and his Wessex warriors against William of Normandy, crafty, cruel, but a wise and able statesman and a man of genuine if superstitious religion. In a dream of 'the doom of England' Edward the Confessor, foreseeing the Norman Conquest, watches a tree shattered, soaked and baptized in blood, and remade to become ever taller and more expansive (III. i). The ethics of Providence are inscrutable, but its actions may at least be dramatized.

Harold is captured by William and next cunningly forced to ransom himself for his country's sake by swearing on the bones of certain Norman saints to support William's claims to the English throne. When he is absolved from his oath by the not quite legally consecrated (III. i) Archbishop of Canterbury, the opposition of a native English against a Continental Christianity makes a subtle Tennysonian point. Harold is ill at ease: told that 'naked truth' is not actable in 'a man of state' he rejects the thought that 'lying and ruling men' should be 'fatal twins' (III. i), but he is caught by circumstance and has internal wars on his hands. The kingdom is unsettled; indeed as a single kingdom it does not as yet properly exist. It has been William's deep aim to bring order from this chaos, to make Angle, Jute, Dane, Saxon, and Norman move to one 'music', so creating a nation greater than France (II. ii); and a ruthless statesman such as William may be better qualified for the task than a man of simple integrity like Harold. Harold breaks his oath, claiming that the old paganism with its Woden and 'warrior-gods' would be preferable to the thought of the holy Norman saints allying themselves with such a 'trickster' (III. ii) as William. Though he has the Pope and 'his master' (III. ii) Hildebrand, afterwards Gregory VII, against him, he answers the Norman emissary with scorn:

> Tell him the Saints are nobler than he dreams,
> Tell him that God is nobler than the Saints,
> And tell him we stand arm'd on Senlac Hill
> And bide the doom of God.
>
> (v. i.)

Before the battle, like Shakespeare's Richard III, he has sleep visions of the saints he has dishonoured, foretelling disaster; and though he remains brave, leaving to England his 'legacy of war against the Pope' (v. i), the doom is fixed. While through a dramatic conception of splendid quality the Latin chants from a chorus of English canons pit their ritual strength against the Norman saints and the Pope's anathema, Harold, the constitutionally elected of his people, pits native English bravery against a foreign invader; and loses. Over his body William honours the superlative courage of Harold and his men:

> Of one self-stock at first,
> Make them again one people—Norman, English;
> And English, Norman; we should have a hand
> To grasp the world with, and a foot to stamp it . . .
> Flat. Praise the Saints. It is over. No more blood!
> I am King of England so they thwart me not,
> And I will rule according to their laws.
>
> (v. ii.)

Harold had, it is true, sinned. For the rest, we watch English virility in union with an English Christianity being subdued by Continental powers for the furtherance of England's future greatness. No dramatist has a more acute insight than Tennyson into the enigmatic workings of the historical process.

As though winding into his problem's heart, Tennyson finally concentrates on the crucial story dramatized in *Becket* (comp. 1879; acted, 1893). From a massive deployment of historical, social, romantic and humorous material flames out the central opposition of Church and State. The range of characters from kings to beggars, both secular and ecclesiastic, old men and children, is wide. Scene after scene, starting with the brilliantly symbolical game of chess, has dramatic lift and tension, and a fierce interchange of speech with speech in a stage verse as professional as that of Knowles and showing a similar skill in colloquial trick and detail.[1] The sub-plot of King Henry's liaison with Rosamund is better integrated than in Darley's version, and the general tone more ennobled, contrasting with Darley as Shakespeare contrasts with Marlowe. The climax of Becket's martyrdom, in which Sir Henry Irving was acting a few hours before his death, ranks among the great moments in British drama.

Both sides have a hearing. The King claims to have cleansed a society rife with brutality and murder:

> I came, your King!
> Nor dwelt alone, like a soft lord of the East,
> In mine own hall, and sucking thro' fools' ears
> The flatteries of corruption—went abroad
> Thro' all my counties, spied my people's ways;
> Yea, heard the churl against the baron—yea,
> And did him justice; sat in mine own courts
> Judging my judges, that had found a King
> Who ranged confusions, made the twilight day,
> And struck a shape from out the vague, and law
> From madness. And the event—our fallows till'd,
> Much corn, repeopled towns, a realm again.
>
> (I. iii.)

Evil churchmen, sheltering under ecclesiastic law, have committed dastardly crimes. But he denies any desire for tyrannic rule; what he wanted—like Dante—was that Church and Crown should function as 'two sisters gliding in an equal dance' (I. iii). He has much reason in this. His main fault is his uncontrollable temper, and Becket's unswerving confidence continually rouses him to verbal fury:

> What did the traitor say?
> False to himself, but ten-fold false to me!
> The will of God—why, then, it is my will—
> Is he coming?
>
> (I. iii.)

---

[1] Tennyson's stage instincts are witnessed by his boyhood drama *The Devil and the Lady* (pub. 1930); and also by the dialect vigour of *The Promise of May* (1882), emphasized by Arnold Matthews (p. 306, note).

Even when he is with Rosamond, Becket is in his thoughts, giving him no rest. These idyllic scenes we need, if only for relief; their humanity, with love as 'king' (II. i), makes a needed contrast, on the humanistic side, to religion; and by a brilliant stroke, after Becket has saved Rosamund from Queen Eleanor and put her in a convent and the King hears of his action without knowing its reason, the accumulated force of Henry's unrestful erotic passions drives his fury, in a fine speech of towering, stuttering wrath, to the fatal 'Will no man free me from this pestilent priest?' (v. i). The dramatic integration is perfect.

Becket is an experienced statesman and soldier who on accepting the archbishopric recognizes a new allegiance: certain omens at his birth pointed to a sacred destiny (I. i). There is no simple egotism, as in Darley; what he asserts is not just himself but himself-as-arch-bishop, as when he charges Lord Leicester to obey 'not me but God in me' (I. iii). He is criticized, with justice, for uncompromising behaviour and John of Salisbury warns him against the possibility of impure motives (v. ii). He is nevertheless the carrier of a great mission. In Europe the Pope had been worsted by the 'fierce Emperor', Barbarossa (I. iii), and the English quarrel is part of a wider conflict. Becket deplores the weakness of Rome. Had he been Pope

> I would have done my most to keep Rome holy,
> I would have made Rome know she still is Rome . . .
>
> (II. ii.)

He is more than a typical ecclesiastic, since he has the qualities of both soldier and saint; he is a man of action dedicated to a purified Christianity. When he refuses to be content with the traditional rights of the Church, emphasizing that there must be a further advance, a further purification (II. ii), we recognize a forecast of Protestantism, the more so since Becket's is a very English Christianity, centred as much in 'the mother church of England, my Canterbury' (v. ii) as in Rome. He is conceived as a man before his time.

His martyrdom is superb:

> Ye think to scare me from my loyalty
> To God and to the Holy Father. No!
> Tho' all the swords in England flash'd above me
> Ready to fall at Henry's word or yours—
> Tho' all the loud-lung'd trumpets upon earth
> Blared from the heights of all the thrones of her kings,
> Blowing the world against me, I would stand
> Clothed with the full authority of Rome,

> Mail'd in the perfect panoply of faith,
> First of the foremost of their files, who die
> For God, to people Heaven in the great day
> When God makes up his jewels.
>
> (v. ii.)

Notice the lines' lift, the dramatic crests, ready for the actor. Again:

> Back, I say!
> Go on with the office. Shall not Heaven be served
> Tho' earth's last earthquake clash'd the minster-bells,
> And the great deeps were broken up again,
> And hiss'd against the sun?
>
> (v. iii.)

He is pressing towards not death but life:

JOHN OF SALISBURY: That way, or this! Save thyself either way.
BECKET: Oh no, not either way nor any way
                 Save by that way which leads thro' night to
                     light.
                 Not twenty steps, but one.
                 And fear not I should stumble in the darkness,
                 Not tho' it be their hour, the power of dark-
                     ness,
                 But my hour too, the power of light in dark-
                     ness!
                 I am not in the darkness but the light,
                 Seen by the Church in Heaven, the Church on
                     earth—
                 The power of life in death to make her free!
>
> (v. iii.)

And last, or all but last:

> I do commend my cause to God, the Virgin,
> St Denis of France and St Alphege of England,
> And all the tutelar Saints of Canterbury.
>
> (v. iii.)

We shall not be true to Tennyson unless we realize that Becket is pre-eminently an English archbishop dying for the Faith with the courage of Harold at Senlac.

All worldly ordinance is built on compromise. From the sadistic agonies of *Queen Mary* a voice cries bitterly for the casting out of all hierarchies, secular and sacred, and all differences in wealth, leaving to man only 'the one King, the Christ, and all things in common, as in the day of the first church, when Christ Jesus was King' (v. iv). That appearing to be impossible, a choice must be made: Tennyson's choice falls on Britain and her constitution and established religion as the solution to 'this long-tugged-at threadbare-worn quarrel of Crown and Church' (*Becket*, II. ii). In these three histories he disentangles the lines of her development. Earlier patriot dramas appear crude in comparison.

In A. C. Swinburne's *Atalanta in Calydon* (1865), Meleager, tormented by an abnormal, at once sacred and shameful, passion, is burned down by love for the angelic, monster-slaying, male-maiden (951–1030) Atalanta. The poetry is beautiful but prolix. *Erectheus* (1876), like *Atalanta* in classic form, is more compact. To save Athens from Eumolpos, son of Poseidon, god of the sea and earthquake, Chthonia, daughter of the Athenian king Erectheus, sacrifices her life. In the following battle the army of Eumolpos is felt within the surging Swinburnian poetry as a semi-supernatural, earthshaking, power:

> Earth groans from her great rent heart, and the hollows of rocks are afraid,
> And the mountains are moved, and the valleys as waves in a storm-wind swayed.
> From the roots of the hills to the plain's dim verge and the dark loud shore,
> Air shudders with shrill spears crossing, and hurtling of wheels that roar.
> As the grinding of teeth in the jaws of a lion that foam as they gnash
> Is the shriek of the axles that loosen, the shock of the poles that crash.
> The dense manes darken and glitter, the mouths of the mad steeds champ,
> Their heads flash blind through the battle, and death's foot rings in their tramp.

It is sea as well as an army, a 'manslaying flood', 'full of the terror and thunder of water'. Athens is victorious, and her futurity saved. She is to be the first to teach man freedom, having the sea henceforth as her friend. Her world mission as a source of human enlightenment is secure. The conception, which inevitably arouses thoughts of Britain's sea-story, is nobly handled; it is obviously better for reading than for the stage, though with its sustained pressure, its action's surge, crest and noble conclusion, it has a lyrical-dramatic quality all its own.

We cannot give such praise to the trilogy on Mary Queen of Scots: *Chastelard* (1865); *Bothwell* (1874); and *Mary Stuart* (1881). These certainly constitute an imposing attempt at State drama but though separate scenes grip they are lost within a prolixity of speechifying almost pathological. Long speeches, some of hundreds of lines, do not gather power through length; they either inform us of details beyond all necessity or repeat themselves. However, there is a strong study of Mary as a woman by turns passionate, unscrupulous, pathetic, endearing, criminal; one fiery-full of natural power and exulting at the thrill of intense living, at movement, action, risk, and danger. When she is with Bothwell she reminds us of Shakespeare's Cleopatra. Mary is opposed by John Knox as a reactionary, her Catholicism running counter to her people's beliefs, and after her removal to England the various interests of Elizabethan England, France, and Spain all cluster round her amazing personality. No one knows what to do with her indomitable yet disrupting presence. She is the centre of one adoration after another, and of plot after plot, and even the author's prolixity cannot altogether prevent this being an exciting treatment of an amazing woman. Even so, it fails: our interest is centred on Mary as a person, dwarfing the rest; and the attempt to see world affairs in pseudo-Shakespearian fashion almost wholly through a single person cannot now succeed. Shakespeare always established a symbolic relation with the community and in Byron and Tennyson the protagonist, however great, is part of a closely intertwisted fabric. With Swinburne we are only interested in the other people as they affect Mary. There is far too little play of his known political feeling; its absence might seem to his credit, but *Erectheus* shows what he could do when the spark was there. He is not deeply engaged in anything beyond Mary as a person: and one woman cannot make a trilogy.

Our State dramas spring from a soil of close contemporary concern. Changes were active at home and yet greater changes were turmoiling on the Continent. First Napoleon and then Bismarck reawakened the imperial dreams of Charlemagne and Barbarossa. This is the concern of Robert Buchanan's *The Drama of Kings* (1871), which simultaneously serves to sum up our recent sequence and by expanding the old theme of personal revenge to international proportions renders it newly relevant to the modern world.

The vast drama, which is to show two nations each crying 'liberty' (Prologue; 14–15) as they labour for each other's destruction, is conceived as a play arranged by Lucifer for God, with choruses of Spirits and others as commentators. It is a kind of sequel to Goethe's *Faust*, expanding Goethe's war prophecy from the vantage-point of a later experience. It is in three parts.

In Part 1, 'Buonaparte: or France against the Teuton', Buonaparte is shown during the year 1808 in the name of his new and enlightened empire defying the Pope and incurring the Church's curse (1; 95–6, 100). The Chorus is baffled; neither Empire nor Church are final; God is mysterious and works slowly, awaiting the 'one free voice' of 'Man' (1; 100–7). Buonaparte consults his Famulus, his daemon or guardian spirit, praying that his actions may replace princedoms by one mighty community of Man enjoying equality with one king and one priestless Temple, to 'spheric music' (1; 113–14). Man, he says, is but a 'foolish Titan', too easily dominated and always failing in self-assertion; and yet he recognizes that in comparison with this Titan he is himself nothing (1; 117–18, 122). Part 1 ends with an elaborate chorus hymning the vaguely apprehended Spirit—

> All have known her, and yet none possess her;
> None behold her, yet all things caress her—
>
> (1; 134.)

towards whom Man, the Titan, is moving.

Part 2, 'Napoleon Fallen', takes us to Napoleon III in the year 1870, after the surrender of Sedan. Napoleon is in distress. Has he been too weak? He recalls the great Buonaparte:

> He lash'd the world's Kings to his triumph-car
> And sat like marble while the fiery wheels
> Dript blood beneath him . . .
>
> (2; 249.)

Even so, says Napoleon, he fell, as do all, whether tyrants or martyrs, Brutus as well as Caesar; but martyrs fare the worse, dying with tortures like Christ. Meanwhile the Teuton replaces 'the blessed Nazarene' by 'that pallid apparition masculine', presumably the superman–conception, and expects the brainless Wilhelm and crafty Bismarck to work a triumph 'mightier than Christ's' (2; 252). The chorus deplores the decadence of England and to awake her strength sings of 'the perfect State', active in the arts of peace, commerce, social justice, and defence of the weak; enjoying a poetic and reverential wisdom unfettered by creeds; an 'Evangel State', God-guided and 'royal' (2; 263–76).

In Part 3, 'The Teuton against Paris', Bismarck in 1871 is claiming to be the implement of 'God's avenging furies' (3; 292) bent on humbling France. He sees himself as the 'hard surgeon' to a 'sick world' and supports himself by a considered anti-democratic philosopy of the various hierarchies descending from God, through Christ to Kings, the wise, and the good, and next the 'merely strong'; below whom are the base and the weak. Without respect to the higher we

have chaos; the democrat has his axe at the roots of the great Tree
(3; 300–5). The Chorus, here Sisters of the Red Cross, is not convinced:

> Because these things have been and are
>   And oft again may be,
> Doth this man swear by sun and star,
>   And oh, our God, by Thee,
> Framing, to cheat his own shrewd eyes,
>   His fair cosmogony of lies.
>
> (3; 317.)

It is a pity that Buchanan, who alone among the world's dramatists
seems to have realized exactly what kind of poetic simplicity is
needed for an audience to respond fully to a chorus, should have
expanded his drama to such forebidding proportions.

In Versailles the Kaiser celebrates his imperial triumph attended
by priests pronouncing the Benediction and organ music: Church
and State are, momentarily, one. The refrain is 'Hark to the song of
the sword'. A priest tells us that it is God's plan that the strong
should strike all that is 'shameful and weak' to ensure strength for
Man's futurity (3; 394, 397). Though temporarily disturbed by
voices of the dead which wail and plead their sufferings, the Kaiser
recovers and proceeds to a formal declaration of his pacific intentions:

> and the bright sword I hold
> May in the strong hands of my son become
> No firebrand but a symbol; not a thing
> Left like the steel of some old warrior
> To rust upon the wall, but ever bright
> And beauteous; not a firebrand, not a threat,
> But part of pomp and peaceful pageantry,
> Flashing with memorable light and fire . . .
>
> (3; 406.)

That may stand as a worthy expression of the state beyond war to
which we may suppose our race to be advancing.

The Epilogue in retrospect regards such as Buonaparte and
Bismarck as lesser evils than effete dynasties and a decaying Catho-
licism. Germany's new strength is honoured; the Kaiser's plea of
'Right Divine', though 'a living lie', 'temporarily' functions as a
'feeble good' because it is based on the 'conscience' and 'will' of an
awakened people. Kings have been used by God to arouse man's
'Titan soul', and now, being awake, that soul will outgrow them
(Epilogue; 427–8). A paean to the future hymns, as in Shelley's
Prometheus Unbound, a City of Heaven flowering from Earth with

as Monarch One called the 'heir of the Crucified', conceived as both the Soul of Man and as a Person: 'He cometh late, this greatest under God' (Epilude;[1] 437–47). Though both Prelude and Epilude are set in a conventional Heaven before God, the author apologizes for this orthodox framework, denying any firm personal faith and pointing to Goethe's *Faust* as an excuse (Appendix: 'On Mystic Realism'). The drama's real faith is in the mysterious 'her' sought by Man the Titan in the choric invocation already noticed (1; 128–36); and in the equally mysterious 'he', who corresponds to Tennyson's 'Christ that is to be' (*In Memoriam*, CVI), of the Epilude. Though too long for the stage in its present form this work comes under no such condemnation as Swinburne's. *The Drama of Kings* is throughout dramatically conceived and built.

V

Our recent discussions have made little contact with the supernatural: Victorian drama of quality has nothing to compare with the semi-Gothic and numinous effects of Emily Brontë's highly dramatic novel *Wuthering Heights* (1847). Verbal poetry has certainly been strong, and abundant, but magic casements have for the most part remained closed. And yet if magic is denied on one level, it will appear on another. Straight drama is only one element in the general output of opera, burlesque and musical fantasy that had been active from the Restoration onwards. The outstanding exponent of Victorian fantasy is J. R. Planché. [I shall give volume and page references to the 1879 Testimonial Edition of his extravaganzas.]

Planché deplored the limitations of the contemporary theatre; its frivolity he relates to 'the decadence of national grandeur and the general disorganization of society' (*The Prince of Happy Land or The Fawn in the Forest*, 1851; IV; preface, 172), while 'the immortal names of Shakespeare and of Byron' only survive with the aid of spectacle (*The Camp at the Olympic*, 1853; IV; 318). Accepting the conditions, Planché does his best with them. For some of his extravaganzas he relies on Greek myth but his best are drawn from the French fairy-tales of Madame D'Aulnoy and others. Though 'the Empire of the Fairies is no more' and 'the poetry of ancient times' is too often profaned by bad burlesques (*The King of the Peacocks*, 1848; III; 267–8), his own contact is re-established in terms of

[1] There is an Epilude as well as an Epilogue.

fantasy and humour, and the poetic tradition revivified by the cunning use of Shakespearian reminiscence and quotation, as when in *The White Cat* (1842) Prince Paragon cries: 'She speaks, she speaks! White Pussy, speak again!' (II; 158). Or this from *The Island of Jewels* (1849).

BELLOTTA: Gracious, papa! don't stand here, if you please.
QUEEN: 'Things that love night love not such nights as these'.
          Persuade him to move on, Prince Prettiphello.
PRINCE: Are you aware, sir, you have no umbrella? [*Rain*]
KING: A thought has struck me, rather entertaining,
          I am a king more rained upon than reigning.

(IV; 41.)

The living impact of Shakespeare is used to focus the Victorian mind to myth and fairy-lore, the humour both measuring a disparity and making a contact. The appeal is of the same kind as that of Aristophanes' *The Birds*, of which Planché did a version (1846).

Nature, ranging from pastoral charm to thunder and lightning and with a goodly deployment of lakes, islands, caverns, deserts and mountains, is elaborately depicted; it shifts and changes and has queer properties, a kaleidoscope of visual poetry. Animals are everywhere: dragons, lions, bees, and pre-eminently cats and birds. In titles alone we have a White Cat, a Blue Bird, Peacocks, a Fawn, Frogs. Animals are prime agents, actors and talkers, and demand respect. In *The Queen of the Frogs* (1851) those who ill-treat animals are incarcerated in a subterranean cavern; the hero of *The Invisible Prince or The Island of Tranquil Delights* (1846) is kind to an adder which turns out to be a fairy with great powers; the king of *King Charming or The Blue Bird of Paradise* (1850), after having been changed for a while into a bird, insists that there shall henceforth be no traps nor cages in his realm; and Felix in *The Prince of Happy Land* finds that the fawn he has shot is his loved Desiderata. All such stories, from the Greeks down, shadow truths concerning the spirit powers existent throughout nature, high or low. An acorn in *The White Cat* contains a tiny dog; in *The Bee and the Orange Tree* (1845) Prince Amiable is turned into an orange-tree which groans and sings.

Inward worth may exist behind apparent ugliness. The kind Beast in *Beauty and the Beast* (1841) is transformed by love into a prince, and because she chooses to make a snake happy rather than win beauty for herself the ugly heroine of *The Island of Jewels* becomes in effect beautiful, since 'such actions beautiful' can transform her (IV; 45). Ugliness changing to beauty is a recurring theme and the subject of amazing transformation scenes, as when in *The Good Woman in The Wood* (1852) a cottage in obedience to a wish changes to 'a pavilion formed entirely of roses' and a potato patch to magnified grounds (IV; 223). When a usurping king enters, the roses turn to nettles, a starling laughs, he shoots, everything tumbles down and the king finds himself in a cage. Planché develops the moral pointings of his sources with full purpose, attacking those who use such stories without preserving the meanings (Preface to *The Prince of Happy Land*; IV; 172). Even more important is the metaphysical truth shadowed by the transformation scenes opening as though to disclose before Victorian London some splendid hinterland to human misery. The world of Shakespearian imagery, or of Coleridge's *Zapolya*, is revived in kings and queens and princes; in the recurring use of gold, as in *The Fair One with the Golden Locks* (1843), *The Golden Branch* (1847), *The Yellow Dwarf and the King of the Gold Mines* (1854), the 'Golden Pinery' (IV; 209) of *The Prince of Happy Land*; and in jewels, as in *The Island of Jewels* with its palace of rich metals, home of King Emerald. But comedy is preserved and the splendour and magic countered by references to contemporary affairs or facts, such as hansom cabs and trains, as in 'the Fairy Atmospheric Down Train' in *The Bee and the Orange Tree* (III; 75). The humour is the condition for tuning in to this world of miraculous nature, wondrous palaces, and beautiful princes; for the human stress falls on the princes, with such names as Prince Perfect, Prince Paragon, Prince Sylvan, Prince Prettiphello. In *The Prince of Happy Land* the heart-conquering Prince Felix is a 'sweet youth' (IV; 179) first seen and loved by the heroine in a dream-vision. Furibond in *The Invisible Prince* is ironically called 'a prince whose beauty takes all hearts by storm' and the hero Prince Leander, disguised as an Amazon, is a 'lover true' who claims with a pun to be both Hero and Leander (III; 117, 141). The old bisexual fascination is strong when a girl in boy's dress offers herself for military service in *Fortunio and his Seven Gifted Servants* (1843):

KING [*aside*]:   No age could ever boast a youth so pretty.
                          That he is not a girl 'tis quite a pity . . .
PRINCESS: Brother, I'm sure you couldn't have the heart
                          To see this stripling to the wars depart.
                          He's much too young and handsome. [*To Fortunio*]
                             You shall be
                          Groom of the bed-chamber, Sir Knight, to me.
KING: Nay, he shall office in *my* household take . . .

                                                                              (II; 201.)

Here our beautiful young man is really a girl, but so in a sense were the others, since the parts were normally played by actresses. We are close to the old drama; the attraction of 'breeches parts' for women was traditional, and we still have our 'principal boys' in pantomime.

Planché also points onwards. In his magical nature, forming and dissolving according to spiritual necessities, we have a world closely resembling that described today by spirit personalities purporting to speak from higher dimensions. When in *Beauty and the Beast* (1841) a lost man prays to his 'protecting genius', the prayer is heard by a 'kind spirit', snow melts from the trees and the forest opens to disclose a banquet; and here the heroine with the help of a ring travels on the wings of thought from fairyland to Brixton (II; 118–19; 133–4). In *The Invisible Prince or The Island of Tranquil Delights* (1846) invisibility is no argument for unreality. All our wondrous journeys and invisibilities and transformations are part of the same spiritualized fabric. When Mordicanta in *Young and Handsome* (1856) complains that the relegation of witches and fairies to fiction by an age of scientific advance will impoverish the human imagination, and her familiar, a cat, observes that men now only worship love and money (V; 153–4), Planché's awareness of the deficiency is evident. He is also aware of Spiritualism. Clairvoyance, trance, and second sight were mentioned in *The Golden Branch* (1847; III; 199) and *The Queen of the Frogs* (1851; IV; 158). There is a wizard's 'séance' in *The Seven Champions of Christendom* (1849; III; 354). As in certain materialization-séances, 'hands, without bodies', moving chairs and vanishing, appear as early as *The White Cat* (1842; II; 145, 157, 159). It is not surprising to find the five volumes of the extravaganzas concluding with the definitely spiritualistic *King Christmas*, called 'a Fanciful Morality' (1871), in a modern setting. 'Fancy' acts as a 'medium' for spirit communication, says that she can materialize a 'hand or foot' and succeeds in raising a spirit (V; 294–6). Though its tone is light and ironic, this concluding fantasy serves to underline the pivotal nature of Planché's work.

PART 4

CHAPTER XII

Nordic

I will fashion a ladder for One whom you know not of.
Henrik Ibsen; *The Emperor Julian*, IV. ii.

I

THE centre of dramatic gravity changes. Italy, England, Spain, France, had been successively its home. At the romantic period Germany had been an influence, and now the power re-arises in Scandinavia and Germany. Having regard to the Scandinavian element in Wagner,[1] we may call the movement 'Nordic'. Its great ancestors are Swedenborg and Goethe.

Emanuel Swedenborg (1688–1772) was an expert mineralogist as well as a religious philosopher. He had personal experience of other planes and of spirit-converse, and has been called the father of modern spiritualism. He influenced the poet-mystic William Blake, and during the nineteenth century mediumistic spiritualism expanded rapidly in America and Europe. The dramatists Henrik Ibsen in Norway, August Strindberg in Sweden and Maurice Maeterlinck in Belgium have affinities with it. With these we may group the rather different challenge of the Danish theologian Sören Kierkegaard and the music of the Finnish composer Sibelius.

Goethe (1749–1832) as poet, dramatist and philosopher was a man of comprehensive wisdom made of a spiritualized paganism and a science in contact with esoteric tradition. Eros was his deity and at the conclusion to *Faust* romantic and Christian symbols blend. His great descendants are: in drama Richard Wagner, and in teaching Rudolf Steiner.

While dogmatic religion was shaken by science, by spiritualism and by other esoteric studies, royal and aristocratic acceptances were being replaced variously by socialism and the demand for great

[1] Edouard Schuré regards Wagner's genius as 'of the Scandinavian type' in view of its 'fierce energy and indomitable self-will' (*The Genesis of Tragedy*, 1936; 85).

leaders and even supermen.[1] 'Supermen' we have already met in the
drama of the Greeks and of Shakespeare, Chapman, Goethe, Byron,
Beddoes, and Browning. An obvious greatness was in Napoleon and
his successor in Germany, Bismarck; but the main drive was for a
more subtle greatness, in descent from past heroism yet with affinities
to art. What was wanted was a fusion of heroism and art to make a
finer social order and a new humanity; a fusion of sexual impulse and
Christianity to make a new religion; and a recognition of occult or
spirit powers. Of all this the most complete exemplar and prototype
was Byron, whose works, name, and legend had reverberated across
Europe.

II

Richard Wagner aimed to re-create western drama in a manner
worthy of its Greek ancestry. Thought and language had become
severed from emotion; traditional opera and oratorio he regarded as
exercises primarily in music; but a new totality was conceived whereby man might regain contact with his deepest personal and communal
selfhood.

Elemental power drives through the ghostly ship legend of *The
Flying Dutchman* (1841); *Tannhäuser* (1844) dramatizes a conflict of
sexual and sacred loves; *Lohengrin* (1848) is made from a Flemish
legend on divine initiation in the ages of chivalry. To Wagner
woman's love is a redeeming force, and in *Tristan and Isolde* (1859)
the twin mysteries of death and love converge.

In the four-part cycle *The Ring of the Nibelungs* (1854, 1856, 1869,
1874; but the whole libretto completed earlier, 1853), Wagner fuses
Norse mythology with Germanic legend for a more general purpose.
The river gold, guarded first by the Rhine maidens and afterwards by
a dragon, perhaps corresponding, like Samson's hair, to some secret
semi-sexual potency, is stolen from the Rhine by the dwarf Alberich
and welded into a ring which offers its owner world domination
provided that he renounces love. For this ring the king-god Wotan,
Alberich and the Giants, typifying respectively authority, avarice and
labour, are henceforth in rivalry. As in *Timon of Athens* the gold is
ambivalently both a high power and a curse. Wotan, trammelled by

---

[1] Eric Bentley's *The Cult of the Superman* (1947) is a valuable study concentrating on Thomas Carlyle and Nietzsche. Carlyle is another, if not exactly
'Nordic', at least northern candidate.

legality and unwilling to renounce love, plans the making of a hero to succeed where he cannot, his divinity being as provisional as that of Zeus in Aristophanes' *The Birds*. Siegfried's birth from an incestuous union of twins suits his function as a new Hercules existing beyond law and expected to release creation from bondage. He is presented as a wonder-youth akin to the royal boys in *Cymbeline*, Home's heroes and Coleridge's Andreas, being like them raised in association with nature and receiving spirit counsel from bird-song. He slays the dragon-giant Fafnir, gains the Ring, vanquishes the old order in Wotan and pierces a circle of fire to win Brynhild, Wotan's armed Valkyrie warrior-daughter, whose dramatic bisexuality personifies a perfect love. This love Siegfried's impetuous desires are in danger of desecrating and before union is achieved he is by villains tripped, like Samson, into sexual laxity; is guilty of refusing to restore the Ring to its home; and dies by treachery. The superman so perfect in other ways fails in the higher reaches of love. Brynhild immolates herself on his pyre and restores the Ring to the Rhine, whose waters inundate the flames.

Water and fire, nature and mind, dominate. We watch first Siegfried and then Brynhild aspire daringly through flames, but their union in earthly terms is withheld, and meanwhile the secret virtue is once again inviolate. Psychologically we can say that man must learn in full consciousness to enjoy and use the beauty of the gold *as it exists within the waters* (see pp. 294–5 below).

Parsifal (1882), with its hero of youthful purity and supporting cluster, recalling the conclusion to *Faust*, of youths and boys as servitors and songsters of the Grail, all opposed to heterosexual seduction and black magic, may be defined as a grand expansion of the 'seraphic'. Therein is its whole purpose and meaning.

Sexual passion, the superman, power, will, and necessity, sacrificial love and a seraphic Christianity: these Wagner arranges and re-arranges to plan. He labours towards the integration of sexual instinct, power, and sacrifice. Love and death draw close. His drama is inflated and stabilized by mystic intimations and a chivalric colouring.

Wagner's loose and vastly conceived deployments come nearer than those of any other artist to a true collaboration and interfusion of sound, scenic-display, myth and thought in direct relation to action and the roots and flowerings of human destiny. Separate sense inlets become a single comprehensive perception. Wagner's theatre holds vast nature, its forests and rocky heights, its seas and storms, its mysterious mines, and cloudy Valhallas. The music realizes, inflates, gives breath-of-life to, what is indeed the truth, as we experience the interpenetration of earthly life by powers not normally apprehended. Wagner's drama is massive, but the ethereal is co-present within its mass. More, the distinction is melted down: colour and music, mass and ethereality, are one.

III

On 21 March 1872 Henrik Ibsen [1] wrote from Dresden to Fredrik Gjertsen:

> It is acknowledged here that German literature required Byron's assistance to enable it to reach its present standpoint; and I maintain' that *we* need him to free us from ours.

Twenty-two years earlier his first play, *Catiline* (1849), had as its hero a man of sexual guilt who was yet ambitious to 'blaze in splendour like a shooting star' (II). Correspondences to Byron, whose legend had fired revolutionary forces throughout Europe, are close. Two women influence Catiline. One is Furia, a ghostly and ominous woman, driving him to dangerous deeds; the other, his wife Aurelia, loving and sweet. Such types recur in subsequent dramas, corresponding respectively to the power quest and Christianity.

Catiline stands alone. After it Ibsen, like Wagner and Yeats, plants his work in native soil. *The Warrior's Barrow* (1850) and *The Vikings at Helgeland* (1858) dramatize conflicts of paganism and Christianity. Hiordis in *The Vikings* is a woman like Furia of violence and unrest, urging Sigurd to heroic deeds. Medea-like she practises witchcraft and dreams of waking storms to lure mariners to death (II). She dresses like a warrior and radiates uncanny powers, hearing the dead on their ride to Valhalla, but fearing the encroaches of the White God, Christ. Only beyond death can her insatiable ambition for Sigurd and herself be fulfilled, and so she slays him, meaning to follow. Dying, he tells her that he has become a Christian; they will be for ever parted. Hiordis kills herself, and as the dead warriors thunder through the sky her son cries: 'Mother is with them' (IV). She is Clytemnestra, Medea, and Lady Macbeth; she will become Hedda Gabler.

---

[1] Quotations and references are given from *The Correspondence of Henrik Ibsen*, ed. Mary Morison, 1905; and, except for *Catiline* (where I quote from Ibsen's 1875 revision), from William Archer's edition of the plays, 1906–9.

The Pretenders (1863) is medieval. Skulë and Haakon are rivals for the throne, the one uncertain and tragically shadowed, the other, like Shakespeare's Caesar as against Antony, predestined for success. Until the assertion of Sigrid at the close there are no strong women to impel the action, but we have instead the half-male strife-stirrer Bishop Nicholas. He is sexually impotent and in compensation enjoys his own disruptive powers, like Virgil's Allecto. He has the negative aspect of bisexuality and genius; in him sexuality is absent and Church and State fused to the ill of both. In its historic conception, especially in the 'great king's thought' of imperial brotherhood (III; IV; V) beating through it, *The Pretenders* forecasts *Emperor and Galilean*. Bishop Nicholas's return as a ghost with his amusing accounts of Hell serves as a link between Byron's repudiation of Hell and the more humorous approaches of Bernard Shaw.

Ibsen's treatment of sex is strongly unorthodox. *Love's Comedy* (1862) moves from satire on marriage to the decision of the well-named Falk and Swanhild to refuse to desecrate their love by a conventional union. Swanhild, successor to Hiordis, urges Falk, as poet, to live his poetry: to 'be', not merely to write (I). Falk, following now the Socratic archetype, starts off with a company of students; and, to clustering associations of art, song and music, they leave for the mountains. In this early drama Ibsen's furthest aim is adumbrated.

That aim now splits into two companion pieces of cosmic drama: *Brand* (1866) and *Peer Gynt* (1867). In the first we meet a fantastical and heroic pastor all dedicated to his vocation. Brand's God combines the beauty of a young Hercules with the awful powers of Jehovah, and his human gospel is a teaching of wholeness or integration, complete being, the necessity 'to be' (I). Following his slogan 'All or nothing' (II; III) he refuses the last offices to his dying mother, who withholds money which his religion demands that she should renounce; his dying child's health he sacrifices to his duties as a priest; his loving wife Agnes tries to maintain the pace, but dies. Still refusing compromise, Brand breaks with all the hypocritical orthodoxies of his community. Climbing the mountains, he sees the spirit of Agnes who tells him, in the manner of spirit messages, that his child is well; and that his 'all or nothing' has been a fault (V); but he remains firm. When, as he nears the mysterious 'ice-church' (I; V), Gerd, the wild mountain girl who has acted as companion and prompter of his spiritual quest, honours him as a man-god, he breaks down and weeps, in contrition; and now at last Gerd kills the

falcon which she has for long been trying to kill and which is found
in death to be white, like a dove. The falcon symbolizes that within
Brand's quest which was in practice cruel, though its essence was
pure.[1] An avalanche crashes down. A voice speaks the words 'God
is Love'. Pagan and religious values jostle, fling apart and join in
this enigmatic but inclusive drama, by turns Hebraic, Nietzschean,
and Christian.

From the cold ice peaks and unhealthy deep-set valleys of *Brand*
we move to the expansive and horizontal world of *Peer Gynt*; it is a
move from religion to humanism. Peer is a care-free romantic, full of
poetic fantasies; he is sexually irresponsible, constituting Ibsen's sole
adventure in the tradition of comoedic sexuality, and nearly sells his
soul to the Trolls, or nature deities. But his warm love for his mother
at whose death he is present, playing a child's game with her whilst
imaginatively willing his love to force the appropriate authorities to
receive her in Heaven, establishes a firm contrast with Brand.
Visiting America he engages in dubious big-business and becomes
rich; back in Europe he reverses the Byronic idealism by planning to
lend money to the oppressors of Greece. He has schemes of irrigating
the Sahara. After becoming a prophet, he qualifies as king in a mad-
house. Returning to Norway he shows himself a coward during a
sea storm, and is eventually told by the symbolic Button Moulder
that, having never properly realized himself, not even in evil, his soul
is likely to be melted down, like useless buttons, his personal integrity
lost. Nevertheless Solveig, who loves him, has been waiting: and her
love, which is simultaneously a mother's love (v. x), may save him.

Peer Gynt, like Goethe's similarly straggling *Faust*, must be read
as a reflection of European humanism; from romanticism, pagan
fantasies and indulgences to an unprincipled capitalism, the nineteenth-century prophets raising their voices and madness not far off.
Meanwhile all soul value appears to have been lost. Peer has followed
the Troll's counsel: 'To thyself be enough' (II. vi); instead of attaining true being, which demands effort, he has remained content. He
has gone 'round about' (II. vii), not direct; he is a thing of unco-
ordinated desires and fantasies; but even so there may be a delayed
arrival. True being is here possessed by two symbolic creatures who
can claim to be '*themselves*'; the indefinable fog-like Boyg (II. vii),
symbolizing amorphous, undifferentiated nature; and the Sphinx
(IV. xii) which holds the answer to life's enigma in that it symbolizes
the higher integration. This symbol is used again in Shaw's *Caesar*

[1] The meaning of this symbolism I have discussed more fully in *Ibsen*, 1962.

and Cleopatra (p. 346 below). Between these man's drama is played out.

Paganism, Christianity, Renaissance—all are active in European man. Meanwhile Bismarck was forging for good or ill a great empire. With one eye on contemporary Europe and another on the womb of Western culture Ibsen composed what he always regarded as his greatest work, *Emperor and Galilean*, in two parts: *Caesar's Apostasy* and *The Emperor Julian* (1873). It aims at the harmonization of Christianity and paganism, of *Brand* and *Peer Gynt*. It has analogies to Buchanan's *Drama of Kings* (pp. 272–3).

Julian, a young prince of the recently converted royal house, is in intellectual ferment. He is attracted by Greek paganism, by its bacchanals and myths, and by the Socratic way of life, now deadly sin. Must truth oppose beauty? (*C.A.*; II). Yet in neither paganism nor Christianity can he find content, books are not enough and there must be some new revelation: 'The time is ripe', for 'the old beauty is no longer beautiful and the new truth is no longer true' (*C.A.*; II). He hears of a certain Maximus at Ephesus who communes with the dead; of the wonders that happen at his séances; this surely, 'communion between spirit and spirit', is 'the end of all wisdom'; he must visit Maximus (*C.A.*; II). Ibsen is writing as a modern, with modern spiritualism in mind.

Julian is at Ephesus, in oriental dress. In Maximus he recognizes the medium for 'the new revelation' and has himself had a mystic experience of the etheric dimension, a placid sea changing to an abyss, and next:

> But above, in the boundless dome, which before had seemed to me empty—there was life; there invisibility clothed itself in form, and silence became sound. (*C.A.*; III.)

He envisages a new state, winning back 'our lost likeness to the god-head' and corresponding to the body-soul harmony of a statued Apollo. He looks for 'a new race, perfect in beauty and in balance' (*C.A.*; III).

This Greek vision is in effect aligned with spiritualism, for we pass next to Maximus' séance (III). He is our new inspirer, succeeding Hiordis, Gerd and Bishop Nicholas. There is a Dionysian hymn, celebrating a 'marriage with the soul of nature'; and a 'countenance' materializes telling Julian that he is to establish an empire by 'the way of freedom' which is yet 'the way of necessity'; and that this is to come through the power of 'willing', not willing anything from choice, but rather a willing of what he 'must'. The empire can only be founded *by one in whom the oppositions of fate and freedom, instinct and ethics, are transcended*. Put otherwise, no instincts are to be rejected but all are to be transfigured. Maximus explains: the Tree of Knowledge and the Tree of the Cross have had their empires; and the new 'third empire' will cover both. We next hear the voices of Cain and Judas, as 'corner-stones under the wrath of necessity', 'great helpers in denial', who may be called archetypes of *all our satanic dramatic themes and persons*. They did what they 'must' and their fruits have been a glorious 'life' founded on 'death'. There is to be a third of these: Julian himself. Ibsen's respect to Cain follows Byron's and forecasts Shaw's in *Back to Methuselah*. Unlike earlier leaders, Christ or Alexander, Julian has been promised a 'pure' woman as wife. His leadership is to be one with this sexual-spiritual partnership.

Julian is made 'Caesar', or prince-elect under the Emperor. From now on his story is simple. For a while, as a general in Gaul, he blends courage with mercy, striking the required balance. But the perfect wife he expected falsifies his expectance; he has no woman to inspire him. After becoming emperor, he aims to be both emperor and high priest in one, and despite liberal intentions is soon an oppressor of Christianity. When he tries to re-engage in pagan rituals in devotion to such deities as Dionysus, Apollo, Helios or Cybele, he only makes himself ridiculous. When he turns pagan philosopher, his academic pamphlets are answered by Christian martyrdoms and miracles. Christianity enjoys the backing of destiny. Julian's failure is diagnosed by Maximus: he has merely tried to reduce the race to its pagan childhood; what was wanted was an advance beyond both 'flesh' and 'spirit' to a third and inclusive empire denying neither and realizing the purposes of both; and this will not happen till 'the right man', the 'twin-natured', comes (*E.J.*; III. iv), one like the Jews' Messiah, an 'Emperor-God' covering what a later age calls State and Church; 'Logos in Pan' and 'Pan in Logos'; one 'who wills himself'; one who, as Nietzsche also counsels (pp. 294–5), dares to *be* (*E.J.*; III. iv). Julian ends like Macbeth, fighting. The spirit of Constantine visits him by night; phantoms are enigmatic and auguries silent. His guiding powers have betrayed him, and there is 'no longer any bridge' between him and 'the spirits':

> Where are you now, oh white-sailed fleet, that sped to and fro in the sunlight and carried tidings between earth and heaven?

> > > (*E.J.*; v. i.)

Once more he glimpses 'a shining ship between heaven and earth' (*E.J.*; v. ii), but there are nightmares too. At his death Maximus admits that he was wrong; Julian was not the man; even so 'The third empire shall come!' (*E.J.*; v. iv).

Throughout we must be prepared to see a nineteenth-century relevance; and when Julian claims that, though himself a rejected 'Dionysus' (*E.J.*; iv. i), he will nevertheless 'fashion a ladder for One whom you know not of' (*E.J.*; iv. ii), he speaks directly for Ibsen himself. Ibsen's subsequent plays are rungs of that ladder, in terms of his own century. Their heroes will be inspired by a succession of powerful women corresponding to the 'pure woman' whom Julian lacked.

Ibsen's political thought outpaced contemporary politics. With liberalism he was soon dissatisfied. What he wanted was 'freedom from the political liberty-tyranny' of his day; freedom, that is, from politics. 'Special' reforms are useless (Letters to Georg Brandes; 20 December 1870; 24 September 1871). In *Rosmersholm* (1886) we hear that the 'true task' of democracy is to make a nation of noblemen (I) and in *An Enemy of the People* (1882) that 'the strongest man in the world is he who stands most alone' (v).

So he concentrates on individuals. *Pillars of Society* (1877) reveals a criminal lie beneath the respectability of a public figure, Consul Bernick; and *A Doll's House* (1879) shows a woman in rebellion against a false marriage, Nora's dancing of the Tarantella serving to equate her, as woman, with the Dionysian energies. The sun, as Helios, was Julian's favourite god, and in *Ghosts* (1881), after conventional valuations have constricted all natural joys, their stifling presence is relieved when dawn replaces cloud and the boy Oswald asks for death: 'Mother, give me the sun' (III). In *An Enemy of the People* Ibsen dramatizes himself as Dr Stockmann, arousing animosity through his insistence on unpalatable facts. And yet in *The Wild Duck* (1884) he deliberately shows an idealist, Gregers, spreading misery while forcing people to face the truth. Why does he do this? The answer lies in his symbolism. Ibsen's modern settings often suggest the claustrophobic as interiors without natural contacts, typifying contemporary civilization; and there is always some symbolism too suggesting the greater, exotic, Dionysian powers: the sea and ships, the 'Indian Girl' and the 'Palm Tree', in *Pillars of Society,* the Tarantella in *A Doll's House,* the gloom followed by sunrise in *Ghosts.* Now in *The Wild Duck* there is the wounded bird loved by the child Hedvig and the loft in which the old Ekdal, once a fine hunter, goes rabbit shooting; and these pathetic reminders of great nature and free life counter, not any one person, but the *whole opposition* of dangerous idealist and ineffectual self-deceivers. This is the real conflict: vast nature against civilization's useless quarrellings. We remember Ibsen's desire to transcend opposition in politics.

Man must transcend himself by enlisting new powers. The portraits in *Rosmersholm* (1886) are of a race that never laughs (III). Rebecca, a free-thinking and advanced woman from the north, like Hiordis associated with witchcraft (III) and sea storms and called a 'mermaid' and 'sea-troll' (IV), entangles herself with Rosmer's life. Old trammellings are loosened by new life infused through a woman, from the feminine and Dionysian, pagan sources. Formerly a pastor, Rosmer renounces Christianity; but the ancestral phantoms, the White Horses, dominate as a threat and the death of Rosmer's wife must be atoned. Rebecca's will weakens and Rosmer loses faith in his mission of ennobling men. Each learns from the other's values and together they plunge into the mill race. In modern terms the theme of *Emperor and Galilean* is given a tragic but purposeful definition.

This feminine power, already so strong in Hiordis, Gerd, Nora, and Rebecca, is given centrality in *Hedda Gabler* (1890). Dissatisfied with her academic husband, Hedda wills to exert power over a Bohemian writer, admiring his anti-social challenge as Hiordis admired warrior valour. Tormented like Medea by a hated society, Hedda becomes a criminal and nihilistic force. Inside her is fire, and in a fearful scene she burns Lovborg's manuscript; many of Ibsen's plays contain some kind of burning, variously symbolizing the fires become destructive because unused. Hedda is a pagan: she would have Lovborg wear 'vine leaves in his hair'—as did Julian—and die 'beautifully' (II; III); and both Dionysus and Apollo are in these words. She ends playing wild music before shooting herself.

But what if the woman inspirer succeeds? Did Julian in part fail through not getting his 'pure' or perfect mate? Can the right woman make a superman? Solness in *The Master Builder* (1892) is an architect genius with strange telepathic powers; he is aware of a 'troll' in himself in contact—folk-lore blending into spiritualism—with 'helpers and servers' or spirit guides beyond (II). He blames himself for a fire which he had desired, but *done* nothing to effect. Did his desire enlist spirit helpers? (II). Is he a *new kind* of man? And now, in middle age, he is guilt-burdened, impeded and unhappy. To him comes the girl Hilda Wangel, fresh mountain air personified; he is her hero; he must awake, recapture his genius, build magnificently and climb, despite his giddiness, to his building's top. There is much talk of a wonderful 'kingdom' and 'castles in the air' (I; III). The play's realistic fabric shimmers with spiritualized meanings. Solness climbs his building, waves and falls. Hilda is exultant; at the moment of his triumph she heard 'harps in the air' (III).

The Master Builder is all height and lightness; in *John Gabriel Borkman* (1896) we have depth and weight. The hero is a miner's son who has become a great industrialist and capitalist, and in pursuance of his ambitions has broken the law and been in prison. Now, freed, he still dreams of great things. His wife is bitter; her sister, once his true love, replaces earlier woman inspirers with a different emphasis, insisting that he killed the love-life in her with his ambitions (II). It is the old opposition of *Brand*: power against love. But he defends himself. There has been a mysticism in his power quest. He first heard in the mines how 'the metal sings down there', and how 'the hammer strokes that loosen it are the midnight bell clanging to set it free', while it sings 'for gladness' (II); and he alone heard its cry for freedom (III). He is nineteenth-century industrialism in all its crime and all its glory, releasing wealth for man. In him 'power' was an instinct, but it was to be used for 'the well-being of many, many thousands' (II). All that he did was done in obedience to a compulsion from within; a true descendant from *Emperor and Galilean*, he has willed 'himself'; but 'I have never found one single soul to understand me' (III). Staggering out in the cold, he climbs. He dreams of the treasures still 'spell-bound in the deeps and the darkness', 'yearning for the light'. He has a vision of steamships across the globe, factory wheels whirling, their bands flashing, and ranges of towering mountains, his 'infinite, inexhaustible kingdom': 'Can't you hear, Ella?' Ella insists that there comes only 'an icy blast from that kingdom' and that having killed love he cannot inherit the glory (IV). He dies. It is a great study of the genius superman in action; of power as against love and ethics; and of these in strict relation not only to the nineteenth century, but, by symbolic extension, to the futurity of mankind.

Ibsen's main cosmic symbols are Byron's: sun, mountains, sea. Mountains suggest aspiration. The sea, symbol variously of freedom and death, dominates in *The Lady from the Sea* (1888) and *Little Eyolf* (1894). In the first Ellida is drawn by sea magic from her conventional marriage towards a seaman lover whose very eyes vary with the sea, but on her husband's granting her freedom she stays with him. Here the sea's lure is a 'craving for the limitless and the infinite', a dark power shadowing Ellida with 'black soundless wings' (v). *Little Eyolf* turns on sea and death. The crippled Eyolf, successor as a wronged child to the various boys, sacrificed or nearly sacrificed, in *The Vikings at Helgeland*, *The Pretenders*, and *Pillars of Society*, and to Hedvig and Oswald, is suffering for his parents' sin: such tragic youth alone, following the Adonis, or Balder, archetype, arouses Ibsen's softer feelings. The mysterious Rat-Wife tells Eyolf how she lures rats to their drowning; their very fear forces the plunge, but the fascination is no deceit, because death is 'soft and dark' and a 'long sweet sleep' (I); and to this same mystery, this otherness, she lures Eyolf, who cannot swim. His unhappily married parents, Allmers and Rita, whose sexual indulgence was the original cause of Eyolf's lameness, are guilt-stricken. They discuss Eyolf sunk in the fiord's 'depths', now swept by the 'undertow' to the 'open sea'. Where, they wonder, is he now? His 'great open eyes' accuse them. So through impressions of water Ibsen realizes the psychic world (II). The second act is deep, by the fiord, beneath a precipice; the third high, on the hill's top, with a flagstaff. Gradually Eyolf's death works in his parents a 'resurrection'. Flowers from the sea bed, strangely, 'blossom' (II). Allmers tells Rita about a mountain lake which he had to cross; his loved ones were far away; he rejoiced—as did the rats—in 'the peace and luxury of death'; and then found himself on the other side of the lake (III). In Asta, Allmers' supposed half-sister, we have Ibsen's one example of bisexual disguise (II). We end with thoughts of spirit helpers, stars and 'the great silence'. *Little Eyolf* expands Julian's mystic experience through water to the great dome (p. 285 above).

So satisfying a use of sea magic leaves Ibsen free in both these plays to give us a conventionally moral conclusion. This is rare. Marriages in Ibsen are normally unhappy or of little meaning; the whole stress is on the spiritual partnership, outside marriage, of inspirer and hero. Such inspirers or plot directors have been: Furia, Hiordis, Swanhild, Gerd, Hedda, Rebecca, Hilda, Ella; and the half-male Bishop Nicholas; and Maximus with his Dionysian ritual and occult practices. Through them the female principle impregnates, spiritually, the male, the sexes' functions being reversed. These agencies have become steadily lighter, more sweet. In *When We Dead Awaken* (1899) Ibsen's themes of inspirer and superman are blended with his death-mysticism to make a fitting conclusion. From Hiordis, who deliberately slays her lover, onwards, death, often suicidal, has been *purposive*, at once sacrifice and self-attainment. Brand's 'In

Death I see not Overthrow' (v) stands central in Ibsen's dramatic thought. Now our understanding is to be clarified.

Rubek is a sculptor genius, famed for his piece 'The Resurrection Day' showing 'a young woman awakening from the sleep of death' (I). His dull marriage is interrupted by meeting Irene, his old model. She has been mad in an asylum, a kind of death, and is watched by a Sister of Mercy. She and Rubek discuss their old relationship. Both have fallen from that spiritual marriage which made the great work, and their guilt is strong. She accuses him of killing her. She recalls how she as a model used to be simultaneously willing and struck with anger; how she was angered at his dispassionate artistry, yet ready to kill him had he touched her (I). That knife-edge between strong sensuousness and absolute asceticism basic to the artistic *moment* is exquisitely dramatized, Rubek and Irene together personifying the inmost coition of artistic creation, at once the dispersal and furthest consummation of biological instinct, with art, here the sculpture, as their 'child' (I). But beyond is still life itself, in time: how can the asexual or supersexual moment be lived? That is the theme always of these matings of inspirer and semi-superman, driving to a marriage beyond marriage, as in *Love's Comedy*, to art as life; to art incarnate, the true selfhood, or being. Rubek and Irene are rising from their half-death to a new life. The setting is mountainous, with a lake and 'blue-white' snow (II). A bright, high world. Children are at play. Irene's inspiration becomes resurgent and strong. She strides 'like a marble statue', looking like 'the Resurrection incarnate' (II); she is art become life, like Hermoine in *The Winter's Tale*. But 'resurrection' means what it says, and is more than metaphor. The statue piece which now comes to life showed a 'pure' woman

> not marvelling at anything new and unknown and undivined; but filled with a sacred joy at finding herself unchanged—she, the woman of earth—in the higher, freer, happier region—after the long, dreamless sleep of death. (I.)

Again, we may recall Julian's trance vision.

Rubek's wife pairs with Ulfheim, the hunter, on the lower, biological plane, the Viking plane. Rubek and Irene ascend through mist and storm like Brand and Gerd, but the adventure holds a promise and a happiness beyond that of earlier conclusions, since in Irene are both the idealism of Hilda Wangel and the love of Ella. Deathly impressions cluster; the 'miraculous' earth life and its love are slipping away; when Rubek burns for her, Irene cries: 'No, no—up in the light, and in all the glittering glory! Up to the Peak of Promise!' She is now 'transfigured' (III). Ahead, beyond mists, is the sunrise. Irene and Rubek are, as it were, caught *up* into the heights by an avalanche. A blazing light is cast back on all Ibsen's former conclusions.

The strange, human and yet inhuman, or superhuman, quest is ended. It is not 'Christian'; Ibsen's clergymen are as clearly distrusted as his doctors are trusted. Yet there is always some guilt from which the hero has to be extricated; Christianity and love are not forgotten; and the death in ascension of Rubek and Irene is given the Church's final blessing through the Sister of Mercy's 'Pax Vobiscum' (III). The Third Empire, we remember, does not repudiate, though it does transcend, the Christian tradition. In Christian terms it could correspond to the return of Christ in glory. Ibsen's standard is high: 'I stamp no copper happiness as gold' (*Love's Comedy*; III).

Ibsen's dramas usually rely, like the *Oedipus Tyrannus,* on a retrospective revelation, and they sink deep as the *Oresteia* into wells of racial heritage and past evil. They are shut in by mountain valleys or nineteenth-century walls, longing for freedom and expanse with Viking impulse, but forced rather to plunge deep and ascend high. Compression forces ascent. There are links with Byron: with *Cain*, with Sardanapalus' dream of a constricting and ghostly past, with Byron's supermen. Ibsen's intuitions of death, though intensely spiritualistic, gain from a poetic projection. He avoids talking of another 'dimension' or a 'spiritual world'; like Peer, he 'goes round about', and uses the sea instead, mountains, the sky dome, the sun. This is often the way of poetry and drama; it was Aristophanes' way in *The Birds*; for etheric experience, being no less rich and nature-planted than earth life, is best approached through earthly colourings. Ibsen's total structure corresponds closely to Shakespeare's: from the fairy-lore and fantasy of *St John's Eve* (1853) and *Olaf Liljekrans* (1857), and the histories. ancient and medieval, to problem plays, tragedies, and re-emergence into light and intimations of something rich and strange within, or beyond, death. At its heart is *Emperor and Galilean*, which is all his own: our one great dramatic statement on the central conflict of the Western world.

IV

In the works of Friedrich Nietzsche the dramatic tradition of Europe becomes self-conscious. His philosophical books are difficult, but their contrapuntal and dramatic meanings are adequately covered by his two symbolic works, *The Birth of Tragedy* (1872) and *Thus Spake Zarathustra* (1883–91). The first we have noticed (pp. 6–7 above); the second acts as a resolution of its problems.[1] The dramatic aim was a harmonization of Dionysian and Apollonian; in the prophet Zarathustra the harmonization is all but incarnate. He is accordingly, like Socrates, a living personification of *that for which drama exists*. The choice of 'Zarathustra' as spokesman follows Byron's use of Mazdaism in *Manfred*. Zarathustra had been the prophet of a religion opposing truth and light to darkness and evil, and now Byron and Nietzsche work instead on their interpenetration. The new Zarathustra is thus the prophet of sublimation in the manner of Alexander Pope's *Essay on Man* (1733–4), which follows his *Essay on Criticism* (1711) as *Thus Spake Zarathustra* follows *The Birth of Tragedy*.[2] The teaching is that instinct, which includes sexual energies and all their concomitant and dangerous fantasies, must be accepted: physical promptings and conscious thought, Dionysian instinct and Apollonian fantasy, are to function in dramatic reciprocity.

Nietzsche insists that all new good has been accompanied by an accusing conscience (56); he assumes conscience, but insists that we may have to surmount it. Man is at present a chaos of unrelated fragments—Ibsen made precisely this point (*Brand*; 1)—and must strive for unity. So we watch Zarathustra in his laboratory of integration. He is lonely, save for his symbolic beasts, Serpent and Eagle, but his teaching ranges wider, avoiding sexual love and, like Plato and Renaissance drama, concentrating on friendship; the friend is a 'foretaste of the superman' and a 'creative' power who, as in one of Shakespeare's Sonnets (p. 67 above), has 'a perfect world in his gift' (16). Chastity is a high value (13), and yet the suffusing tone is strongly erotic and the female principle contained, various allegorical female persons appearing to Zarathustra as lovers, almost as part of

[1] My detailed study of *Thus Spake Zarathustra* occurs in the chapter entitled 'The Golden Labyrinth' in *Christ and Nietzsche*, 1948. In my present account I again rely on the Everyman translation by A. Tille and M. M. Bozman, but in numbering the sections for reference I have on this occasion followed the standard English edition under the general editorship of Oscar Levy, leaving the Introductory Discourse unnumbered.

[2] Pope's philosophic poems are analysed in my *Laureate of Peace*, 1954.

him. He is a poet, and poetry is associated with the 'eternal feminine' (39) or regarded as sexually indeterminate, 'male or female' (74). He is being led by an inward 'voluptuousness' to a marriage with that in him which is 'more strange to himself' than are men and women to each other, this love of oneself being the supreme art (54; 55). A primary emphasis falls on the physical, the body's 'great intelligence' and 'bliss' being the source of a secret cosmic wisdom (4; 22), rather as in Shakespeare's 'My brain I'll prove the female to my soul' (*Richard II*; v. v.). Zarathustra's soul is a 'well' of love and sometimes he addresses it as a different being (31; 58; 70). We have accordingly a kind of internal coition and ever active self-ravishing, expressed in a varied dance drama of words and images. At high moments he attains a joy surmounting all negations, energy and reason being melted together to create a higher state which includes laughter (56; 73). Dionysian powers are married to an Apollonian and semi-Christian sensibility with love and laughter as constituents to the 'Golden Wonder' (58) of a perfected self-integration.

Ibsen and Nietzsche are mutually interpretative. Within his own bisexuality Zarathustra is acting something very like the drama of an Ibsen hero and heroine. In announcing that woman's happiness consists not in 'I will' but in 'he will' (18) he might be thinking of Ibsen's women inspirers. Like Ibsen, he demands 'a new nobility' (56). Ibsen's dream of a poetry not written but lived is given its technique. In both this higher state is symbolized by mountains.

But precisely because he is on the way to making himself an incarnation of poetry, or drama, Zarathustra, though admitting that he is a poet, speaks like Plato slightingly of poetry (39; 56; 74). What drama does circuitously is being done directly, and bull fights, tragedies and crucifixions are grouped together as unnecessary mechanisms (57). Much of Nietzsche's opposition to Christianity can be defined as a rejection of all such external reliances in favour of the inward battling referred to in Byron's *Manfred* and *Cain* (iii. iv. 129–30; ii. ii, 463–7). Since the Renaissance our dramatic tradition has already split the one archetypal tragedy or sacrifice into innumerable personal adventures, and Nietzsche is carrying the process a step further: selfhood must be achieved by the self.

As to the technique required, which involves the individual's sex life, the expression is guarded. Zarathustra admits to shame and fear; he would rather 'die' than confess his 'midnight' fantasies (79), yet he knows that only he who shall dare to speak more openly, saying 'Thus shall ye flow, ye great and small streams', will, like Ibsen's

Third Empire hero who 'wills himself' (p. 286 above), be 'lord of the earth' (79; and see 44; 47; 54). Private dramas of orgasm and fantasy, corresponding respectively to the Dionysian origins and Apollonian dream pictures of Nietzsche's *Birth of Tragedy*, may be supposed to function. 'To the knower all instincts are hallowed' (22), and such a self-acceptance gradually matures into universal acceptance and ratification, recognizing that 'the most evil thing in man is necessary to the best in him' (57) and that 'the wickedest is needed for the superman's best' (73). The aim is not dark. Such a shameless self-creation, or re-creation, has its reward:

> Thou goest thy way of greatness: now is that become thy final refuge
> which hath been hitherto thine extremest peril.   (45.)

'Passions' become 'virtues'; 'devils' become 'angels' (5; 17). The very thing which was most feared as worst is found to be *the one and only key to the best*. Dangerous actions are not being counselled; it is all purely a drama within the individual's sex life, fantasy life and soul life, his 'secret love' (34).

The driving force within creation is called 'the will to power' (34). This 'will', which is a poetic power (22), must be related to the Dionysian, which include the sexual, energies and which have as their implanted aim the achievement of a high state of self-surmounting like, yet beyond, art; the state, that is, that we find dramatically defined by Ibsen in *Love's Comedy* and *When We Dead Awaken*. This will give us the 'superman', a conception that may be directly related to Nietzsche's reading of Byron's *Manfred* and *The Prophecy of Dante*.[1] The superman is far more than a conventionally great man. He is pre-eminently beautiful (16; 24), blending strength with gentleness, a creature of artistic harmony and angelic grace (35).

Nietzsche rejects religious faith as usually understood. Nevertheless, Zarathustra has as his supreme love a lady he calls 'Eternity' (60) and she is the goddess of his central belief, the doctrine of 'the Eternal Recurrence' (57). 'Recurrence' means the unending repetition of all that is, both good and bad, like the repeated performances of a great tragedy. It means the eternity of every 'now'; but since this involves not a repetition *within* time but a repetition *of* time, the repetition must exist in *another sort of time;* vertical, we may say, instead of horizontal (*Christ and Nietzsche*; V. 191). It sounds fearful, but it is

---

[1] See Walter Kaufmann, *Nietzsche*, Meridian Books, U.S.A. and England, 1956, XI. 266; and Ernest Rhys, The Everyman translation of *Thus Spake Zarathustra*, 1933, viii.

regarded as the first step to a supreme insight and joy. In *The Birth of Tragedy* the numinous was our origin and man its projection; here, starting from human instinct, we wind upwards into the eternal.

The Superman himself is clearly related to futurity as the purpose and end of human creation (Int. Disc.; 20; 56; 61; 73), and yet he need not be limited to the evolutionary, or time, process. Man is to propagate not only 'onwards' but also 'upwards' (56), creating from hîmself a 'higher body' (3). The Superman comes out of man like lightning from a cloud (Int. Disc.). He has an 'angel's eye' and is lifted on the 'ether'; in him power 'condescendeth to the visible' (35). Like Christ, he will seem 'terrible in his goodness' (43). The impressions are transcendental, or spiritualistic, and Nietzsche may well be drawing inspiration without knowing it from the etheric and seraphic orders. The exact relation of the Superman to the Eternal Recurrence is not clear. Provisionally we can say that time is to give birth to the timeless. Even Zarathustra's own 'will' is said to be 'unburiable' and 'a thing that blasteth rocks' (33).

We are faced by a kind of Christology asserting, as did St Paul when he called Christ the 'first-born of a great brotherhood' (Romans viii. 29), that we are *to make Christs of ourselves*. In so far as we concentrate on Nietzsche's two artistic and visionary books —and he himself once warns us to put first trust in a man's *poetic* wisdom (22)—we shall find many correspondences with the New Testament. Zarathustra is a self-giving, self-sacrificing, type (22; 30; 56; 58); he repudiates revenge and even judicial punishments (19; 29; 42); and sees himself as a universal lover (Int. Disc.; 45; 75). This love has little in common with pity, or ethical duty, but comes rather from a superabundance and an overflowing (22; 54) such as seems to have existed in Christ. Both Ibsen (to Brandes, 24 September 1871) and Nietzsche stress the all-important half-truth that you can best help others by first coining the gold within yourself. Sun and gold are Nietzsche's dominating symbols: 'Only as an image of highest virtue came gold to be valued highest. Golden is the glance of the giver' (22).

That there are dangers is clear. We shall do well to presuppose a sensitive self-criticism, or conscience, which Nietzsche assumes as one element in the process, though it may have to be surmounted (56); and also the help of prayer or a prayerful state. We should probably assume a Christian upbringing as constituent, seeing the Nietzschean gospel, like Ibsen's Third Empire, as an incorporation and redirection rather than a wholesale repudiation of established good. Of spirit helpers, Ibsen's 'helpers and servers' (p. 288 above), we hear nothing, though they may be covered by Zarathustra's Sun and Mountains, his Serpent and Eagle (Int. Disc.; 74), and his lady personifications of Life, Wisdom and Eternity (32; 59; 60). Zarathustra cannot himself deliver a precise ethic since he is concerned mainly with self-making from a reliance on cosmic powers welling from body and soul, and it is *for these powers to direct*. A critical interpretation will be needed to receive and adjust the message, and it is all far from easy. To 'obey' oneself is harder than to 'command' oneself, and to 'become that thou art' is the crown of wisdom (56; 61). St Paul might have understood this; and Hamlet with his 'To be or not to be'; and Ibsen. My exposition of Pope's teaching in *Laureate of Peace* (p. 293, note) does something to obviate the dangers. The central challenge of both Pope and Nietzsche might be defined as the assertion that eternal life can be better attained by sublimation than by abnegation.

Nietzsche is by nature an individualist and as little at home with party politics as Ibsen: both dislike the State. But self-acceptance must expand and in so far as he touches politics Nietzsche accepts the hard facts to which our dramatic story introduces us. He can admire the Italian Renaissance and its dangerous men and respects the aristocratic values. To him Christianity appeared to have by-passed both the energies and the compulsions of earthly existence as we know it, and was in consequence cut off from the true sources of power. Looking ahead he foresaw government by a wise oligarchy, so following the thought of Plato and Milton. His political thinking occurs mainly in the scattered and unrevised jottings posthumously incorporated into *The Will to Power*, and is not developed.[1] Once he touches the solution of *Emperor and Galilean*, hoping for 'the Roman Caesar with Christ's soul' (*The Will to Power*; 983). The only contemporary system which at all suits the whole tenor of his thought is the royalistic democracy of Great Britain; a second-best possibly, but Caesar-Christs are not easy to come by.

We may sum up: Nietzsche, like Ibsen, would have men develop from pagan energies and heroisms through and beyond art, drama, and philosophy to a new self-surmounting and a greatness as yet unknown.

[1] On the unreliability of the collection posthumously entitled *The Will to Power* see Walter Kaufmann's *Nietzsche*, XIII. 346. For another good account of Nietzsche's thought, see F. A. Lea, *The Tragic Philosopher*, 1957.

CHAPTER XIII

Transitional

> The only difference between the saint and the sinner is that
> every saint has a past and every sinner has a future.
>
> Oscar Wilde, *A Woman of No Importance*, III.

I

TOWARDS the end of the nineteenth century our national imagination enjoyed what may be called a 'renaissance'. Values were in the melting-pot. Prophetic voices had for long been attacking Victorian acceptances; religious belief had been shaken by science; sexual taboos were now weakening. It is no simple revolution, or reversal. Life tingles as excitingly in patriotism as in socialism; national revivals are active in Scotland, Wales and Ireland; and the powers stirring on the Continent have their analogies in Britain. The rights of Roman Catholicism are now established and Spiritualism rises to importance. Theories of evolution open vistas of human greatness; woman asserts her rights; there is purpose, hope, and drive. But nothing is simple. Literary influences from French 'decadence' mix with the astringent idealism of Nietzsche; the aristocratic tone of the Restoration jostles with a romantic socialism; wit is brilliant and thought daring. There is often an element beyond ethic, a touch—or more—of satanism, of Gothicism; but it is a satanism newly accepted, civilized, and bright. The result can only be compared to the age of Elizabeth I.

In tragedy our first great name is not a writer's but an actor's, Sir Henry Irving, who from the seventies onwards brought grandeur to sombre themes: Shakespeare had never died out, but Irving's importance lies in his recapturing and by his genius transforming the romantic energies dormant in other works. We again face guilt, terror, and the occult. He was drawn to such dramas as W. G. Wills's *Eugene Aram* (1873), *Vanderdecken* (on 'the Flying Dutchman', 1878) and *Faust* (from Goethe, 1885), wherein the macabre mysteries dominated: Irving, like Kean, was always happy with the macabre.

A more psychic interest was in his revival of Boucicault's telepathic melodrama *The Corsican Brothers* (1880 and 1891; originally 1852) and his greatest success a gripping study of mental agony adapted from the French by Leopold Lewis as *The Bells* (1871). In this the protagonist is shown in dream seeing himself being forced by a mesmerist to reveal his crime. That most powerful means of inward realization, sound, makes of the recurring sleigh bells a terrifying symbol of conscience and fear, and Irving's genius did the rest. Mesmerism was to have another triumph in Paul Potter's dramatization of George du Maurier's *Trilby*, under Beerbohm Tree (1895). All dramatic art, and Irving's pre-eminently, is mesmeric; Euripides' Dionysus was a mesmerist. From this centre of histrionic power Irving brought mastery to the greater classics, to Shakespeare and to Tennyson's *Becket*.

More directly spiritualistic was *Mind or More than Matter*, called 'a Spirit Drama', by 'Pro and Con' (Thomas Herbert Noyes, jun., and Gustave de Mirelles Soares; 1873). The hero Raolo expounds modern spiritualism to a Cardinal, arguing that it descends from Plato, Pythagoras and Socrates (I. i). This drama is as a hinge for the swing over from the Faust tradition to twentieth-century spiritualism.

The relevant metaphysic is correctly set out: space, the 'boundless ether', is full of invisible entities, which the perfect man would—like Prospero—control; there's 'a mysterious bond' between 'mind and matter', and the spirit world is merely a 'gradation' higher, as the butterfly to a chrysalis:

> The time is coming, nay, is near at hand,
> When many eyes shall open to the light,
> And spirits be our most familiar friends;
> And death, no more a terror, but a joy,
> Be hailed by all as but a second birth.
>
> (II. i.)

Love is 'the fount of all philosophy'.

And we have drama as well as philosophy, for Raolo's spiritualism is used to uncover a crime. His method is to mesmerize the girl Viola, who in trance becomes clairvoyant. He is cautious, warning us that what her 'psychic lens' correctly focuses she may well mistranslate, and that her spirit counsellors themselves lay no claim to divinity but are 'simply fellow workers with ourselves ' (III. ii). However, she reads all that is necessary from the criminal's mind and the murder is re-staged, as in *The Bells*. We may recall similar examples in the more magical contraptions of Greene and Webster (pp. 62, 106) and the appearance of the victim's spirit is certainly a concession to dramatic effect nearer to old traditions than to modern spiritualism. When the criminal confesses the Cardinal is duly impressed (III. ii). This attempt to make drama from the new advances in psychic knowledge is fascinating and the note struck of triumphant, beyond-tragedy, certitude an important pointer to future dramas: 'A new and blessed era dawns in this!' 'Intellect' will gain 'new wings' to meet the 'blessed spirits', and Mind come to maturity (III. ii). Nothing similar had been felt since the Florentine Platonists of the Renaissance (p. 44 above). Our new dramatic period is to show a buoyancy unknown since the Elizabethans.

This 'buoyancy' characterizes the melodic dramas of W. S. Gilbert and A. S. Sullivan. Gay used old tunes and Gilbert old ballad forms, and the best song music of the Savoy operas has an Elizabethan freshness. In joyousness or pathos it possesses affinities to folk art and it has become a kind of folk art for twentieth-century Britain.[1]

The operas introduce us to an irrational world countered on choice occasions by an exaggerated logic, as when in *The Pirates of Penzance* (1880) the hero's attainment of his twenty-first birthday is denied on the ground that he was born on the twenty-ninth of February. Satire is often contained, but there is no settled satiric aim; the satire exists mainly in revealing inconsequences beneath convention. The Savoy operas are in harmony with the new, non-moralizing, movement; and, as surely as did Irving, they build from evil. Irving gave us terrors in a grand style; the Savoy operas horrors in a light one. Their main achievement is the mastery of the sadistic by melody.

W. S. Gilbert's most powerful straight drama was *The Hooligan* (p. 250 above), and the Savoy operas often concentrate, like the light operas of Gay and Colman, on some form of judicial punishment. Legal satire occurs in *Trial by Jury* (1875) and, on the Court of Chancery, in *Iolanthe* (1882). The harshness of naval discipline exposed in Jerrold's *The Mutiny at the Nore* is comically reversed in *H.M.S. Pinafore* (1878). The approach may be carefree, with light understatement, as when being buried alive is called 'such a stuffy death' in *The Mikado* (1885; II) or the King in *Utopia Limited* (1893), hearing of a public whipping, admits that 'I shouldn't like it myself'

---

[1] Attention is drawn to the operas' 'folk' affinities by Audrey Williamson in *Gilbert and Sullivan Opera*, 1953.

(II); or when in *The Gondoliers* (1889) an expression of sympathy for a woman awaiting interrogation in the torture chamber of the Grand Inquisitor is countered by the remark, 'She has all the illustrated papers' (II). But the subjects handled are grim. An execution and an execution block dominate *The Yeomen of the Guard* (1888) and we hear about his craft from the assistant tormentor in the Tower, though he claims not to have undertaken the work from any particular liking:

> In the nice regulation of a thumbscrew—in the hundredth part of a
> single revolution lieth all the difference between a stony reticence
> and a torrent of impulsive unbosoming . . .   (I.)

The recently appointed Lord High Executioner in *The Mikado*, Ko-Ko, is the more embarrassed for being a soft-hearted man who has never killed so much as a bluebottle (II). There is here a peculiarly interesting co-presence of sympathy and fascination, together with a peculiar identification of fun and fear:

> To sit in solemn silence in a dull, dark, dock,
> In a pestilential prison, with a life-long lock,
> Awaiting the sensation of a short, sharp, shock,
> From a cheap and chippy chopper on a big, black, block!
>   (I.)

The Mikado's aim to make 'the punishment fit the crime' as a means to rendering 'each evil liver' the 'unwilling' source of 'harmless merriment' to the community (II) is obliquely relevant to the enjoyment of punitive suffering so widespread in our society. Ko-Ko's attempt to satisfy the Mikado by description of a supposed execution has a grotesquerie too horrible for cold quotation. This is more helpful:

> KATISHA: And you won't hate me because I'm just a little teeny
>   weeny wee bit bloodthirsty, will you?
> KO-KO: Hate you? Oh, Katisha! Is there not beauty even in
>   bloodthirstiness?
> KATISHA: My idea exactly.   (II.)

Is human cruelty a necessary part of nature's 'beauty' and 'grandeur', like the fierce winds and the tiger's lashing tail (II)? Perhaps. But we may be lifted into purer airs where

> The flowers that bloom in the spring, tra-la,
> Have nothing to do with the case.
>   (II.)

The Mikado is in substance the most horrible and in manner the gayest and most buoyant of the operas. Its costumed orientalism does much to subdue the horrors to a scintillating whole, and the bright music, though not the humour, is our guide. The humour is itself macabre: we are not experiencing the purification of horror by humour, but rather the purification of a horrible humour by melody.

Ruddigore (1887) is in Gothic vein. During the tortures inflicted on her by one of the hero's ancestors, a witch has laid on each of his descendants in turn the curse that he must commit one crime every day, or die like her in torment. The mad burlesque shadows the thought that criminality may be arbitrarily caused by ancestral and ghostly conditioning, or obsession, and that the guilty may be, as are our executioners, kindly people at heart. So may, as is well known, the sadist; and such psychological insights tend to subvert all moral systems. In *The Pirates of Penzance* (1880) we are told that the policemen's lot 'is not a happy one' precisely because they know that criminals are in most respects just like their neighbours (ii). The pirates themselves are failing in their profession from good nature and finally turn out to be noblemen. In Gilbert's world justice may be horrible and the criminals not only kindly but respectable. We draw near to mad old Lear's 'None does offend; none, I say, none' (*King Lear*, iv. vi).

Since the sadistic complex is the root paradox of man and his society, any full consciousness of it is likely to start more and still more salutary paradoxes rippling outwards. Politics are an obvious field for them. In *The Gondoliers* two socialists become in effect kings and are shown comically serving their servants (ii). Both here and in *Utopia Limited* a constitutional monarchy is shadowed; and when the Utopian society, having been forced by its own perfection to the brink of disaster, decides to adopt the party system of Britain with its deliberate preservation of human confusions, we have in burlesque terms a just conclusion: the only system that fits a paradoxical world is one that functions in terms of paradox. In politics burlesque is truth, since the world we live in is in fact Gilbertian.

The method of the more famous operas is not strictly satiric, but rather one of catharsis, or sublimation, through melody. He who would make people wise, says Jack Point the jester in *The Yeomen of the Guard*, 'should always gild the philosophic pill' (i). When he and Elsie sing what is really a prophecy of his own tragic love for her, the little drama lifts into a lilting, happy tune in which both

scorned and scorner, sadness and merriment, as from some higher
dimension, participate:

ELSIE: It's the song of a merrymaid, peerly proud,
     Who loved a lord and who laughed aloud
     At the moan of the merryman, moping mum,
     Whose soul was sad, and whose glance was glum,
     Who sipped no sup, and who craved no crumb,
       As he sighed for the love of a ladye!
         Heighdy! Heighdy!
       Misery me, lackadaydee!
     He sipped no sup and he craved no crumb,
       As he sighed for the love of a ladye!

                                         (I.)

Repetitions of the refrain assert a harmony, a mastery, a triumph.
It is a melodic ride, the joy an air-borne joy, loving while over-riding
the anguish. Throughout these operas the treatment of pathos and
horror has the impersonal, uninvolved quality of old ballads, of
folk-art, or a Shakespearian song.

II

Irving and the Savoy operas both contribute to the new, beyond-
good-and-evil, drama. And what of social drama? T. W. Robertson's
homely pieces are carefully made, and convincing in Victorian terms.
Perhaps their chief interest today lies in their interweaving of society
with war; the Crimea in *Ours* (1866); the Indian Mutiny in *Caste*
(1867) and *The Nightingale* (1870); and the Franco-Prussian War in
War (1871). Robertson's social thinking, though superficial, is in
advance of his imperialism, which is crude. In *The Profligate* (1889)
and *The Second Mrs Tanqueray* (1893) Sir Arthur Pinero handled
sexual irregularities in man and woman with honesty, and in *His
House in Order* (1906) showed what technical skill could do in a plot
of suspense and excitement to reveal the falsities of a rather too
obvious respectability. Life was perhaps less technical and more real
for Henry Arthur Jones, whose *Michael and his Lost Angel* (1896)
shows a moralizing cleric brought to face his own fall under temptation. In *Mrs Dane's Defence* (1900) the laws of sexual morality are,
after a tough contest, maintained; but the contest *is* tough. *The Liars*
(1897) is a keen, semi-satiric, comedy. Both Pinero and Jones revealed
challenging truths in contemporary, if ephemeral, terms.

More important than these is James Albery, whose first success *Two Roses* (1870) has humour of timeless quality:

> MRS CUPPS: I don't care for all your fine talk. I'll have my money, or I'll know the reason why.
> GRANT: What can be fairer? You shall know the reason why. I haven't got it. (I.)

Again:

> That's a very impudent young man, and he don't seem conscious of his affliction. They say 'pity the poor blind'; but he seems determined not to feel his own suffering, which is most impious; for when tribulation comes we ought to tribulate, and not fly in the face of Providence and be happy. (II.)

The main attraction is the penurious Digby Grant, one of Irving's earlier parts, delightful in his unprincipled and aristocratic self-confidence and atrocious snubbing of his former friends when he becomes wealthy. Satire is contained, but the stage appeal is in this utterly unmoral fascination. The setting is countrified. Albery loves country settings: cottages, orchards, and flowers. The old gardener in *Forgiven* (1872) is a grand study and *Apple Blossoms* (1871) lives up to its title. A key-setting in *Genevieve* (c. 1875) is a house built over a boat-dock, endangered by floods, and fresh air blows through its psychology and wit. We have a monstrously selfish parent and an adventurer and big-game hunter of Restoration bearing and more than Restoration interest:

> I have been struggling with a white-winged angel, canting virtue, and I have conquered. The arrogant devil that has led me safely by the slippery edges of wild precipices, and on the tiger's stealthy track, is my guide *now*. I *will* have my *will*. You shall be mine.
> (III.)

Without any dilution of its ugliness the psychology of rakery is honestly, sympathetically, and convincingly presented. The thought, which ranges in exquisite prose over a wide field, covering religion too, is daring.

Albery's gifts were too advanced for his time and his accomplishment suffered. His finest achievement was his first, *The Jesuits* (c. 1864; *Dramatic Works*, ed. Wyndham Albery, 1939; I; xvi), which was never produced. Set in the reign of Charles II, it starts on the wave-length of Restoration wit, as in this, on the new science: 'It's plaguy hard a poor planet can't move without being watched. What right has a man to poke his nose into the affairs of Jupiter, and see

how many moons he keeps?' (I). The main story is tragic, having
as hero a young man brought up by a stern Jesuit to avenge and
prevent persecution by challenging a certain Sir John Flaxman.
Henry falls in love with Belinda, Sir John's sister:

> Just as a deaf man, if he were to hear
> Apollo strike his harp, would sit and wonder
> At his fantastic fingerings, but, if
> The heavy weight were lifted from his ear,
> And all the music rushed in on his soul,
> How would he wonder then! I have been deaf
> To Nature's voice and now I hear her music.
>
> (IV.)

Warned by his Jesuit master of his sacred obligation to crush the
devil active within erotic temptation, Henry is in agony, praying to
the 'spirits of air' who hover over 'poor mortals' and pick from
their human lusts

> Some little precious thought or holy prompting,
> And bear it up to heaven to plead for us . . .
>
> (v.)

And yet, when Belinda is with him, the glory is irresistible. Under the
starlit skies he swears to her that he will not hurt her brother. He
swears

> By yon grand page of heaven's history

and continues:

> Spirit of beauty, how is night arrayed!
> She has not left a jewel in her casket
> But wears them all. 'Tis a review in heaven
> Before the King of Kings . . .
>
> (v.)

A conquering strength, together with an utterly undated and un-
datable, Shakespearian, freshness, is in this love poetry. This early
conflict of love and religious duty may be related to Albery's
later daring; his is a challenge from a far deeper level than Pinero's
or Jones's. He writes from the centre.

Nothing comparable is to be reported before Oscar Wilde. He too
started with a strong but unsuccessful drama, *Vera or the Nihilists*
(1880), with an action set in Russia in 1795–1800. The liberal-minded
prince, Alexander, joins a revolutionary group and falls in love with
its leader, the girl Vera. On the death of his tyrannical father,
Alexander inaugurates a just rule, but is now condemned as a traitor

by the nihilists and Vera chosen to assassinate him. Like Albery's Henry, she solves the insoluble by her own death. Scene on scene has power; characterization is excellent, rhetoric is adequate, the dialogue often crisp and the romance moving. Without sentiment or propaganda a full consciousness of European politics and sociology is felt to be in control. The opposition of the stern and cold revolutionaries and the heartless brilliance of the aristocracy is replaced by Alexander's will to build from his marriage a reign serving his people. All the relevant lines of force active in Wilde's day are correctly deployed; and so his anachronistic reference to trains may be forgiven.

The Czar's neurotic tyranny is comic:

> Who is that man over there? I don't know him. What is he doing? Is he a conspirator? Have you searched him? Give him till tomorrow to confess, then hang him!—hang him!   (II.)

The cynical statesman, Prince Paul, though deplorable, has dignity. When, sick of 'the people and their rights', he remarks that in any 'good democracy' 'every man should be an aristocrat' (II), his thought touches that of Ibsen and Shaw; and when he is in danger among the nihilists his cool talk and aristocratic poise show to advantage. Alexander is idealized. To him the crown, 'this little fiery coloured world', girdling earth and sea with power, is as nothing compared to 'the meanest serf' who is loved (IV). Passionately he explains to Vera how their love might use their royalty to spread freedom across Russia. For a moment, before the tragic climax, love and power are at one.

Wilde has left nothing else so good, at least in conception. *The Duchess of Padua* (1883) is a neat enough projection of Renaissance villainy, controlling a subtle interplay of good and evil. *Salomé* (1892; translated by Lord Alfred Douglas from Wilde's French in 1894 and finally revised by Wilde) is a *tour de force* of atmospheric pressure. In the exotic, bejewelled and moonlit paganism of Herod's court Salomé's powerful sensuousness is challenged by the prophetic voice of Jokanaan (John the Baptist). Against the static and enervate paganism with its repetitive remarks, the voice of Jokanaan is dynamic. But the atmosphere is stifling.[1] The exotic sensuality points on to Flecker's *Hassan*.

Of the well-known comedies, *Lady Windermere's Fan* (1892) and

---

[1] The imagery and atmosphere of *Salomé* have been sensitively handled by Arnold Matthews in *A Study of Imaginative Speech in Modern Prose Drama*, Thesis, University of Leeds, 1959.

A Woman of No Importance (1893) are not very happy blends of conventional plot and original wit. In *A Woman of No Importance* our moral sympathies and intellectual admiration, both so exactly placed in *Vera*, drag apart, disrupting the artistry. Lord Illingworth's wit is attractive:

> All thought is immoral. It's the very essence of destruction. If you think of anything, you kill it. Nothing survives being thought of.
>
> (III.)

The usual aim of Wilde's wit is to reverse some moral valuation by a sharp paradox containing an element of truth. The trick can tire us; but in so far as we applaud it, we are embarrassed to find its exponent meeting a rigidly conventional condemnation within a conventionally conceived plot. *An Ideal Husband* (1895) is more harmonious; the exponent of wit has a more suitable place; the action, turning on the revelation of the statesman Sir Robert Chiltern's guilt, is strong; and the conclusion makes a moral compromise of a kind unusual in drama but refreshingly true to life. In *The Importance of Being Earnest* (1895) Wilde's paradoxical genius is allowed full freedom to make its own fantastic world under a brilliantly ironic, because self-condemnatory, title.

Wilde's plays can in parts be read as oblique expressions of his inner torment, using Lord Illingworth and Sir Robert Chiltern as masks. His true interests, over-bold for public drama, were more directly expressed in the narratives *The Happy Prince* (1888) and *The Picture of Dorian Gray* (1891); and also in *The Portrait of Mr W. H.* (1889), wherein he related the boy actors of the Elizabethan stage to those sonnets of Shakespeare which his own passion for Lord Alfred Douglas so closely recalls. Unable to implement the meaning of *The Happy Prince* by using the seraphic fires to right the social injustices of his time; unable to resolve that nerve-jarring opposition of pagan and Christian dramatized in *Salomé*; in these anxieties Wilde snapped the tension by plunging into an underworld of youthful criminality. Confronted on trial with one of his own letters containing the seraphic phrase 'your slim gilt soul', he based his defence on the great names of David, Plato, Michelangelo, and Shakespeare. His *De Profundis* (pub. 1905) sounds the deeps of pathos and tragic paradox. His life's story illumines wide areas of our drama and is itself, like Byron's, toweringly dramatic; and if as it seems he half willed his own tragedy, he can now say of it with Webster's Lodovico, 'I limn'd this night-piece, and it was my best'.

CHAPTER XIV

Edwardian

We take the Golden Road to Samarkand.
James Elroy Flecker; *Hassan*, v. ii.

I

THE florescence is from now on rich. The Edwardian era has a buoyancy and flair all its own, evident on every level of stage artistry, from music halls and musical comedy to the highest reaches of cosmic speculation. Poetic dramas such as Stephen Phillips's *Nero* (1906), Laurence Binyon's *Attila* (1907) and Rudolf Besier's brilliantly activated *The Virgin Goddess* (1906), were staged with honour. Passions are coloured and action vivid. Typical achievements are the melodramas of Hall Caine, the macabre fantasies of Lord Dunsany, the Dartmoor crime plays of Eden Phillpotts, and St John Ervine's dour masterpiece *John Ferguson* (1915). Meanwhile Alfred Sutro moves at ease in contemporary high life and knows how to pierce its defences. Stanley Houghton's *Hindle Wakes* (1912) is symptomatic of a new sexual and feminist daring. Moral conventions are under fire and society itself impugned. Progress, and sometimes the superman, is expected. Nietzsche was the presiding genius.

Edwardian drama shows two related trends, Dionysian and Apollonian: (i) a colourful enjoyment of the tragic and (ii) the will to human advance. Of the first, Phillips's Nero, though the play's verse lacks quality, may serve as a personification. Nero is a semi-Freudian conception, an artist type close bound to his mother Agrippina and still near the child-consciousness; in whom self-indulgence and egotism are one with his artist's dreams; for whom all life, including empire, is play-acting; who somehow manages to keep his filial devotion intact while arranging Agrippina's murder; and who ends up, at a magnificent climax, exulting in his city's 'crimson sepulchre' while Rome, which he has set on fire to appease his mother's spirit, burns (IV. ii). This Nero's lurid irresponsibility exaggerates certain aspects of what Nietzsche looked for in a 'tragic' civilization; a civilization able to enjoy life's terrors as an aesthetic phenomenon, to see the tragic as, provisionally, a good (*The Birth of Tragedy*, trans. W. A. Haussmann, 1909; Appendix, 194). Edwardian drama knew this enjoyment.

That such acceptances may paradoxically condition advance will be the clearer from a consideration of the social dramas of John Galsworthy. Drama is loath to reject, to deny; its instinct is to accept and balance opposites; justice is its recurring theme and the judicial its proper tone. No social dramatist has preserved these qualities with a finer integrity than Galsworthy.

Feeling bitterly the injustices, he refuses all facile strokes. In *The Silver Box* (1906) and *Justice* (1910) the law's essential injustice is exposed yet blame withheld. The strike in *Strife* (1909) is maintained by the will-power of the antagonist leaders, while others suffer, and in the conflict of gentility and the new-rich in *The Skin Game* (1920) both sides are at fault. The anti-imperialist attack in *The Mob* (1914) is itself a patriotism. Subtlest of all is *Loyalties* (1922), on the relation of the British upper class to a Jew; but the Jew's unfortunate manner is not forgotten.

Each play is a trial; counsels for prosecution and defence have their say; and an unseen presence—the 'presence' conjured into existence by all true dramatic conflict—sums up. Quietly, judicially, the sentence is pronounced in our minds and society, without rancour, condemned.

Galsworthy's plays are limited to the rational and to the surface. Our greater dramatists aim to penetrate deeper and we shall now consider four of philosophic tone: Hardy and Davidson, Granville-Barker and Zangwill. All labour to forge purpose from the tragic, to weave cosmic and human colours into design. The Edwardian note is struck by Edward Carpenter, author of *The Intermediate Sex* (1908), in his drama of Moses' burning faith and troubled leadership *The Promised Land* (1910; originally published as *Moses* in 1875). Though Moses dies wearied and uncertain as to the future, the fire passes to Joshua as 'the silver clarions of the morning sound'.

II

Though Thomas Hardy's bitter survey of the Napoleonic wars in *The Dynasts* (1903–8) is more dramatic panorama than drama, its concentration on so outstanding a personality as Napoleon and so grave a crisis in British history gives it importance in our tradition.

And it goes farther; Hardy is wrestling in modern terms, as did Aeschylus for ancient Greece, with the problem of cosmic justice. Like Buchanan's *Drama of Kings*, he has his choric spirits called 'phantom intelligences', divided into separate groups representing Time, Pity, Irony, and Rumour. For God we have the apparently unconscious 'Immanent Will', corresponding to evolutionary science.

The patterning of events shows a semi-dramatic mastery and the cinematographic directions create a mental theatre. But the human persons lack vitality and their blank verse is often flat. They are dwarfed both by the panoramic over-view and by the attendant philosophy. Napoleon is the plaything of powers beyond his understanding (e.g. 3; I. i). He is no superman:

> To shoulder Christ from out the topmost niche
> In human fame, as once I fondly felt,
> Was not for me.
>
> (3; VII. ix.)

People fight as 'people in a dream' (3; VII. vii). The role played by Britain as a nation is more strongly presented, Pitt and Nelson being accorded poetic approval as her agents. The Spirit of the Years recalls to Napoleon how once 'well-nigh every monarch' in Europe was his vassal:

NAPOLEON: Saving always England's—
Rightly dost say 'well-nigh'—Not England's—she
Whose tough, enisled, self-centred, kindless craft
Has tracked me, springed me, thumbed me by the
     throat,
And made herself the means of mangling me!
                              (3; VII. ix.)

In British action alone do we receive any real sense of power.

The choric spirits are more exciting, their poetry barbed, and their attempt to interpret man's relation to the cosmos the drama's heart. The Spirit of the Years offers a clairvoyant introduction:

A new and penetrating light descends on the spectacle, enduing men and things with a seeming transparency, and exhibiting as one organism the anatomy of life and movement in all humanity and vitalized matter included in the display.   (1; Fore Scene.)

'Gossamer', yet 'irresistible', threads are seen 'twining and serpentining' into man and earth alike from the 'Immanent Will', whose brain is 'the Everywhere' (1; Fore Scene). Later, on a battlefield, 'the controlling Immanent Will appears therein, as a brain-like network of currents and ejections, twitching, interpenetrating, entangling, and thrusting hither and thither the human forms' (1; VI. iii). Again, 'the unnatural light' before seen usurps that of the sun, bringing into view, like breezes made visible, the films or brain tissues of the 'Immanent Will' that move Napoleon and others to 'Its inexplicable artistries' (3; I. i). Once the clairvoyance shows Wellington 'acting while discovering his intention to act' (3; VII. vii). The Will is generally regarded as unconscious; better that, we are advised, than evil (2; VI. v); or it may correspond to a human mass-consciousness (2; I. iii). Once it is said to be super-conscious:

> In that immense unweeting Mind is shown
> One far above forethinking; processive,
> Rapt, superconscious; a Clairvoyancy
> That knows not what It knows, yet works therewith.
>
> (1; v. iv.)

It is 'in-brooding' (1; v. iv). But what has this appalling Frankenstein monster,

> Whose furthest hem and selvage may extend
> To where the roars and plashings of the flames
> Of earth-invisible suns swell noisily . . .
>
> (3; After Scene)

to do with the softer values hymned by the Pities? However, despite the worst arguments of the darker spirits, the Pities too have logic:

> Yea, Great and Good, Thee, Thee we hail
> Who shak'st the strong, Who shield'st the frail,
> Who had'st not shaped such souls as we
> If tendermercy lacked in Thee!
>
> (3; After Scene.)

There is one only solution: that the age-long agonies 'shall be cancelled', and that, as in Shelley's *Prometheus Unbound*, nature should awake, 'Consciousness the Will informing, till It fashion all things fair' (3; After Scene).

Though moulded within the art-form for its own purpose, the spirits are created from spiritualistic concepts. More, they sometimes act directly on persons. They whisper to Napoleon (1; I. vi; 2; VI. iii; 3; VII. ix) and others (1; v. vi; 2; VI. vii), attempting to influence them, functioning as Homer's deities or the spirit guides of modern spiritualism.[1] Both clairvoyance and clairaudience contribute to Hardy's metaphysic, and this alone precludes a final pessimism. Despite its weakness in human delineation, yet in the ambitious scale

---

[1] These voices have been discussed by J. O. Bailey in *Thomas Hardy and the Cosmic Mind*, University of North Carolina, 1956.

of its conception, its sense of a spiritualized unity and its final evolutionary hope, Hardy's *Dynasts* has the thrust if not the trust of Edwardian drama.

The Dynasts forms a natural introduction to the Scottish dramatist John Davidson who, working on much the same material and with a similar rejection of traditional religion, reaches different conclusions. He is strong where Hardy is weak; energy replaces fatalism; the horrors which so pain the one, the other fiercely embraces.

Davidson wrote various dramas, pastoral, historical and prophetic. *Smith*, subtitled 'a tragic farce' (1886), brings fervour and a straining ambition to bear on modern life; *Scaramouch in Naxos* (1888) is a poetic fantasy critically dramatizing the relation of the modern theatre to the Greek god Dionysus; and *Self's the Man* (1901) has a hero of power, vision and superlative abilities, with high designs above all normal categories of good and evil, a force of light refusing to use the death penalty, a believer in immortality. As he advances, Davidson's dramatic poetry becomes more and more powerful and his thoughts more dangerous. In *The Theatocrat* (1905) the decadence of modern drama is symbolized by an actor-manager in difficulties, a drunken leading actor and the failure of an attempted production of *Troilus and Cressida*; and new life is sought in a religious work by the actor-manager's friend, a bishop, whose prophetic message is directly opposed to Christianity and causes an uproar on the first night. The message is Davidson's; now he has his thoughts clear; the commercial theatre and orthodox religion are together attacked by a new, semi-Nietzschean, gospel of frightening power.

Davidson's mature teaching, as set out in the introduction to *The Theatocrat* and the epilogue to *The Triumph of Mammon* (1907) and the texts of both plays, rejects orthodox concepts of God and sin and all transcendent categories: the universe is quite unmoral (*The Theatocrat*; 26). But the recognition is happy: we are urged to accept, and respond to, life's magic. The teaching has affinities to Wordsworth's, to which he refers, and to all poetry: 'all convincing imagery is scientific truth' (*The Triumph of Mammon*; 160). Time is rejected and the eternal now—the 'now' basic to dramatic art—alone real (p. 316 below). Davidson's metaphysic, relying on the omnipresent and invisible ether, the bisexual yet creative electricity (*The Theatocrat*; 25) and matter, is in part derived from nineteenth-century physics, but it may also be related to occult and spiritualistic thought: light and colour are identified with sound and music, all together making 'the ethereal warp and woof of the matter of which we ourselves are woven' (*The Triumph of Mammon*; 156–62). Similar statements are found in the accounts of other dimensions received through trance mediumship, and also in Gordon Craig's theories of dramatic art. We are urged to become newly conscious of life's elixir. Matter has become in turn 'subconscious, conscious, and self-conscious' (*The Theatocrat*; 9) and the language of the new self-consciousness is poetry: 'It is a new poetry I begin, a new cosmogony, a new habitation for the imagination of men' (*The Triumph of Mammon*; 167).

Davidson is in line with Ibsen's prophecy of the man who 'wills himself' in *Emperor and Galilean*; and with Nietzsche, though he rejects doctrines of a superman as too idealistic (p. 315 below), insisting instead on his own mystique of the actual and the now. All that is needed is a full consciousness of what we, which is the universe, are. Both Hardy and Davidson aim to break the opacity between man and nature, but whereas the one looks for a new consciousness in nature the other looks for it in man. Hardy wants the cosmos to respect human valuations; Davidson wants humanity to attune itself to the cosmos.

So much for philosophy; drama is a more severe test. Drama is as a laboratory for testing such theories. In *The Triumph of Mammon* and *Mammon and His Message*, the first two parts of a projected but uncompleted trilogy called *God and Mammon*, Davidson attempts a dramatic exposition.

The setting of *The Triumph of Mammon* is contemporary, in a Nordic country called 'Thule'. Battleships, flags, and colour enliven our first stage direction. We are in a modern world of State affairs and power. King Christian is opposed by his eldest son, called 'Mammon' because of his atheistical and immoral beliefs:

MAMMON: That which I am
                I am, and would be under any name,
                Immanuel, or Siddartha, or Herakles,
                A new force in the world. My title, Mammon,
                Delights me: I shall make this name renowned
                For things unprecedented through the earth.
KING CHRISTIAN: What things?
MAMMON: Things sifted from the stars in nights
                Of travail—exiled moons; things that shall change
                The thoughts of men and renovate the time.
                                                    (II. iii.)

'Mammon' was the god of riches, desire, war, adventure, discovery, power; his splendour has been degraded to a supposed 'inferior devilry' by Christianity, which humbles pride, smirches sexual love, dilutes virility and tyrannizes over the intellect (II. iii). His blasphemies arouse wrath: the Abbot Gottlieb, symbolizing, as Mammon mockingly observes, the Christian tradition, suggests that, instead of being put to death, he be castrated. King Christian visits him in the Chapel Royal to perform the act.

Mammon (III. ii) is alone, tied to a pillar facing a crucifix on which he has been meditating. Though Christ may be honoured above all rivals hitherto, yet now the world 'wearies of you'; economic theory and idealistic reforms cannot patch up a decaying order; new life is wanted. His father approaches, with a knife. After all, he says, God's elect are the virgins and celibates like Christ; life in Heaven will be a 'single ecstasy' of 'undesirous ravishment'; earthly sex 'is sin, is Hell'; and from this he will deliver his son (III. ii). Great issues are being dramatized. Is humanity to take sexual fulfilment or its denial as its highest aim? Both Christ and Nietzsche's Zarathustra were without it and it is once agreed in *The Theatocrat* (I) that the artist is better celibate, like a priest. We shall find this issue faced again by W. B. Yeats.

The scene develops. Mammon thinks of Gwendolen, his love:

> O father, sex is soul,
> The flower and fragrance of humanity,
> More beautiful than beauty, holier
> Than any sacrament, greater than God—
> I tell you, father, greater than all the gods,
> Being the infinite source of every thought
> Worth thinking, every symbol, myth, divine
> Delight of fancy.   (III. ii.)

The King says that thrones are falling, civilization disintegrating through irreligion and atheism; God is the only 'keystone'; and God has ordained 'this Christian surgery'. Mammon in reply reasserts his own faith: 'The Universe unveiled is there, there, there!' He 'cannot speak such greatness'. But he is terrified at the thought of being 'a sapless thing'. At the last moment he cries 'God help me then! Christ save me!' The King stops. Mammon expresses repentance. The King cuts his bonds, whereupon Mammon 'takes the knife and seizing King Christian by the throat stabs him'. Then:

> Now, old, vain, foolish Christian man, who saw
> My terror—I, afraid!—go up to Heaven!

> Glare at me! Heart of Hell, what awful eyes!
>
> [*Stabs again*]
>
> I would you were the soul of Christendom!
>
> [*Stabs a third time*]
>
> I would you had been God!
>
> (III. ii.)

We hear much of literary dramas not dramatic enough for production: here we have a scene too dramatic for production.

From now on Mammon's progress is rapid. Various parties solicit his approval (v. i). The Nietzschean Guild is repudiated on the grounds that Nietzsche's superman is really a Christology in disguise; the Teutonic god wanted by others is an artificial conception; reformers from 'the Isles' (i.e. Britain) are rejected, theories of equality are denied. Most of what Mammon dislikes he regards as parasitic on the corpse of Christendom. What he looks for is an acceptance and intensification of the actual. He wills

> to make
>
> This mighty world a hundredfold itself.
> There shall be deeper depths of poverty,
> A more distressing toil, more warlike war,
> An agony of spirit deadlier
> Than that which drenched Gethsemane in blood . . .
>
> (v. i.)

And yet, too, a 'rapture', a 'beauty', and a 'glory' hitherto unknown, corresponding, we may suppose, to the state of being including, yet beyond, suffering announced in Shelley's *Prometheus Unbound*.

At a ceremonial gathering in St Olaf's Hall Mammon is denounced for his father's murder by the Abbot Gottlieb, and the Papal Legate excommunicates him. With the help of machine-guns he establishes himself, remarking that 'secular change' inevitably demands a 'crimson baptism'. He crowns himself and announces his gospel. His philosophy has no room for the transcendent:

> No world but this, which is the Universe,
> The whole, great, everlasting Universe.
> And you are it—you, there, that sweep the streets,
> You that make music, you that make the laws,
> You that bear children, you that fade unloved.
> Oh, if there be one here despised and mean,
> Oppressed with self-contempt and cursed with fear,
> I say to him:—Not any where at all
> Is there a greater being than you—just you:
> You are the lustre of a million suns—
> The fuel of their fires, your flesh and blood;

> And all the orbs that strew ethereal space
> Are less than you, for you can feel, can know,
> Can think, can comprehend the sum of things:
> You are the infinite Universe itself
> Become intelligent and capable . . .
>
> (v. ii.)

His words pour out, an amazing blend of precision and excess, in intoxicating torrents, concentrating on the 'ether', 'lightning', 'electric lust for ever unconsumed', 'twisexed fertility' and man

> The intellect, the passion and the dream,
> The flower and perfume of the Universe . . .
>
> (v. ii.)

This Earth is Heaven and Hell; every moment is judgement day; time is a delusion; eternity is now. Since in man the whole universe has become self-conscious, labour for the future is nonsense: we ourselves are 'posterity'. It is all wonderful; its assertions, though not its denials, are mostly true; but the central thought is hard to hold for long and yet harder to translate into action.

In *Mammon and his Message* (1908) we see Mammon at work. For beggars and criminals he plans a humane extermination; prostitutes, only needed under Christianity, are to change their ways; the capitalist system he intends to destroy. His conscience sometimes makes him see, like Macbeth, his past victims. However his recoveries are firm. He has Gottlieb tortured mainly in order to overcome his own inhibitions and master a full self-realization (see p. 362 below). He naturally arouses opposition, which he meets with arms, emerging again victorious. There was to have been a third play but Davidson's suicide left the trilogy uncompleted. The last piece was presumably to have been tragic, since a note in his preface to the second indicates that it would have shown Mammon as strong in suffering as in power.

Under dramatic expansion Mammon's gospel of total acceptance and total living reveals its contradictions: if all men are so splendid, why tyrannize over them? Why disbelieve in social equality, if each man is the universe? So comprehensive an attempt to base a life-plan on tragic exultation inevitably forces paradox. Mammon certainly serves as a retrospective comment on three centuries of dark persons in drama and history, while also being prophetic of modern Europe. Davidson must not be supposed to subscribe to all Mammon's actions, and he is aware of objections to his philosophy, recognizing that the Catholic doctrine of the Real Presence is a profound symbol of the magic in matter he is announcing, and that his own system of 'dynamic ether', material creation and atomic 'force', 'the polar tension couched and wed in every atom', is already covered by the Christian Trinity (II. ii). A Catholic might argue that what Davidson is telling us is both so true and so dangerous that it must for the present remain limited by dogma and locked in symbol.

Hardy and Davidson offer respectively negative and positive readings of man's relation to the cosmos; our next two dramatists, again a contrast of pessimism and optimism, work closer to normal experience.

Though Harley Granville-Barker may have aimed beyond his reach, the aim was worthy. The eighteenth-century heroine of *The Marrying of Ann Leete* (1899) breaks through social distinctions to marry a gardener, true life asserting itself against convention. The terms are simple and scarcely adequate to the complexities of the new century, which Granville-Barker next faced in a number of heavy and intricate problem plays without either the cosmic colourings of an Ibsen or the humour of a Shaw to relieve their pain. In *The Voysey Inheritance* (1905) a man of principle is forced to lower his pride and compromise with the web of financial dishonesty in which his father has left him. For are not most incomes, in essence, theft? (III). And do not 'splendid criminals' (V) possess a vitality we can respect? *The Madras House* (1910) cleverly uses a fashion business to pillory the tinsel and titillation of sex attraction and all the various suppressions, flirtations, seductions and pseudo-romanticisms that characterize our approach to women, a Mohammedan harem being regarded as more honest. The attack on an over-cerebralized sexuality forecasts D. H. Lawrence. Granville-Barker's heroes can be deeply disturbed by the presence of women. Trebell in *Waste* (1907) is a statesman-genius, his eyes set prophetically on progress, vitalism, and a well-planned transfer of government support from Church to Education. Women he dislikes and sexual intercourse he despises; and when he falls into adultery the child, which would to him have justified the otherwise stupid action, dies through the mother's fear of childbirth rendered the more unbearable by the father's coldness towards her. The scandal ruins Trebell's career, and being left with neither a biological nor an idealistic justification, he commits suicide. Was his loveless genius at fault? Or shall we blame the universe for waste?

In *The Secret Life* (1923) Strowde, a politician who has turned to writing in which he only half believes, realizes that he is a failure. On 'chilly' heights he and Joan have loved, Ibsen-wise, 'the unattainable in each other', without marriage and without achievement.

There is a truth or hope beyond animality and all outward 'tokens of our living' which we touch, but deny (I. iii). What of politics in such a world? The only strength flowers from 'the secret life' in each of us (I. iii), but our minds are 'prisoned', though there exists—following the thought of Ibsen's *Emperor and Galilean*—'a world of power to be wielded that might stagger the purpose of a Caesar' (II. iii). Meanwhile what is the worth of 'this sacred self that cannot yield to life'? Perhaps death can make us fruitful (III. ii). When the wise Kittredge hints that after death 'that inmost thing we were so impotently may but begin, new breathed, the better to be' (III. ii), he may be right, and yet this is no political solution. Not until *His Majesty* (1928) did Granville-Barker touch a convincing hope. A mid-European king has been forced from his throne. Offered the chance of reinstatement, he returns to prevent civil war and disappoints his supporters by refusing power on terms which his conscience does not approve. He is innately royal; once his sword, thrown on the floor, exerts strong dramatic radiations, no one daring to touch it. As a voice of enlightenment he resembles Byron's Sardanapalus, Wilde's Alexander and Shaw's Magnus. Only under this royal principle does Granville-Barker's political drama find rest.

His work is strangely undramatic, with much dead dialogue and the greater things half spoken, as though afraid to speak; yet in it there burns a gem-like flame, willing the liberation of man's imprisoned self and the interpenetration of society by spiritual power.

A more impulsive force drives within Israel Zangwill's *The Melting Pot* (New York, 1908; London, 1914). A young Jewish musician from Europe sees America as the crucible for the fusion of races and even perhaps 'the coming superman' (I); as at least a great human republic and kingdom of God (II), where all racial animosities are forgotten. When he discovers that his love Vera is the daughter of a Russian nobleman who was in part responsible for the pogrom in which his mother and sister died, all his old bitterness is re-aroused. While his music wins acclamation, he realizes his fall:

And *my* soul? What of *my* soul? False to its own music, its own mission, its own dream. That is what I mean by failure, Vera. I preached God's Crucible, this great new continent that could melt up all race-differences and vendettas, that could purge and re-create, and God tried me with his supremest test. He gave me a heritage from the Old World, hate and vengeance and blood, and said, 'Cast it all into my Crucible'. And I said, 'Even thy Crucible cannot melt this hate, cannot drink up this blood'. And so I sat crooning over

the dead past, gloating over the old blood-stains—I, the apostle of
America, the prophet of the God of our children. Oh—how my music
mocked me!   (IV.)

Zangwill, himself a Jew, has Hebraic fervour. *The War God* made a
strong impression when produced by Beerbohm Tree in 1911. Set in
militaristic 'Gothia' planning war against 'Alba', it has a saintly
pacifist Frithiof standing in contrast to the King, to his Bismarckian
Chancellor, and also to a revolutionary movement, for Frithiof
rejects all force. His denunciation to the revolutionaries goes deep.
Society is rotting and peace with its 'starved and frozen workers' is
as bad as war. Even so, bloody means solve nothing:

> You talk of killing off the Holks and Torgrims,
> Blind instruments of blinder social systems!
> But first kill off your Christless Church and State,
> Your standing hosts of soldiers, landlords, lawyers—
> And, worst of all, the evil in yourself.
> Reformers must begin with self-reform—
> 'Tis not so pleasant as reforming others.
>   (III.)

The Chancellor's opposing philosophy recalls Buchanan's Bismarck
(p. 271 above). Equality and comfort will never alone satisfy man's
aspirations, always pining for the heights:

> Life is fight, thank God!
> Come, bare your forehead to the fierce salt Truth.
> Take war away and men would sink to molluscs,
> Limpets that wait the tide to wash them food.
> The nations would grow foul with lazy feeding.
> What Heaven loves is breeds with life a-tingle,
> Swift-gliding, flashing, darting death at rivals,
> Men fearing God and with no other fear.
>   (IV.)

There is no final contradiction, since Frithiof's 'evil in yourself'
corresponds to the Chancellor's 'life-a-tingle'. Set between the
extremes is the mild King seeing arbitration as 'the next stage in
human evolution' (IV). *The War God* was prophetic.

The Next Religion (1912) rises to a strong conclusion. A prophetically minded clergyman, Stephen Trame, loses faith in orthodoxy,
and after a period of destitution is helped by a rich man to establish
a new, rather Davidsonian, religion based on the laws of nature,
science, the arts, and such leaders or thinkers as Mazzini, Emerson,
and Swinburne. He repudiates prayer and immortality. He is

throughout pathetically inefficient but is helped by his demure wife, Mary, though she does not accept his religion. The final act is in the vestry of the new St Thomas's Temple, on a day of grand ceremonial. Stephen Trame, now blind, is the high priest and his musician son Wilfred, the organist. We are to watch the new religion under attack.

First his wife reveals that it was her prayer that brought the millionaire's gift on which everything for the religion hostile to prayer has depended; and next Trame's old friend, Hal, a Christian convert, levels a series of scathing attacks against the new faith, pointing out that its liturgy is traditional and that the central mysteries of life and death remain while the findings of science are always changing. So much in preparation. Stephen's son, Wilfred, is suddenly killed. The youths of the choir, in golden mantles, perform a ritual, setting a seraphic tone for what is to follow. Mary is distraught. While to her her boy's immortal shape is now that of 'an eager and beautiful youth', haloed and for ever making holy music, her husband is to deliver his sermon on the True Immortality, which is no more than survival within the memory of others. The argument between father and mother grows, pointedly interspersed by music and chant from the choir off-stage. What else, says Stephen, can we conceive? Is everyone, insane and all, to survive? Passionately his wife asserts the infinitude of possibilities: 'And is there not Time enough and Space enough and Power enough to set all these blunders straight?' (III). She denounces his 'miserable religion'; his ideal of 'a world of peace and perfection' leaves her cold. In ecstasy, claiming a mother's insight, she asserts that 'Wilfred lives'. This humble woman, so long the meek follower of her brilliant husband, now blazes. What of those in whose memory he is to live? It is admitted that they too must die:

> MARY: All of us turning like him into loathsome logs! And our
> successors on the planet—logs in *their* turn. And so on and so on
> till this revolving graveyard is shrivelled up by a wandering star.
> And this you call an inspiring reality!   (III.)

It sounds like a criticism of Davidson's denials. She refuses to let him, blind as he is, infect others with his spiritual blindness. She herself will preach the sermon:

> Yes, I. Let them hear a woman for once. You and your dried-up
> thinkers! I tell you that the great live world will never *take* your
> religion, and that even if you deluded all male humanity, the *mothers*
> would rise up and tear it to pieces.   (III.)

The feminine assertion, so strong in Edwardian drama, in Hall Caine's *The Eternal City* (1910), in Shaw and Barrie, has here its supreme moment. Opening the door, Stephen lets 'the triumphant Requiem'—his son's composition—burst forth. 'Wilfred's music', he says. She cries 'The Resurrection and the Life'.

The early acts are undistinguished; the conclusion, so flamingly redramatizing the ancient Adonis theme of slaughtered and surviving youth, is magnificent. The criticisms of orthodoxy are strong; the new and needed religion fails only for its rejection of prayer and immortality. The play has been banned for performance in Great Britain.

III

In health the heart is not heard; in a nervous state it may be. The works just discussed leave us conscious of their intellectual heart-beats: we pass now to dramas wherein man's relation to his universe is more objectively dramatized and the numinous more concretely embodied.

The importance of the numinous or Dionysian element in dramatic composition is well illustrated by the dramas of Henry James. Confining himself to a limited social surface without help from either nature or the occult, or from humour, and yet with a genius not to be satisfied by a Galsworthy's plain dealing, he is, as a drama-tist, in a difficult position. Once, however, he plunged deeper and composed a one-act drama, *The Saloon* (1908), with as strong a central theme and as convincing a use of the supernatural as we shall anywhere find.

Young Owen Wingrave refuses a military career on pacifist principles, so incurring the wrath of his grandfather, who disinherits him. Owen is rational and enlightened, opposing 'The Scandal of History; the Dead Waste of Power; the Sin and Shame of the World'. His fiancée Kate is against him, being a militaristically minded girl who plays wild martial music of exotic and Dionysian tone; the ancestral warrior values are in her and her music. In the old house the ghost of one of Owen's ancestors who had beaten to death a similarly recalcitrant young idealist is still known to be active. In dialogues of great intensity Owen and Kate argue the matter late at night. They are at cross-purposes: he suspects her of wanting the inheritance he has lost, while she in answer calls him a coward. They are both unjust, since her convictions are sincere and he is superlatively brave. Gradually, in dialogues lit first by lamp and candle and afterwards only by the 'dim blue starlight' from a large window, they begin to understand each other. She has once seen the ghost, and knows that the testing hour has now come; she is in terror for Owen, who accepts the challenge, wildly and fearlessly cursing the ancestral portraits on the walls. At the climax Kate shrieks. There is

> a great quick Blackness of deeper Darkness, completely obscuring the cold light from the high window, which passes, like the muffling whirlwind of an Apparition, and has come and gone as a great flash of light.

Out of it has sounded 'like a ringing cry of Battle' Owen's last gasp of recognition. He lies dead. He is called a 'soldier'. The end is just: though the ancestral powers are the stronger, he dies, like Byron's Sardanapalus, as a martyr to civilization.

This is not merely a technical *tour de force* on James's part, though it is not less. His main interests are covered; an old house, European tradition, new civilization; and yet only through an occult realization can they attain dramatic pointing and detonation.

James writes from the extreme of civilized sophistication, from the new world. But the more mysterious powers were natural elements for the older, Celtic consciousness active in Irish and Scottish folk-lore and legend. From these drama flourished naturally in the Irish dramatic movement under the inspiration and guidance of Lady Gregory, whose own stage writing covered a wide range of comedy, history, tragedy and fantasy.[1] We shall review three Irish dramatists: Martyn, Synge, and Yeats.

The hero of Edward Martyn's *The Heather Field* (1899) is a mystic whose delight is in nature and that which is seen through nature: 'Have you ever seen on earth something beautiful beyond earth?' (III). He hears spirit voices from 'choristers singing of youth in an eternal sunrise' (II). In *Maeve* (1900) the heroine is dominated by a similarly seraphic intuition. She feels the presence of the 'beautiful dead people' (I) and has mystic intimations of a past wherein Celtic youth possessed the delicate perfection of the Greeks (I), and of such

---

[1] An account of Lady Gregory's life and work is given by Elizabeth Coxhead in *Lady Gregory, a Literary Portrait*, 1961.

beauty is the Spirit Lover who now draws her from a conventional marriage:

> There he lives in never-fading freshness of youth. I am haunted by a boyish face close hooded with short gold hair—and every movement of his slender faultless body goes straight to my heart like a fairy melody. (II.)

Greece is again a prepossession in *An Enchanted Sea* (1902), with not only the same thoughts of a Greek choir like angels, but the living presence of the golden-haired and 'wonderful' sea-boy Guy, whose 'genius' is both Irish and Greek (II), who sings of sea magic and is taken back into the sea. Martyn's fusion of the Socratic and the Celtic is fascinating.

John M. Synge's dramas, in a prose pitched on an idiom and rhythm caught from peasant speech and imagination, are strong in natural perception. There is no metaphysical discussion: we are just among people whose minds are close to nature.[1] It is not all happy. *The Shadow of the Glen* (1903) is heavy with thoughts of human loneliness: 'It's many a lone woman would be afeard of the like of me in the dark night, in a place wouldn't be as lonesome as this place . . .' Here you live

> seeing nothing but the mists rolling down the bog, and the mists again and they rolling up the bog, and hear nothing but the wind crying out in the bits of broken trees were left from the great storm, and the streams roaring with the rain.

A tramp invites the lonely woman to come away: there are larks and thrushes 'when the days are warm'. Strength is drawn from nature; and, helped by a human companionship, it can be sweet. Synge is powerfully aware of man's loneliness in a mysterious but wonderful universe.

In *The Well of the Saints* (1905) the blind pair avoid healing because the country's sounds and smells have for long built in their minds perception of a yet grander nature than others perceive (III). The inward imagination, built on the Dionysian, the numinous, the sound values of nature rather than its Apollonian sights, tunes us to Wordsworthian intimations, though Synge himself never philosophizes.

The powers of imagination are dramatized even more vividly within the serio-comic *The Playboy of the Western World* (1907). Christy Mahon, the suppressed and nervous young man, gains

---

[1] Synge's nature mysticism has been admirably discussed by U. M. Ellis-Fermor in *The Irish Dramatic Movement*, 1939.

respect in a new village community for having, as he supposes and
relates, killed his tyrannical father with a spade. This new respect
infuses power and self-realization; he wins in the local races and his
love for the girl Pegeen is returned. He has, like Nora, been 'lonesome': the word is reiterated (II). Now he is a splendid lover:

> It's little you'll think if my love's a poacher's or an earl's itself, when
> you'll feel my two hands stretched around you, and I squeezing
> kisses on your puckered lips, till I'd feel a kind of pity for the Lord
> God is all ages sitting lonesome in His golden chair.   (III.)

But when his father turns up safe after all and in the general hurly-
burly Christy again strikes him down, things change: as Pegeen says,
'There's a great gap between a gallous story and a dirty deed' (III).
It is true: so too *there is a vast, if only provisional, difference between
our various literary satanisms and their correspondences in actual life*.
However, as the villagers, including Pegeen, become cruel, Christy
becomes admirable. There has throughout been an ugly emphasis on
hanging, brutally and half enjoyingly described; now they noose his
neck and burn his leg; they are round him as yelping hounds. He
fights it out and maintains his new self-reliance: 'if it's a poor thing to
be lonesome, its worse, maybe, go mixing with the fools of earth'; he
has learned to speak 'words would raise the top-knot on a poet in a
merchant's town' (III); if Pegeen is lost, he is not; and when he and
his father go off, he asserts his new self-assurance, even over him.
Imagination has won; he ends up lonely, but victorious. So richly do
fantasy and fun play above the depths.

The tragic *Deirdre of the Sorrows* (1910) takes us to a past age, and
impressions of rich and primitive colour. Deirdre prefers simple love
with Naisie to acceptance of King Conchubor's throne; they are
formally married under the blessing of 'sun and moon', 'earth', 'air',
and 'sea' (I); after seven years of love both know that age and
weariness will come, and they return to the King, to meet death.
Fatalism dominates; action is half paralysed; the drama is mainly
verbal till the end, when Deirdre, her love killed, follows him to
death. She thinks back to their union with nature: 'it's many a dark
night among the snipe and plover that you and I were whispering
together'. Now all nature speaks his loss; the moon itself will be
'lonesome', looking for them; and she goes to a 'cold place' to join
him (III). The impressions are dark; and yet somehow love, death,
and nature are felt in close and not all unhappy association. Love has
been, and there will be no failing, nor age.

Synge never interprets the mystery which he so beautifully expresses. His people have superstitious fears, but the dramatic guidance is agnostic. A pagan fatalism counters the Catholic tonings of *Riders to the Sea* (1904). The action is brief and the conception vast: the Sea is our off-stage protagonist, demanding, like Death itself which it serves to symbolize, all old Maurya's sons. It is as unfeeling as Hardy's Immanent Will, yet it and humanity are mysteriously interlocked and the only strength is acceptance: 'They're all gone now, and there isn't anything more the sea can do to me ...' But there is one appearance, unique in Synge, which with full dramatic ratification counters the rest. Maurya sees her last son Bartley riding seawards and leading a pony on which the recently drowned Michael appears 'with fine clothes on him and new shoes on his feet'; and she knows that Bartley is doomed. This once, Synge's world view is invaded by spirit perception.

W. B. Yeats's dramatic world of brief, usually poetic, plays is deliberately concerned with the spiritual. He uses Irish legend in *The Countess Cathleen* (1892) and, with strong national meaning, in *Cathleen ni Houlihan* (1902); and also in the powerful *Deirdre* (1907). The mythical hero Cuchulain, who in *On Baile's Strand* (1904) fights and kills his own unrecognized son, is conceived as a man of free-hearted generosity and heroic strength. Yeats believes in heroism and the supernatural; for him poetry is the right means of approach; and his central dramatic quest looks accordingly for some type of super-hero symbolizing the incarnate imagination.

In *The King's Threshold* (1904) Seanchan, a poet rejected from the council, asserts the rights of poetry against King, State, and Church. He resists passively, refusing food; the King pleads with him, but he remains firm and dies. King and poet each claim to be wielding a power which was the origin of progress and civilization, but Seanchan's claim is the more impressive in that 'those that make rhymes have a power from beyond the world'. He is prophetic, foreseeing a race of supermen:

> The stars had come so near me that I caught
> Their singing. It was praise of that great race
> That would be haughty, mirthful, and white-bodied,
> With a high head, and open hand, and how,
> Laughing, it would take the mastery of the world.

The 'laughing' is Nietzschean (p. 294 above). Seanchan's opposition to society, his curses and final refusal to make terms with the State when it woos his collaboration, follows the stories of Sophocles'

Oedipus and Shakespeare's Timon. Like Oedipus, he dies mysteriously, his weakened frame shattered by 'some strange triumphant
thought'. Love he has renounced for death, telling Fedelm that
otherwise 'the kiss of multitudes in time to come had been the
poorer'. His disciples read his death variously in terms of (i) the
great new race to come and (ii) the hero's passing to another world.

Yeats's most comprehensive dramatic achievement is *The Unicorn
from the Stars* (1908). While polishing a golden coach with an
emblem of Lion and Unicorn young Martin has fallen into a trance
wherein he saw 'white shining riders' on white horses which became
unicorns trampling grapes into wine, and heard a 'command' with
'laughter', recalling the laughing superman of *The King's Threshold*;
but what the command was he forgets. He is told that the Unicorn
symbolizes 'virginal' and 'tireless' strength. Suddenly an exclamation
'Destruction on us all', spoken by a thieving beggar, Johnny, acts as
a release: destruction was the command (i). Aiming to bring men
back to 'the old splendour' of life in contact with 'the wildness
of the clean green earth', Martin joins with the beggars under the
standard of the Unicorn to destroy the Law and the Church (ii).
Enthusiasm rises; there is an orgy of drunkenness; all work stops.
From boyhood Martin has seen the 'shining people', or spirits (i;
ii). The spirits are active, but do not work, enjoying their 'secret
frenzy'; and all great events, he says, are 'begotten in joy' (ii). The
riot of destruction starts. Houses are burned down. Then Martin has
a second trance. On waking he murmurs of

> sweet marvellous music—louder than the trampling of the unicorns;
> far louder, though the mountain is shaking with their feet—high
> joyous music.   (iii.)

It is 'the music of Paradise'. He sees his mistake. Though the music
is made of battle with a 'thousand white unicorns trampling' and
riders with drawn swords clashing, on earth the fight must remain
mental. Only in Paradise will action be free, with yet greater passions
and love, a swifter riding and fiercer battling; there only the Nietzschean gospel is to be realized. There will accordingly be no return to
ancient heroisms; rather we advance, as Timon advances, beyond
sense perception and the extinguished 'sun' and 'moon' to 'nothing'
(as at *Timon of Athens*, v. i); and through Nirvana to 'God' (iii). The
ambivalence of *The King's Threshold* is provisionally clarified.

The Unicorn symbolizes an ideal pervasive in Edwardian drama:
but does it stand for mental or physical action? Is it sexually, as are

Nietzsche's Zarathustra and Davidson's artist (p. 314 above), chaste, or, as Davidson's Mammon, ardent? Like Bernard Shaw, Yeats next approaches his superman ideal through comedy. In *The Player Queen* (1922), the recluse queen is said to be secretly visited by the Unicorn; that is, as Psyche is visited by Eros in the old myth, symbolizing sexual fulfilment without a human partner. Now the drunken poet Septimus is shocked: he will have no scandal said of this noble, religious, milk-white and blue-eyed beast. True, much virtue has made it 'cross-grained', but its character must not be maligned. The Unicorn symbolizes the unity of self-realization and integration, with consequent loneliness: recalling a metaphor applied to Nietzsche's superman (*Thus Spake Zarathustra*, 43) it is imaged as bathing, to music (I). But is this chastity the final wisdom? Septimus is in doubt: 'I announce the end of the Christian era, the coming of a New Dispensation, that of the New Adam, that of the Unicorn; but alas, he is chaste, he hesitates, he hesitates'. It should trample man to death and 'beget a new race', yet its very intoxication is 'cold'. What it most dreads is 'a blow from a knife that has been dipped in the blood of a serpent that died gazing upon an emerald', the words signifying presumably some union of the sensual and the spiritual. Though the Christian era has now ended, the 'machinations of Delphi', the inmost nature of poetic psychology, prevent the Unicorn from becoming the New Adam: it remains a 'violent virginal creature' (II). Here Yeats is within the territory of *When We Dead Awaken*, Nietzsche's Zarathustra, and the castration scene of *The Triumph of Mammon*. He is worrying as to the compulsion of sexual abstinence, already touched in *The King's Threshold*.

Such fiery physical-spiritual intuitions are difficult, and Yeats's drama, apart from a few minor references, has no other important unicorns. Most of his remaining dramatic work is directly spiritualistic. The realization of fairyland in *The Land of Heart's Desire* (1894) was a forecast of both Martyn's *Maeve* and Barrie's *Mary Rose*; *The Shadowy Waters* (1911), driving towards an ideal, mystic, love—a 'unicorn' love perhaps—is strongly and supernaturally atmospheric. In *The Hour-Glass* (1914) an angel comes as messenger from the other world to shatter a rational scepticism. *The Resurrection* (1931) uses an incident from spiritualistic materialization—'the heart of a phantom is beating' [1]—to dramatize the impact of Christ's

---

[1] See A. Norman Jeffares's quotation of Yeats's reference to Sir William Crookes' *Studies in Psychical Research* in *W. B. Yeats, Man and Poet*, 1949, 269; also Virginia Moore's account of Yeats's spiritualistic interests in *The Unicorn*, 1954.

reappearance on contemporary philosophers. There are three grim dramas on earth-bound spirits compelled to relive their former experiences: *The Dreaming of the Bones* (1919), the séance piece *The Words upon the Window Pane* (1934) and *Purgatory* (1939). Use of spiritualism makes possible a compactness otherwise unattainable, as in the Nō dramas of Japan.[1]

Fiercer pulsations throb within the poetic plays of Gordon Bottomley. Though he was himself a Yorkshireman, his strongest work adopts the Scottish scene. He looks for the jagged outline, the human power, and the coloured passion. Like Yeats he moves from legend and folklore through a more human emphasis to spirit plays. But he puts greater reliance on tradition, on already existent superstitions, established legends or real events warm with centuries of human emotion. His two best-known dramas derive from Shakespeare and all are passionate. Action may be violent. Bottomley prefers the ferocities of a barbaric age to the diluted activities of civilization.

In *The Crier by Night* (1900) Celtic superstition and supernature accompany dark passions, cruelty, and murder. *The Riding to Lithend* (1909) is a fierce study of Icelandic heroism. The people in *King Lear's Wife* (1915) are hard. We meet Shakespeare's Lear in middle age. While his neglected queen is dying he engages in an affair with the servant-girl Gormflaith. Goneril is a virgin huntress in love with slaying, who has learned hardness from her father's tyranny. At her mother's death she murders Gormflaith in righteous indignation and determines that the deed's thrill shall guide her life. Perhaps some opportunities are missed, but none are missed in the more colourful, varied, and brilliantly activated *Gruach* (1921). Gruach is a mysterious girl, restive and uncontrollable, a kind of Emily Brontë at home in her wild Scottish setting and its dangers:

> When a fierce bird is beautiful it is then
> More beautiful by its fierceness; and that rare flower
> Is thus more beautiful by its wickedness.
>
> (i.)

On the eve of her marriage to an unloved husband a young messenger from the King, Duncan, asks hospitality. She, dressed in her white and gold wedding gown—ironic colours—faces him. He tells her his name: 'Macbeth' (i). The dark undercurrents of her mind come up in her sleep; she walks and speaks, revealing to him her love. They elope. She, not he, is the controlling force, practical, incisive, ruthless.

[1] See Arthur Waley's *The Nō Plays of Japan*, 1921.

Every twist of psychology, every accent of speech, is weighted with dramatic irony from our knowledge of the future. The recreation of a primitive society and of ancient Scotland and its snow-bound wastes is masterly.

Other Scottish pieces followed in a more spiritualistic vein. Like Yeats, Bottomley took inspiration from the Japanese Nō plays, but he developed the formal elements with a stronger understanding of their Dionysian potentialities, the words of his choric introducers suffusing the action with mesmeric force. In *Towie Castle* (1929) the spirit of Jean Forbes, who had been the victim of an appalling atrocity, has forgotten the agony and does not want to be 'haunted' by the slayer's grief. She can recognize the loyalty which prompted the deed and even half sympathizes with his 'fierce part', and accordingly pardons him. We are told that the deep life of the past, with all its pain and pity, compares favourably with modern vacancy. In the dread but wonderful *Marsaili's Weeping* (1932) a mother whose children have been hideously murdered by a rejected suitor learns through agony to forgive. Behind the criminal action was an insatiable love. So—to transpose a quotation—we are made to feel that

the sickening thing
Which has been done to me, had to be done;

and that 'the final courts of judgement are not seen'. Attaining forgiveness, Marsaili feels her murdered children near and can almost touch them. Their dead uncle's presence is witnessed by a spirit-light on the waters. Again we are warned that the 'unhesitant deeds' of the past, whether light or dark, were part of a 'virtue' and a 'pride' now gone. Bottomley's fearless dramatic thinking illuminates much that is both fine and fierce in Western drama.

Through Bottomley's power we are attuned to a ghostly nature, to sense of old actions clinging pitilessly to their localities and to the undying witness of the dead. We are gripped by emotions of iron, by phantasmal presences and by an eternity transmuting pain.

The Celtic sympathies of the Scot Sir James Barrie were sifted through a more sophisticated intelligence. The peculiar blend of humour, sentiment and irony that made *Quality Street* (1902) and *What Every Woman Knows* (1908), has proved ephemeral, but his fantasies endure. He is at his happiest when turning normality inside out with puckish enjoyment, as in *The Admirable Crichton* (1902), wherein a forced stay on a Pacific island turns a butler into a master, and various aristocrats into his followers and servants. The island is as a magical power revealing values. *Peter Pan* (1904) blends a boy's adventure-reading with fantasy to create a 'Never Land' that has proved an undying joy to Christmas audiences. *Peter Pan* is not only made of fantasy. Its moving spirit-light, Tinker Bell, its levitations, flights, and forming and dissolving objects, are happy developments from the phenomena of Spiritualism: the child-imagination is naturally close to clairvoyance.

The action of *Dear Brutus* (1917) is controlled by Lob, who is Shakespeare's Puck grown old. On Midsummer Eve his garden changes to a magical wood where his guests have a second chance in life. The philosophy has its interest, but more important is the firm realization of the wood and what happens there. Barrie's people never become truly alive until dipped in magic. The wood is a dream, a 'might-have-been' (II), a spirit land; and it is wonderfully convincing. In *Mary Rose* (1920) the magic island of the Outer Hebrides, known as 'The Island that Likes to be Visited' (II), is a spirit land which claims Mary Rose and tragically interrupts her young life. Intimations both sad and gay are in her story and she becomes a pathetically child-like, earth-bound ghost. Her son is found, and she is released, passing to happy music. A strange, pathetic, wistful, half-frightening and half-entrancing story, whimsical and tragical by turns.

Spirit knowledge is generally best when freely moulded and manipulated into art; otherwise colour and warmth may be lost. Once, however, in *A Well-Remembered Voice* (1918), Barrie attacked it more directly, showing a fine skill. A mother gets answers from her son Dick in a séance, and the message 'Love Bade Me Welcome'. The boy's father is a disbeliever, and is visited afterwards by Dick in person, whose general account of life beyond the veil is in line with spiritualistic reports. And yet he knows *nothing whatsoever* about the séance. He explains that personal manifestation is very difficult, and that he only got the necessary pass-word by chance. Asked what it was, he replies: 'Love Bade Me Welcome'. It is a brilliant little study of the mysteries involved.

Barrie enjoys acting like Lob or the host in *Shall We Join the Ladies?* (1921), leaving us to guess. And there is more than guesswork. His finest achievements are in what might be called his 'magical geography'; in his 'Never Land' and wonderful islands and the Midsummer Wood, in Mary Rose's talk to her island trees. These are true, if delicate, creations.

IV

For a nearer and more daylight poetry we turn to two English dramatists: W. W. Gibson and John Masefield.

Gibson's pocket-size playlets in the collection *Daily Bread* (1910) treat of the hazards of workmen in various industries; and one, *The Garret*, the horrors of unemployment. Suffering and death may be accompanied by clairvoyance: in *The Firstborn* a fisherman at sea sees his child who has died on land, in the waves. More gripping is the heightening of the normal to macabre effect, as proletarian heroism is shown contending with the elemental powers of modern industry. Sound, the Dionysian language, may be fearful, as in the ominous junction clashings and express-train thunder of *The Shirt*. The riveter of *The Wound*—'the hammers break a man before his time'—crashes from a girder after nerve strain at home. *The Call* takes us to the engine-room of a fire station. The furnace man dying from burns in *The Furnace* sings deliriously of the monster's red eyes and insatiable greed, always roaring for more food, till in his dreams he becomes again a little child, loving the pretty flames and planning to be a furnace man, and stops moaning, at peace. *Mates* honours the heroic comradeship of miners. In *The Night Shift* a young wife, weak in bed, clairaudiently hears and describes the tappings of her husband lost in the mine, and feels the damp and the stifling, as the taps grow fainter. There is a continual interweaving of domestic, woman's, suffering with the claims of the man's appalling and tragic livelihood. Perhaps nowhere else is proletarian heroism rendered so grimly dramatic nor the Dionysian basis of modern industrialization so vividly apprehended.

Elsewhere Gibson favours atmospheric, sometimes snowbound, nature settings on the border wilds of north England. In *Bloodybush Edge* (1913) bleak nature, ghostly presences and memories of fierce men are the stronger for contrasted reminiscences of warmth and safety in the Old Kent Road of London. *Lovers' Leap* (1924) is a grim study of passion and violence and *Kestrel Edge* (1924) a short drama of gripping suspense on love and murder. Like Bottomley, Gibson can admire masterful passion and instinctive deeds. His best dialogue is rich in colloquial idiom and a strongly localized characterization.

John Masefield dramatizes humanity, spirit power and nature in strong interactivity. *The Camden Wonder* (1907) is a ghastly story of innocence brought to the gallows, and no less grim are the external events of his masterpiece, *The Tragedy of Nan* (1908).[1] Nan is a sensitive country girl in a mean-souled society. Hearing that her father had been hanged for sheep-stealing her lover Dick Gurvil rejects her, but when the authorities discover their error and send money in recompense, Dick's feelings change. Nan, embittered by her father's execution, the miserable payment, Mrs Pargetter's cruelty and her lover's worthlessness, kills Dick and drowns herself in the rising Severn 'Bore', or flood.

Through two acts Nan's lonely suffering accumulates; in the third it overflows. The hideous execution agonizes her memory. Her father was a good singer:

> And that strong man was killed. Sudden. That voice of his'n was choked out with a cord. And there was liars, and thieves, and drunken women, and dirty gentlemen. They all stood in the cold to see that man choked.   (III.)

In recompense she receives 'little yellow rounds of metal'. The contrast between gold and human emotion follows *Timon of Athens*; she is driven to Timon's insight. And yet, as in Shakespeare, there are two golds, metallic and symbolic. Nan's terrible deed is countered by the mutterings rising to ecstasy of the half-crazed old Gaffer, whose mind simultaneously dwells on his own long-dead love and interlocks with Nan's emotions and destiny, to act as a choric voice. He speaks of the flood, driving fishermen's nets with golden flag-flowers and apples 'Beyond Glorster. Beyond 'Artpury':

> NAN: And fish, Gaffer?
> GAFFER: Strange fish. Strange fish out of the sea.
> NAN: Yes, strange fish indeed, Gaffer. A strange fish in the nets
>   tomorrow.   (III.)

He talks of a Gold Rider coming and a horn, and these symbols refer to both his own wandering reminiscences and to Nan's emotional experience:

> The horn. The horn. Gold hoofs beating on the road. They beat like
> the ticking of a 'eart. Soon. Very soon. The golden trump.   (III.)

---

[1] An earlier study of mine on *Nan* appeared in *The New Hyperion*; and see my general 'appreciation' in *John Masefield, O.M.* Both volumes (1950 and 1960) were compiled by Geoffrey Handley-Taylor. The second contains some interesting programme facsimiles of Masefield productions.

Somehow, despite the sordid action, within—or beyond—is a death-conquering triumph:

> Twelve. Twelve. Us rang out a peal at twelve. Angels. Gold angels.
> The devil walks the dark at twelve. Ghosts. Ghosts. Behind the
> white 'eadstones. Smite 'em, gold rider. Smite 'em with thy bright
> sharp spear. (III.)

The Gold Rider is contrasted with 'the devil' and 'ghosts': with evil and death-as-death. Though highly symbolic, the Gaffer's thoughts are nature-rooted, with talk of cows, rabbits, flowers, the 'night-owl laughing in the woods' and the roaring waters. He gives Nan roses for her hair. We remember Synge, but there is a difference. In Synge, nature, even his sea, is passive, enigmatic, withdrawn. Here the Severn Bore is an oncoming power; an agent. So too with the symbolic powers. Yeats's unicorns and heaving battle music were lively enough, but they were distant, remembered from a dream. Here the Gold Rider is felt to be closely engaged.

The last act introduces the symbols; falls back to harsh realization of injustice and avarice; and then surges up, synchronizing the harsh and the golden. It is as a musical composition. Actual music is suggested by the Gaffer's fiddling, Nan's father's singing, the jingle of the coins like 'bells', the nearing horn. Music, symbol, and human emotion—all are of a piece. Symbols of victory are not imposed on the human action but are felt flowering from within. The hoof-beats *are* the heart-beats to which they are compared; the Severn Bore *is* Nan's passion. Everything has a realistic basis: 'You'll hear the horn long before the coach is due' (III). This is far more than a technical trick; it is a way of saying that the otherness is not outside realism, but another dimension of it. This is why symbolic drama such as this has a higher value than the spiritualistic alone. The Gaffer's consciousness is tuned in not to a different world, but to one of greater richness interpenetrating the actual, revealing what is already there, a radio releasing otherwise unheard significances. So he chants of the waters 'a-roaring', the tide 'singing', or murmurs

> There be a music on the sea, a soft music. The ships be troubled at
> the music. (III.)

When Nan, loveless and lonely save for the old man's wild poetry, is about to murder the lover whose miserable soul has shattered her faith in human love, at this very moment the Gaffer glories in an ecstasy of insane, unmoral, Shakespearian knowledge: 'O Love, you be a King. A King'. Its successful blending of humanity, nature and transcendental symbolism in mutual interdependence and interaction within a unified and living universe may be said to lift this third act to Shakespearian status.

With this remarkable use of symbolic action we may compare the equally remarkable use of spirits in *Melloney Holtspur* (1922). Masefield has an exact insight into the relation of the spirit world to humanity; and his semi-dramatic narrative *King Cole* (1921) is a beautiful statement on spirit guidance. Spirit apprehensions are often limited to the vague and enigmatic. Here and in *Melloney Holtspur* the spirits are actively and purposefully engaged, like the symbolic powers of *Nan*, in the human drama.

Melloney had been deeply wronged by her dissolute yet finely tuned artist lover Lonny Copshrews, and after both have died she, now a spirit, takes revenge by causing his misdeeds to be revealed by a human agent to his daughter, so spoiling her hopes of marriage. There are three dramas: the spirit drama, the earth-plane drama, and that which is made of their interaction. Lonny wants the 'old stain washed away' by young happiness (II). But Melloney, together with the Man in Armour functioning as the voice of eternal law, decrees his torment. At the limit Lonny denounces this inhuman law passing on, as in Greek drama, the sufferings of one generation to the next. Atonement comes, not easily, at the end, through Melloney's forgiveness and love. With a beautiful precision Masefield brings to bear on our long dramatic tradition of evil, revenge and judgement, and all its unrestful ghosts, the more exact knowledge today attainable regarding earth-bound spirits and the law of recompense: *Melloney Holtspur* illuminates the *Oresteia* and *Hamlet*. There are weaknesses; the conclusion is not so clear as it might be, yet in the main the realization of spirits in relation to each other, in influencing lives on the earth-plane, or in being seen or heard by them, is done with both spiritualistic knowledge and dramatic mastery. Perhaps most exquisite are the children; not only is child-clairvoyance finely treated, but the talk of children among themselves was never more delightfully rendered.

Masefield's work is innately, though not doctrinally or moralistically, Christian. Of his Christian dramas, *Good Friday* (1916), on Jesus' crucifixion, is the weightiest. Jesus himself does not appear, his personality being created by the opinions of others: Pilate, his wife, Herod, the Jews, and a Centurion. These are very ordinary people, at their ordinary tasks and interests, though experience of the Crucifixion and following earthquake makes of the Centurion's account a

messenger speech of darkly terrifying power. Our real protagonist is
the Madman, once a lord and now a blinded beggar, having suffered
martyrdom for his wisdom. As a personification of tortured insight
throughout the centuries, he functions as both protagonist and
chorus. During the Crucifixion he is on the stage alone to express its
meaning. Wild duck whose 'green necks glitter as they fly' have their
ways, but no sooner does the 'wild' soul of man find its true path
than it meets brutality and torture. Only the brave persist:

> Darkness, come down, cover a brave man's pain,
> Let the bright soul go back to God again.
> Cover that tortured flesh, it only serves
> To hold that thing which other power nerves.
> Darkness, come down, let it be midnight here,
> In the dark night the untroubled soul sings clear.
>   [*It darkens.*]
> I have been scourged, blinded and crucified,
> My blood burns on the stones of every street
> In every town; wherever people meet
> I have been hounded down, in anguish died.
>   [*It darkens.*]
> The creaking door of flesh rolls slowly back;
> Nerve by red nerve the links of living crack,
> Loosing the soul to tread another track.

This must not only be spoken, but acted; the second 'come down'
demands a voice and gesture greater than the first; the Madman
holds, and will raise with dramatic power, a staff or stick. Voice and
facial expression change before 'another track'. And then, the voice
again changing:

> Beyond the pain, beyond the broken clay,
> A glimmering country lies . . .

There the 'golden ones' await to receive the sufferer. There is no
doctrinal emphasis; the conception is earth-rooted, nature-rooted;
and from earth and nature it flowers into the spirit realm. We are at
the heart of Christianity, antecedent to and conditioning dogma.
Subject and impact considered, we can say that no more powerful
stage poetry has been composed in English.[1]

Of Masefield's other dramas *Philip the King* (1914), recalling
Aeschylus' *Persae*, is a penetrating study of Philip's religious
imperialism; metaphysical powers are active in the avenging spirit
voices from those whom Spain has wronged; and the King's acceptance of defeat has a severe beauty. Historic insight combines with

---

[1] See p. ix above.

numinous perception to give the drama grandeur and weight. *The Tragedy of Pompey the Great* (1910) sees Pompey as a man of political wisdom; and *The Faithful* (1915), set in Japan, breathes nobility and courage.

Masefield's later dramas, mostly brief and on religion, have their excellences. The lyrical Christology of *The Coming of Christ* (1928) and *Easter* (1929) possesses a freshness beyond the doctrinal born of the fusion of spirit knowledge with tradition. Especially notable in the convincing simplicity of its dramatization is the hero's arrival beyond death in *A Play of St George* (1948):

> GEORGE: I know not whither I am going . . . I am falling through a great darkness.
> [*Two Gleaming Spirits dance down Right and Left to him, one to each side.*
> THE SPIRITS: We have been sent to guide. Hold fast to us.
> GEORGE: O help. O strength.
> THE SPIRITS: The worst is past. Can you hear the music now?
> GEORGE: I hear. I hear.
> THE SPIRITS: That is the language here. You forget the pain now.

These dramas may show less of the sap and vigour, less urgency, than *Nan* and *Good Friday*. The vision is now captured, tamed rather than tugging. Even so they mark an achievement: from the sordid and the brutal Masefield has advanced through vision to serenity.

V

Our last dramatist is James Elroy Flecker. His *Don Juan* (1911), bringing the old myth to bear on modern life, contains some exquisite poetry, some well-turned prose, and a denunciation of war comparable with James, Galsworthy and Zangwill. Influences from Byron, Wilde and Synge are apparent. Juan is beautiful, unfaithful and enlightened. The alternate rhyming of his duet with Tisbea has charm and strong clear lines:

> Kiss long and deep while guardian overhead
> The noiseless constellations turn and tread.
>
> (I. i.)

His gipsy idyll passes and he is a young lord associating with statesmen. The commercial and militaristic organization of modern society he repudiates, foreseeing 'an avenging socialism' followed by an 'iron' bureaucracy leaving 'little sweetness in the world' (II. ii).

War with Germany is felt to be near, and if it comes 'it will be a long
time before England is merry again' (II. i); and to prevent it he shoots
the Prime Minister (II. ii). His dream is 'a land where beauty and
reason are no longer at strife'. A combination of sexual freedom and
idealism has taught him—Byron-like—'how to live' and thence to
become a universal lover of 'the whole'. Old theology having been
successfully surmounted, he has

> revealed
> A pagan sunrise on a Christian field.
> (II. iii.)

A line that might serve as a text for many of our Edwardian dramas.
More important is *Hassan* (comp. 1913-14; prod. 1922).[1] With less
wild urgency than Masefield's *Nan*, its sophisticated insight, exact
patterning and extraordinary inclusiveness serve to sum our period,
if not our tragic tradition. A vast content is brilliantly, almost
lightly, handled, the more easily for its projection into an exotic
and colourful culture. The high civilization that once ruled from
Morocco to Persia is here admirably re-created: *Hassan* is of those
rare dramas which make an important epoch live. The courts of
oriental potentates were admired and copied by the Italian princes
of the Renaissance, whose culture did so much to inspire our
dramatic tradition. Flecker's imaginative ground is well chosen and
he adds territory since won to enrich the composition.

The story is as follows. A simple, carpet-loving and artistic con-
fectioner, Hassan, is shown enduring *a purgatorial experience*. At a
moment of passionate jealousy at his betrayal by a friend and the
taunts of the desired Yasmin, he gives way to a sadistic fury, threatening whippings and impalings, and falls in a fit by a fountain (I. ii).
On waking he finds himself with the Caliph, whose life he saves from
the revolutionary Rafi. As a court favourite he sees Rafi and Pervaneh
choose one night of love followed by torture and death rather than
the alternative of freedom for the one and the Caliph's harem for the
other. Having angered the Caliph by his outspoken criticisms he is
made to watch the young pair endure their torments, and again faints.
He awakes, again by a fountain (v. i), and with Ishak, the poet, leaves
Baghdad for the Golden Journey to Samarkand.

Judicial torments from Aeschylus (p. 9 above) on, in the
medieval plays, in Marlowe, in Restoration drama, in Sheil and
Davidson, in operas of Colman and Gilbert, have been a recurring

[1] I have published a more detailed study of *Hassan* in *The Wind and the Rain*,
II, iii, Winter, 1944.

dramatic horror. Colman and Gilbert use an oriental setting, as did Wilde in *Salomé*, not merely to distance horror for comedy, but still more to provide richness and colour to correspond to the sadistic fascination; to hook, so to speak, the instincts to be sublimated. 'Agony', says Ishak, 'is a fine colour' (III. iii); and throughout *Hassan* colours are vivid, especially reds for roses, sunset and blood. In 'The Procession of Protracted Death' the victims are 'half naked', and the torture is conveyed by the rich tones of violin music (V. i): the aesthetic and the sadistic are close. Hassan is himself a keen amateur of the arts and the Caliph a connoisseur. Like many a tyrant the Caliph claims to be kindly; he sees himself as performing the natural functions of a ruler and when Hassan is horrified at his cruelty warns him not to 'leave the Garden of Art for the Palace of Action' or concern himself with the tyranny of princes (III. i). The contrast is firm. The Caliph's cruelty is an extension of all official justice: the revolutionary Rafi's threats were originally just as cruel. But Hassan is simple and soft-hearted, and finds that he cannot take his revenge on Yasmin when the chance offers. And what of Ishak? As poet he must observe and record agonies for which 'the exalted Designer of human carpets' (IV. i)—God, or the Caliph as his instrument in weaving the multi-coloured 'carpets' of human happiness and agony (III. iii)—is responsible: 'Thus I corrupt my soul to create—Allah knoweth what—ten little words like rubies glimmering in a row' (IV. i).

Rafi and Pervaneh endure a romantic Calvary, Pervaneh in ecstasy seeing Rafi as transfigured and one with 'the Eternal Lover, the Friend of all the World'; she—for Rafi is no visionary—would suffer so that great nature may endure, the as yet unborn children may conquer, and 'the Trumpeter of Immortality' be not shamed (IV. ii). We are reminded of *The King's Threshold* and the horn in *Nan*. But what is the relation of this 'Eternal Lover' to the Caliph-as-God?

Answers to such insoluble questions can only be shadowed by symbolism. Our two main symbols are: (i) carpets and (ii) fountains. The first symbolizes man's more passive being: his character, his soul pattern, his life story and destiny, objectively viewed. Hassan had at first a loved carpet; next a gaudy one with scarlets and tigers, defiled by the torture; and he finally recovers an 'old' one, presumably the first, with its 'gentle flowers' (I. i; III. ii; V. i). The Caliph's own simple but fine carpet decorations (III. i) correspond to his unified, though cruel, personality and exquisite taste. The fountains, symbolizing man's sexual and biological self, are more dynamic; and what is here most important is the thought of the fountain designed by the Byzantine artist executed by the Caliph's father running with blood (III. i). At the climax this happens. It suddenly 'runs red':

> HASSAN: The fountain—the fountain!
> ISHAK: Oh! alas! it is pouring blood! Come away.
> HASSAN: The Garden is alive!
> ISHAK: Come away: it is haunted! Come away: come away! Follow
> the bells! (v. i.)

The horror is as the horror of the life force, the sexual origins, desecrated by the sadistic; horror springing from the very origins of life. The bells are the bells of the Samarkand caravan.

The disembodied spirits of Rafi and Pervaneh question the ghost of this Byzantine artist as to their future. Their memory, he says, will dissolve; he himself remains near the earth he loved by the fountain which he made, but they, being more spiritual, will be homeless and adrift. He knows nothing of 'justice' or 'reason', only that the wind will come and that they will be cold. The wind, the traditional stage accompaniment of the ghostly,[1] rises. Pervaneh, the stronger of the two in love's idealism and still set on finding the Eternal Lover, calls to Rafi, who can only wail: 'Rafi—Rafi—who was Rafi?' She cries 'Speak to thy love—thy love' (v. i). Is survival proportional to love's faith? The Byzantine's knowledge was only that of an earth-bound ghost and Pervaneh is not actually shown, as is Rafi, as losing her selfhood.

The ghost-wind rises, but it seems now only to be ringing 'more wildly' the bells of the waiting caravan. Here is our final symbolism, the bells and Golden Journey to Samarkand, contrasting with our ghosts, with death-as-death, as the Gold Rider with the Devil and graveyard ghosts in *Nan*. Spiritualism in modern drama is as yet weak: even *Melloney Holtspur* radiates no power comparable to that of *Nan*. Dramatic positives come best through an incarnated and energic realization. The Golden Journey is such a positive, functioning as the Third Person of the Christian Trinity to resolve the dualism of the Caliph-as-God and the Eternal Lover. It is Nietzschean too, corresponding to the golden impressions of *Thus Spake Zarathustra* and to Ibsen's 'I cross the barren desert to be free' in *Love's Comedy* (III). Much of the Edwardian quest, ranging from the fierce insights of

---

[1] This association appears to derive from a psychic fact. Cold airs are sometimes felt at séances. There was a wind at Pentecost.

Davidson through Yeats's Unicorn to Masefield's Gold Rider and subsequent Christian affinities, is covered by Flecker's Samarkand; though it must be admitted that problems of State are left unsolved with the Caliph.

Horror has driven Hassan beyond both sexual and artistic desires and Ishak has broken his lute to leave poetry in praise of kings for the desert and its 'barren' path 'as yellow as the bright seashore' (v. i). Scarlets of love and lust, and all the variegated tints of art, give place to a golden asceticism. It is a state beyond poetry which now becomes, as Ibsen so often wished it to become, action. As pilgrims to the sacred city Hassan and Ishak mix with the caravan merchants. Chant is raised to the rich merchandise covering the arts and pleasures of civilization, and after our hothouse and half-paralysed experiences the Samarkand chorus is keen and astringent, marking purpose and movement. The two pilgrims are in rags. Like Masefield's Madman they are scorned, yet dedicated:

> We are the Pilgrims, master; we shall go
>   Always a little further: it may be
> Beyond that last blue mountain barred with snow,
>   Across that angry or that glimmering sea.

> White on a throne or guarded in a cave
>   There lives a prophet who can understand
> Why men were born: but surely we are brave,
>   Who take the Golden Road to Samarkand.
>   (v. ii.)

'White' and 'throne', images for God in *Don Juan* (III. iii), are contrasted with the darkness of 'cave'; and beyond both is the *golden* journey, undertaken 'for lust of knowing what should not be known'. Human loves, families, girls, and 'Syrian boys' are left behind; beyond art, beyond lust and love, men follow their 'dreams', leaving the 'dim-moon city of delight' to their women.

The poetry's resonance must not be smothered by alien music such as Delius's well-known setting. The gradually distancing camel bells and 'Samarkand' refrain demand careful timing and staging. Given those, we shall receive the music and the vision.

These greater dramas grow from a dramatic soil rich on all levels in warmth and purpose. In the preface to *Scaramouch in Naxos* John Davidson suggested that our drama should look to pantomime for reinvigoration; by which he probably meant beauty, fairy lore and delight, desiring to blend these with weightier themes. In the best stage work of the period this union was achieved. It can be recognized as well in Gordon Craig's theories of atmospheric staging and the aesthetic originalities of Granville-Barker's Shakespearian presentations at the Savoy, as in the spiritualized showmanship of Sir Herbert Beerbohm Tree. Tree was the presiding genius. Under him His Majesty's Theatre became a recognized temple for spacious productions. *Nero*, *Attila*, *The War God*, *King Lear's Daughter* and— after Tree's death—*Hassan* were all staged at His Majesty's. Tree's *Macbeth* opened with the Weird Sisters floating in mid air through driving clouds; and the forum of *Julius Caesar* filled the auditorium with incense. Spectacle and pageantry were elaborate; some of it would seem ill advised today, but not all; and at the best there was a grandeur since lost.

CHAPTER XV

Shaw

When a thing is funny search it for a hidden truth.
Back to Methuselah, v.

I

BERNARD SHAW combines the offices of critic, humorist and
visionary. His thinking may be related economically to Marx,
metaphysically to Goethe and Lamarck, and dramatically to Wagner,
Ibsen and Nietzsche. Nietzsche's works he regards as the Bible of
the modern consciousness (*The Quintessence of Ibsenism*, 1913;
'An Ibsen Theatre'). He is as much Continental as British, his Irish
humour bridging the gap; in terms of humour he engages in a daring
which British audiences would not otherwise have allowed. His
obvious attacks are levelled against middle-class values and professions; doctors and science, politicians and British democracy.
Widowers' Houses (1892) and *Mrs Warren's Profession* (1893)
handle the evils of slums, prostitution and tainted money. *The
Philanderer* (1893) lays the basis of Shaw's advanced sexology. Like
other satirists, he regards self-deception as more dangerous than open
criminality. He has the usual sympathy with energies, with the
satanic, his preface to *On the Rocks* (1933) stating that dangerous
thoughts are allowable though they must be distinguished from the
corresponding *actions*: a helpful comment to students of drama. His
thought varies from satanism, through attacks on hypocrisy, to
religious mysticism: he has strong religious sympathies, and is an
admirer of Bunyan. Comedy, so often limited to the sexual, is
brought by Shaw to bear on the subjects *generally regarded as the
domain of tragedy*: statesmanship and world affairs, wars, and such
great persons as Caesar, Napoleon, and St Joan. His is a large-scale
comedy like Aristophanes'; and like Aristophanes' it touches vision.
Comedy is often our best approach to the mysteries (pp. 13–17 above,
and pp. 391–2 below).

His considered philosophy is evolutionary. He believes in the Life

Force, affirming an optimistic recognition of its miraculous nature as it travails to create a greater humanity, of which certain great men of history are the precursors. Its power is strong in women, who are impelled by it, as *Man and Superman* (1903) shows, to win a husband and bear children. In *Back to Methuselah* (1921), where man is shown gradually evolving towards a spiritualized and immortal being, the personification of the bisexual Life Force is Lilith, a female figure who speaks the epilogue. Women are central powers and man's prided intellect often childish in comparison. Shaw's Life Force corresponds to the Living God of the Bible.

II

Such is the context in which we must understand Shaw's dramatic socialism. Reform is not easy. In *Major Barbara* (1905) the Salvation Army heroine finds that in her work for the poor she is forced to accept assistance from both a whisky magnate and her millionaire father, Undershaft, who has himself created an ideal little society of his own from the proceeds of his armament factory. Shaw has his eyes on the real lines of force, involving money: good and evil do not in practice exist apart from their context, and Undershaft, the great industrialist, has the necessary drive and wealth. Such powers we must respect, expanding the evil into good:

> Yes, through the raising of hell to heaven and of man to God, through the unveiling of an eternal light in the valley of the Shadow.
> (III.)

Advance depends on such men as Undershaft, we need more and not less of them, and the revolutionary who thinks otherwise impedes progress. In 'The Revolutionist's Handbook' appended to *Man and Superman* we are reminded that 'what Caesar, Cromwell and Napoleon could not do with all the physical force and moral prestige of the State in their mighty hands, cannot be done by enthusiastic criminals and lunatics', and that 'whilst Man remains what he is there can be no progress beyond the point already attained' (VII); so 'national Christianity is impossible without a nation of Christs' and 'man' must be replaced by 'superman' (IX). *Back to Methuselah* dramatizes the evolution.

Shaw's dramatic socialism contains strong aristocratic sympathies. The aristocratic connections of so central and admired a person as

Lady Cecily in *Captain Brassbound's Conversion* (1899) are intrinsic to her dramatic stature. In *Misalliance* (1910) democracy and aristocracy are regarded as interdependent. *On the Rocks* delights in relating a modern attempt at 'Platonic communism' to the ruling class, a duke and leading figures of the services and of finance embracing the change while the voices of proletarian socialism reject it. Under the proposed system the police will 'have a status which they feel to be a part of the status of the Duke here' (II): the aim might almost be called a 'royalistic communism'. *The Apple Cart* (1929) is a dramatic essay on aristocratic and royal valuation. King Magnus regards his royal office as a safeguard of the long-range and eternal values as opposed to the politics of ephemerality and expedience (I). As we see him turning the tables on his socialist cabinet we watch a flowering of the great man from its symbol, which is royalty: even the old supposed divinity of kings housed a truth, since man has a 'divine spark' in him (I), and it is this human and divine reality within the political order that the crown symbolizes. The next step is to use the divine spark in actuality. That is the task of the great man, the leader.

This greatness is a matter of integration. Power must be bisexual. In the preface to *Good King Charles's Golden Days* (1939) it is suggested that votes should be given not for the individual but for man-with-woman, called 'a bisexed couple'; or bisexuality may be found or felt within the individual, and perhaps that is why Mrs Basham in this same play is found regretting the use of 'abandoned females' in place of the far more convincing boy actors who 'could make you believe'—as the others could not—'that you were listening to real women'. Shaw regularly counterbalances male traditions by forceful women: as bearer of the life-force woman is an almost impersonal power in *Man and Superman*, and Mrs George in *Getting Married* (1908) is a medium who in trance speaks inspiredly of sexual relations, covering both the female and the male contributions. The more obviously feminine qualities do not exhaust feminine potentiality: Candida in *Candida* (1894) and Lady Cecily in *Captain Brassbound's Conversion* are both natural commanders. Such women intuitively recognize the folly of men: they are always realists and in some sex as such may be surpassed. 'How could I manage people', says Lady Cecily, 'if I had that mad little bit of self left in me? That's my secret' (III). Sexual principles may be fused within the individual and this sexual blend, or integration, has much to do with what we call 'genius'. In *The Philanderer* membership of The Ibsen

Club is limited by the exclusion of any manly man or womanly woman (I). 'All good women' are 'manly' and all 'good men' are 'womanly' (*The Quintessence of Ibsenism*, 'What is the New Element?'). 'Genius' is part-feminine and a poet naturally has the 'temperament' of 'an old maid' (*Man and Superman*, Epistle Dedicatory; also IV).

We accordingly have a number of part-feminine men. The artist Dubedat in *The Doctor's Dilemma* (1906) is 'pretty' but not 'effeminate'; 'a man in his thoughts, a great poet and artist in his dreams, and a child in his ways'; and he is 'one of the men who know what women know' (II; III; V). Such artist types are preferred to the normal appetite-driven and convention-bound man, though women may have the strength either of their sex or of its surmounting, or both. In *Misalliance* the boy Bentley is one of those 'who from seventeen to seventy' preserve the appearance of age in mind and of youth in looks. He is a mixture of emotionalism and insight, an artistic type, contrasted with his brother's normality, and at the conclusion he masters his nervousness to face danger with Lina, the Polish acrobat, a woman of action called 'a man-woman or woman-man', averse from love-making. Bentley, also, will 'never marry'; they follow the thought pattern of *The Philanderer*. Bentley is of similar make to the 'effeminate' (I) yet disturbing eighteen-year-old poet Marchbanks in *Candida*, who renounces his love and realizes his true power and destiny, a 'secret' (III) akin to Lady Cecily's. In *Saint Joan* (1923) we have the saintly heroine in male dress making a man of that beautiful study in querulous non-masculine sensibility, the inadequate yet fascinating Dauphin, the understanding between them as underlined in the Epilogue being one of the most attractive themes in the play. Highly developed types may be older, like the Irish mystic Keegan in *John Bull's Other Island* (1904) and old Captain Shotover in *Heartbreak House* (1916), who has no family emotions, thinks being married 'up to the hilt' is 'hell' and yearns for a land with 'no women', for 'strength' and 'genius' flower from independence (II). Keegan, despite his years, has the face of a young man (II) and the aged Shotover believes in 'youth', 'beauty', and 'novelty' (I). Both have the secret of enduring vitality.

The complications of Shaw's sexology make of his Don Juan in the Interlude in *Man and Superman* (III) what might be called a kind of esoteric justification of Restoration comedy. This Don Juan, descended from Charteris in *The Philanderer*, repudiates marriage vows in terms obliquely reminiscent of Etherege's Dorimant as illogical and impractical, while putting trust in an astringent philosophic quest leading to the superman. The Life Force, he says, impels sexual unions, coming as a sudden invasion from without; but he has no mystique of sexual union: there is just a sudden irruption for the purposes of procreation strangely antithetic to his astringent philosophy. This—we find it again in *You Never Can Tell* (1896; III)—may be unsatisfactory, though in *Getting Married* Mrs George, as spokeswoman of sexual intercourse, does something to right the balance. In contrast to Don Juan the Devil and Hell stand for conventional values and pleasures, for sentiment and romance; for all the more obvious, though superficial, positives. Our various esoteric types are precursors of the Ancients in *Back to Methuselah*.

Integration conditions male leadership. If we are not to be left with the plea advanced at the conclusion to *Too True to be Good* (1931) for the 'woman of action' to solve our difficulties, the female powers and insights of a Lady Cecily must somehow be functioning within the man. Napoleon in *The Man of Destiny* (1895) shows promise and tries to 'act like a woman', but is indecisive and worsted by a woman in boy's dress. King Magnus in *The Apple Cart* is near integration; his wife is now mainly a loved companion and his relations with his dream mistress Orinthia are 'strangely innocent'. He is beyond dangerous desires: 'I never resist temptation, because I have found that things that are bad for me do not tempt me'. Orinthia regards him as either a 'child' or a 'saint', with the 'makings' of a 'woman': 'There is more of you in me than of any other man within my reach. There is more of me in you than of any other woman within your reach' (Interlude).

Our firmest realization of an integrated leader is Caesar in *Caesar and Cleopatra* (1898). He addresses the Sphinx:

> I am he of whose genius you are the symbol: part brute, part woman, and part god—nothing of man in me at all. Have I read your riddle, Sphinx?   (I.)

Though ageing, Caesar has a 'child's heart' (I) and is called 'boyish' (III). He makes friends everywhere, and 'has no hatred in him' (IV). But his unattachment can be maddening: Cleopatra means little to him; at the close he has forgotten her. Like Byron's Sardanapalus and Ibsen's Julian in Gaul—and Magnus who hated death-warrants —he is clemency personified; slaying in hot blood he can forgive but he loathes judicial punishment (V). Clemency he regards as a matter of practical common sense and it is suggested that his views fore-shadow Christ (iv). Shaw is aiming to create a personality in whom *Christ's teaching becomes political wisdom*. Though kindly, Caesar is strong and master of every situation. He is an artist in action. When the aesthete Apollodorus compliments him on being an artist as well as a soldier, the very contrast angers him. Told that Rome produces no art, he replies:

> What! Rome produce no art! Is peace not an art? is war not an art? is government not an art? is civilization not an art? All these we give you in exchange for a few ornaments. You will have the best of the bargain. (v.)

The reply is unanswerable.

Shaw likes soldiers. Bluntschli in *Arms and the Man* (1894) is highly original and Private Meek in *Too True to be Good* is a genius. Soldiers may be associated with religion. The Salvation Army title *Major Barbara* makes a sexual blend which typifies the ideal that gave us Saint Joan. Anthony Anderson in the last act of *The Devil's Disciple* (1897) is a pastor turned soldier, and the relationship of the Roman captain to the Christian Lavinia in *Androcles and the Lion* (1912) is beautifully developed. In Caesar we have hints of that 'soul of Christ' demanded by Nietzsche (p. 297 above). That the treatment is light marks, in Shaw, no lack of purpose: rather the reverse.

The approach may be mystical. In *Getting Married* Mrs George is a woman of promiscuous sexual experiences and also a 'clairvoyant' who speaks poetically in 'trance' of woman's surrender to man and what it does for him. She is a medium, a 'pythoness'; ecclesiastics are doubtful whether to call it demoniac 'possession' or 'the ecstasy of a saint'. She taps the creative powers, as a human analogue to Lilith in *Back to Methuselah*. We first meet Keegan, the Irish patriot-mystic of *John Bull's Other Island*, in a 'trance' by sunset (ii). Though ageing, he has 'the face of a young saint'. He loves all animals, like St Francis, and talks to a Grasshopper (ii) as Caesar talks to the Sphinx. Formerly a Catholic priest, he has since derived wisdom from a dying Hindu who explained earthly suffering to him by the great law of Karma (iv). To him this world seems to be Hell. What he craves is a state where priest and worshipper, work and play, human and divine, are one (iv). Beside Keegan we have Captain Shotover in *Heartbreak House*, whose wisdom is similarly given exotic support; he was once married to a West Indian negress who 'redeemed' him and is said—though he has his own version—to have sold himself to the Devil in Zanzibar, getting in return a 'black witch' for a wife (I; II). He is supposed to possess uncanny powers of divination and clairvoyance (II); he is a man of 'vibrations', 'magnetic' (II), striving to attain 'the seventh degree of concentration' (I). His powers have natural sanction: like Timon, he is averse from humanity and challenges society in the name of vast nature and Heaven's 'dome' as 'the house of God' (I). Man is, or should be, free: 'The wide earth, the high seas, the spacious skies are waiting for you outside' (II). England he sees as being driven on the rocks by crass inefficiency. 'Navigation' alone can save her: 'Learn it and live', he says, 'or leave it and be damned' (III). But he is not himself now a supporter of forceful government (III), his interests having become more purely psychic. When he sees the Church as severed from 'God's open sea' (III), he may mean that it has lost contact with the natural psychic powers, but they exist as strongly as ever and he is labouring to invent a psychic ray as a defence against human iniquity and stupidity; a 'mind ray' able to explode his enemy's ammunition (I), like Prospero's weapon-negating magic. His mind varies from thoughts of destroying his fellow creatures to a dislike of force. He is a figure of *spiritual* force. He is as frightening as Oedipus in the *Oedipus Coloneus*; a 'supernatural old man' (I). In *Heartbreak House* we are on the edge of the numinous and strange psychic forces, of explosions and death. We end with an air-raid, in which each member of the mixed but well-defined community has an allegorical fate. To some the drumming in the sky is Beethoven music; suicidally they make the house lights blaze, embracing danger after paralysis (III). Shotover himself only knew the true intensity of living when risking his life at sea (II). On death's brink we touch life. We are reminded of the mystique of risk and courage in *Misalliance*.

The mystical insights of *Saint Joan* are obvious enough: the miracles, the sense of power, the voices and clairaudience, and best of all the wonderfully composed Epilogue, where Joan's spirit talks to the earth people who are travelling in the astral while their bodies sleep. Joan contains nearly all Shaw's favourite qualities: bisexuality, soldiership, occult powers, saintliness, common sense, efficiency.

The other-worldly metaphysic follows the teaching of Spiritualism. The visual and musical directions to the Don Juan Interlude in *Man and Superman* are exquisite realizations of the etheric dimension; music is used as a language, and the account of Heaven and Hell, where we hear that the state beyond death corresponds so exactly to what we are that Heaven would be no pleasure for one unfit for it, is closely spiritualistic. In *Back to Methuselah* the superman quest is given a cosmic and mystic range. Adam and Eve, like Joan, hear voices. Adam chooses death rather than an unbearable eternity of himself and Eve embraces procreation as an alternative. Cain, prototype of soldiership and force, is given, as in Byron and Ibsen, a case; but man must mature; he must live longer; and we see this happening, in different stages, until at the last we watch him graduating through the artistic intelligence to the stature of the Ancients. The artists are beyond the sexual, and must next, like Ishak in *Hassan*, pass beyond art. The attempt at a living sculpture recalls Shakespeare and Ibsen. The Ancients themselves correspond to Prospero, as Shotover to Timon. They are nearly sexless, the She-Ancient having a man's breast; their life is mental, beyond sex and art and even food and sleep, with mesmeric and magnetic powers corresponding, like Shotover's, to Prospero's magic. Their experience cannot be described except by analogy; telepathy replaces language; they can create and re-create and change their bodies by mental or spiritual power. Though sounding cold it is an 'ecstasy' one moment of which would strike the lower people dead (v). It corresponds point by point to accounts from higher planes in and beyond the etheric as received today through trance mediumship. We are in a world of new sense-powers and 'ears with a longer range of sound than ours' (v). The Ancients refer to the 'astral body' in which earlier men believed and their own destiny is 'to be immortal' in a world not of people but of 'thought', which is 'life eternal' (v). Lilith, the bisexual creative power torn asunder for creation, speaks the Epilogue, recapitulating the whole story from the Fall when man refused 'to live for ever': 'They did terrible things: they embraced death, and said that eternal life was a fable'. So man chose death and mutual slaughter, but through the labours of creation he will at last 'disentangle' his 'life from matter'. This will be the true 'life'; 'and for what may be beyond, the eyesight of Lilith is too short. It is enough that there is a beyond'. This great work is one long concentration on the breaking of the opacity shutting man from the immortality, or eternal life, which is his birthright.

Shaw has used Spiritualism to fill out his evolutionary statement, and we can always ourselves use it, should we so choose, to make sense of superman claims: they, and Ibsen's 'third empire' too, may be unrealizable in this dimension, and point to another. Both processes are rational; more, they converge. For, as Shaw says in his Preface ('The Artist-Prophets'), 'We aspire to a world of prophets and sibyls'.

His aim is never for long limited to the religious or occult. His desire is to blend inspiration with sociology, politics and, above all, with great men. That is why he compares himself to Shakespeare, to awake us to his true message, which exists strongly within the unfurling humanism of Renaissance drama.

III

Shaw's dramas are shot through with comedy. His humour is bright, kindly and exciting. He contrasts with Ibsen in his peculiar forwardness; dramatic revelations from the past do not interest him. He refuses to take old compulsions and clogs seriously: Shotover is angry at one who probes into 'old wounds' (*Heartbreak House*, III) and Caesar would let the race's memories be destroyed and build the future on their ruins (*Caesar and Cleopatra*, II). The trial in *Saint Joan* opposes prophecy in Joan to tradition in the Inquisitor, and tradition, as the Epilogue demonstrates, loses. Jesus, dramatized before Pilate in the preface to *On the Rocks*, is all for newness:

> The beast of prey is not striving to return: the kingdom of God is striving to come. The empire that looks back in terror shall give way to the kingdom that looks forward with hope.

The mysterious 'lady' who visits the Prime Minister in *On the Rocks* (I) introduces herself, by a profoundly Shavian paradox, as a 'ghost' not from the 'past' but from the 'future'. Believing in a beneficent cosmic process Shaw allows scant respect to ingrained evils, to hereditary and ghostly compulsions. What he likes best is to show a false and backward-looking valuation rendered ridiculous by the ever-new and up-bubbling Life Force. True humour derives from the overthrowing of superficialities by the orgiastic, or some derivative in the realm of facts and forces; sex, its usual theme, is as 'sex' only part of Shaw's concern, but his humour obeys the same law, with the Life Force as feminine and cosmic agent.

Vengeful and judicial retaliations are accordingly repudiated, as in *Thus Spake Zarathustra*. The embittered and revengeful Gunner in *Misalliance* is comically bested by one woman and mothered back to sense by another. The avenging pirate in *Captain Brassbound's Conversion* finds his melodramatic outbursts constricted by the trying on of his newly mended coat by his captive Lady Cecily, who has been tidying him up. Here neither the Pirate with his revenge nor later the Judge with his law is allowed respect; both think in terms of retribution and our only trust is in Lady Cecily, whose controlling function recalls Shakespeare's Portia. Shaw pays no respect to horrors. The Crucifixion, symbol of that whole gamut of sin and torture throughout our blackened world which he tends to regard as unnecessary folly, he naturally repudiates, complaining that we have turned Christianity into 'Crosstianity' (Preface to *On the Rocks*). Following Byron and developing the humour of Ibsen in *The Pretenders*, he likewise repudiates that prodigious symbol of retribution, Hell. In *Man and Superman* we are startled to hear from the Devil that anyone can go to Heaven who wishes to, though if we are not fit for it, it will be as boring as classical music to the uninitiated. Laugh after laugh is raised by replacing the traditional by a more spiritualistic eschatology, and much the same happens in the Epilogue to *Saint Joan*. No intellectual argument could disprove the traditional threat of Hell; but humour acts differently; it dissolves it. Whatever our beliefs, we must recognize that, in so far as we respond to the fun, some deeper health in us has already ratified the reversal.

Superficialities of all sorts are overturned, *including many of Shaw's own most cherished allegiances*. The advanced Shavian opinions of Tanner on unmarried love are toppled over at the brilliant climax of the first scene of *Man and Superman* (I). Despite Shaw's Marxist interests, Mrs Tarleton in *Misalliance* takes Gunner's communist terms such as 'capitalist' and 'bourgeoisie' as swearing: 'All right, Chickabiddy: it's not bad language; it's only socialism'. Shaw's humour often appears suicidal. After all the accumulated profundity, bitterness and scorn of Keegan's denunciation of England in *John Bull's Other Island*, the very crassness of Broadbent's typically British impenetrability and capacity for adjustment wins unconditionally with nine words: 'I think these things cannot be said too often' (IV). That is great humour, depth beyond depth. In *Candida* the Christian socialist Morell is a stuffed dummy beside the esoterically conceived Marchbanks, and yet even this, Shaw's inmost and cherished sanctity, the 'secret' of Marchbanks and Candida, does not escape. In *Too True to be Good* Colonel Tallboys speaks to Private Meek, the soldier-genius:

> TALLBOYS: No doubt you are an extraordinary soldier. But have you ever passed the extreme and final test of manly courage?
> MEEK: Which one is that, sir?
> TALLBOYS: Have you ever married?
> MEEK: No, sir.   (III.)

Is the Christian and Nietzschean celibacy to be our highest ideal or not? Is it, after all, a retreat? That 'No, sir' raises as deep a problem of racial destiny as any two words in our drama. Such strokes indicate that Shaw's real message is *in the humour itself*. When in *Androcles and the Lion* we enjoy the muscular Christian convert's shame at having let himself go against the gladiators in the Roman arena instead of turning the other cheek, we recognize that in spite of what we mumble in church we did not want him to restrain himself; we exult in his comic fall from grace; and from that paradox is momentarily born some flaming sight of a Christianity not humble but triumphant.

Nietzsche's Zarathustra insisted on humour as necessary henceforth to the highest wisdom; the conclusion to John Cowper Powys's study *Rabelais* (1948) develops the attendant philosophy and Shaw is our grand exemplar in practice. Keegan's way of 'joking' is 'to tell the truth', for 'every dream is a prophecy' and 'every jest is an earnest in the womb of time' (*John Bull's Other Island*, II; IV). 'When a thing is funny', says the He-Ancient in *Back to Methuselah*, 'search it for a hidden truth' (V).

Such humour startles us into unexpected possibilities which on reflection may be found reasonable. Shaw's dramatic technique throughout relies on startling; comic surprise replaces the tensions, suspense and expectancies of tragedy. In *Misalliance* an aeroplane containing a Polish woman acrobat suddenly crashes into the conservatory of a middle-class Surrey house: nothing could have been more unlikely. *Heartbreak House* is called 'a house of surprises' (I), and they certainly occur; the entry and amazing message of the American ambassador in *The Apple Cart* is a typical example and so is the irruption of a twentieth-century cleric from Rome in the Epilogue to *Saint Joan*. Joan's miraculous powers give us the comic climax to her first scene, though these very same powers raise tears in her third. Shaw's use of humour and surprise is of a piece with his beliefs; all events, natural or miraculous, come from the one Life Force, the normal expressions of life 'ever renewing itself' being a 'continual miracle' (*The Apple Cart*, I). Our dramatic surprises, functioning variously in terms of farce, high comedy, philosophy and the sacred, come from the inexhaustible stores of futurity, and to this we must trust. The humour is never cruel: the laughter raised by the extraordinarily funny incident of the pig in *John Bull's Other Island* only confirms the sensitive Keegan in his belief that our earth itself is Hell (IV). Never in Shaw are man's physical and cosmic instincts degraded, but only, as in Byron's *Don Juan*, his mental follies. Hence our sense of well-being, of a sun dispelling fogs, of a golden quality. Yet there is little of the warmth we feel in O'Casey's humour; Shaw's is rather made of light, it is like mountain air, or the golden asceticism of Flecker's Samarkand; and by its light we see colour.

Shaw's prose style may be bare but his total drama is colourful. Setting and costume may be as important today as was poetry to the Elizabethans, and to read Shaw for his 'ideas' without visualizing his stage directions is like reading Shakespeare in a prose paraphrase for children. Shaw loves contrasting stuffy interiors with the wide-open spaces of God's creation. The sea-captain Shotover and Lina the Polish acrobat both long for open spaces. At a crisis the wise King Magnus deliberately arranges to meet his cabinet out of doors. *Too True to be Good* takes us from neurosis and a sick-room to a north African sea-beach with a coloured pavilion backed by mountains. *The Simpleton of the Western Isles* (1934) is all South Sea expanse, ready for the descent of the Angel of Judgement who after being shot at by a terrified humanity lands safely and proceeds to shake the bullets out of his feathers. Localities are many: Balkan highlands, Moroccan castle, African desert, the Sierra Nevada, tropical jungle (in *Buoyant Billions*; 1947), Hindhead in Surrey. Settings include the Sphinx, a Roman arena, Rheims Cathedral, Covent Garden, The Hague; and there is a wide range of costume. The wise Keegan and Shotover have travelled widely and are associated with warm lands: Jerusalem, India, Zanzibar, Jamaica. Shotover's black wife serves an imaginative purpose; Shaw's religious anti-self gives us *The Adventures of the Black Girl in her Search for God* (1932). This exploitation of geographic colour—not colour for its own sake as in O'Casey—reaches an extreme in the exotic orientalism of *Buoyant Billions*. But colour is not limited to foreign lands: when the action is in England Shaw does his best with terraces, deck-chairs, gardens and views. *Caesar and Cleopatra* is richly inlaid, its directions are little poems: against a 'vivid purple' sky changing to 'pale orange' a colonnade and a vast image of the god Ra show 'darklier and darklier' (IV); and Caesar's ship is 'so gorgeously decorated that it seems to be rigged with flowers' (V). *Heartbreak House* has its first setting designed as the poop of an old-style sailing ship, but for the air-raid we are outside with hammocks lit by 'an electric arc' like 'a moon'. These effects are of man, his civilization and the cosmos; of earth contact as such we find less, though it is finely established by Keegan's talk to the grasshopper and the beautiful direction describing Roscullen (*John Bull's Other Island*, II), where colour is felt in depth. Or we may touch other dimensions, as when in *Man and Superman* (III) the Spanish setting at nightfall melts into an etheric world of violet light and ghostly music. Newton in *Good King Charles's Golden Days* rates above his scientific labours 'the elixir of life, the magic of light and colour, above all, the secret meaning of the Scriptures'. Costumes alone are of an extraordinary richness and variety. The colourlessness of Shaw's prose dialogue acts as a transparency through which we view a wider range of geographic and other colours than has been deployed by any other of our major dramatists.

CHAPTER XVI

Georgian

The world I knew, the world worth living in, vanished in 1914,
and since then we've all existed in a series of vast mad-houses,
shrieking with hate and violence, stinking of death.

J. B. Priestley, *Music at Night*, II.

*Our selection of dramatists is limited to those who achieved maturity
during the years between the two wars.*

I

THE fiery strength active within Edwardian drama broke loose in the
First World War. Dramatically it was a turning-point. After the war
a number of leading actors and actor-managers were gone; the world-
view of authors and public had changed; the age of anxiety had come.
'There's a great gap', said Synge's Pegeen, 'between a gallous story
and a dirty deed'; and the war was, or seemed, little better than that.
Patriotism and heroism were soiled values; cynicism, light or bitter,
was rampant; sexuality despised convention, and nerve strain was a
mark of good sense. Psychology had become public property and the
subconscious mind a recognized power. Jazz revues replaced musical
comedy. In drama the seraphic intuition pales, while the old Adonis
theme of prematurely slaughtered youth comes into its own. Bereave-
ment brings strength to Spiritualism.

John Drinkwater, who had composed poetic dramas of human and
natural violence in *Rebellion* (1914) and *The Storm* (1915), produced
a little masterpiece in *X=O: A Night of the Trojan War* (1917),
driving home the paradox of war. *Abraham Lincoln* (1918), a study
in leadership, gained a striking post-war success:

> Two years of darkness, and this man but grows
> Greater in resolution, more constant in compassion.
> He goes
> The way of dominion in pitiful, high-hearted fashion.
>
> (I. ii.)

355

Lincoln's loneliness is emphasized. Great individuals dominate in *Mary Stuart* (1921), *Oliver Cromwell* (1922), and *Robert E. Lee* (1923). Drinkwater's dramas read as an attempt to preserve faith in greatness.

Four strong dramas study the war and its results. Zangwill's *The Cockpit* (1921) and *The Forcing House* (1922) together, as their titles indicate, show social iniquity and political war-mongering giving place to the terrors of a tyrannic and inefficient communism, the only redeeming power being in the royalty of the young queen, whose goodness nevertheless remains ineffectual. In *The Cockpit* Zangwill maintains his Edwardian flair, but the sequel is laboured. Heavy too are the prolix diagnoses of C. K. Munro in *The Rumour* (1922) and *Progress* (1924), though keen in satiric grip and insight into the trickery and self-deceptions of high policy and big business. Both Zangwill and Munro wrote from direct concern with the war and its aftermath. So did J. Middleton Murry, whose poetic drama *Cinnamon and Angelica* (1920) is notable for a strong development of the Adonis archetype in description of a young soldier's death, together with some scathing satire on an irresponsible press.

Typical of the post-war period were the early plays of Noel Coward. He could draw fun and satire—as did Zangwill in *We Moderns* (1924)—from the newly unashamed sexual freedoms, but he could also delve into the 'Oedipus' psychology of a mother-son relationship in *The Vortex* (1923), dramatize violent passions in *Sirocco* (1927), and survey modern decadences in *Post Mortem* (1930). He was at ease in the new whilst feeling nostalgia for the old. *Cavalcade* (1931) traces the change: 'Something seems to have gone out of all of us, and I'm not sure that I like what's left' (II. x). People dance mechanically to the rhythm of 'Twentieth Century Blues' (III. ii). *Bitter Sweet* (1929) contrasts old melody and romance with the superficiality and cacophony of post-war pleasures. Coward has the right key. The new mode is barbaric. The jungloid and negro basis of popular dance rhythms may be aligned with such ruling influences as the atavistic revelations of Freud, Jung and Frazer's *The Golden Bough*. Typical poems strike similar notes: a grim modernity is related to ancient ritual in T. S. Eliot's *The Waste Land* (1922) and to savagery in Edith Sitwell's *Gold Coast Customs* (1929). At the climax of James Joyce's drama *Exiles* (1918) sexual passion, darkness and summer rain together challenge morality—'no law made by man is sacred against the impulse of passion' (II); and a long dramatic movement within his famous portmanteau novel *Ulysses* (1922) resurrects the dead and upturns the obscene underworld of man's nature to phantasmagoric effect. D. H. Lawrence has his 'dark gods' and in his dignified if laboured drama *David* (1926) tries to see King Saul as their representative (xi, xvi). These movements were not wholly new but the war gave them new impetus. A surface was shattered to reveal territories of the brutal and the irrational, and force their acceptance. Results are fear, and a sense of inward accusation. In the theatre the typifying atmospheric effect is the drum or tom-tom, as ominous as the bell in Gothic drama. As a *summoning* sound it dominates Eugene O'Neill's *The Emperor Jones* (1921).

Though American, O'Neill's play demands a brief comment here. Jones, a westernized Negro who has established his mastery in a southern island, is a man of natural power. He is also a capitalist, profiteering mightily:

> Dere's little stealin' like you does, and dere's big stealin' like I does. For de little stealin' dey gits you in jail soon or late. For de big stealin' dey makes you Emperor and puts you in de Hall o' Fame when you croaks. If dey's one thing I learns in ten years on de Pullman ca's listenin' to de white quality talk, it's dat same fact. (I.)

Though he has been a member 'in good standin' o' de Baptist Church', that makes no difference. 'I'se after de coin, an' I lays my Jesus on de shelf for de time bein'' (i). Jones, though a Negro, may be regarded as typifying Western civilization. The local, aboriginal natives rise against him; their tom-toms are heard, demanding his blood. Trying to escape, he gets lost in the jungle; his various past crimes in America rise before him; abject fear grips him; piece by piece he strips away his clothes; his revolver bullets are used in dispelling the visions; and all the time the insistent tom-toms summon the trapped superman. Finally he is a shivering, naked, savage in distant Africa facing an alligator and a witch-doctor to whom he abases himself. Layer on layer gone, he is at his ancestral origins. Last, his remaining bullet, a silver one, is used on himself. Despite his agonized attempts to escape he has gone in circles and is back at the forest's edge, where the natives await: their mesmeric powers have won. Jones is Western civilization, trying to escape itself, going in circles, brought to judgement; he is a would-be superman reduced in an hour or two to a savage. It is a remarkable drama, compact of colour, sound and mystery.

II

We turn to R. C. Sherriff's *Journey's End* (1928), our greatest modern war play.

The setting is a dug-out near the German lines. The people are a young company commander, Stanhope; his officers; and Mason, the cook. In terms of colloquialisms, snatches of song, humour, peace-time reminiscences, moral laxity, courage and food, their talk distils the life-view of the 1914 war. Characterization has an almost magical life. Osborne, the public-school master of perfect, if rather avuncular, tact and understanding; the lower middle-class Trotter, of blunt sensibility but genuine worth; Hibbert, the cowardly wreck who prefers death to war; young Raleigh fresh from school and as yet unsoiled, whose premature death, in the old Adonis tradition, is actually dramatized; Mason, the cook of Cockney wit; in each, character study flowers into a living personality. There is no social favouritism: there is something ever so slightly wrong about the Colonel's attitude, while Mason at a crisis shows a sensitivity comparable with Osborne's. Through this uncanny rightness realism touches profundity, but such profundity could not have been touched in a different context.

Everything stands out against the war setting in rounded completion, like costumes before a black curtain. Here peace-time interests are automatically revalued. Raleigh's admiration of Osborne's international rugger status leads inevitably to: 'It doesn't make much difference out here' (II. i). But Osborne's playing with his children on leave and Trotter's ''olly'ock' (II. i) stand the test. On his first fateful entry down the dug-out steps the Colonel's 'Spring's coming' (II. ii) does more in its context than a volume of nature odes together with another volume of war satire. Osborne's dialogue with Raleigh when waiting to go on the raid, his unfinished pipe, the ring he leaves for his wife—all have an intensity almost too keen for art. The steps to the trenches are impregnated with violent radiations, more powerful than poetry, or even action. The raid is staged by sound; impacts are inward and Dionysian. Throughout a host of unspoken energies and emotions swarm round each careless remark, so that we have a maximum of photographic realism combined with a maximum of numinous power. The usual tragic process of showing human energies enlocked with some beyond-human antagonist—god, nature-force, or death—which is yet felt deeply to be one with those human energies, is realized here not as a process but as a situation. The tragic mystery is implicit at every moment and all the minute particulars known *sub specie aeternitatis*. It is precisely because the persons are shadowed by death that they are so individualistically alive; the mystery of death points the mystery of personality; death and human personality converge.

The only person fully conscious of this impingement of death on life is the protagonist Stanhope, who exists as a bridge, or medium, between the worlds of daylight existence and war, or death. He is conceived differently from his companions: they are known objectively as 'characters', Stanhope is a spiritual force. In him passion and intellect are less hidden, breaking out and dying down like flickers on a dark horizon, as though the fires in some unseen psychic world had chosen this lonely eminence through which to flare their fantastic eruptions. His behaviour is volcanic. The deeps simultaneously hinted and veiled by the others are in him nakedly apparent, though controlled: his speech should be given a slightly husky voice and a controlled intensity. Realism is preserved by a cause in addition to war strain: drink. Clytemnestra and Pentheus were possessed, Lear mad. Such conceptions touch layers beyond the normal, as though the close in-knitting of psychic forces to the pin-point of sanity obscures those depths where alone the human essence exists; where Osborne, Trotter and the rest are not different, but similar:

> STANHOPE: I envy you, Trotter. Nothing upsets you, does it? You're always the same.
> TROTTER: Always the same, am I? [*He sighs.*] Little you know—
> (III. ii.)

It is magnificently true. We do *not* know, and the mystery of a Trotter goes as deep as the mystery of Hamlet. Hamlet is a voice for it, that is all, and so is Stanhope. He is himself conscious of the fear that makes of Hibbert a nervous wreck:

> STANHOPE: I know what you feel, Hibbert. I've known all along—
> HIBBERT: How *can* you know?
> STANHOPE: Because I feel the same—exactly the same! Every little noise up there makes me feel—just as you feel. (II. ii.)

He is a generalized personification of British manhood in war: 'Other men come over here and go home again ill, and young Stanhope goes on sticking it, month in, month out' (I). He is mankind engaged in ruthless and brutal slaughter; in hourly terror of death;

in strength of will nerving itself to bear its agony in service to a blind yet demanding purpose. Stanhope is Europe crucified.

He is already close to death: 'It can't be very lonely there—with all those fellows. Sometimes I think it's lonelier here' (II. ii). His mind-state is that described by the returned spirit in Barrie's *A Well-Remembered Voice*: 'When one has been at the Front for a bit, you can't think how thin the veil seems to get'. Stanhope discusses himself with Osborne:

> STANHOPE: Whenever I look at anything nowadays I see right through it. Looking at you now, there's your uniform—your jersey—shirt—vest—then beyond that—
> OSBORNE: Let's talk about something else—croquet, or the war.
> STANHOPE: [*laughing*]. Sorry! It's a habit that's grown on me lately —to look right through things, and on and on—till I get frightened and stop.
> OSBORNE: I suppose everybody out here—*feels* more keenly.
> STANHOPE: I hope so. I wondered if there was anything wrong with me. D'you ever get a sudden feeling that everything's going farther and farther away—till you're the only thing in the world—and then the world begins going away—until you're the only thing in— in the universe—and you struggle to get back—and can't?   (II. i.)

The experience, which is a kind of clairvoyance, resembles that recorded in one of J. B. Priestley's dramas: 'When we were face to face with the great reality of Death, everything seemed to be part of an illusion' (*People at Sea*, 1937; I). Stanhope describes how the feeling came over him at dawn:

> I was looking across at the Boche trenches and right beyond—not a sound or a soul; just an enormous plain, all churned up like a sea that's got muddier and muddier till it's so stiff that it can't move. You could have heard a pin drop in the quiet; yet you knew thou-sands of guns were hidden there, all ready cleaned and oiled— millions of bullets lying in pouches—thousands of Germans waiting and thinking. Then gradually, that feeling came—   (II. i.)

Osborne brings him back with:

> I never knew the sun could rise in so many ways till I came out here. Green, and pink, and red, and blue, and grey. Extraordinary, isn't it?   (II. i.)

But there can be no real return: Stanhope has gone too far.

War overstands the drama like the curse on the House of Atreus or the Ghost in *Hamlet*, fearful and fascinating. The exquisite directions make it a living presence. We hear the rattle of machine-guns, the whine and crash of shells, the deep boom of distant artillery.

Through the dug-out opening we see the red and green of rockets, the steel-blue and grey of Very lights, intermixing with the cosmic lights of stars and moon; or there is bright sun; and at the climax a rosy dawn awakening to an 'angry red' (III. iii). The dug-out opening acts as an opening into another dimension. The terrified Hibbert in his misery would prefer death; it is the half way, the uncertainty, the tone quality of war, which he cannot stand. But Stanhope is obsessed by war; it alone wakes his efficiency; it owns him. The death of Raleigh, whose sister awaits Stanhope in England, cuts the last thread. This is right, for he is marked out for another and a mightier whom he loathes yet loves, and whose immensity and terror are his destined mate.

The tragic dramatist's business is to stage some convincing objectification of the agonies, fears and insights which we all experience, and never had a dramatist one more communally convincing than this. No heroic drama in our tradition has so convincingly shown us real courage, as well in the German prisoner, even in Hibbert, as in the rest. The appeal outspaces war. Stanhope's words about 'sticking it because they know it's the only thing a decent man can do' (II. ii) and his 'You think I don't care. . . . To forget, you little fool—to forget!' (III. ii), need be limited to no particular time or place. True, the setting is unique and the dug-out a death trap, but then life itself is, at its best, no more. As students of tragedy we make that our start, searching for a further revelation; and among the most powerful of such revelations *Journey's End* is likely, as the years pass, to hold its own.

Of our other war plays J. R. Ackerley's *The Prisoners of War* (1925), on a group of officers interned in Switzerland, is a powerful study in nerve strain. An older man suffers from a passionate attachment to a younger and ends in mental collapse, projecting his thwarted emotions on a plant. Reginald Berkeley's *The White Château* (1927) has a strong first act on the German invasion of Flanders.

The First World War stimulated studies of war, the most profoundly universal dramatic example being probably Laurence Binyon's *Boadicea* (1926), viewing its action as part of the eternal conflict of the will to civilized order and the frenzied instinct—'the wild religions of the world are born of this force' (VI)—for freedom, explicitly reading history from the contesting principles, *male* and *female* (VII), basic to dramatic art. Situations are strong, the poetry loaded, and the conception profound. Roman-Britain also gave us

H. F. Rubinstein's *Britannia Calling* (1930) and, after the Second World War, Gordon Daviot's *Valerius* (pub. 1953) and R. C. Sherriff's *The Long Sunset* (1955).

III

In this period the demarcation between prose and poetic drama means little: our poetic dramatists strive for colloquial idiom and engage freely in doggerel rhyme, as well as chorus work, dance, and anything else that comes to hand. We shall discuss some leading writers who have brought poetic insight to the contemporary consciousness.

T. S. Eliot has been for long an accepted voice for contemporary anxieties. His poem *The Waste Land* (1922) has dramatic quality of a high order, not only in dialogue and character creation but in tone of voice: 'I will show you fear in a handful of dust' (i). Sexual instinct, with water as its symbol, is regarded as an ultimate threat: 'Fear death by water' (i). Advance is through desert and fire to religious grace, as rain. The only explicit religious commitment is conveyed by a use of Sanskrit quotations (v) to denote a spiritual mastery corresponding presumably to the bisexual Tiresias, in whose consciousness, as the author's note informs us, the poem's various sexual engagements are contained: 'the two sexes meet in Tiresias'. Eliot's first drama is *Sweeney Agonistes* (1932), composed of two 'fragments', using a mixture of modern colloquialism and jazzy rhythms for a comically satiric critique of south-sea romance on a 'crocodile' island. Sexual desire is identified with cannibalism; modern jazz life, sex life, all the barbaric tom-tom beats, are repudiated; on this plane we are left with nothing better than 'birth and copulation and death' (ii). The references to cannibalism have point, since sexual desire is here voracious. Sweeney, our main speaker, ends in maudlin half-drunkenness, narrating, or confessing, a sex murder:

> I knew a man once did a girl in
> Any man might do a girl in
> Any man has to, needs to, wants to
> Once in a lifetime, do a girl in. (ii.)

This recalls Davidson's Mammon on torture:

> First, I must torture some one ere I die:
> The thing possesses me; and once for all
> I'll have it done and out of me.
> (*The Message of Mammon*, iii. i.)

The same psychological compulsion is being expressed. *Sweeney Agonistes* concludes with a nightmarish chorus in terror of execution: 'And you wait for a knock and the turning of a lock for you know the hangman's waiting for you'. This playlet is dynamite.

The Family Reunion (1939) is its sequel. *Sweeney Agonistes* bears as its text Orestes' words on the Furies or Eumenides, in Aeschylus' *Choephoroe*: 'You don't see them, you don't—but *I* see them: they are hunting me down, I must move on'. Our new hero Harry uses the same words: 'Look there! Can't you see them? *You* don't see them, but I see them . . .' (I. i). They actually appear. We are to watch the 'moving on'.

Harry has returned to his ancestral home Wishwood in a state of neurotic obsession, thinking that he has murdered his wife, who fell overboard from a liner: whether he did or not is not established or important, since we are concerned, as in Byron's *Manfred*, only with his soul-state. The drama is on the Gothic pattern: we have the past, mysterious, crime; the guilt; the ancestral home, with its 'spectres' and grounds going 'to rack and ruin'; and Harry on his travels 'jostled by ghosts' (I. i). His trouble is deeper than 'conscience'; he knows himself contaminated in a 'diseased' world (I. i). And now, coming home, he feels the haunting presences nearer (I. i). So do we, through a strongly evocative poetry:

> That apprehension deeper than all sense,
> Deeper than the sense of smell, but like a smell
> From another world . . .
>
> (I. ii.)

We watch his penetration of the horror, his living into it, and its reversal. Causes are analysed. His aunt tells him that his father hated and wished to murder his mother (II. ii), and he remembers his mother's possessiveness (II. i). The old 'Oedipus' complex is at work. But precise causes do not matter; all we want is some sense of the evil being implanted and general, perhaps ancestral or perhaps going back to yet deeper origins, the hero's life being no 'isolated ruin' and rather 'part of some huge disaster' and 'monstrous mistake' (II. i). Gradually he wins release; his personal 'prison' becomes a public 'liberty' (II. ii). The Furies appear, but now *outside* him, objectified; now instead of running away he will 'pursue'. With them he will be 'safe', for they have become their opposite: 'I must follow the bright angels' (II. ii).

The victory is not given a Christian formulation; comedy is made from attempts at a Christian interpretation (II. iii) and Harry knowingly risks and presumably causes his mother's death from heart failure in order to further his quest of personal integration. The sublimation dramatized we do better to relate to the golden 'kalon' of Byron's *Manfred* (p. 233 above) or to Flecker's Golden Journey in *Hassan*. Eliot has pointed more exactly than any earlier dramatist the meaning of our many dramatic horrors: their substance is *potentially angelic*. This is the Nietzschean doctrine in *Thus Spake Zarathustra*: 'Thou goest thy way of greatness: now is that become thy final refuge which hath been hitherto thine extremest peril': in Nietzsche too 'devils' become 'angels' (p. 295 above).

So consciously possessed a wisdom does not lend itself easily to drama, and the play has its weaknesses. The sudden appearance of the Furies is not dramatically strutted, self-communing tends to replace action, and there is little colour:

> The bright colour fades
> Together with the unrecapturable emotion,
> The glow upon the world, that never found its object;
> And the eye adjusts itself to a twilight.
>
> (I. ii.)

Release is won, slowly, painfully and inwardly. But the victory is not fully exploited elsewhere. Eliot's best humanistic and Nietzschean insight occurred in a lonely and fascinating six-line glimpse in the short poem *Triumphal March* (1931). Perhaps the only full imaginative affirmation in this period of the flowering of bright from dark power occurs in Francis Berry's poetic narratives, *Fall of a Tower* (1943) and *Murdoch* (1947).

Beside the quotation from Aeschylus in *Sweeney Agonistes* was one from St John of the Cross: 'Hence the soul cannot be possessed of the divine union, until it has divested itself of the love of created beings'. Eliot has two distinct directions: humanist and religious. Before *The Family Reunion* he had written *The Rock* (1934) and *Murder in the Cathedral* (1935), both severely orthodox. *The Rock*, a pageant revue on contemporary society in relation to the Church, is chiefly notable for the poetry of its choruses warning us that our demure respectability hides 'the tooth of the dog' and 'the talon of the cat', and culminating in a marvellous invocation to Light.

Murder in the Cathedral dramatizes Becket as a type of Christian heroism conquering pride and attaining martyrdom. As in *The Family Reunion* the dramatic conflict is almost wholly within the hero, at times almost as a monologue, and we must not expect a contribution to our dramas of Church and State on the lines of Tennyson's *Becket*. Becket's murderers are, it is true, allowed a strongish defence in a modernized idiom sparking off a genuine and sympathetic humour, and this might have established a valuable comoedic relation were the effect not subsequently spoilt by an arbitrary attempt to twist humour into ridicule. *Murder in the Cathedral* is a devotional morality and as such must be received: at its heart is a sermon. But it is no ordinary morality. Lines are spoken from a Dantesque over-view, knowing and fore-knowing events as from the eternal dimension. It is a drama beyond drama written as from within the spiritual self-conflict of a saint, at a far remove from normal experience. A heavy responsibility falls accordingly on the Chorus, needed to link the action to the audience. The Chorus expresses twentieth-century fears in a world sliding to irreligion. In the past there was always hope, but now 'a new terror has soiled us', the terror of nature unredeemed, of animality, of romantic vision which cheats and degrades with

> Rings of light coiling downwards, descending
> To the horror of the ape.
>
> (II.)

And beyond that, the void. The terror is mingled with disgust, like Harry's 'What matters is the filthiness' in *The Family Reunion* (II. i). The Chorus's 'sickly smell' (I) and 'I have smelt them, the death-bringers' (II) resemble Harry's 'smell from another world' (p. 363 above). We establish this important conclusion: what is common to Eliot's religious and humanistic dramatic poetry is a certain territory of fear and horror related to sinful instinct and dark presences. This fear is reversed by Harry's sublimation and by Becket's martyrdom; by the Nietzschean and by the Christian ways respectively.

Of Eliot's later dramas the most important is *The Cocktail Party* (1949), which represents a convergence of his humanistic and religious directions. Much depends on Sir Henry Harcourt-Reilly, functioning as a central authority made from a composite of modern psychology and traditional priestcraft. The attempted fusion fails: what was common to the two earlier dramas lay within the realm of the numinous and the occult, *and only in such terms can dogma and science today be reconciled*. Now Sir Henry does not house these powers. He has no such aura of mystery as had the Stranger in Jerome K. Jerome's *The Passing of the Third Floor Back* (1910). Once, too late, he asserts clairvoyant gifts (III); for the rest, despite his intellect, he is made from the joining of externals. On the psychological level we have an incisive study of neurosis, Celia's confessional speeches (II) are superb writing, and the balancing of marriage contentment against heroic martyrdom rings true. But the general tone remains didactic; we are told more than we are made to experience; and the teaching is the less dramatically authoritative from the absence of Dionysian power where the actual opens to the unseen. Such a criticism could not be made against Eliot's poetry. The poetic wisdom of the *Four Quartets* (1944) possesses an authenticity to which the later dramas, as dramas, only intermittently correspond.

Eliot's awareness of the more brutal instincts grows from a contemporary poetic soil. Gordon Bottomley's plays contrast the virile brutalities of the past with the effete dilutions of modern civilization (p. 328 above). Lascelles Abercrombie is no less macabre. He has a strong sense of the sadistic, together with other twisted and dangerous passions. In *The End of the World* (1922) destruction is expected from a comet; the scorching horror is grimly realized, and its implications driven home. One hitherto morally minded person derives consolation now only from the memory of certain lascivious and daring thoughts, though he never put them into practice. Another meditates on his acceptance hitherto of the good-and-evil basic to existence in trust that it pointed to 'wonders' ahead for which man could strive, so helping nature 'towards its masterpiece'; and now this Nietzschean hope is to be shattered by a meaningless annihilation (II). *Phoenix* (1923) develops a longer action, showing fierce sexual passions in strong antagonism.

Yet another variation on dangerous instinct comes in the Passion Play at the heart of John Cowper Powys's *A Glastonbury Romance* (1933). Though described within a novel, its dramatic importance is great. For here, working from a basis of no particular religious allegiance, Powys instinctively drives his central interest in the sadistic to a Christianized climax. Mr Evans is a mild man intermittently afflicted by a murderous obsession; and it is probable that no such profound study of human evil exists in our, or perhaps any, literature. In order to come to terms with this obsession Mr Evans elects to act the part of Christ, and whilst he is on the cross the deepest issues of pain and evil are fought out. *A Glastonbury Romance* sends a shaft of light down our whole dramatic tradition, including the Crucifixion itself as a symbolic power throughout the centuries for the exorcising of this particular demon.

W. H. Auden is less sombre; he prefers to work from the surface; but he is not superficial. He writes from what might be called the 'newspaper' consciousness, with a wide command of modern idiom and slang, but it is all used with cunning overtones and a probing irony. His brief impressionistic drama *The Dance of Death* (1933) acts out a progress from sun-bathing to a half-hearted attempt at a specifically British brand of social revolution, followed by a return to nature and an attempt at mysticism leading to an ironical conclusion at the entry of Karl Marx, who knows 'the economic reasons for our acts'. It is a gripping little piece: drums, music and dance contribute. *The Dog beneath the Skin* (1935), written in collaboration with Christopher Isherwood, is an expanded satire on contemporary European and British civilization covering, among much else, callous State executions, brothels catering for abnormal sexuality, night-club exhibitionism, and the desecration of classic art; also a lunatic asylum, used for satire as in *Peer Gynt*. The doggerel verse can simultaneously amuse and sting, as when a court lady plays a new variation on the Adonis archetype when commenting on an executed revolutionary:

> He can't have been more than nineteen, I should say.
> He must have been full of Vitamin A.
>
> (I. iv.)

The village community of Pressan Ambo in England is amusingly handled. The hero, Francis, finally denounces everyone. Hitherto disguised as a dog, he throws off the disguise and the others become animals instead. Francis prophesies a country

> Where grace may grow outward and be given praise
> Beauty and virtue be vivid there.
>
> (Epilogue.)

The action throughout is interspersed with serious sermon-choruses pointing the manifold psychological inadequacies of us all, as when we are found 'reading the reports of trials, flushed at the downfall of a fellow creature'. Means of escape, including political programmes, are exposed; regeneration must come from within; we are told to 'repent', 'unite', and 'act' (after II. iv).

Clearly, much depends on enlightened leaders like Francis, and in *The Ascent of F6* (1936) our collaborators study leadership and the great man. Michael Ransom is disillusioned; being both 'scholar and man of action' (I. iii) he engages in the innocuous heroism of mountain-climbing, in which he shows his genius for leadership.

Urged by his statesman brother Sir James to attempt the climbing of the demon-haunted mountain F6 for international and imperial reasons, he refuses until his mother, functioning like Volumnia in *Coriolanus*, persuades him. On the slopes of F6 is a monastery of Tibetan sort; the monks' chanting acts like the tom-toms in *The Emperor Jones*, as a numinous threat; a crystal 'which glows faintly with a bluish light' (II. i) is brought by the Abbot. In this crystal each sees his unadmitted tendencies:

> Nothing is revealed but what we have hidden from our selves; the treasure we have buried and accursed.   (II. i.)

The Demon is said to be a 'gnashing accusation'. For Ransom the danger lies in the temptation to exploit his genius for leadership. Even though it be his aim to help a suffering humanity, such secular power acts in terms of 'the human will' which is from the Demon, and the Abbot counsels a 'complete abnegation'. But, while recognizing his personal failure (II. i) and accusing himself of 'pride' (II. ii), Ransom goes ahead. Three of the party die during the ascent. He reaches the summit, whereon is a veiled figure.

The action becomes symbolical, all the people reappearing. The Abbot retracts his diagnosis and instead accuses the veiled figure, which is now revealed as Ransom's mother who, after the rest have dissolved, sings a baby lullaby, recalling the conclusion to *Peer Gynt* and perhaps also the Madonna, to the Chorus's comment that 'Love' is 'greater than all' (II. v). Finally Ransom is dead, alone, on the summit. Temptations of power were superficial: the 'Oedipus complex', so often supposed a constituent to genius, has been the true motive. Our key is accordingly psychological. And in a more general way the mountain itself, the mysterious monastery, and the nerve strain, reminiscent of *Journey's End*, in Ransom's party, all make strong drama. Mountains have for long been off-stage, or subsidiary, powers and here at last one takes on a protagonist importance. *The Ascent of F6* has significance beyond Auden's psychological satire and sermons through its involvement in matters of heroism, vast nature, and the occult.

Stephen Spender's *Trial of a Judge* (1938) takes us to Germany. The Judge is made by political pressure to reverse the sentence he has pronounced on Fascist or Nazi troopers for their murder of a Jew, while some Communists far less guilty remain condemned: so 'justice is murdered' (III). The Judge sees brutality ascendant, and cannot stop it. He is soon himself arbitrarily tried and condemned, knowing that all he believes in is crumbling. Sympathy goes both to him and to the Communists, who die bravely for the future without expecting personal honour. But we recognize that the Judge is weak and that the Communists themselves aim at an equally violent revolution. The various issues are faced and intricately discussed. The Judge ends in a half-mystic state, rejecting all thought of force as merely the 'stupid opposite' (v) of what is hated, and at a high moment his suffering blossoms 'in a single flower of fire' (v) to a recognition of universal good. However, we are aware of brutality victorious; more, it has dramatic compulsion and stature; the Fascists alone radiate power. Drum-beats are continual, a summoning threat which the Judge recognizes:

> Always through my life I heard
> Behind the music of the summer hills
> The measuring distance of a drum.
>
> (v.)

The Fascist troop-leader contrasts his party's life-power backed by a people's will with the Judge's belief in an abstract justice which is merely part of his personal 'mental pattern' (v). He and his generation have been irresponsible; the power they have neglected to use has gone to those who have the will to revivify and guard the nation. Nor will they stop there, but finally 'burst over Europe as a bomb' (v). The threat is impressive; brutality rises as a force of nature, a Dionysian upthrust hitherto suppressed, for which the Judge shares responsibility; its symbol is the drum.

The movement is a little heavy and weighted by argument, but it is a State drama, demanding contrapuntal discussion. The verse varies, often too congested for public speaking though on occasion detonating:

> Your clever bullets which streamed through him
> Put out the universe where it hung in his mind
> And future time.
>
> (III.)

What comes across most is the appalling power being unleashed and rampant. The Red prisoners can only whisper of freedom and peace to come. Three loud drum taps bring down the curtain. As a document of its time *Trial of a Judge* is impressive, and its challenge is universal.

Communist revolution is given a firm declaration in C. Day Lewis's *Noah and the Waters* (1936). The point by point correspondences of flood and revolution are well maintained, at least for the literary understanding, though an audience's appreciation might be harder to win. However, this unpretentious little morality fulfils its purpose, standing out with honour from the dearth of successful Communist drama in contemporary Britain.

Among these inter-war dramatic diagnoses the most clear statement is also the most traditional: Clemence Dane's *Adam's Opera* (1928). Many of our recent themes are contained and something added: royalty.

She had already written *Will Shakespeare* (1921), a poetic study of Shakespeare and Elizabeth I in mutual relationship and joint dedication to England. The Queen expects from Shakespeare, who is caught in the trammels of a passionate love, a self-surmounting, for England's sake, like her own:

> I know the flesh is sweetest, when all's said,
> And summer's heyday and the love of men:
> I know well what I lose. I'm head of the Church
> And stoop my neck on Sunday—to what Christ?
> The God of little children? I have none.
> The God of love? What love has come to me?
> The God upon His ass? I am not meek,
> Nor is he meek, the stallion that I ride,
> The great white horse of England.
>
> (IV.)

She bows rather to the courage of Jesus, the 'man', in the style of Masefield's *Good Friday*. So she demands from Shakespeare a dedicated life of austere labour, however great the burden:

> Carry it!
> Or, if you choose, flinch, weaken, and fall down,
> Lie flat and howl and let the ones that love you
> (Not burdened less) half carry it and you!
>
> (IV.)

As for reward she offers none; she believes in nothing beyond death; even love ends. But her words rouse Shakespeare to a less agnostic faith and to the service of Love as God, or God as Love, in terms of suffering. His greater dramas are envisioned. Not only does *Will Shakespeare* contain poetry of Elizabethan freshness; it offers a humanistic guidance absent from our other dramas. This comes from the standpoint taken: the acceptance of royalty as above, yet counselling, the poet, who nevertheless may see a little deeper; together with a fusion of State and Church in terms of courage.

After three centuries of experiment we find our best answer given in Elizabethan and Shakespearian terms.

Our understanding of *Adam's Opera* will be helped by recognition of Clemence Dane's true strength, which could be defined as a variation of the bisexual. The Queen in *Will Shakespeare* is superhumanly strong and in the later study of Elizabeth and Essex, *The Lion and the Unicorn* (1943), she 'has the heart of a man, not a woman' (I. i). So too Emily Brontë in *Wild Decembers* (1932) has the mind of a great 'navigator' or 'discoverer' and 'thinks like a man' (I. ii). Though *Adam's Opera* is highly symbolic, and built round a fairy story, it is born less from fancy than from realism and from strength.

Adam's Opera (1928) is a comprehensive reading from a view similar to Zaı gwill's and Munro's of post-war Britain after the apparent failure of President Wilson's world idealism. Adam represents modern idealism: supported by Tom Tiddler for capitalism and Tom Fiddler for the arts, he searches for, finds and awakes the Sleeping Beauty; marries her, and is crowned. Next his eye is deflected from the one Vision by the drag of human selfishness and greed; he is worn out; his followers hound him down and he dies a martyr. Tom Tiddler is installed as president; he and his supporters grow drowsy; Beauty returns to her slumber. In her child by Adam, Eros, there remains a hope.

Much is done through chorus work and other songs of simple and popular rhythms such as Auden uses, often directly drawn from nursery rhymes and folk tradition, particularly effective in choruses by 'They', or the community, to suggest the confusions and mechanical responses of crowd psychology. A recurring refrain is 'We do as we're told'. There is no simple diagnosis in terms of social or political systems. The satire is directed on humanity itself, its inertia and selfishness. Men have their opportunity: 'I gave you the kingdom and the glory' (II), but it is rejected. All three political parties, Conservative, Liberal and Socialist, fail to realize what is happening; they play a card game punctuated by 'Grab, grab, grab' (II). Tom Tiddler thinks only of profit and opposes innovations which endanger the activities of the civil service, big business, armament factories and political agitators (II). Post-war art is mercilessly described in the direction to Act II; Tom Fiddler's portrait of Beauty is unrecognizable (II). Ladies' fashions and society chatter are mocked in a satire resembling Coward's in *Bitter Sweet* and *Cavalcade*.

The ideal, or vision, is one of world brotherhood. Beauty's kingdom involves a free-hearted opening up of resources and removal of barriers, a letting in of 'fresh air', a world treaty, a 'heaven-on-earth' (II). The child's name 'Eros' is chosen to preserve the romantic magic, or thrill, and to avoid a decadent religiosity: to the annoyance of Mrs Grundy, who would have preferred the name Love, it was born not on a Sunday but a Friday. Its nurse is Mother Earth, to whom as guardian Adam gives it, angering Beauty by his recognition that its time has not yet come: 'God himself cannot make him come again before his time' (II). For Adam has endured a Timon-like disillusion:

> I do not know friends from foes, Tom Fiddler! Woe's me, I had no foes a year ago. Is this the rat's work also? Has he gnawed away my faith? Who of you are my friends? Who are my foes? Are you one, old friend? Will you too sell Beauty for gold?   (II.)

At his martyrdom by the yapping crowd Beauty, angered by his inability to put her first beyond all social and international claims and by his subsequent parting with their child, throws the first stone and kills him. Tom Tiddler's attitude is that of the knights in *Murder in the Cathedral*: 'You know, I'm cut up about all this. He was a good fellow in his blind, blundering way' (II). The martyrdom, regarded here (I) as the normal reward of the visionary in action, recalls the Madman's speech in *Good Friday*.

When twentieth-century scepticism in Tom Tiddler rejects the vision as outside common sense and reason, Tom Fiddler tells him that 'your reason is my devil' (II). But, as in *Will Shakespeare*, more than poetry is involved; though Tom Fiddler as artist has worked and starved (I) for the vision of Beauty, Adam, the active visionary, is his master and 'leader' (II), and the symbol of such mastery is inevitably the crown, though it may be a crown of a new kind. Adam is given by Beauty a crown of briars and roses and a sceptre of lilies, and kingship is thenceforward emphasized. Adam's aim is to be 'a true king' (II). When the people turn against him they first suggest reducing him to a president; and when the deplorable Tom Tiddler succeeds him, it is as president of a republic, not as king. We have a trinity: Beauty, whom alone Adam worships (II); Adam as King, her servant on earth; and the child Eros. Eros is of the future:

> Here shall he stand where I stumbled.
> Saviour and Prince is he.
>
>   (II.)

The strength of *Adam's Opera* lies in these symbols of universal appeal which yet remain independent of religious dogma and political programmes. Strangely few of our post-Caroline dramatists have understood the imaginative powers of kingship; most offer us nothing better than a succession of unhappy tyrants. Royalism was a main source of Shakespeare's strength; Byron transmitted it to a new age; Mary Russell Mitford, Wilde, Shaw, Zangwill and Granville-Barker knew its meaning; Masefield strikes metaphoric fire from it. In *Adam's Opera* it assumes a symbolic centrality. Remembering *Will Shakespeare* we may suppose that Christianity is contained too, but if so it is a Christianity nearer to *Good Friday* than to *Murder in the Cathedral*. Though it antedates the works just discussed and though some of these dramas contain much, especially in revelation of evil depths, that *Adam's Opera* does not, we can yet say that it pin-points, as does none of its rivals, the imaginative powers on which contemporary advance depends: Beauty, King, Eros.

IV

Though Eire is no longer British,[1] we shall nevertheless review the plays of Sean O'Casey, who has for long made England his home. O'Casey is in the main a war dramatist; he uses in turn every modern fight, social, civil, or international, that comes within the range of his experience and on each lavishes his art. In *The Shadow of a Gunman* (1923) he describes the poetical Donal Davouren as one devoted to 'the might of design, the mystery of colour, and the belief in the redemption of all things by beauty everlasting' (I; Direction). The words serve as a text for O'Casey's drama, which labours to make harmony from chaos.[2] In peace he diagnoses the central conflict of our society as the conflict between sex love and the Christian Church.

Juno and the Paycock (1924), O'Casey's first full-length success, takes us to the Dublin slums in 1922 during the conflict between the new Irish Republic and the still dissatisfied Die-Hards or Extremists. Captain Boyle claims to be an experienced sea captain but it is mostly fantasy, and he cannot be made to work, preferring to idle with his

---

[1] This must be my excuse for not finding space for a discussion of the recently published collected plays by Denis Johnston, whose reputation was established in 1931 by *The Moon in the Yellow River*.

[2] Much new biographical material on O'Casey's personal experiences in relation to his dramas is soon to be published in Saros Cowasjee's *O'Casey: The Man behind the Plays*.

companion Joxer, a comic waster. Mrs Boyle is devoted and tireless, keeping the home and trying to rouse her husband. Their son, Johnny, is in a state of nervous terror and is eventually taken out to his death for the betrayal of a comrade. Mary, the daughter, is deserted by her lover. The painful story is shot through with comedy. Boyle's absurd reminiscences are accompanied by Joxer's heroic quotations: 'Let me like a soldier fall—me breast expandin' to th' ball!' (II). A socialist reformer who claims to stand for the 'new life' is found to lack humanity in face of a human and sexual problem (III). Against all falsities stands Mrs Boyle: calm, tireless and heroic. O'Casey's women are strong and brave; his men vary between vision and fatuity. Maternal and religious emotions are a surer guide than men's conflicts:

> Sacred heart of the Crucified Jesus, take away our hearts o' stone . . .
> an' give us hearts o' flesh! . . . Take away this murdherin' hate . . . an'
> give us Thine own eternal love!   (II.)

God himself can do nothing against 'the stupidity o' men' (III). And yet from this slum hell of folly and cruelty breaks rich comedy, warm and human; O'Casey's language has an almost Shakespearian resource, ranging from humour to terror; flashes of philosophy and poetry counter the degradation; even Joxer's quotations have their lustre. Song and music come in, too, and dominating all is the pictured Virgin and before it a crimson bowl in which floats a votive light, to burn red as the action advances, and then flicker and fade. Such central symbols are favourites with O'Casey; and he loves colour.

The Plough and the Stars (1926), on the Easter Rebellion of 1916, is more complex, with a violent action and multi-radial pointings. Among the Irish are revolutionaries, a world-communist and the pro-British Bessie Burgess. The Dublin fighting is vividly dramatized: we are in a city torn by modern war. The best soldiers are afraid: 'His very soul is cold . . . shiverin' with th' thought of what may happen to him' (III). This horror the women must reject or 'they're lyin' against God, Nature, an' against themselves' (III). Male activity is comic, as well in Peter in his uniform 'like th' illegitimate son of an illegitimate child of a corporal in th' Mexican army' (I) as in the Covey talking of 'Jenersky's *Thesis on th' Origin, Development, an' Consolidation of th' Evolutionary Idea of th' Proletariat*' (I). The Dublin fighting becomes a chaos of looting. But the woman, Bessie, is brave: while men are out to slaughter each other the hero's wife,

Nora, is in labour and Bessie goes 'firmly and swiftly' through the firing to get a doctor, with a prayer (III).

At the start the love of Jack Clitheroe and his wife Nora expresses itself in ballad poetry, and at the close Bessie and Nora dominate. Jack has been killed. The sky is red, the city burning. Nora, her husband and new-born child dead, is mad. She sings, like Ophelia, in her madness. Bessie is shot and dies, singing a hymn, the phrases broken. Ultimate horrors are mingled with melody. There is a jagged realism but scarcely satire; the British soldiers are not unsympathetically presented. Humour and pathos are in violent alternation. Asserting itself in blood and battle, from madness and meaningless death, is the half-strangled instinct for melody and song; there is woman's love, and woman's courage; and, though it seems futile, a religious trust. The dominating colour is red.

Colour and song henceforward assume a primacy. O'Casey's wide sympathies necessarily expand, and *The Silver Tassie* (1929) treats of the European war with a far greater emphasis on formality and design. The first act, in Ireland, has the old realism; the second takes us to France, and the manner changes. The setting shows a ruined monastery with a Virgin in stained glass and a broken life-size Crucifix; also a gunwheel and a gun. In the sky is sometimes a green, sometimes a white, star. Dramatic speech is melodious, soldiers and ambulance men interweaving their chants to express themselves and their situation. Satire against an important—presumably political—visiting civilian is crude: 'Keep 'em moving much as possible. Too much rest—bad' (II). But the artistic purpose has temporarily lost all contact with human individuality. The dramatic aim is to master the horror of war by subduing it to an aesthetic harmony; there is even a long hymnal invocation to the Gun, and the final direction for its *silent* flashes in a reddened sky makes of it a temporary and fearful protagonist.

Instead of heroism we are aware primarily of pathos. Our main concerns are now the blinded Teddy and the mutilated Harry. They are back home, at a football club dance. Their miserable plight is contrasted with the decorations, the coloured lanterns and streamers. Harry is roused to an agonized jealousy at his girl's unfaithfulness and a cruel and irrevocable contrast is felt between the healthy and the maimed, who are necessarily now 'in another world'. Speech is often studied and stylized:

> HARRY: The rising sap in trees I'll never feel.
> TEDDY: The hues of branch or leaf I'll never see. (IV.)

The dangers of self-pity are obviated by their speaking rather as choric voices than as themselves. The painfulness is relieved by one of O'Casey's glorious incidents of protracted humour concerning the manipulation of a telephone and by Harry's ukelele bringing to mind black bodies in a jungle dance and tom-toms; but our prevailing impression is that of a callous destiny together with an acceptance. Living, to have 'flavour', means either a 'kiss' or a 'blow', and the ebbed life must give place to the 'full life on the flow' (IV). O'Casey's uncompromising belief in the right to happiness for those who can find it resists even his sense of suffering in those who cannot. This is high dramatic thinking. No victory is wrenched from the suffering itself; our only catharsis comes through the suffusion of colour, melody and design, into which the people are dissolved.

Stylization and patterning are developed yet further in *Within the Gates* (1934), where design is brilliantly used to pack contemporary London into a single play. The scene is a park, with a war memorial figure of a soldier in the background. The four acts are set successively in the four seasons and at a corresponding hour, and the human themes are entwined with nature and thought of natural fecundity. We have dances and choric songs, the verse forms using refrain and repetition of a maze-like fascination and a bird-like recapturing. Colour is everywhere. Sky, foliage, stars, costumes are exactly pictured; stage directions riot in colour; the memorial figure changes in appearance according to the season and the light. In the first act there is a maypole with coloured ribbons. Colours may be ominous, as when evangelists come in with red and black posters on death and judgement. The richest intuitions are golden, corresponding to the 'golden and purple pavilions', laburnum and lilac, of spring (IV): we have 'the golden flame of love' (III), the 'golden meshes of a poet's song' (II), and all the 'golden' youth of England lost in the war (IV). Gold is close to nature. From the tree-boys' and flower-girls' fertility chorus 'Our mother the Earth is a maiden again' (I) and the Dreamer's

> Gay, white apple-blossoms her breast,
> Her legs golden branches of willow,
>
> (II.)

to the tragic end on a winter's night, nature rules. The ancient fertility origins of drama are revivified in the heart of modern London.

Nature is associated with sexual energies in contrast to contemporary religion. Satire on the Church can be strong and also amusing, as in an old woman's sarcastic address to the Bishop's sister:

> ... and grant us grace to have faith in thy dignity and importance,
> per benedicite pax hugger muggery ora pro puggery rigmarolum!
>
> (IV.)

The main attack is against the gloom and joy-killing qualities of contemporary religion, especially that of the Protestant 'evangelists' who honour 'pain' and smother joy with 'sighing' (IV). But O'Casey is saturated in religious tradition and his humour does not preclude reverence. The incense of the Church is 'golden' (III). The conflict between sexual energies and Christianity is at the heart of today's civilization and the thrust and withdrawal of O'Casey's satire against a Church that has failed to master it merely reflects that heart's pulsations.

We have only two real negatives. There are the newspaper readers, devotees of the sadistic and the sensational, with their headlines of murder, rape, suicide and divorce; and there are the Down-and-Outs whose muffled drum-beats and mournful chant come nearer act by act, functioning as a ghostly, inhuman, threat; for these 'challenge life no more'; in them hope and faith are dead; life with her flaming colours has passed them by, and now they have 'but a sigh for a song and a deep sigh for a drum-beat' (III; IV). This nightmare group is a stage conception of uncanny power.

A wide range of semi-stylized people appear and we have a number of theological, social and scientific arguments, but the main human interest is in Jannice, a young prostitute who has adopted the profession in revulsion from an upbringing in a repressive church home, and in the Bishop whose youthful lapse was the cause of her birth. Both are costumed in black and red. The Dreamer, descendant from Davouren in *The Shadow of a Gunman*, personifies poetic wisdom. Jannice has heart trouble and expects to die soon; meanwhile she is tortured by her way of life and by both a sense of guilt and a scorn of insincere respectability. She scorns the newspaper readers, the respectable addicts of sensation:

> You bunch of high-minded toads, don't look at me long, for there's only venom for a woman in the things ye think of her. The dear joy of a sin ye turn to a sting and a bruising . . . In your looking after a woman there is no kindliness . . .
>
> (III.)

The Bishop tries to reclaim her, but the Dreamer makes a contrasted appeal:

> The Dreamer calls you to the deep kiss and clutch of love; to sing our song with the song that is sung by a thousand stars of the evening! (III.)

The Down-and-Outs, who symbolize not simply unemployment but all who have accepted defeat, nearly engulf her in their 'marching misery', yet she resists and will die 'game' and 'dancing' (IV). The Dreamer, wearing a 'vivid orange', or golden, scarf, dances with her to flute music, *against* the ghastly chanting of the Down-and-Outs. It is a magical, ritual, contest, essence against essence, music against music. She falls and asks the Bishop to guide her hand to sign the Cross, and dies trusting in 'the golden mercy of God' (IV). Her death is not as the living death of the mournful and defeated. It is not the death meant by the Dreamer's

> Way for the strong and the swift and the fearless:
> Life that is stirr'd by the fear of its life, let it die . . .
> (IV.)

We end with the Bishop's 'She died making the sign of the cross' (IV) and the Dreamer's 'You fought the good fight, Jannice' (IV).

Within the Gates is O'Casey's most comprehensive achievement. His experience as a war dramatist enables him to master the far harder task of dramatizing peace through a number of *ritual conflicts*; and the interest never flags. All O'Casey's feminine trust is in his pathetic and yet indomitable young whore. Her words blaze; she has tragic stature. The Bishop is as a man weak, though he is kindly, and in this context it is to his credit that he was in youth human enough to have an illegitimate child; he has the dignity of his office and his voice at the close is authoritative, representing O'Casey's blessing, through the Church, on his unregenerate yet trusting heroine. The most bitter words here are the Bishop's to his self-righteous sister: 'Go home, go home, for Christ's sake, woman, and ask God's mercy on us all!' (IV). The Dreamer is a voice of poetic wisdom. The rest are mainly types. With a careful selection and exploitation of themes O'Casey uses 'the might of design' and 'the mystery of colour' to pack contemporary city civilization into a three hours' performance and also, while relating it to the natural universe, to expose its central conflict and point a direction. The diagnoses offer hope; patterning and harmonization endue the whole with 'beauty everlasting'.

Within the Gates succeeds magnificently. O'Casey's return in subsequent dramas to the arena of ordinary action is less successful.
Religion remains a centre, in verbal tone, biblical reminiscence,
symbol, and as subject for attack. Catholicism is contrasted to its
disadvantage with social advance and young sexual love, but little is
made of the approved powers. The patterned mingling of Communism and Christianity in *The Star Turns Red* (1940) does more than
the leader Red Jim, who is drawn in terms of a rather too obvious
perfection; and as for the sexual, it remains no more than the 'sexual',
without esoteric or seraphic pointings. O'Casey's men lack virility,
and his most successful reformer is the poetical Ayamon, an artistic
type, successor to Davouren and the Dreamer, in *Red Roses for Me*
(1943); and yet even so the stage vision of a transfigured Dublin
does more to convey the revolutionary atmosphere than the man
does. The symbolisms of revolution in *Purple Dust* (1945) are less
satisfying. O'Casey's concentration on the visionary, the symbolic
and the religious marks a craving for supernatural solutions. In
Cock-a-Doodle Dandy (1949), where he tries through the agency of
his Cock to endue youthful sexuality with an effective magic as against
the ineffectual healing of Catholicism at Lourdes, two age-old
traditions, comoedic and tragic, are rather arbitrarily opposed. *The
Bishop's Bonfire* (1955) gets us no farther.

O'Casey can find nothing human to meet his vision. Neither sex
love nor Communism can bear the final strain. The problem resembles that posed by Eliot's psychiatrist, and in both instances the
proper solution exists within the spiritualistic, or seraphic, sphere.
O'Casey drew near to this solution in *Oak Leaves and Lavender*
(1946).

This is a work of exact and impersonal integration showing the
impact of the numinous on a realistic and historically significant
action. We are in an old English mansion during the Battle of
Britain in 1940. Purple is the colour of death: spirits appear and a
lavender song acts as a bridge between the two worlds; the sign for
air-raids is purple. At the start and finish we see dim eighteenth-
century ghosts from a past aristocracy, and from time to time during
the action the lavender perfume is sensed and the swish of their
garments and a faint music are heard (II; III). Death is close; its
meaning and the life beyond are discussed; and when the building
shakes we are not sure whether it is a bomb or the impingement of
the other dimension on this. So Death's presence exquisitely conditions a bustling, sometimes amusing and sometimes tragic,

realization of Britain at war. Her great past is remembered and great names: Marlborough, Nelson, Wellington, Shakespeare, Milton (I; III). The Irishman Feelim O'Morrigum is anxious to recall what Ireland has done in British wars (III); he is O'Casey's voice for that respect for Britain's traditions and literature that so strikingly accompanies his Irish and Communistic allegiances. He can assimilate so much: in a sharp dialogue he generously allows an attractive young Communist to get, or seem to get, the worst of it (I); and the hated Nazis are given the honour of Wagnerian Valkyrie music to accompany an air-raid (II). Central to the action is Dame Hatherleigh, believer in the Israelite origins of Britain (I), personifying British history and being half identified with Time (III). There is little or no plot; we neither need nor expect one. But in terms of dialogue and impressions Britain in her hour of danger, quivering on the edge of death, is beautifully apprehended; and never more so than when O'Casey's glorious humour is the medium of transmission. The only breath of bitterness comes from one of the Spirits who, seeing our modern uniforms, cries: 'Gracious God! Has colour gone from life?' (III).

The Drums of Father Ned (1960, discussed more fully in *The Christian Renaissance*, 1962, Appendix) serves as a clarification. Though it makes gestures towards Communism and youthful sexuality and a strong Protestantism as antagonist to the Irish priesthood, its only ultimate and inclusive authorities are (i) the numinous background figure of Father Ned, whose drumming, together with the mysterious Echo, signalizes an inclusive religious force; and (ii) the seraphic Eros-equivalent of 'thin poetic face', Angus the Young as 'Keltic god of youth and loveliness', depicted emblematically with a gold-stringed harp and a bird of symbolic colouring (III). These two, aural and visual, Dionysian and Apollonian, serve as generalized symbolisms relating O'Casey's more personal religious and sexual interests to our dramatic tradition.

V

Byron's *Cain* developed two main strains of post-Renaissance advance: (i) space travel and (ii) the occult. Of these the first is not widely represented in modern drama; the second is. Science is not a natural dramatic subject. We have Charles Morgan's *The Flashing Stream* (1938) and *The Burning Glass* (1953), on war inventions, scientifically toned, though *The River Line* (1952) offers a more normal human interest and a more inward penetration, leading at one point to thoughts of immortality; and in this sphere modern drama is active enough. But the occult, from the Faust stories through Byron's *Cain* to our own day, has been regularly regarded with moral suspicion. Its mysteries grade through fear into evil, and it is significant that the two strongest lines of development that remain to be discussed concern (i) criminology and (ii) the occult; and that dramatists good at the one are likely to get involved in the other.

In descent from the old Faust and Don Juan myths modern drama brings the analytic and critical intelligence to bear on accepted morality. Attacks on convention and hypocrisy, starting with Pinero and Jones, had been gathering strength. Zangwill in *Plaster Saints* (1914) could see a clergyman's sexual lapse as impelled by a 'strange transfiguration, when all the world grew golden', while 'the sin seemed not in the loving, but in letting the love go by' (1). Similar insights combine with war excitement and war revulsion to make the dramatic challenges of Somerset Maugham.

Maugham's strength lies in his honesty. Asked whether he is a humorist or a cynic one of his people in *The Circle* replies:

> I'm neither, my dear boy; I'm merely a very truthful man. But people are so unused to the truth that they're apt to mistake it for a joke or a sneer. (III.)

This is true of Maugham himself. Emotional honesty empowers his best social and marriage dramas, *Our Betters* (1917), *The Circle* (1921), and *The Constant Wife* (1927). *For Services Rendered* (1932) is a bitter and successful indictment of society's disregard for a war hero. Maugham's masterpiece is *The Sacred Flame* (1928), as brilliant in construction, as emotionally compelling, and as firm in sense of womanly heroism, as Clemence Dane's *A Bill of Divorcement* (1921). A war-disabled and paralysed son is given an overdose by his mother to prevent the suffering of three people through the discovery that his wife is with child by his brother, whom she now loves. Mrs Tabret's quiet assurance from a viewpoint beyond conventional judgements is contrasted with the black-and-white valuations of the unlovable Nurse Wayland. All motherhood is in her, and all her motherhood dictates the crime. She has wisdom. Speaking of her son's wife she says:

> She was as kind as ever, and as gentle, but it was an effort, and what is the good you do worth unless you do it naturally as the flowers give their scent? (III.)

Agreement seems easy, and yet within that quiet statement lies an explosive force.

Mrs Tabret is wholly sympathetic and her action artistically approved. But there are more general implications, suggesting that 'the most law-abiding and decent person' may be driven to commit a crime (III). That is our new note. Beyond the general run of crook and detective dramas post-Nietzschean psychology bears fruit in a number of crime plays of insight and distinction. R. C. Sherriff, J. B. Priestley and Emlyn Williams have all contributed to the psychology of crime. In Emlyn Williams's *Someone Waiting* (1953) Fenn is a mild man to whom life has been unkind; events entice him to murder; and once started he shows a semi-insane cunning, functioning like 'a man in a trance' without 'dread' or 'horror'; like 'the practical trance of a great doctor' at work on some 'miraculous operation' (II. ii). Criminology takes us across the threshold of sanity into the occult. In Clemence Dane's weirdly powerful *Granite* (1926) the heroine's criminality is impelled by a demoniac person.

The dramas of the one-time doctor, James Bridie, concentrate on criminality or supernature, or both. No modern dramatist has a deeper insight into criminality. He is primarily interested in the relation of criminality to genius, especially medical genius. In *The Switchback* (1929) a humble but brilliant doctor with a new discovery is thwarted by the higher professionalism of the Medical Council; and when its attitude changes he refuses their offer in Timon-like scorn, rejects civilization and leaves for the Asian desert to find communion with the dead past and the infinities of 'space'. In *The Anatomist* (1930) a great doctor compromises with criminals to get bodies for dissection. He is ruthless, having one aim only: 'God's work' (I), 'divine science' (II. ii). He believes in Machiavelli and like Wordsworth's Oswald regards the hostility of the herd-consciousness as the test of greatness. In *A Sleeping Clergyman* (1933) an immoral and dissolute but brilliant medical researcher has an illegitimate daughter who is responsible for a shameless murder and commits suicide after giving birth to an illegitimate son who becomes a great doctor destined to save mankind from a world-annihilating plague. It is remembered that great poets are often diseased and that war heroism and crime have a single basis (II. ii). The great doctor's sister speaks our moral:

> And my mother had the courage to do what was to be done and the courage to kill and the courage to die. And my grandfather had the key to all the mysteries.   (II. ii.)

The creative scheme works on a system independent of human valuations. These are as likely as not to thwart what is best, which is always close to what we regard as the worst, while both are equally hostile to mediocrity. On such dangerous qualities depend progress and even security. The irrelevance and unawareness of contemporary religion is symbolized by the Sleeping Clergyman whose snores punctuate the dramatic narrative.

Dr Angelus (1947) is composed from a more strictly criminological viewpoint. The doctor murders first his mother-in-law and next his wife because they fetter his freedom. He has the qualities of a 'great man' (II) and a half-convincing goodness: 'Whenever he talks to me I sort of know in my bones that he's all right' (III). At his arrest he is first proudly scornful and next cringing and pathetic. He can in all seriousness invoke his wife's spirit to support his innocence. Even in so clear a case, we are aware that crime may be close to, if not born from, the divine spark: the name 'Angelus' is a pointer. So is that of Sir Gregory Butt, the established professor of conventional repute who tries only to avoid trouble for himself and is easily placed:

> No? Because you're an old tin idol and a pompous old quack. Angelus may be a murderer and I may be a bloody coward, but you're not fit to black our boots. (III.)

Angelus might be called a split personality; the problem is really too deep for any but a dramatic definition.

From the Faust story down, criminality and the occult are closely related: they are both aspects of the irrational, both offend the daylight, Apollonian, intellect, and yet this very offence conditions, again and again, dramatic power; for it is drama's task to tap these deeper sources. In Bridie's *Mr Bolfry* (1943) a minor devil is raised in the home of a Presbyterian minister and announces a gospel, which he relates to the teaching of William Blake, on the necessity and rightness of evil as well as good, the importance of their conflict and the inevitability of its reflection in human warring. *Marriage is No Joke* (1934) shows us a burly and unrestful divinity student who does not discover his true self until during the war he becomes the leader of a band of bloodthirsty Kurds in north Persia, the experience eventually making of him an effective minister, able to battle for good.

Of Bridie's many supernaturally impregnated plays *Tobias and the Angel* (1930) ranks first. It has rightly become the most popular of his works, having an embodied warmth beyond the rest. A delightful humour creates in the old Tobit that rarest of dramatic phenomena, a wholly good and lovable man—with women it is easier—in whom we can believe. His son Tobias is a timorous weakling who with the help of an archangel makes a dangerous journey, routs a demon, executes a business transaction and wins a wife. The myth is given a modern interpretation, the Archangel being called Tobias's personal 'daemon' (III. i). If we fear the darker adventures of dramatic thought we must, like Tobias, gain strength from our spirit guardians. The powers of darkness can only be mastered by the powers of light.

The most striking advance of modern drama, starting with *Mind* in the last century (p. 299 above), is its use of Spiritualism or other kinds of extra-dimensional insight. We have already noticed the contributons of John Masefield, the ghostly atmosphere of *The Family Reunion* and the crystal-gazing of *The Ascent of F6*. Sometimes we find resemblances to the spiritualist Nō plays of Japan, as in Yeats's *Purgatory* (p. 328 above), Bottomley's dramas, and Sturge Moore's interesting *Medea* (1920). In *Medea* we are first reminded that such spirits as those known to have attended 'clay-clogged' men in ancient Greece can still today be apprehended by minds not 'hoodwinked' by modern scepticism, and we next watch Medea in conversation with her murdered children, childlike and mischievous as when on earth, while she is baffled. This is our message:

> Death is life veiled
> By the pang which destroys the senses.
> Passion survives: and more daintily limbed,
> Man has to ail as he ailed:
> His new habiliment, though dimmed,
> Yet shines, by turns, transfigured again
> As immortal beauty recovers from pain.

Lawrence Binyon's *Ayuli* (1923) concludes movingly with a spirit dream. Many of our dramatists write from direct knowledge of modern spiritualism.

The ghostly may occur simply for sensation, as in Arnold Ridley's *The Ghost Train* (1925). There is usually more to it than that. The coming alive of a past age in Drinkwater's *Mary Stuart* (1921) or of Robert Emmet in Denis Johnston's *The Old Lady Says 'No!'* (1929) might be called dramatic devices. The same may be said of Clemence Dane's ghost in *A Traveller Returns* (1927), but her *Come of Age* (with Richard Addinsell, 1934), on the poet Chatterton, grippingly dramatizes Death and skips the centuries for a reincarnation; and *The Lion and the Unicorn* (1943) is given a spirit conclusion. In O'Casey's *Oak Leaves and Lavender* the eighteenth-century spirits are well realized and functional; the same century comes alive in Harcourt Williams's spiritual playlet *Au Petit Trianon* (1929); and also in John L. Balderstone's *Berkeley Square* (1926), where the hero's adventure into the past is worked up to a strong climax blending metaphysics and romance as hero and heroine are forced to separate across the centuries. A ghostly past is powerfully dramatized in Robert Ardrey's *Thunder Rock* (1940).

We may have séances, as in Yeats's *The Words upon the Window Pane* (p. 328 above), with Swift as communicator. Eric Linklater's *The Devil's in the News* (1934) opens with a séance and his *Crisis in Heaven* (1944) takes us to Elysium. On the plane of melodrama Bayard Veiller's *The Thirteenth Chair* (1917) interweaves criminal investigation with a séance. Aldous Huxley has written one crime play, *The Gioconda Smile* (1948) and a séance play, *The World of Light* (1931), in which the originating source of a medium's messages turns out not to have died after all, though the charge of fraud is negated by the accuracy with which his living thoughts and doings have been reported, the authenticity of mediumistic messages being to this extent supported rather than questioned. Telepathy is the theme of Ashley Dukes's *Return to Danes Hill* (1958). Barrie's *A Well-Remembered Voice* (1918) is an acute study of séance communication (p. 330 above); and in *Mary Rose* spiritualistic truth is contained within an art-form of fantasy design. Coward has two extremes: spirit return is basic to both his farce *Blithe Spirit* (1941) and to his strongest drama of social denunciation *Post Mortem* (1930). In Emlyn Williams's *Trespass* (1947) the atmosphere of a Welsh castle and two mediums, one fraudulent and one authentic, contribute to a sinister action which suggests that it may be wiser not to complicate earthly emotions by revelations from the spirit dimension. The return of an earth-bound spirit in Sherriff's *The White Carnation* (1953) poses some amusing problems on the relation of earth law and government to the world of the dead. We have an excellent passage on psychic science:

> We always think of this other world as something remotely up in the sky somewhere. I suppose that's because we've always been taught to look up when we think of heaven. But it may not be up there at all: it may be all round us—separated from us by some kind of blindness in our understanding . . . just as sounds in wireless waves

are silent and television blind to us until we turn the knob on a machine. The other world may move in some kind of wave like that —very close to us—then something happens: some tiny upset that disturbs the delicate order of it all.   (II. i.)

It could not have been better expressed.

Sutton Vane's *Outward Bound* (1923) starts grippingly with a company of baffled people on a ship gradually discovering that they are dead; and closely related to it is *Fear No More* by Diana Hamilton, widow of Sutton Vane, and Conrad Aiken (1946). The state of death is briefly dramatized at the conclusion to Maugham's *Sheppey* (1933). Saloman Ansky's *The Dybbuck* (comp. 1914; pub. after performance, in English, 1927) is a powerful study in spirit possession. Insanity, clairaudience and crime are grouped together in Lord Dunsany's playlet *Atmospherics* (1937). Many of our spirit plays are a little ominous, since the impact of the one order on the other tends normally to arouse disquietude. G. K. Chesterton's *Magic* (1913), written from a Catholic standpoint, neatly uses the damnable powers —for so they are regarded—of modern spiritualism to prick the bubble of a twentieth-century cleric's rationalism. Astral travelling in sleep and spirit converse are optimistically realized in the Epilogue to Shaw's *Saint Joan* and the conception of the Ancients and their abnormal faculties in *Back to Methuselah* appears to owe much to accounts of life on other planes received through spiritualistic communications. The concluding scene of Clifford Bax's *Socrates* (1930) supports Plato's account of Socrates' beliefs, his *daemon* and views on death, with knowledge drawn from modern communication.

Of all our spiritualist dramas the most important remains Masefield's *Melloney Holtspur* (p. 334 above), though our most comprehensive metaphysical dramatist is J. B. Priestley.

In the third act of *Time and the Conways* (1937) there is irony from our knowledge of the future dramatized in the second. But we are warned not to allow sequence to tyrannize: 'There's a great devil in the universe, and we call it Time' (II). Again:

No, Time's only a kind of dream, Kay. If it wasn't, it would have to destroy everything—the whole universe—and then remake it again every tenth of a second. But Time doesn't destroy anything. It merely moves us on—in this life—from one peep-hole to the next.
                                                                      (II.)

The thoughts are drawn from J. W. Dunne, and *I have been Here Before* (1937) is even more successful in using the age-old philosophy

GEORGIAN

of recurrence supported by Nietzsche and P. D. Ouspensky. Dr Gortler, a German professor, arrives at a north country inn where according to his calculations certain crises in the lives of certain people are due to develop. The interaction of abstruse but exciting theory with a warmly conceived human action is quite remarkable; metaphysics become dramatic. More, metaphysics *are* the drama, for drama depends on free will, and Dr Gortler's aim is to indicate the possibility of getting off the rails of recurrence and turning the circle into a spiral; in other words to make drama replace fatalism. Time is constituent to dramatizations of chance in *Dangerous Corner* (1932) and moral judgement in *An Inspector Calls* (1946); and also, though differently, to the communion through clairvoyance of *The Long Mirror* (1940). These plays witness a unique identification of metaphysics and drama.

In *Music at Night* (1938) music arouses reminiscences and conversations with the dead, which develop into open confessions and a recognition, following Nietzsche's philosophy of the Dionysian music in *The Birth of Tragedy*, of the littleness of separate egos in comparison with the one great mind and heart of which each is an expression (III). Among the people is a successful journalist who had money to invest for his mother but used it for himself. She died before it was repaid: 'And now all the time she watches me' (III). The wealthy self-made Sir James Dirnie built his fortunes on betrayal: 'Years ago I got myself a job by ratting on a pal. It gave me my start, but it finished him. He drowned himself' (III). Others are tortured by thoughts of nightmarish existence after death and of pain as the ruling principle of the universe, from which there is no escape in this life or another (III). The Communist poet Peter Horlett is a materialist who believes that thought 'is only a change in the cell-structure of the brain' (I) and romance an aberration of 'the leisured class'. But he too is caught by recognition that

> there is a heart
> Feeding the imagination with strange blood . . .
>
> (II.)

and speaks of Helen, Deirdre and Guinevere:

> O heart
> That does not beat this side of the moon yet draws
> The very red out of the rose, leave me in peace!
>
> (II.)

Sir Charles Bendrex is an unhappy cabinet minister who dreams back to the Edwardian age, the age of straw hats. He talks to his valet

Parks, who had died in 1913 and who now offers him a straw hat, which he refuses (II). The play concludes with Bendrex's death. His body is alone. Parks enters in 'a ghostly suggestion' of 'sunshine light', wakes him from death and offers him the hat, which this time he accepts, happily.

Johnson over Jordan (1939), inspired by Tibetan spiritualism, is more comprehensive. The hero is an unspectacular business man, who has just died. We see first his family and the funeral arrangements, and next we are with him. He is in a dream world of money anxieties which quickly become a hell of complication, dominated by torturing commands to answer questions and complete forms. A Figure representing Death as Fear directs him to another room which becomes a night club, where he is among his lusts and is brought to shame. Hearing his own funeral service he wants to assure his family that he is not dead, but he must pass on to the Inn at the End of the World where he finds whatever has 'illuminated' his 'mind' and 'touched' his 'heart' (II). Here he meets those he has loved and helped, re-experiencing his better moments. There is music: 'I've heard that before, in the strangest places, and it never lasts long' (III). He can choose 'what time and place he'd like this to be while he's having his supper' (III); he is in the etheric world, wherein objective reality is created by thought. The Figure, now illumined by 'a golden shaft of light' and with 'the face of a handsome young man, like an Apollo', speaks: 'Robert Johnson, it is time now'. The Figure is 'smiling like an angel'. To majestic music, the 'small and forlorn' Johnson faces the great blue light, and the stars.

Priestley's later works concentrate more on the specifically human and sociological, though the higher perceptions, once established, maintain their influence. We are not allowed to forget that 'what we see and what science investigates is merely a three-dimensional cross-section of a four or multi-dimensional reality' (*People at Sea*, 1937, II. i). Through all burns the one ideal of a better world, which is less simple than it sounds since the rights of both vast nature and ethical vision must be maintained. In *Home is Tomorrow* (1948) Sir Edward Fortrose, representing the United Nations in control of a savage island, sees his organization as an outpost of light in primeval darkness; and we applaud what he stands for. But his flighty and faithless wife would prefer the savagery and the darkness: 'At least it's real—it's life—full of scents and sounds—with wind and rain and starlight. It responds to something in our heart and blood'.

To her this international organization is 'sterile, arid, lifeless' (1). Nature must not be slighted. Nor must the fourth dimension. For the lovable professor in *The Linden Tree* (1947) history is no mere narrative of events, however important, but also 'the record of man as a spiritual creature, with a whole world of unknown continents and strange seas, gardens of Paradise and cities lit with hell-fire, within the depths of his own soul' (II. ii).

Priestley's development from metaphysics to a more normal concern with society has point. To stay for long within the otherness is both difficult and unwise; indeed the surest sign of having touched it, in life or drama, may be to show that you are equally or more interested in incarnate existence. T. S. Eliot's dramatic progress is interesting: from sex crime through religion and the occult to social, or society, doctrine. The ground won for drama by Spiritualism is firm, and it will yield rich harvests, but at present our greatest achievements are such as have on them *as well* the bloom of earthly life. So Flecker's Golden Journey succeeds his ghosts; *Nan* has a glory lacking to *Melloney Holtspur*; and similar contrasts are in *Mary Rose* as against *A Well-Remembered Voice* and *Tobias and the Angel* as against *Mr Bolfry*. Though spirit perception must be functioning within, the supernatural is generally better remade, as Shakespeare and Ibsen remake it, in semi-natural terms, even at the cost of some falsification of known spirit fact, lest vitality and colour are lost. The otherness must be felt, as it is in Aeschylus, Shakespeare and Masefield, in active interpenetration with, not merely in opposition to, the natural. This is the point of all our seraphic persons, from Plato downwards. The difficulty arises from the necessity of interweaving that which is beyond earth-law with life as we know it; and it is in their beyond-law quality that the occult and evil, from the Faust story onwards, draw so close, since both equally appear to offend daylight reason; and there is always the possibility of demoniac possession to be remembered, which opens vast fields of speculation.[1] Both *The White Carnation* and *Trespass* drive home the embarrassment in earthly terms of a returned spirit. On all these matters we must preserve open minds unclouded by prejudice.

Spiritualism itself does not leave us in this impasse. Earth-bound spirits, though they may act behind life's scenes as do those in *Melloney Holtspur*, do not materialize so permanently and uncompromisingly as Beddoes's or Sherriff's, and a censorship appears to be

---

[1] See p. 151 note; also Geraldine Cummins, *Beyond Human Personality*, edition of 1952, XVII.

set up from the other side to preclude dangerous revelations. Its philosophy preserves as great a respect for the earth-plane as does Christianity itself. Besides, nothing is more important to the spirit dimension itself than colour; in Lady Gregory's *The Dragon* (1917) it is once defined as 'the many-coloured land' (III); and it is our, not its, fault if we regard it as abstract or ghostly. Our only contemporary dramatist who could have rendered the etheric in its true nature is probably O'Casey. For the rest much may be learned from Masefield's narrative *King Cole* (p. 334 above) and Bridie's *Tobias and the Angel*: there *are* spirit guardians ready to help in life's difficulties, to infuse courage and master demons.

Christianity, with its concentration on the Incarnation, and all the attendant earthly-warm and homely qualities, has many advantages. And yet religious dramas based on dogmatic belief are too often merely fabrications of the devotional intelligence, without the Dionysian under-thrust; and Dionysus, like Jehovah, is a jealous god who knows only too well how to sterilize an art disloyal to his deity. Charles Williams's *The House of the Octopus* (1945) certainly succeeds; its high Christian doctrine flowers from a dramatic soil rich in jungloid idolatry and atheistic statecraft; and the savagery, though not the statecraft, is accorded a degree of sympathy. The Eucharist is subtly related to blood sacrifice and pervading the whole is the key thought of spirit life beyond death, to pagan superstitions dark but in Christian terms active and purposeful, returning to help on earth, as in Masefield. So, though at one extreme we have the ultimate biological horror of the Octopus, symbol both of torture and of state strangulation, and at the other the Flame of the Holy Spirit, the elements are dramatically entangled; and dramatically it is the entanglement rather than the doctrine alone that is important.

The Christ story itself is so firmly distanced by reverence and dogma that it is almost impossible to make it live. Masefield through his Madman achieved success in *Good Friday* and more recently Emlyn Williams has given us *The Wind of Heaven* (1945).

This fascinating drama tells of the reincarnation of Christ during the last century as a Welsh peasant boy aged thirteen, two years younger than the similarly conceived Guy in Martyn's *An Enchanted Sea*. We are among the mountains in the land of British origins, of Shakespeare's princely boys in *Cymbeline*, and of John Cowper Powys. The people are modern, some agnostic or irreligious, and weighted by thoughts of death, and among them exists this simple yet miraculous being. Central to the action is the mourning lady,

Dilys Parry; in her hall is an old Welsh harp, and her striking of it accompanies the early scenes, sounding as a heavenly premonition. The stress is on sound, not sight. What is so mysterious about the boy Gwyn is this: that in his presence there has been heard on occasion a strange music, and yet as much wind, or ethereal breath, as music, and hard to describe; as magical as the music Shakespeare's Glendower draws from the air. All Wales and its love of music are here and perhaps no other land could have been the soil for such a story. Nor could any dialect so convincingly report the marvel of it as the Welsh lilt of Gwyn's simple mother and the countryman, Evan Howell.

Meanwhile Ambrose Ellis, a circus director from Birmingham, has come wanting Gwyn for his circus, since his drawing-power might be great. He is, or tries to pose as, a vulgar, self-made, man, of Napoleonic drive, and he certainly has great abilities. Himself of Welsh birth, he gradually begins to recall his own boyhood and its gleams of mysticism; and he is drawn to change his ways and serve the Christ-boy, whose powers are being used to heal men dying from a plague, and even to raise the dead, though at the cost of his own death. Henceforward Ambrose Ellis dedicates his life and powers to the cause; but the cause is to be less religious than educational, on the lines of the author's other Welsh piece, *The Corn is Green* (1938).

The Wind of Heaven is a Christ play of a new and compelling kind, but it is also firmly rooted in Renaissance tradition. For in it are again our two old companions in descent from the fierce passions and angelic intuitions of the Middle Ages: the power man and the seraphic boy; Shakespeare and his Fair Youth, his tragic heroes and boy-girls; Massinger's Sir Giles Overreach and seraph Angelo; Empedocles and Callicles. These represent man with his passions and purposes and the ideal to which these passions are to be attuned. The ideal must be unsullied and so young, but in *The Wind of Heaven* an advance in religious emblem is marked by replacing the traditional Christ-child by boyhood; for manhood, unless tragic, is still far ahead.

To conclude, we cross the Atlantic for Eugene O'Neill's *Lazarus Laughed* (1926), a great play speaking Christ-truth from Dionysian soil. To the accompaniment of choric laughter rising from the mystique of that life-joy active within all great comedy, we attend the impact of the resurrected, laughing, and joyous Lazarus on the tyrannies and sadistic neuroses of imperial Rome. Emperor and Galilean, the tragic and the comoedic, death and life, pagan and

Christian, power and seraph, all are variously opposed, balanced and blended under the final sovereignty of the immortal and radiant hero who as the action advances grows gradually younger and more beautiful, and his laughter more silvery, from man to youth and from youth to boy. The drama is made as much from massed grouping, chorus and mime as from dialogue. Great scenes demand from the leading persons the furthest resources of the actor's art. Rooted in our dramatic origins and levelling our whole tragic and comoedic tradition against the last frontiers of earthly experience, *Lazarus Laughed* is as near to a total drama as any we possess.

So with this extraordinary work we close our volume. And if we ever suffer fear or horror from the daring thought-excursions and brutal actions of great drama; if we need a reminder that its single purpose is the marriage of the Dionysian energies to Apollonian forms, so that we have the one music sounding through earthly and beyond-earthly creation, and all the magic as natural as the tint on a flower; if we need to be assured that, though many ghouls must be met and loved—as O'Neill's Lazarus loves and half redeems the sub-human Caligula—yet sweetness and not ghoulishness is our aim; we can do no better than turn to *Lazarus Laughed*, wherein so much of our long dramatic story is compacted.

INDEX

INDEX

References to play titles are included in the page numbers for the playwrights.
Main entries are denoted by heavy type.